THE RISE OF
ROME

*The Making of the
World's Greatest Empire*

ANTHONY EVERITT

RANDOM HOUSE
New York

Published in the United States by Random House,
an imprint of The Random House Publishing Group,
a division of Random House, Inc., New York.

RANDOM HOUSE and colophon are registered trademarks
of Random House, Inc.

Grateful acknowledgment is made to Penguin Group (UK) for permission to reprint approximately
1,202 words from *The Rise of the Roman Empire* by Polybius, translated by Ian Scott-Kilvert, selected with
an introduction by F. W. Walbank (Penguin Classics, 1979), copyright © 1979 by Ian Scott-Kilvert;
approximately 856 words from *The Early History of Rome: Books I–V of The History of Rome from Its
Foundation* by Livy, translated by Aubrey de Sélincourt with an introduction by R. M. Ogilvie (Penguin
Classics, 1960. Reprinted with a new introduction 1971), copyright © 1960 by the Estate of Aubrey de
Sélincourt, introduction copyright © 1971 by R. M. Ogilvie; approximately 146 words from *Rome and
Italy: Books VI–X of The History of Rome from Its Foundation* by Livy, translated and annotated by Betty
Radice, introduction by R. M. Ogilvie (Penguin Classics, 1982), copyright © 1982 by Betty Radice,
introduction copyright © 1982 by the Estate of R. M. Ogilvie; approximately 439 words from *The War
with Hannibal: Books XXI–XXX of The History of Rome from Its Foundation* by Livy, translated by Aubrey
de Sélincourt, edited with an introduction by Betty Radice (Penguin Classics, 1965), copyright © 1965
by the Estate of Aubrey de Sélincourt; approximately 137 words from *Rome and the Mediterranean: Books
XXXI–XLV of The History of Rome from Its Foundation* by Livy, translated by Henry Bettenson,
introduction by A. H. McDonald (Penguin Classics, 1976), copyright © 1976 by Henry Bettenson,
introduction copyright © 1976 by A. H. McDonald. Reprinted by permission of Penguin Group (UK).

Library of Congress Cataloging-in-Publication Data

Everitt, Anthony.
The rise of Rome: the making of the world's greatest empire/Anthony Everitt.
p.   cm.
ISBN 978-1-4000-6663-6
eBook ISBN 978-0-679-64516-0
1. Rome—History—Empire, 30 B.C.–284 A.D.   2. Rome—
History—Empire, 284–476.   I. Title.
DG276.E84 2012
937'.63—dc23   2011048318

Printed in the United States of America on acid-free paper

www.atrandom.com

2 4 6 8 9 7 5 3 1

First Edition

Book design by Jo Anne Metsch

In memory of
the poet
José-Maria de Heredia,
my forebear
and
another student of Rome

LA TREBBIA

L'aube d'un jour sinistre a blanchi les hauteurs.
Le camp s'éveille. En bas roule et gronde le fleuve
Où l'escadron léger des Numides s'abreuve.
Partout sonne l'appel clair des buccinateurs.

Car malgré Scipion, les augures menteurs,
La Trebbia débordée, et qu'il vente et qu'il pleuve,
Sempronius Consul, fier de sa gloire neuve,
A fait lever la hache et marcher les licteurs.

Rougissant le ciel noir de flamboîments lugubres,
A l'horizon brûlaient les villages Insubres;
On entendait au loin barrir un éléphant.

Et là-bas, sous le pont, adossé contre une arche,
Hannibal écoutait, pensif et triomphant,
Le piétinement sourd des légions en marche.

J-M H

PREFACE

ROM EDWARD GIBBON ONWARD, HISTORIANS HAVE pondered the decline and fall of the Roman Empire. But how was the empire won? What was it that enabled a small Italian market town by a ford on the river Tiber to conquer the known world? I seek to answer these questions by telling the story of the rise of Rome. This is the first time in many years that an account of the Roman Republic has been written for the reader with a general interest in history, and more particularly in the origins of the West. It is a taster of the treasures in store for anyone who wishes to dig deeper into the subject.

THIS REMOTE PAST is worth the trouble of exhuming because the Romans remain relevant to us. They still inspire us, still have an effect on how we view social, political, and moral values. We live in a world they made.

The idea of Rome is imprinted on our genes. It has generated proverbs, maxims, and phrases that we use in our everyday lives with scarcely a thought for their old significance: all roads lead to Rome, the grandeur that was Rome, when in Rome do as the Romans do, Rome wasn't built in a day, Rome the eternal city.

Every few years, Hollywood produces a film that re-creates this vanished civilization—among them *Gladiator, Spartacus, Ben-Hur,* and *Quo Vadis.* We stand in awe of Roman power and ruthlessness. We are frightened, but also enthralled, by their "Games"—the bloodstained entertainments in which gladiators fought one another for the amusement of huge audiences.

The Romans were a practical people fascinated by engineering. They pioneered the art of building long-lasting roads. They showed how living in towns could be comfortable and civilized, even if mainly for the rich.

A community is not just about bricks and mortar. The Romans were practical in another way, for they believed deeply in the rule of law. From their earliest years, they created a legal system, which they went on improving throughout their history. Roman law has influenced the legal systems of many modern European countries and also that of the United States.

Although Latin died out as a living language after the Western Roman Empire came to an end in the fifth century A.D., it has had a long afterlife. Until the 1960s and the Second Vatican Council, the religious services of the Roman Catholic Church were conducted in Latin. Even today, flowers and plants, and medical names for parts of the body and for diseases, are in Latin. The constellations in the night sky are called by Latin names and reflect the heroes and heroines of Greco-Roman legends. The names of many American institutions—such as Senate, Congress, and President—come from Latin. Courses in Latin are still offered in some high schools and in many colleges and universities. Translations of Rome's poets and historians are on sale in American and European bookshops.

The founding fathers of the United States of America were brought up on the classics of Roman literature. They were fascinated by the Roman system of republican government. They liked its balance between three sources of power: kingship (all-powerful Roman consuls); oligarchy, or rule by a few noble families (the

Roman Senate); and democracy, or rule by the People (the Roman citizens' assemblies, which passed laws). The first Americans imitated this model and designed a three-part government, full of checks and balances, with a President, a Senate and a Chamber of Representatives, and a judicial system.

THE CITY'S FOUNDATION myths and the events of its early centuries are almost entirely unhistorical, but they were what Romans believed of themselves. They are a rich and poetic feast that has nourished European civilization for two thousand years. It is only in the past few generations that our collective mind has begun to jettison them. If this book serves any purpose, it is as a reminder of what we are losing.

I reflect on the big themes and analyze the development of Roman politics, warfare, and society. But above all this is history as *story,* and I seek to bring to life the extraordinary personalities who lived it—from Tarquin the Proud to Marius, from Coriolanus to Sulla, from Scipio Africanus to the brothers Gracchi. The most charismatic of them all was not even a Roman but the man who came closest to destroying Rome—the great, tragic, embittered Hannibal.

One of the curious features of Roman history is that it often suggests parallels between then and now, but such comparisons can be dangerous, and I leave readers to make their own connections unaided.

AN UNQUENCHABLE LEGEND underpins the hopes and ambitions of many of the actors in this long drama—that of the siege and sack of the city of Troy (or Ilium, as Homer had it in his epic poem the *Iliad*) and the tragic heroism of the Greek warrior Achilles, doomed to die young but glorious. A latter-day Achilles, the astounding Alexander the Great, also blazed a trail that many young Greeks and Romans, from Pyrrhus to Pompey, did their best to emulate. And it was generally agreed that Rome was Troy reborn, ready to avenge itself on the once victorious Greeks. When he invaded Italy, Pyrrhus (also the name of Achilles' son), the king of Epirus, believed that he was refighting the Trojan War, and mythical divinities, such as Jupiter's wife, Juno, and the demigod Hercules, were deployed by Hannibal as weapons in his propaganda campaign against Rome.

One of my protagonists is the city of Rome itself. Its temples, statues, rituals, and symbols were a visual register of collective memory. The Romans were fascinated by the historical associations of the places, shrines, temples, and statues of their city. Ceremonial customs often included enigmatic allusions to events that took place along ago. Interpreted carefully, the urban landscape was its own history book. The past was reincarnated in the present. The living sensed that they were treading in the footsteps of greater ancestors and that distant happenings had a way of repeating themselves, in a light disguise.

The Romans were fighters and spent much of their time battling with their neighbors in Italy and then with powers beyond the Mediterranean Sea. Politics and warfare were inextricably intertwined in their system of government. Ambitious men had to combine the art of the public speaker at home with that of the general in the field if they meant to attain power. And power, *imperium,* was what they were educated to seek—less for the general good than for their own *gloria,* or public esteem.

My stress on narrative and the deeds of famous men (it *is* usually men) is, in fact, how the Romans saw their past, and I aim to offer not so much a complete history as a portrait sketch, which they themselves would recognize. Inevitably, there is much war, death, and blood to wade through in these pages, but, as occasion offers, I attend to the diversions of peace as well.

By great good fortune, many of the private letters of the first-century orator and politician Cicero have survived. They open a window into the minds of men faced with the collapse of their state. As a remedy against pessimism about the present, they studied the history and antiquities of early Rome. If he and like-minded friends had not pursued their researches, not only would we know less about their city's history; we would know less of what this city had about it that meant so much to them.

SCHOLARS HAVE, RIGHTLY, questioned the historicity of events in the literary sources. Ancient historians did their best with the materials at hand; where there were information gaps they were tempted to fill them in with what seemed plausible. The greatest of them, Livy, was as much an artist as a scholar and his masterwork, the multivolume *Ab urbe condita* (*From the Foundation of the City*) possesses some of the qualities of a good historical novel. He is a wonderful author, but not always a trustworthy guide.

On occasion, contemporary academics overreach themselves. They dismiss incidents because they are, to the rational mind, simply implausible; they must have been made up. Unfortunately, much in history is implausible. It is in the nature of human affairs that this should be so.

Throughout the time span of this book and especially in the first centuries, academic crux succeeds academic crux. Sometimes agreement has been reached, elsewhere debate continues, often fierily. Every now and again, one suspects an excess of ingenuity. While I nod in the direction of these uncertainties, if not in the main text then in the endnotes, I do not spend too much time on difficulties of interpretation, which are of little interest to anyone but the specialist.

Taking the variable nature of the literary sources into account, I have divided the book into three parts: Legend, the age of the kings, where most of the events never took place, at least not in the manner described; Story, the conquest of Italy and constitutional conflict, where fact and fiction cohabit; and History, the Republic as a

Mediterranean power, where the literary sources make a serious attempt at objectivity and accuracy.

I CLOSE MY narrative with the bitter civil war between Sulla and Marius in the first century B.C., and the statesmanlike eastern settlement of Pompey the Great. The contrast between external triumph and domestic collapse could scarcely be greater.

Although more conquests were to come, the Republic was now the undisputed ruler of a vast Mediterranean empire; at the same time, it was on the verge of a final and irrevocable constitutional breakdown. The men who governed the world were unable to govern themselves.

Readers who want to know what happened next may wish to consult my lives of Cicero and Augustus, which trace at some length Rome's bloody transition from a partial democracy to a total autocracy.

When I refer to a year or to a particular century, it should be understood as B.C., unless specified otherwise.

Roman nomenclature is complicated and requires an explanation. Most male citizens had three names. The first was the given name, or *praenomen.* In the late Republic, only eighteen of these were in general use, the most popular being Aulus, Decimus, Gaius, Gnaeus, Lucius, Marcus, Publius, and Quintus. As a rule, an eldest son took his father's praenomen—annoyingly, because it requires care to distinguish between different historical figures with identical names.

Then followed the *nomen,* or family name, the equivalent of our surname. After this came the *cognomen.* Originally, this was a nickname attached to a particular person (thus *Cicero* means "chickpea" and presumably referred to a pimple on the face of a once-upon-a-time Tullius), but over the years it came to denote branches of the larger family, or clan. A successful general would be given an additional cognomen, or *agnomen,* which referred to the enemy he overcame. So, after defeating Hannibal in northern Africa, Publius Cornelius Scipio became Publius Cornelius Scipio Africanus.

The subordinate status of women was exemplified by the fact that they were allocated only one name, the feminine version of the family nomen. So the daughter of Marcus Tullius Cicero was called Tullia. Sisters had to share the same name, which must have caused confusion in the family circle. They usually kept their *nomina* after marriage (so Cicero's wife was called Terentia, not Tullia).

When using his full official designation, a Roman citizen inserted after his nomen his father's praenomen and his tribe. So the complete Cicero was Marcus Tullius M[arci] *f*[*ilius,* or "Marcus's son"] Cor[nelia *tribu,* "in the Cornelia tribe"] Cicero.

When readers use this book's index, they should refer to the nomen. So when looking up Cicero, they will find him listed under the *T*'s as Tullius Cicero, Marcus. Tiresome, but that is how it is.

CONTENTS

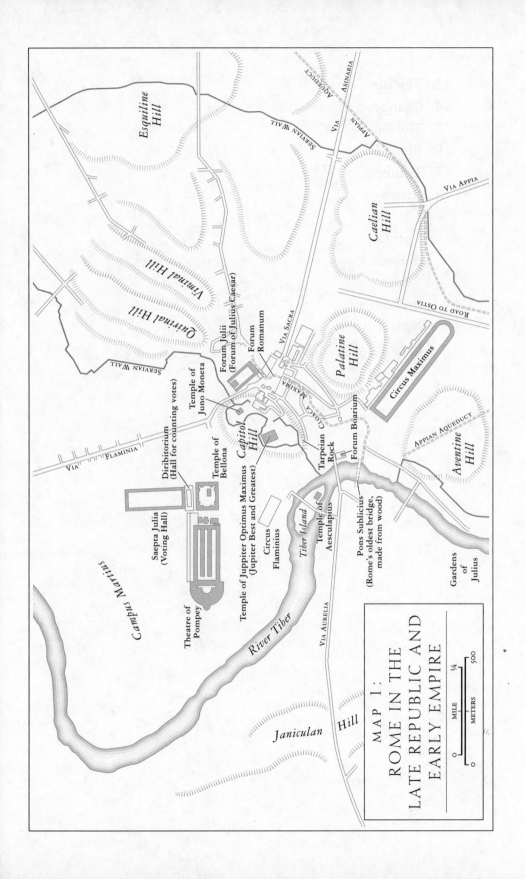

MAP 1:
ROME IN THE
LATE REPUBLIC AND
EARLY EMPIRE

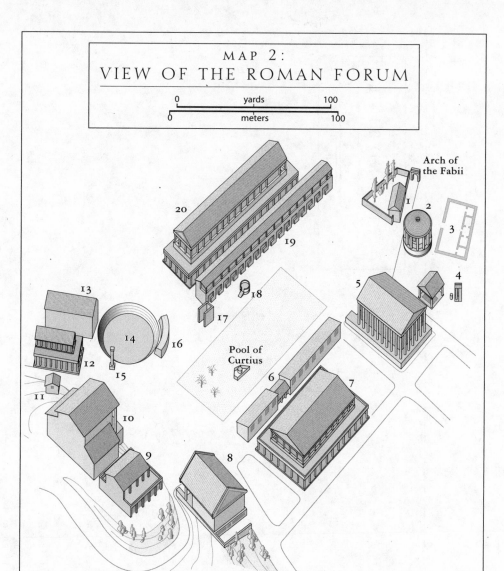

| 0 | yards | 100 |
| 0 | meters | 100 |

Arch of
the Fabii

Pool of
Curtius

A reconstruction of the Roman Forum in the second century. Beginning from the top right, then clockwise. The triangular Regia (1); the circular temple of Vesta (2); in plan the House of the Vestals (3); the Pool of Iuturna (4), a long narrow trough; the temple of Castor and Pollux (5); the Old Shops (6), a row in front of the Basilica Sempronia (7); the temple of Saturn (8), Rome's treasury; the Basilica Opimia (9); the temple of Concord (10); the tiny state Prison (11); the Basilica Porcia (12); the Senate-House or Curia (13), which looks out on the circular Comitium (14), a gathering place for meetings of the People's assembly; the Column of Gaius Maenius (15), victor of a naval battle against Antium in 338; the speakers' platform or Rostra (16), named after captured ships' prows from Maenius's victory; the shrine of Janus (17); the shrine of Venus Cloacina (18); the line of New Shops (19), behind which stands the Basilica Aemilia (20).

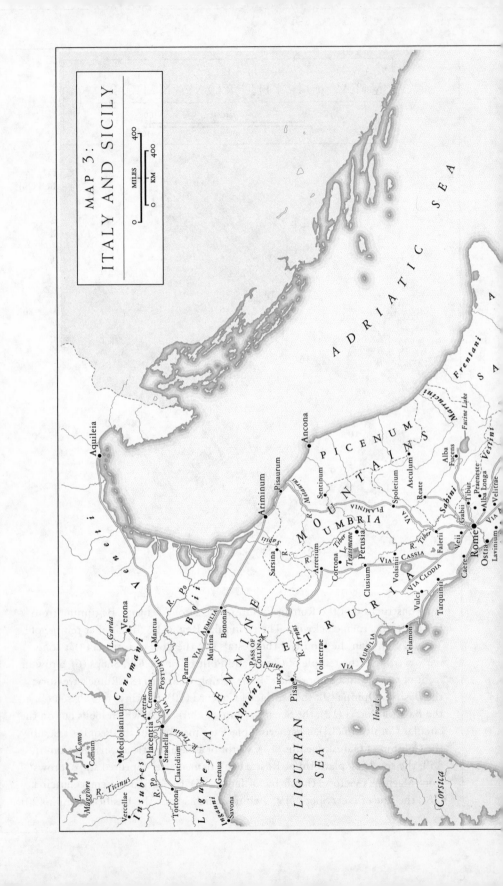

MAP 3:
ITALY AND SICILY

MILES   400
KM   400

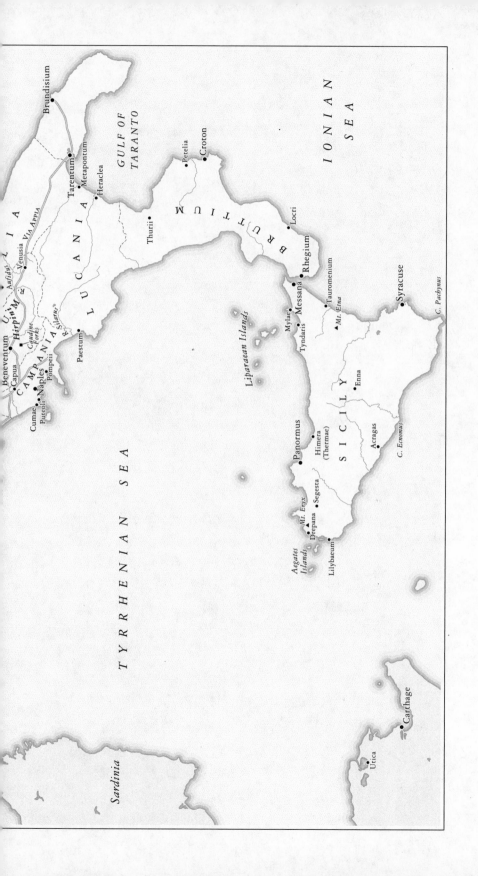

Brundisium

GULF OF
TARANTO

Tarentum
Metapontum
Heraclea

Petelia • Croton

Thurii

B R U T T I U M

Locri

Rhegium

Messana
Tauromenium

Syracuse

C. Pachynus

I O N I A N

S E A

Mylae
Tyndaris
Mt. Etna

Liparaean Islands

Paestum

Pompeii

S I C I L Y

Enna

Panormus
Himera
(Thermae)

Acragas

C. Ecnomus

Segesta

Mt. Eryx

Drepana

Aggates
Islands
Lilybaeum

T Y R R H E N I A N   S E A

Brundisium

Venusia VIA APPIA
Aufidus

L U C A N I A

Beneventum U I A
Capua
HIRPINI
Caudine
Forks
CAMPANIA Silarus
Cumae Naples
Puteoli

Sardinia

Carthage

Utica

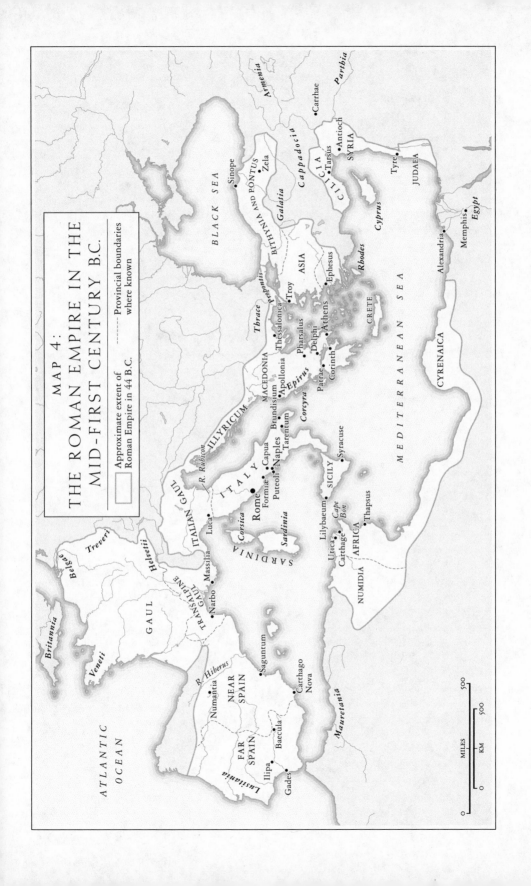

MAP 4:
THE ROMAN EMPIRE IN THE
MID-FIRST CENTURY B.C.

Approximate extent of
Roman Empire in 44 B.C.

Provincial boundaries
where known

INTRODUCTION

TWO OLD FRIENDS, NOW GETTING ON IN YEARS, WERE looking forward to meeting each other again. The year was 46 B.C. and Marcus Terentius Varro, the most prolific author of his day, was on his way to his country house a few miles south of Rome. A shrewd, practical man, Varro was no deep thinker, but he did try to know all that was known. His neighbor Marcus Tullius Cicero was a great public speaker, whether in the law courts or in the political bear pit of the Senate House. Self-regarding, eloquent, and sensitive, Cicero was vinegar to Varro's oil. For all that, they liked each other, largely because they shared the same interests. One of these was a passion for Rome's past.

By a happy chance, a few of Cicero's letters to Varro have survived the bonfire of time. In one note, Cicero urged Varro to hurry up: "I am coming to hope that your arrival is not far away. I wish I may find some comfort in it though our afflictions are so many and so grievous that nobody but an arrant fool ought to hope for any relief."

The "afflictions" Cicero had in mind stemmed from a civil war among Rome's governing élite. Leading personalities were at risk of losing life and limb. What were they to do, they asked themselves anxiously, in an age when the Roman Republic, the ancient world's lone superpower, omnipotent abroad, seemed bent on destroying itself at home?

MOST OBSERVERS OF the day thought that the rot had set in a century or so previously. Rome's conquest of Greece and much of the Near East released unimaginable quantities of gold, not to mention that human gold, uncounted numbers of slaves. Wealth flooded into Rome, which became, in effect, the capital of the known world and grew into a multicultural melting pot and megalopolis of up to one million souls.

This was the unintended consequence of winning an empire, and it is perhaps no accident that the serious study of Rome's past began at about this time. To men like Varro and Cicero, the once tough, socially responsible, resourceful, and plain-living Roman was being softened and subverted by the Oriental vices of greed, luxury, and sexual license. The city's constitution had served it well for centuries. A lawmaking citizens' assembly balanced a small ruling class of nobles. But for this system to work effectively a capacity for compromise and reasonableness was essential—and now this capacity had been lost.

The crisis came when Cicero was a young man. In 82, the Republic's bloodbath of a civil war, which was waged on and off for fifty years, reached its first horrific climax. Soldiers were forbidden to enter Rome, but a vengeful and ambitious general, Lucius Cornelius Sulla, led an army of Roman citizens into the city and conducted a massacre of his opponents.

The uncertainty about who was to be a victim paralyzed high society. Eventually, a young man plucked up his courage and approached Sulla.

"We don't ask you to exempt from punishment those you have decided to kill, but at least free from suspense those you have decided to spare," the young man said.

"I don't yet know whom I'm going to spare."

"Well, then, at least make clear whom you're going to kill."

Sulla took the point, and saw to it that from time to time white-washed notice boards were put up in the Forum, Rome's central square, on which were written the names of those who were to die. There were no formal executions, and anyone who chose to was permitted to carry out killings, and qualified for a handsome reward upon the production of a severed head. A victim's estate was forfeit. The process was called a proscription (the Latin for "notice board" is *proscriptio*).

SULLA'S OBJECT WAS to eliminate his opponents, but his supporters often took the opportunity to settle private scores or to enrich themselves. One hapless property owner complained, "What a disaster! I'm being hunted down by my Alban estate."

Cicero, an ambitious lawyer in his twenties, had direct experience of this cruel and fraudulent behavior. In his first criminal case, he courageously exposed the activities of a member of Sulla's circle, a Greek former slave named Chrysogonus. He revealed a plot to pretend that a dead landowner had been proscribed; this allowed his estate to be confiscated and sold at a knock-down price to Chrysogonus.

At some risk to his personal safety, Cicero drew an unforgettable portrait of a ruthless fixer on the make:

> And look at the man himself, gentlemen of the jury. You see how, with hair carefully arranged and smeared with oil, he roams around the Forum, accompanied by a crowd of hangers-on who (humiliatingly, he implied) are all Roman citizens. You see how he despises everybody, how he considers no other human being to be his superior and believes that he alone is rich and powerful.

Luckily, the authorities left Cicero alone, and it may be that the general had not been aware of the advantage men like Chrysogonus were taking of a confused situation.

Sulla was not simply a mass murderer; he was also a thoughtful politician. He introduced reforms designed to strengthen the powers of the ruling class and to ensure that nobody else would be able to copy his example and hijack the state at the head of an army. They failed, and the careers of politicians loyal to the constitution, such as Cicero and Varro, were thrown off course by a succession of would-be Sullas, the last of whom, Gaius Julius Caesar, launched the civil war that brought down the Roman Republic. Caesar's victory meant there was no longer room for them on the public stage.

How was a patriotic Roman to respond? As far as Varro and Cicero were concerned, there was no alternative but to withdraw into a life of scholarship. In particular, this meant writing histories of Rome, or composing political treatises, or becoming an antiquarian.

"Only let us be firm on one point—to live together in our literary studies," Cicero told Varro in April:

> If anyone cares to call us in as architects or even as workmen to build a commonwealth, we shall not say no, rather we shall hasten cheerfully to the task. If our services are not required, we must still read and write books on the ideal republic.

Varro certainly did pursue his researches. He is credited with writing a phenomenal 490 books, although only one complete work survives—a handbook on agriculture. He lived to a very great age, completing one of his most celebrated tomes, *Country Matters* (*De re rustica*), toward the end of his life. He told his wife, "If man is a bubble, all the more so is an old man. My eightieth year warns me to pack my bags before I set out on the journey from life." In fact, he managed to survive for one more decade. Among other achievements, Varro established a chronology, which fixed the foundation date of Rome at 753 B.C.; although it contains errors, it remains the traditional time line to this day.

Varro and Cicero continued to meet, sharing black views of the current state of affairs and recalling Rome's past glories. They visited each other in one or another of their rural or seaside villas. Cicero could be a persnickety and demanding guest. "If I have leisure to visit Tusculum," he wrote, "I shall see you there. If not I shall follow you to Cumae, and let you know in advance, so that the bath be ready." A little later, he jokingly threatened, "If *you* don't come to me *I* shall run over to you."

His admiration for his learned friend shines through the correspondence: "These days you are now spending down at Tusculum are worth a lifetime by my reckoning. I would gladly leave all earthly wealth and power to others, and take in exchange a license to live like this, free from interruption by any outside force. I am following your example as best I can."

ROME'S HISTORIANS AND antiquarians did not regard themselves as professional scholars but, like Cicero and Varro, tended to be unemployed members of the ruling class. Their purpose was to educate the degenerate generations of their own day. They wanted to be truthful, but when they were handicapped by a lack of facts they accepted legends and were not beyond filling gaps with what they felt must, even should, have happened.

They shaped the story of Rome's early years as they, the despairing politicians of the Republic's last gasp, wanted it to be. It was meant as an alternative to the ruinous present. Thomas Babington Macaulay, the nineteenth-century English poet, historian, and politician, imagined that the foundation myths of Rome were originated as folk ballads, and he re-created some of them in unforgettable verse.

Better than anyone else, he has evoked the stern spirit of the Roman patriot:

> To every man upon this earth
> Death cometh soon or late.

And how can man die better
Than facing fearful odds,
For the ashes of his fathers
And the temples of his gods?

The tales men such as Varro and Cicero told not only illustrated lost virtue but also included horror stories of long ago, worked up if not made up, which were intended to be a dreadful warning to the wrongdoers of their own day, who were set on destroying the state. Their version of events is only loosely connected to the truth (insofar as we can discern this nearly three millennia later), but its historical unreliability is much less important than the light it casts on what a Roman saw when he examined himself closely in an idealizing mirror.

I

LEGEND

1

A New Troy

THE ORIGIN OF ROME CAN BE TRACED BACK TO A giant of a wooden horse.

FOR TEN YEARS a coalition of Greek rulers besieged Troy, a mighty city-state at the foot of the Dardanelles, on the coast of what is now northwest Turkey. The expeditionary force was there largely thanks to the machinations of three deities: Juno, the wife of the king of the gods, Jupiter; Minerva, whose specialty was wisdom; and the goddess of sexual passion, Venus. They were competing for a golden apple inscribed with the words "A prize for the most beautiful." Not even their fellow gods dared to judge among these potent and easily offended creatures, and so it was decided that the poisoned choice would be handed to a mortal, a young shepherd named Paris, who tended his flock on the slopes of Mount Ida, a few miles from Troy. His only qualification appears to have been astonishing good looks, for there was nothing in his character to mark him out from the crowd.

The goddesses duly turned up without a stitch of clothing on among them. Not being above bribery, they offered, respectively, the gifts of power, of knowledge—and of access to the most beautiful woman in the world, Helen, the queen of Sparta. Feckless and

randy, Paris accepted the third offer and awarded the apple to
Venus. The losers stormed off, plotting vengeance.

It transpired that Paris was actually of royal blood. His father
was Priam, the king of Troy. When his mother was carrying him,
she dreamed that she would give birth not to a baby but to a flaming torch. This was a serious warning from the gods of future disaster, and the couple arranged for a shepherd to leave the baby exposed
on a mountainside (a regular means of eliminating unwanted infants in the classical world), to be eaten by wild animals. The shepherd didn't have the heart to obey, and brought the boy up himself.

Once the youth's true identity was revealed, his parents put the
bad dream to the back of their minds and acknowledged him as
their son. Priam dispatched him with a fleet to conduct a friendship tour of the isles of Greece. Paris had a better idea. He made
straight for Sparta and the court of Menelaus and his wife, Helen.
Helen was even more beautiful than he had imagined. While
Menelaus was away on a visit to Crete, he eloped with her and
sailed back to Troy with his prize.

Although Priam recognized that his son had broken the laws of
hospitality by stealing another man's wife, he unwisely received the
couple within his walls. He should have realized that he was welcoming a lighted torch into his city, just as his wife's dream had
foretold.

The cuckolded husband's brother was the federal overlord of in-
numerable Greek statelets. Together they won the support of their
fellow rulers and a combined army set off for Troy, to retrieve Helen
and punish the city that had taken her in. Ten wearying years
passed, full of incident but without a decisive victory for either
side. The most notable event took place in the ninth year of the
siege. This was a prolonged sulk by the Greeks' greatest military
asset, the youthful but hot-tempered Achilles.

A handsome redhead, he was brought up as a girl among a sister-
hood of girls, according to one tradition. This was because his

mother, Thetis, a granddaughter of the sea god Poseidon (the Roman Neptune), foresaw that his fate was either to win eternal fame and die early or to live a long life in obscurity. As a loving parent, she opted for longevity. Achilles, who was given a female name, Pyrrha (Greek for "flame-colored," in tribute to his hair), was pretty enough for the ruse to go undetected for some time—until the boy got one of his fellow schoolgirls pregnant. Once permitted to be male, he rejected his mother's wishes and opted for glory. He soon became known as a great warrior and went happily off to fight at Troy, in the full knowledge that he would never return.

Battles in this heroic age were not fought by disciplined groups of men, according to epic poets such as Homer, but were in effect a series of simultaneous individual combats or duels between kings and noblemen. The rank and file took their cue from the success or failure of their champions. After a quarrel with the commander-in-chief, Achilles stayed in his tent and refused to join the battle. However, he allowed his dear friend, and (some said) lover, Patroclus, to borrow his armor and fight on his behalf. Patroclus was killed, and his death brought the Greek hero raging back onto the battlefield, where he dispatched Hector, Troy's bravest champion and Priam's firstborn son.

Achilles was soon dead himself, shot by an arrow from the bow of Paris. Then Paris, the cause of all this woe, was felled, the victim of another archer. The war had arrived at a stalemate.

Openhearted and fearless, honorable but unrelenting in revenge, Achilles was an iconic figure in the ancient world. Young Greeks and Romans through the centuries admired him and wanted to be like him. The Macedonian conqueror Alexander the Great kept by his bedside a copy of Homer's *Iliad,* whose unparalleled poetry celebrates the wrath of Achilles.

ONE MORNING, TROJANS manning the walls looked seaward and were amazed by what they saw. The Greek camp alongside the beach was deserted and the fleet was gone. It was evident that the war was over and the invaders were on their way home. The people flooded out of the city in a state of great enthusiasm. They were puzzled by the sight of an enormous wooden horse, but a Greek deserter told them that it was an offering to Minerva. Apparently, a seer had announced that if the Trojans destroyed it they would provoke her resentment, but if they brought it inside the city she would become their protector, despite the unpleasant business of the golden apple.

A few voices argued that the horse should be burned or pushed into the sea, but it was eventually decided to drag it into Troy. The city gate was too small to admit it, so part of the wall had to be knocked down to make room. The evening was given over to feasting and drinking. Sentries were not posted, and when the revelers at last went to their beds the sleeping city lay defenseless beneath the stars.

OF COURSE, THE Greeks had not departed. Their fleet had harbored behind the offshore island of Tenedos, a few miles down the coast, and awaited nightfall before returning to Troy. Ulysses, the crafty ruler of Ithaca, an island in the Ionian Sea, had devised a cunning plan. The wooden horse was his idea, and it was designed with an internal compartment capable of housing twenty armed men. He briefed the soi-disant defector to tell his entirely fictional story. In the early hours, the man opened a hidden door and let out the soldiers who were locked inside. Meanwhile, a Greek force marched from the shore and entered the city without let or hindrance.

Aeneas, a member of a junior branch of the Trojan royal family and the son-in-law of Priam, had gone to sleep that night in the house of his father, Anchises, in a secluded quarter of the city. His mother was Venus, active as ever in the affairs, and the *affaires de coeur,* of Troy, who had seduced Anchises in his youth and detained him for nearly two weeks of nonstop lovemaking. Aeneas had a nightmare in which Achilles' victim, his body covered with dust and blood, warned him that the city had been captured and was in flames; it was his duty to escape. He woke up to find that this was indeed the case. Climbing to the roof of the house, he saw fires blazing in every direction.

Aeneas realized that nothing could be done to reverse the catastrophe. As the dream had told him, it was his sacred obligation to lead a party of survivors, and refound Troy elsewhere. He took with him the city's *penates,* images of its household gods, and (some said) the celebrated Palladium, an ancient, sacred wooden statue of Minerva that had fallen from the sky.

The small company, which included Aeneas's aged father and his young son Ascanius, also known as Iulus, made its way to one of the city gates, using dark side streets and avoiding Greek marauders. The Trojan prince suddenly realized that his wife was missing, and rushed back to look for her, without success. Returning empty-handed at dawn, he was surprised to find a large crowd of refugees awaiting his orders.

According to another narrative, Aeneas was in charge of allied reinforcements that withdrew to Troy's citadel and prevented the enemy from taking the entire city. He created enough of a distraction to allow much of the civilian population to escape and, after negotiating a cease-fire with the Greeks, marched his people out of Troy in good order.

One way or another, a fair number of Trojans had survived, and under Aeneas's command a decision was taken to leave their native land forever. A fleet was built, and the party sailed away with no certain destination. The idea was to find somewhere to settle and establish a new national home.

This was more easily said than done. Abortive attempts were made to found a city in Thrace and Crete. Aeneas spent some time with a relative who had become ruler in Epirus, on the western coast of Greece, after the assassination of Achilles' son, Pyrrhus, the country's brutal young king. This relative advised Aeneas to make for Italy. However, the unforgetting goddesses Juno and Minerva were determined to prevent a rebirth of the hated Troy, and Aeneas was forced to undergo many dangerous adventures. Like Ulysses before him on his long journey back to Ithaca, he had a narrow escape from the one-eyed giant Polyphemus. Finally, the Trojans were blown off course by a storm and shipwrecked on the coast of North Africa.

THEY FOUND THAT they were not the only refugees seeking a new world. A group of Phoenician expatriates were building a settlement on a strip of coast leased from local tribes. They originated from the great island port of Tyre, in what is now Lebanon.

Tyre was a monarchy. Its unscrupulous ruler had arranged the murder of a wealthy landowner and confiscated his estates. The dead man's widow, Dido, assembled a large community of people who either hated or feared their king and (prompted by her husband's helpful ghost) unearthed a secret hoard of gold to fund her expenses. Seizing some ships in the harbor, she and her followers made good their escape.

They were building Carthage (Phoenician for "new city") on part of a large promontory backed by two lagoons to the north and south when the Trojans arrived, storm-shaken, caked with brine, and exhausted. They were amazed, and doubtless a little jealous, at what they saw.

Virgil, Rome's national poet and the author of the *Aeneid,* an epic poem on the adventures of Aeneas, imagines the scene:

Aeneas looked wonderingly at the solid structures springing up where there had once been only African huts, and at the gates, the turmoil, and the paved streets. The Tyrians were hurrying about busily, some tracing a line for the walls and manhandling stones up the slopes as they strained to build their citadel, and

others siting some building and marking its outline by ploughing a furrow.

Dido welcomed the strangers and, hearing their story, sympathized with Aeneas for his misfortunes. The goddess Juno now
found herself in an uncomfortable position; if Aeneas could be persuaded to make Carthage his home, he would abandon the glorious
future in Italy that had been prophesied for him and there would
no longer be any risk of a new Troy rising from the ground. Unfortunately, though, the despised Trojan would have to marry Dido, a
favorite of hers, as indeed was Carthage. This was a bitter sacrifice,
but she had no choice but to make it.

Arrangements were made with the cooperation of Venus, and the
queen of Carthage duly fell in love with the exile. On a hunting
expedition in the hills, Juno arranged for a fortuitous thunderstorm
and the couple took refuge in a cave, where nature followed its
pleasant course. Dido called the encounter a wedding.

Unfortunately, a local African chieftain had had his eye on Dido
for himself, and did not want to lose her. He was a great devotee of
Jupiter and prayed to him for help. He complained, "Now this
second Paris, wearing a Phrygian bonnet to tie up his chin and
cover his oily hair, and attended by a train of she-men, is to become
the owner of what he has stolen."

Jupiter had known nothing of his wife's plot and was furious. He
immediately dispatched a messenger to warn the Trojan prince to
remember his destiny and leave at once for Italy. Aeneas the True
(so called because of his reputation for loyalty) was thunderstruck
by the rebuke and abandoned Dido without delay.

Thoroughly embarrassed, he tried to justify himself to her, placing the blame on the king of the gods. "So stop upsetting yourself,
and me too, by these protests," he said. "It is not by my own choice
that I voyage onward toward Italy."

Dido, spurned, chose to die. She had a great funeral pyre built, letting it be known that her purpose was to incinerate a sword Aeneas had left behind, some of his clothes, and his portrait. This was a ruse, for the pyre was for her own use. She climbed up onto it and stabbed herself. Before dying, she uttered a curse, predicting eternal enmity between her new city and the one her Trojan lover and his posterity would found in Italy:

> Neither love nor compact shall there be between the nations. And from my dead bones may some avenger arise to persecute with fire and sword these settlers from Troy, soon or in aftertime, whenever the strength is given! Let your shores oppose their shores, your waves their waves, your arms their arms. That is my imprecation. Let them fight, they, and their sons' sons, for ever!

At long last, Aeneas and his companions reached Italy. As they sailed along its western coast, a large wood came into view through which the yellow waters of the river Tiber poured into the sea; and here the Trojans disembarked. Their voyage was at an end. They were greeted by Latinus, the old and henpecked king of the Latini, a tribe living between the Tiber and Anio rivers, from which Latium (today's Lazio) gets its name. He and his people were of Greek origin. Thanks to his wife's influence, his daughter Lavinia had been promised to Turnus, the young and energetic chief of the Rutulians. The king for once stood up for himself; he now changed his mind and gave her to the Trojan newcomer.

War was the inevitable outcome, and Aeneas killed Turnus in single combat. Following this victory he founded the city of Lavinium, named after his wife. The Rutulians were down but not out. Hostilities were resumed and a great battle was fought beside the river Numicius, near Lavinium. There were many casualties, and when night fell the armies separated.

Aeneas, though, had vanished. Some thought he had been translated to the gods, others that he had drowned. His mother, never knowingly worsted, arranged for him to be deified. Dionysius of Halicarnassus, an antiquarian who flourished in the first century A.D., reports that, in his day, a memorial was still standing on the site of the battle. It was a small mound around which stood regular rows of trees. An inscription read, "To the father and god of this place, who presides over the waters of the river Numicius."

Seven years had passed since Aeneas left the smoldering ruins of Troy.

2

Kings and Tyrants

THE RIVER TIBER ROSE FROM TWO SPRINGS IN A beech forest in the Apennine Mountains, which run down Italy like a rocky spine. In three great zigzags, it crossed a plain for some two hundred and fifty miles and emptied itself into the Mediterranean. About fifteen miles from the coast it wiggled into the shape of the letter *s* as it made its way around a cluster of wooded, sometimes precipitous hills. These overlooked and encircled a wide marshy space crossed by a stream, and on some of them stood poor-looking villages, each consisting of a handful of wattle-and-daub huts. These settlements were easily defended and enjoyed clean air, rather than the humid miasma of the valley. The semi-nomadic inhabitants mainly tended livestock, moving them upstream to summer pastures and back to the plain during winter.

It was here that one of the greatest heroes and demigods of the ancient world, Hercules, slew Cacus, a fire-breathing monster who lived on human flesh and made his home in a cave in one of the hills. A larger-than-life figure, Hercules had numerous lovers of both sexes. He was the son of Jupiter by a mortal woman and so incurred the hatred of Juno, seldom one to control her emotions. Driven mad at her instigation, Hercules killed his own children and in expiation undertook twelve "labors," or feats requiring superhuman strength and bravery.

Hercules became known as a protector of Greek colonists and traders who voyaged dangerously across the Mediterranean, and the story grew of a long wandering, as labor succeeded labor. He began his journey in the city of Gades (today's Cadiz), which he founded in southwestern Spain; this was a community of Phoenicians, merchants who competed with the Greeks and revered Hercules under the name of Melqart. He made his way up Spain, along the south of Gaul (today's France), across the Alps, and down into Italy, then over the sea to Sicily and ending up in Greece. According to Dionysius of Halicarnassus:

> Hercules, who was the greatest commander of his age, marched at the head of a large force through all the territory that lies on this side of the Ocean [meaning the Atlantic Ocean], destroying any tyrannies that oppressed their subjects, or states that outraged and injured their neighbors, or organized bands of men who lived like savages and lawlessly put strangers to death. In their place he established lawful monarchies, well-ordered governments and humane and sociable ways of life. In addition, he mingled barbarians with Greeks, and inland communities with those who lived on the seacoast, groups which had previously been distrustful and unsocial in their dealings with each other.

The hero arrived at the cluster of hills by the Tiber, driving the cattle of a fearsome, three-faced giant he had killed in his tenth labor. He crossed the river and, heavy with food and wine, fell asleep on a grassy bank. Cacus seized the moment and stole a number of the finest bulls. He dragged them into his cave by their tails, so that their hoofprints would point in the wrong direction. When Hercules woke up, he noticed that some cattle were missing but could not work out where they were (demigods were evidently of a dimmer wattage than mere mortals today). However, some heifers mooed when the herd moved off and the captive bulls lowed in response, betraying their location. Cacus tried to resist the infuriated hero but was struck down by his club. Hercules fortified the hill, later known as the Palatine, and went on his way.

THE RIVER, SWOLLEN by heavy rains, often flooded, transforming the hills into islands. On one such occasion, a wooden trough containing newborn twin boys could be seen, washed up against a slope. As the waters ebbed, it hit a stone and overturned, throwing out the babies, who whimpered and wallowed in the mud. They lay beneath a fig tree, a popular resort for animals seeking the shade.

A she-wolf who had just whelped appeared, her teats distended with milk. She licked off the mud and allowed the boys to suckle. A woodpecker arrived to lend assistance and stood guard. Now that the way was passable, some herdsmen came by driving their flocks to pasture and were dumbstruck by what they saw. Unabashed and unafraid, the wolf stared at the humans, then loped calmly off and vanished inside a cave, arched over by a dense wood, out of which a stream flowed.

THIS EXTRAORDINARY SCENE marked the next great step in the long process that culminated in the foundation of Rome. Three hundred years had passed since the arrival of Aeneas in Latium. The Trojan prince's son, Ascanius, reigned for nearly forty years in a town he founded, Alba Longa, beneath the Alban Mount, an extinguished volcano (now called Monte Cavo). A line of kings ensued who accomplished little of note and eventually, in the early eighth century B.C., the succession devolved on two brothers, Numitor (the firstborn) and Amulius.

Amulius cheated his elder brother of his throne. He did not harm or imprison Numitor, but killed his son and took steps to prevent his daughter from having offspring who might challenge him for the kingdom when they grew up. He compelled her to become a priestess of Vesta, bound to spend her life as a virgin. The trick did not work, however, for the young woman attracted the attentions of Mars, the god of war, and nine months later she gave birth to healthy twins, Romulus and Remus. The boys were taken from her and a servant was ordered to do away with them by leaving them open to the elements somewhere in the countryside.

It was at this point that the she-wolf came across the boys. One of the shepherds passing by was named Faustulus, keeper of the royal flock. He brought up the infants, and as the years passed they grew into young men with attitude—risk-taking, fearless, and foolhardy. They had hot tempers. According to the biographer Plutarch:

> They were on friendly terms with their equals or superiors, but they looked down on the king's overseers, bailiffs and chief herdsmen. They applied themselves to . . . physical exercise, hunting, running, driving off robbers, capturing thieves and rescuing the oppressed from violence.

When the brothers were about eighteen, a dispute arose between them and some of Numitor's herdsmen. Each side accused the other of grazing meadowland that did not belong to them. They often came to blows. Numitor's men, some of whom had been badly hurt, lost patience and decided to arrest Romulus and Remus and hand them over to the authorities.

Among the group of hills by the Tiber, the centermost, the Palatine, had steep sides, in one of which could be found the cave where the she-wolf had taken refuge. It was a place sacred to the god of shepherds, and every February an ancient festival in his honor was held. The local youths ran around the hill naked except for loincloths made from the skins of animals that had just been sacrificed. Amid much hilarity, they lashed out at bystanders with leather thongs. The purpose of the ritual was to purify the community's flocks, but in later centuries, at least, it was believed that it also fostered human fertility: in Varro and Cicero's day, women stood in the young men's way, supposing that, if they were struck, sterility would be prevented and the pains of childbirth eased.

On this occasion, two groups of boys took part in the ceremonies, with Remus in the first and Romulus with the others, bringing up the rear. The angry herdsmen lay in wait at a narrow section of the roadway; with a loud shout, they rushed on the first group when it came up, throwing stones and spears. Remus and his companions were taken completely by surprise and, bereft of clothes and weapons, were soon overcome and taken prisoner. Romulus escaped and gathered a force with which to rescue his brother.

Remus and the others were brought before the king, who was happy to make an example of them. Wishing to please his brother, Numitor, who shared the herdsmen's exasperation, the king remitted the punishment to him. Numitor watched the captives being led away, hands tied behind them, and was very struck by Remus's good looks and his quiet dignity in misfortune. He could not believe the young man was anything but nobly born, so he took him aside and asked, "Who are you? Who are your parents?"

The young man replied that all he knew was that the man who had brought him up had found him and his twin brother exposed in a wood soon after their birth. Numitor suspected the truth of the matter and, after a short pause, reminded Remus that his punishment had yet to be decided, and that it could be a death sentence. "If I free you, would you be willing to help me in a project that could be to our mutual benefit?" he asked.

Numitor then explained how Amulius had stolen his birthright. He asked Remus to help him regain his throne. Remus, game for anything, jumped at the chance. He was told to await instructions and, in the meantime, to send a message to Romulus asking him to join them as soon as possible. When Romulus arrived, he confirmed his brother's version of their origin.

Meanwhile Faustulus, fearing that Remus's story would not be believed, decided to bring to Numitor as corroboration the trough in which the baby siblings had been placed. He carried it into Alba Longa hidden under his clothes, but as he walked through the town gate he aroused the suspicions of a guard, who could not understand why he was concealing such an everyday object. By an unhappy chance, the man who had originally taken the infants to the river was present and recognized the trough, and Faustulus was immediately hauled before the king to explain himself.

He revealed the whole story. Amulius reacted in a suspiciously friendly manner, so when he asked where the boys were Faustulus pretended that they were watching their flocks in the fields. The king sent him to find them and bring them to the palace, where they would be given a warm welcome. The old shepherd was joined by some guards, who had been given secret instructions to place Romulus and Remus under arrest. In the meantime, the king sent for Numitor, to keep an eye on him until the twins had been properly, and no doubt finally, dealt with.

However, the messenger told Numitor what was afoot and he alerted the boys, their companions, and his own retainers and friends. They forced their way into the town, which was poorly defended. Amulius was easily found and killed. His brother resumed the throne.

Skeptics who believed, as Dionysius of Halicarnassus noted, that "nothing bordering on legend or fable has any place in historical writing," told a different tale. Numitor switched the twins with two changelings; he feared that Amulius would have them killed, and that was exactly what he did. He handed his real grandchildren to Faustulus and his wife. She was a woman of loose virtue and was nicknamed Lupa, or she-wolf, a slang term for a prostitute. The boys received a good education and were ready for public life when the coup against Amulius succeeded.

ONE WAY OR another, this brought to a satisfactory conclusion the story of one brace of brothers but left the future of the other pair in some doubt. What was to be done with these headstrong youths? They were eager for political power, but with the restoration of their grandfather that was not on offer at Alba Longa. However, the population in the kingdom was growing and there were enough adventurers to found a new city. Here was a suitable task for Romulus and Remus (and one that, one may guess, prompted Numitor to heave a sigh of relief).

The brothers decided that the group of hills on the Tiber would be an ideal place for a new city. The ford would allow those who controlled it to manage traffic going up and down the western plain; the hills would assure easy defense from attack; and the Tiber, navigable up to this point, would enable trade and access to salt flats where it met the sea; later, a road to the river mouth was to be called the *via Salaria,* the Salt Road.

Cicero, looking back from the first century B.C., was in no doubt that the choice of site was crucial to Rome's later success:

A river enables the city to use the sea both for importing what it lacks and for exporting what it produces as a surplus; and by its means too the city can not only bring in by sea but also obtain from the land, carried on its waters, whatever is most essential for its life and civilization. Consequently it seems to me that Romulus must at the very beginning have had a divine intimation that the city would one day be the seat and hearthstone of a mighty empire.

The brothers decided that, as a start, they would fortify one of the hills, but they could not agree on which one. Romulus opted for the Palatine, and Remus the neighboring Aventine. Neither would give way, so they went back to Alba and asked their grandfather's advice on how to resolve the quarrel. He proposed that each stand on his chosen hill and, after making a sacrifice to the gods, watch for the flight of birds, a traditional method of discovering the divine will. The decision would go to the one who saw the most auspicious kind of bird.

Remus struck lucky first, for six vultures flew past his vantage point. Romulus, not to be outdone, falsely claimed to have seen twelve vultures. Remus didn't believe him. But when he walked over to the Palatine and challenged his brother, he saw that twelve vultures had in fact just put in an appearance. The question remained undecided, for both men had seen the same kind of bird. Remus claimed victory because he had been the first to spot vultures, and Romulus insisted that he had won because he had seen the largest number of vultures.

Remus lost his temper and made some unkind remarks about a defensive trench Romulus had begun to dig on the Palatine. He jumped scornfully across it, and his brother, now furious as well, attacked him. Their friends and followers joined in the fight. Faustulus, who was present, threw himself unarmed into the melée in an attempt to separate the combatants. He was struck down and killed for his pains. Remus, too, lost his life, at his brother's hands. In Varro and Cicero's day, an old stone lion in the Forum was believed to mark Faustulus's grave.

As calm returned, Romulus realized what he had done. He had founded his new state on a crime. And not just any crime, for he had broken one of the most sacred taboos by committing fratricide. The rivalry of brothers was a common theme in the ancient world—the sons of Oedipus, Eteocles and Polynices, killed one another in a duel—and in the Bible story Cain murdered Abel. But it was something new when the foundation myth of a state originated in brotherly hatred and violence. For Romans in the dying years of the Republic, this was a fearful anticipation of the fratricidal civil wars that led to the decimation of Rome's ruling class.

FILLED WITH GRIEF and remorse, Romulus lost all desire for life—at least for a while. Ambition returned, and he finally built his city on the hill. This was a religious as well as a political act. A foundation pit, the *mundus,* a symbolic entrance to the underworld, was dug, in which clods of earth and first fruits were deposited. Then Romulus, as leader or king, yoked a plow to a bull and a cow and drove a deep furrow around the boundary lines. This marked the *pomerium,* or city limits; it was sacred, and only from inside it could priests watch for the movement of birds and so determine the pleasure of the gods. The city walls, or fortifications, were laid out behind this line and the space on either side was kept free of buildings, graves, and plants. (This ceremony was repeated whenever Rome, in later times, founded a *colonia,* or colony town.)

Romans of the late Republic were eager to determine the date of the foundation of Rome. There was widespread agreement that it took place in the eight century B.C., but there was fierce argument about the exact year. Computations included 728 and 751 B.C., but the date that won the most support came from Cicero's greatest friend, a learned multimillionaire named Atticus, and Varro, who proposed 753 B.C. Even today, this year appears in modern histories as Rome's traditional birthday. Varro was the kind of antiquarian who was fascinated by obscure calculation; he once invited an astrologer to work out from the study of Romulus's life the date of his birth. In what was in effect a reverse horoscope, the man concluded:

[Romulus] was conceived in his mother's womb in the first year of the second Olympiad, in the month Choeac of the Egyptian calendar, on the twenty-third day, and in the third hour, when the sun was totally eclipsed; and . . . he was born in the month Thoth, on the twenty-first day, at sunrise.

Or, in other words, 772 B.C.

This first Rome housed a preliminary population of little more than three thousand Latins. If Romulus was to build a viable community, able not only to man its defenses but also to supply labor for the variety of trades that people would expect of it, he needed more citizens. He established a policy of offering foreigners the gift of Roman nationality, a welcoming approach that lasted a thousand years.

His first measure was to open a sanctuary where exiles, the dispossessed, and criminals and escapees of every kind, freemen or slaves, could take refuge. A miscellaneous rabble soon collected. (The story bears some resemblance to the beginnings of Australia.) It now emerged that there were too few women to go around the growing number of male citizens. Something urgent and decisive had to be done to achieve a one-to-one gender balance.

The king issued a proclamation that an underground altar had been discovered at the racecourse (the Circus Maximus). It was dedicated to Consus, the god of good advice. Romulus proposed a splendid sacrifice, with games and a spectacle open to all the people. Not for the first time, Romulus was playing a trick. Once a large audience had gathered, not only Romans but also members of the neighboring tribe of Sabines, the king took his seat at the front. This was the signal for unleashing a large force of armed men, who kidnapped all the unmarried Sabine women who had come with their families to enjoy the show. Their menfolk were left unharmed and encouraged to make good their escape.

Roman historians could not agree on how many women were taken in this way: estimates varied among 30, 527 and 683. But one thing was clear: every one of them was a virgin.

The Sabines were a warlike people, but before taking military action they sent an embassy to Rome asking for the return of the women. Romulus refused, and counterproposed that marriage between Romans and Sabines should be permitted. Three indecisive battles ensued, and finally, under a general named Titus Tatius, the Sabines invaded Rome and captured its citadel, the Capitoline Hill (or Capitol). A young Roman woman, Tarpeia, betrayed her compatriots by opening one of the gates at night in return for "whatever the Sabines carried on their left arms." By this she meant their golden armlets; instead, loving the treachery but hating the traitor, the men used their shields, worn on their left arms, to crush her to death. A steep cliff on the Capitol was named the Tarpeian Rock after her, from which those convicted of murder or treason were thrown to their deaths (and also people with serious physical or mental disabilities).

A fight ensued in the marshy valley between Rome's hills (the present Forum). The Romans had the worst of it and withdrew toward the Palatine Hill. Romulus was hit on the head by a stone, but picked himself up and shouted to his men to hold their ground. This they did, at a spot by the Via Sacra (Sacred Way) where a temple was later built in gratitude to Jupiter the Stayer. The tide of battle turned and the Romans pushed forward to where the Temple of Vesta now stands.

At this point, an extraordinary thing happened. The Sabine women came pouring down into the valley from every direction. They had been kidnapped and forcibly married, but they now accepted their fate. Interposing their persons between the combatants, they imposed an end to the struggle. A treaty was formed, acknowledging that the Roman husbands had treated their Sabine spouses with due respect, and all who wished to maintain their marriages were allowed to do so. Most of the women stayed where they were.

Romulus (following his old policy) and the Sabines made an even more radical decision. They agreed on a merger of their two states. All Sabines would be awarded Roman citizenship and equal civic rights. Tatius was made co-ruler with Romulus.

ROMULUS WAS AN obstinate and self-willed man. As king, he expected to get his own way. His colleague on the throne died after five years. From then on, Romulus ruled alone. His achievements fall into two classes. First, he established a basic pattern of administration—

the king commanded the army and the judiciary and was advised by a (possibly ad hoc) committee, the Senate (ultimately two hundred strong). Members were drawn from an aristocracy of birth—patricians, the fathers, or *patres,* of the state. They enjoyed important religious privileges. Only they could become priests, and they administered the major cults. They had the authority to consult the gods (by conducting the auspices, or *auspicia*), and they determined the yearly calendar, which included a large number of holy days on which public business could not be conducted. They also supervised the interregnum that followed the death of a king, organizing the election of a successor.

The citizenry was divided into three tribes based on kinship—two of which were composed of Latins and Sabines. Each tribe elected a tribune to represent its interests and commanded tribal levies in times of war. In turn, the three tribes were each subdivided into ten *curiae,* or courts, individually named after thirty of the kidnapped Sabine women. These formed a popular assembly, the *comitia curiata,* which voted by *curiae* on proposals that the king or the Senate placed before it. A *curia* was further subdivided into ten *gentes,* or clans. When considering a proposal, these assemblies cast one vote each, and so by a majority determined the *curia*'s one vote, a majority of which then determined the *comitia curiata*'s decision.

City-states in the Mediterranean in the early classical period tended to be direct democracies, where citizens met in assembly to make all the important decisions, one man having one vote; or oligarchies, where a minority ruling class managed the state; or monarchies or tyrannies (from *turannos,* the Greek for "autocrat," and not necessarily a derogatory term). Quite often, they moved violently from one type of government to another. What was interesting about this early Roman constitution was that it found an ingenious, albeit complicated, formula for combining all three forms of government.

Romulus was as vigorous in the field as he was in the committee room. He set the tone of military aggression that marked Rome's collective personality throughout its history. For more than twenty years, he fought wars with the new state's neighbors, extending territory and expanding the population.

NONE OF THIS meant that the king's fiat was entirely unchallenged. He was generous to his soldiers, assigning them land and giving them a share of the spoils of battle, but as the years passed he became more and more peremptory in manner, especially toward the Senate. On one occasion when they could not come to an agreement, he remarked, "I have chosen you, Senators, not for you to govern me, but for me to have *you* at my command." He presented himself in public in some style, wearing a crown and carrying a scepter with an eagle on the top; he wore scarlet shoes and a floor-length white cloak with purple stripes.

In the thirty-seventh year of his reign, the king went to the Campus Martius, an open space north of the Capitol, and held a military review near the Goat's Marsh (now the site of the Pantheon). Suddenly, a storm came up with loud thunderclaps and darkness fell from a clear sky (perhaps an eclipse). A thick mist formed, and Romulus disappeared from view. When the air cleared, he was no longer sitting on his throne and in fact was nowhere to be found. The senators who had been standing beside him claimed that he had ascended into the skies. One or two said that he had become a god, and soon all present hailed him as divine.

Another version of Romulus's death gained currency. This was that patrician members of the Senate had become so disgusted with his tyrannical ways that they plotted his assassination. They struck him down in the middle of a Senate meeting. They then cut him up into pieces and each "father" carried a body part under his clothes when leaving the meeting. Hence the vanishing.

The Senate was unpopular with ordinary citizens, but their attention was distracted from rumors of conspiracy when, as the historian Livy put it, "the shrewd device of one man is said to have gained credit for the story [of the apotheosis]." A leading politician, he claimed at a People's Assembly that Romulus had descended from heaven and appeared to him. The ghost said that he was to be worshipped under his divine name of Quirinus and promised that "my Rome shall be the capital of the world, so let the Romans cherish the art of war." According to one of Rome's earliest historians, this was a cynical trick, but it certainly worked.

The official version of a deified Romulus was the one that gained the greatest currency. Even experienced and skeptical commentators like Cicero were inclined to believe it. He observed that in the distant and uncivilized past there was a "great inclination to the invention of fabulous tales and ignorant men were easily induced to believe them . . . but we know that Romulus lived less than six hundred years ago when writing and education had long been in existence."

Strangely, the unofficial account of the king's passing was to receive an uncanny echo during Cicero's own lifetime, when in 44 B.C. the great tyrant of *his* age, Gaius Julius Caesar, was struck down by his colleagues during a session of the Senate. Indeed, Cicero was present in the meeting hall at the time, and he must surely have wondered at the coincidence. Then, for seven days, a new comet was seen in the sky, which the common people held to be Caesar's soul; like Romulus, he had ascended into heaven and joined the company of the gods. In Rome's end was its beginning.

THE MONARCHY WAS not handed on by birthright but was an elective post in the gift of the People's Assembly (with some input from the Senate). Most Roman kings were not related to one another and were foreigners or, at least, outsiders; this had the fortunate consequence of removing senators from competition and stabilizing the Senate as an institution.

According to Cicero, the Senate tried for a while to rule without a king, but the People wouldn't have it. An election was held, and the winner was Numa Pompilius, a Sabine from outside the city. If Romulus had been a warrior king, *he* was a priest king. He distributed land to every citizen, writes Cicero, to discourage brigandage and to foster the arts of peace. He was especially interested in religion, which he envisaged as a complex system of rules, ceremonies, and superstitions designed to discover the will of the gods and to ensure their favor. He was advised on these matters by a friendly water nymph named Egeria, whom he consulted privately in her sacred grove (near where the Baths of Caracalla were built in the third century A.D.), but many of his innovations were drawn from Etruscan religious observance. Cicero wrote:

> He wanted the proper performance of the rituals themselves to be difficult, but that the necessary equipment should be readily available, for he provided that much should be learned by heart and scrupulously observed, but made the expenditure of money unnecessary. In this way, he made the performance of religious duties laborious but not costly.

"Laborious" is the word. Senior Romans holding public office spent much of their time on ceremonial business. If any error was made—misspoken or forgotten phrases or interruption of any kind, even the squeaking of a rat—the whole rigmarole had to be repeated until the performance was perfect. On one occasion, a sacrifice was conducted thirty times before the priest got it right.

Numa was followed by a king, Tullus Hostilius, who was even more warlike than Romulus. His reign was marked by a long struggle with Alba Longa, the city built by Aeneas's son and from which Romulus and Remus had emerged to found Rome. It was, in effect, Rome's first civil war. The two sides agreed on a treaty according to which the loser of the conflict would consent to unconditional surrender. The Romans placed a high value on their collective word and, typically, devised an elaborate religious ritual for treaty-making. The king swore that if the Roman People departed in any way from the terms of an agreement with a foreign power he would implore Jupiter, king of the gods, to smite its members, just as he smote a sacrificial pig. With these words, he struck down the pig with a flint.

To avoid a full-scale battle with all the attendant casualties, a duel was agreed on between two sets of triplet brothers—the Curiatii for Alba and the Horatii for Rome. In the fight, all of the Curiatii were wounded, but two of the Horatii were killed. The surviving Horatius, Publius, then reversed the fortunes of battle by killing all his opponents. He was able to tackle them one by one, for they had become separated because of their wounds.

Publius was the hero of the hour, and he marched back to Rome carrying his spoils, the three dead men's armor. At the city gates, he was greeted by his sister. She happened be betrothed to one of the Curiatii, and when she noticed that Publius was carrying his cloak she let down her hair, burst into tears, and called out her lover's name.

In a fit of rage, Publius drew his sword and stabbed his sister to the heart. "Take your girl's love and give it to your lover in hell," he shouted. "So perish all women who grieve for an enemy!"

He was condemned to death for the murder but reprieved by the People, which refused to countenance the execution of a national hero. However, something had to be done to mitigate the guilt of such a notorious crime. The Horatius family was obliged to conduct expiatory ceremonies. Once these had been performed, a wooden beam was slung across the roadway under which Publius walked, with his head covered as a sign of submission.

Typically, two ancient memorials survived that were believed to mark the event. Livy, writing at the end of the first century, observed:

The timber is still to be seen—replaced from time to time at the state's expense—and is known as the Sister's Beam. The tomb of

the murdered girl was built of hewn stone and stands on the spot
where she was struck down.

For men like Cicero and Varro, Rome was a stage on which great
and terrible deeds had been done. People of the present were energized and uplifted by the invisible actors of a glorious past. Horatius did a very Roman thing: he committed a crime that illustrated
not vice but virtue—in this case, the noble rage of valor.

The war with Alba stimulated not only individual but also collective rage. After a resumption of hostilities, the war eventually
ended in a Roman victory. The enemy population was brought to
Rome and, as usual with defeated foes, given Roman citizenship.
But its city was destroyed. Livy wrote: "Every building, public and
private, was leveled with the ground. In a single hour the work of
four hundred years lay in utter ruin." It was as if Alba Longa had
never existed. This would not be the last time that Rome annihilated an enemy city, giving full rein to the hatred caused by fear.

THERE WERE TWO ways of crossing the Tiber. One could walk or
drive a vehicle across a ford that led to a river island, the Insula
Tiberina, and then another ford by which one reached the far bank.
This was not very convenient, though, and the alternative was a
ferry much used by traders in salt on their way to and from the salt
flats at the river mouth.

One of the achievements of Ancus Marcius, Tullus's successor,
was to replace the ferry with Rome's first bridge, the Pons Sublicius. It was made of wood and, for some forgotten ritual scruple,
the use of metal in its construction was strictly forbidden. Its repair
was the responsibility of Rome's leading college of priests, the pontifices (the name means "bridge builders"). It was frequently destroyed by floods, and its rebuilding was a religious duty. The
bridge survived for about a thousand years and was probably not
removed until the fifth century A.D.

Religion also entered into the process of declaring war. The Romans believed that they would arouse divine anger if they went to war on a false prospectus. The cause had to be just. Ancus Marcius was credited with devising a ritual formula that kept Rome on the right side of the law.

When some offense, some casus belli, had been committed, the head of a delegation, or the *pater patratus* ("father in charge"), accompanied by three other colleagues (drawn from a college of priests called *fetiales*) traveled to the border of the state from whom satisfaction was sought. He covered his head in a woolen bonnet and announced, "Hear me, Jupiter! Hear me, land of So-and-So! I am the accredited spokesman of the Roman People. I come as their envoy in the name of justice and religion, and ask credence for my words." He then spelled out the particulars of the alleged offense and, calling Jupiter as witness, concluded, "If my demand for the restitution of these men, or those goods, be contrary to religion and justice, then never let me be a citizen of my country."

The embassy then crossed the frontier and the *pater patratus* repeated the formula to the first (presumably somewhat startled) person he met, and again at the state's city gates, and one final time in the marketplace. If his demands were not conceded within thirty days, he proceeded to a formal declaration of war, calling on not only the leader of the gods but on the god of gates and doorways, of beginnings and endings: "Hear, Jupiter; hear, Janus Quirinus; hear, all you gods in heaven, on the earth and under the earth: I call you to witness that the people of So-and-So are unjust and refuse reparation. But concerning these things we will consult the elders of our country, how we may obtain our due."

If their complaint was not accepted, the envoys returned home and discussed the position with the Senate. Each member was asked his view and, typically, replied, "I hold that these things be sought by means of just and righteous war. Thus I give my vote and my consent." If a majority agreed, then one of the *fetiales* returned to the enemy frontier and formally declared war. He flung a spear across the frontier as a sign that hostilities had begun.

In later years, with the enlargement of Rome's territory this procedure became increasingly difficult to apply. A piece of land was therefore acquired in the city which was symbolically designated as hostile soil and into which the spear could be thrown. A specially appointed senator replaced the *fetiales*. But the principle of ensuring that a war was just remained obligatory, at least in theory.

Ancus Marcius was also responsible for enlarging the city by bringing two hills inside its boundary, the Aventine and the Caelian. He founded the port of Ostia, at the mouth of the Tiber, a clear sign that Rome was developing trade.

The tiny settlement on the Palatine Hill was beginning to find its feet.

3

Expulsion

NORTH OF ROME LIVED A MYSTERIOUS AND HIGHLY cultivated race. These were the Etruscans and their homeland, Etruria, occupied, roughly speaking, modern Tuscany. They first appeared on the scene between 900 and 800 B.C. Their language used a form of Greek script, but it was not an Indo-European tongue, as in most Mediterranean and Middle Eastern societies, and has not yet been fully deciphered. To this day, its origin is unknown.

In fact, it is still not altogether clear whence the Etruscans themselves originated. Some said they came from Lydia, a kingdom on the Turkish coast (where later, in the sixth century, Croesus ruled, a byword for enormous wealth), and were led by the king's son, Tyrrhenus. The Greek for Etruscan is Tyrrhenian. This account is perfectly plausible; for hundreds of years, the Italian peninsula was an archaic America, a new world open to successive waves of colonists. Enterprising Phoenician and Greek traders patrolled the seas looking for business. Aristocrats saw themselves as an international class and networked with one another across state borders. There is no particular reason that a force of Lydians (or, more generally, Asiatics) should not have invaded Italy—in much the same way that Duke William and his handful of Norman knights expropriated Anglo-Saxon England.

It is tempting to envisage a melting pot in which the native population was enriched by Greek and Phoenician aesthetic styles, new techniques in metalworking, and a sophisticated knowledge of town planning. However, modern scholars have been more skeptical, supposing the slow indigenous development of a community of villages into a loose federation of small city-states. Others have thrown up their hands and walked away from the debate, seeing the question as being on a par with the name of Hecuba's mother—"neither capable of being known nor worth knowing."

One way or another, by the eighth century the Etruscans had graduated from being simple farmers into an urban society of merchants and craftspeople. They were organized as a federation and each of their city-states was ruled by a king, or *lauchme,* who governed with much pomp, donning a purple robe and a gold crown. He was attended by servants, who carried *fasces,* bundles of rods tied around a one-headed ax. The Etruscans were militarily active and built up a sizable empire in central and northern Italy that reached Bononia (today's Bologna) in the north and parts of Campania in the south. Rome seems to have retained its independence, however, although much influenced by Etruscan art and architecture, and, above all, by its religious practices.

According to Livy, Etruscans, "deeply learned as they were in sacred lore of all kinds, were more concerned than any other nation with religious matters." Their doctrines were set out in a series of books much used by their disciples at Rome, called *Etrusca disciplina* (*The Etruscan System*); these covered such topics as the scrutiny of the entrails of animals, the interpretation of thunder and lightning, and "rules concerning the founding of cities, the consecration of altars and temples, the inviolability of ramparts, the laws relating to city gates, the division into tribes, *curiae* and *centuriae,* and all other things of this nature concerning war and peace."

Inside every ordinary object or event lay a secret and sacred meaning. It followed that the world was a forest of symbols. The most innocent animals or plants concealed unexpected threats or promises. So, for instance, some kinds of tree were ill-wishing and flourished under the protection of the underworld powers. The eglantine, the fern, the wild pear, the black fig, and any bush that produced black fruits or berries had to be rooted out and destroyed as soon as they were seen to sprout. By contrast, the laurel brought good fortune. The dreams of pregnant women could foretell triumph or disaster, as could eccentricities in the internal organs of sacrificed animals. A model bronze liver has been found divided into forty-four areas, marked with the names of the gods, showing the place allotted to each god in the Etruscan cosmos. Celestial phenomena required particular attention. Storms, rain (especially if of an unusual color or consistency), comets, and the flights of birds and bees all called for careful study and required expert interpretation. Etruscan nobles were trained as *haruspices,* or diviners, and were much in demand in Rome throughout most of its history.

The Etruscans laid out their cemeteries as well as their towns in orderly grids. In their heyday, the tombs of the rich were reconstructions of the houses they lived in when alive, containing corridors and rooms. All kinds of household objects were stored in them. In the burial chamber of one great lady, archaeologists found

gold ornaments, little toilet vases for oil and perfumes, *pyxides* [round boxes with separate lids] imitating wooden coffers for keeping small objects in: all things which could only have been dedicated to a woman for a life beyond the tomb. But together with these objects were indispensable kitchen utensils: andirons [metal supports for fire logs] and spits, a cauldron with a tripod to support it; finally a whole dinner service, the very one which had been used for the funeral feast in honor of the deceased: jugs, amphorae [two-handled jars for storing wine or oil], vases for drawing water or for mixing liquids, drinking cups and dinner plates.

Bright-colored frescoes on tomb walls illustrate the daily life of the Etruscans. Although these sometimes depict frightening demons of the underworld, they mostly evoke with beguiling joie de vivre all manner of humane fun—banquets, young men dancing and making music, horse racing, fishing, wrestling, and other athletics.

One of the most widely read and influential historians of the ancient world, Theopompus, has left a frank, if overly graphic, description of sexual intercourse Etruscan style. Apparently, women took gymnastic exercise naked. They were very good-looking, he wrote, but drank too much wine. Children were brought up by a woman's family, whoever their father was. Men waxed and shaved themselves at establishments that were as common as barbershops.

And they are so far from regarding sex as shameful that when the master of the house is engaged in making love and someone asks for him, they say: "He is fucking so-and-so," referring to the act by its name without any embarrassment. When family or friends hold a party, this is how they carry on: first of all, when they have finished drinking and are ready for bed and while the torches are still alight, the servants bring in call-girls, handsome boys, or their own wives. When they have taken their pleasure of the women or the men, they make strapping young fellows sleep with the latter. They make love and pursue their pleasures in full view of everyone, but usually surround their couches with small frames of woven branches over which they drape their cloaks. They often have sex with women, but they always enjoy themselves better with boys and young men.

There is evidence that women were respected members of Etruscan society. They were given personal as well as family names, unlike their Roman counterparts. Tomb frescoes show wives attending dinner parties, something that would shock a Greek, and depict apparently happy marriages. This is not necessarily inconsistent with general licentiousness and, in its way, Theopompus's X-rated account does tend to confirm women's relative independence.

IT WAS FROM this sophisticated, culturally somewhat overwhelming society that a complete stranger arrived in Rome and won the throne. The surprising thing was that he was not even of Etruscan descent but the son of an aristocratic Greek exile from Corinth, a powerful and famous city in Greece.

Greece was a snake pit of tiny, fiercely competitive states, of which Corinth was the wealthiest at the time. Standing on the narrow isthmus connecting mainland Greece and the Peloponnese, it was ideally situated as an international entrepôt and its merchants traded eastward with Asia Minor and westward with Italy. Corinthian pottery and perfumes were famous throughout the Mediterranean and much sought after among the Etruscan upper classes.

The city was governed by a ruling clan, the Bacchiads, but between about 620 and 610 they were overthrown by a dissident member. This was Cypselus, who set himself up as a popular leader: he was a tyrant, or *turannos,* who opposed the aristocracy and ruled in the interest of the lower classes, especially small farmers. He confiscated the wealth of his opponents and extended the civil rights of the masses.

The Bacchiads bitterly resisted their expulsion, and many of them were executed. One of those who escaped the bloodbath was Demaratus, a rich merchant-noble who had sailed to Etruria, where he had commercial contacts. He arrived with a treasure chest and a large entourage, including a famous painter and some ceramic artists. He began producing fine pottery in the Corinthian manner and established himself in the major Etruscan city of Tarquinii (today's Tarquinia), or possibly neighboring Caere. He received a warm welcome, and the geographer Strabo even claims that he became the city's ruler.

This international career was not as astonishing as might be imagined. Inscriptions have revealed the presence in Etruria of high-ranking individuals of Greek, Latin, and Italic origin. A man's wealth and family tree were more important than loyalty to a particular community, city, or homeland.

Demaratus married a local woman, of noble birth but poor, with whom he had two sons, Aruns and Lucumo (this latter name may be a mistake, for it is close to Lauchme, or "king"). He taught his boys all the arts according to the Greek system. When he grew up, Lucumo decided to emigrate to Rome, where he fancied that a man of energy, like himself, might find more opportunities to better himself than were possible in his hometown. He changed his name to Lucius Tarquinius (or, in English, Tarquin); he was later given the additional title of Priscus, or the Elder, to distinguish him from the next king but one, another Tarquinius. For Cicero, his arrival was a historic turning point, for it introduced Hellenic ideas and artifacts into a provincial backwater—everything from an inexhaustible curiosity about the world to political theory, from beautiful pottery to the poetry of Homer, whose epics, the *Iliad* and the *Odyssey,* were regarded as authoritative guides to the good and courageous life. Above all, they glowed with what seemed to Romans the glamour of a higher civilization. Cicero remarked, "It was indeed no little rivulet that flowed from Greece into our city, but a mighty river of culture and learning."

Lucius's move to Rome met with the warm approval of his highborn Etruscan wife, Tanaquil. She resented snobbish disdain of her marriage to an exile and a foreigner. She felt that in Rome, a new foundation where there were no old families, she would receive the respect she deserved.

Her optimism received a boost when the couple, en route from Tarquinii, were traveling in a covered wagon on the Janiculum Hill on the far side of the Tiber from Rome, not far from the new bridge. An eagle hovered above them, then dived down and plucked off Lucius's cap. The bird soared into the sky, then swooped again and deftly replaced the cap on its owner's head. Tanaquil, who, like most Etruscans, was an expert interpreter of portents and prodigies, saw this as a sign of imminent greatness.

She did not have to wait long to be proved right. The arrival in town of a man as wealthy as Lucius attracted attention, and he was presented to the king. Genial, well-informed, and with great personal charm, he soon became a trusted friend and counselor, and helped finance Ancus Marcius's military campaigns.

The king had two sons, who were approaching manhood and expected to inherit the throne. Tarquin had other ideas. On Ancus Marcius's death, according to the king's will, he was appointed the boys' guardian. He immediately arranged for them to be sent off on a hunting expedition. Having got them out of the way, he persuaded an assembly of the People to elect him as the new king.

Like his predecessors, Tarquin fought wars with his neighbors, and defeated an alliance of Etruscan cities. Plucky and aggressive, Rome was becoming a force to be reckoned with. Its rising wealth relied on military victories over its neighbors, the enlargement of its territory, and the expansion of its citizen base. Plunder enriched the city, and a number of important construction projects were begun. These included Rome's great racetrack, the Circus Maximus, in the valley between the Aventine and Palatine hills, and work began on draining the valley between Rome's hills. The king had made a vow during a battle to build a temple to Jupiter Best and Greatest on the Capitoline Hill, and now he could discharge it. Where there were gaps in the city's fortifications, walls were erected, laid with huge, carefully squared blocks of stone.

Tarquin was the first Roman commander to hold a triumph, a military procession to celebrate a victory. He entered the city, riding a four-horse chariot at the head of his troops. He wore magnificent clothes and insignia, consisting of a toga and tunic, purple all over and shot through with gold, a crown of precious stones set in gold, and an ivory scepter and chair. His face was daubed with cinnabar (red lead, poisonous if a regular cosmetic), reddening his features like those of the statue of Jupiter on the Capitol. Like an Etruscan king, he was attended by twelve *lictors,* men who carried the *fasces,* symbols of punishment and execution.

All these emblems of power were the natural marks of self-assertion by an autocrat who relied on the People's support. Splendor awes and attracts. As an Italian version of the Greek *turannos, we* may wonder whether Roman patricians—"old blood" from the time of Romulus—were any more enthusiastic about their king than the Bacchiads of Corinth had been when confronted with Cypselus. Tarquin was surely trying to weaken their position when he recruited an additional hundred senators from outside the patriciate.

He also enlarged the number of cavalrymen, or *equites,* in the army; these citizens were wealthy enough to pay for their own horses and represented another nonpatrician power center. He tried to bolster their position further by enrolling them into three new "tribes" or voting groups, in the Assembly. A leading patrician, Nevius, opposed the reform. The king was infuriated and decided to take his revenge.

Nevius was an augur, a priest responsible for the interpretation of the flight of birds. Tarquin wanted to show him up as a charlatan who did not speak a word of truth. He summoned Nevius into his presence and said, "I have a project in mind and would like to know if it is feasible or not. Please take the auspices and come back quickly. I will sit here and wait for you."

The augur did as he was told and reported that he had obtained favorable omens and that the undertaking was possible. "You have convicted yourself of openly lying about the will of the gods," crowed the king. "I wanted to know whether if I strike this whetstone with a razor I will be able to cut it in half." This feat was obviously out of the question, and a watching crowd laughed.

Unabashed, Nevius replied, "Go ahead, strike it and you will cut it in half. If not I will submit to any punishment you choose." Tarquin did so, and the steel sliced so easily through the stone that it nicked the hand of the man holding it.

Wisely, the king acknowledged defeat. He canceled his planned reform and had a bronze statue of Nevius erected in the Forum as recognition of his accomplishments. Dionysius of Halicarnassus recalled: "This statue remained down to my time. It stands in front of the Senate House near the sacred fig tree. It is less than life-size and the head is covered with a mantle [like a priest at a sacrifice]. A little way off, the whetstone and the razor are said to be buried under an altar."

LUCIUS TARQUINIUS HAD not touched Ancus Marcius's sons. Over the years, their sense of grievance grew and from time to time they plotted unsuccessfully against him. Loyal to their father's memory, he always pardoned the offense. Now, when Nevius unexpectedly disappeared from the city, the sons drew the obvious conclusion that there had been foul play and the king was to blame. They financed bands of partisans who accused Tarquin of murder. Such a man, they said, should not be allowed to pollute the religious rituals over which he presided as king. It only made matters worse that he was "not a Roman, but some newcomer and a man without a country."

Tarquin, now an old man in his eighties, went to the Forum and defended himself vigorously against the charge. The public supported him, viewing the accusation as self-interested slander. Ancus Marcius's sons apologized to the king, who, as usual, forgave them. Three years passed without incident, and then they entered into a new conspiracy.

They dressed up two of their most fearless accomplices as shepherds, armed uncontroversially with billhooks, and gave them instructions on what to do and say. Then they sent them to the palace at midday. As the men approached the building, they apparently fell into an argument and came to blows. A crowd, ostensibly of people from the countryside, gathered and cheered on the quarrelers.

Eventually, Tarquin had the two men brought before him. They pretended that their dispute was about some goats, and bawled at each other, saying nothing to the point. Amid much laughter at the horseplay, they suddenly attacked the king and one of them hit him on the head with his billhook, a mortal blow. Leaving the weapon in the wound, the assassins ran out of doors but were caught by the lictors. Under torture, they revealed the authors of the plot, who fled into exile, and were then executed.

The king was dead, but the regime was more than capable of handling the crisis. Tanaquil, the queen, closed the palace doors and ejected all witnesses. She then sent out for medical supplies, as if Tarquin were still alive, and hastily summoned her son-in-law for an urgent consultation.

This was Servius Tullius, about whose origins there are various traditions. According to most acccounts, he was the son of a slave woman who belonged to the queen; his father was unknown or quickly forgotten. Cicero writes:

> Though he was brought up as a slave, and served at the king's table, yet the spark of genius, which shone even then in the boy, did not remain unnoticed, so capable was he in every duty and in every word he spoke. On this account Tarquin, whose children were still very young, became so fond of Servius that the latter was popularly regarded as his son; and the king took the greatest care to have him educated in all the branches which he himself had studied, in accordance with the most careful practice of the Greeks.

Portents added to the favorable impression that the boy made on the king and queen. Some report that Servius's mother had a very surprising experience when sacrificing at the palace's hearth. A phallus rose up from the hearth and inserted itself inside her. She told Tanaquil what had happened. The queen realized at once that a god must have been responsible. She watched over the woman's pregnancy and tried to ensure that her baby's divine parentage was kept a secret. This was no easy task, for portents continued to intervene. Once, when the child was asleep, his head burst into flames without his being harmed in any way, and from time to time people noticed a nimbus around his head. It was generally understood that his father must have been the fire god, Vulcan.

Tanaquil advised her husband that young Servius obviously had great promise (greater than that of their own children, incidentally). The boy was brought up as their son, and in due course the adult Servius married the king's daughter.

In the wake of Tarquin's murder, his widow advised Servius Tullius to seize the throne. Outside the palace, a crowd was shouting and pushing, so she went to a first-floor window and gave a short speech. "The king has been stunned by a sudden blow, but the steel has not sunk deep into his body," she announced. "He has already recovered consciousness, the blood has been wiped off and the head examined. I assure you that you will soon be able to see him. In the meantime everyone should obey Tullius, who will dispense justice and perform the other duties of the king."

For the next few days, Servius acted as regent. This gave him time to strengthen his political position and appoint a strong guard. When everything was ready, lamentations were heard from inside the palace, signaling Tarquin's death. Although he had not yet been endorsed at an assembly of the People, Servius's claim to the throne was backed by the Senate and from then onward he acted as king both in name and in deed. He later took care to win popular endorsement and astutely married his two daughters to the dead king's sons, Lucius and Aruns, hoping by this precaution to avoid his predecessor's fate.

Servius Tullius, like great men later in Rome's history, believed devoutly in his luck. He claimed a special relationship with Fortuna, the goddess of chance, to whom he dedicated numerous shrines throughout the city. An ancient temple has been discovered in the Forum Boarium, or Ox Forum (a traffic hub where various streets met, it was so named after the statue of a bronze ox, not because it was a cattle market), and may be one of the king's foundations. The goddess was said to visit him at night, climbing through a window to enter his bedroom. He may have conducted a ritual called "sacred marriage," whereby a ruler had sex with a divinity in her temple, legitimizing his authority and ensuring the fertility and well-being of his realm. (Naturally, a female slave or temple prostitute would stand in for the goddess.)

IT IS WRONG to suppose that Rome at this early stage in its history was a primitive society. City-states like Rome could not develop without widespread literacy, at any rate among the élites. Servius Tullius is known mainly for his bold reforms of the state. These were absolutely dependent on the information technology of the time—not simply writing (both alphabet and numerals) but a technical capacity to store data in an archive and to access and manipulate it for many different purposes. Otherwise, the central management of military and political activity would have been next to impossible. Nor would it have been easy to establish the complicated institutions of government for which Rome became famous.

The king abolished the three tribes and thirty *curiae* of Romulus and replaced them with territorial tribes—four for the city and an additional number in the surrounding countryside. Managed by a senior official, or "commander," these individuals were responsible for organizing local defense, the payment of taxes, and army recruitment.

Tribes also conducted a regular census. An ingenious method

was found for counting the population. The commander of each tribe held a sacrifice and festival, and everyone was asked to contribute to its cost. Men gave a small coin of a certain value, women one of another, and children of a third. In this painless way, when the coins were added up, the number of tribe members, by age and gender, was ascertained.

Also, all Romans were obliged to register their name and that of their father, their age, and the names of their wives and children. On oath, they had to assign a monetary value to their property. Anyone found to have made a false declaration forfeited all his goods and was sold into slavery.

With even greater ingenuity, Servius Tullius devised a system that simultaneously controlled voting at popular assemblies and decided citizens' military responsibilities. The idea was, while maintaining the democratic vote, to give more voting power to the rich—and also to require a substantial financial outlay when the rich served in the army.

How was this achieved? We begin with the word *centuria,* or "century"—literally, a group of one hundred men (although, in practice, not necessarily so many). This was the smallest unit of the army's main military force, the legion; sixty centuries, or up to six thousand men, made one legion. (This number fell over the years to between four thousand two hundred to five thousand men in the second century.) It was also the name given to the voting units of the Assembly. There were eighteen centuries of horsemen and a hundred and seventy of foot soldiers (*pedites*). The foot soldiers were divided into five classes, according to their wealth and ability to pay for armor and weapons. The first and richest class was allocated eighty centuries, the second, third, and fourth twenty each, and the fifth class thirty. (Noncombatants such as trumpeters and carpenters were allocated to one or another of the five classes.) In each class one half of the centuries were made up of older men between forty-seven and sixty, and the other half of younger men between seventeen and forty-six: The age range was much smaller in the first group than in the second—an arrangement that privileged years and experience. Anyone with property below a minimum level was listed separately and was not allowed to serve in the army.

When it came to voting at the Assembly, each century balloted its members and then cast a single vote for or against the motion. The count began with the first class, and so on down. As soon as a majority had been reached, the voting stopped. The arrangement meant that the rich controlled more centuries than the poor. Indeed, centuries in the lower classes found that they seldom had a chance to cast a vote at all.

But if the wealthy won more power in the assembly than was equitable, they had more duties on the battlefield. They were subject to frequent conscription and, serving as heavily armed troops, had to buy their own expensive equipment (bronze helmets, greaves, breastplates, and spears and swords). The lower classes fought as light-armed skirmishers. The principle underlying the Servian reforms was timocratic—that is, they were a property owner's charter. The idea was that only those with much to lose would make careful and well-considered decisions. It goes without saying that the patricians were not pleased with these reforms, for *their* ascendancy rested on birth, not money; they claimed the exclusive right to compete for power.

For Cicero and moderate conservatives hundreds of years later, Servius Tullius was a second founder (*conditor*) of Rome, for he had discovered a way of taming the revolutionary forces of democracy. "[The king] put into effect the principle which ought always to be adhered to in the commonwealth, that the greatest number should *not* have the greatest power," he noted approvingly. "While no one was deprived of the suffrage, the majority of votes was in the hands of those to whom the highest welfare of the State was the most important."

ACCORDING TO LIVY, Servius's census revealed about 80,000 citizens—that is, adult men capable of bearing arms. This was a substantial number, and the king extended Rome's boundary and the *pomerium,* the sacred space behind the city walls, or ramparts, to accommodate a growing population and the seven hills now contained in Rome with a continuous wall. These great Servian fortifications survive in part to this day. (The dating is a mistake; in fact, the walls were constructed in the late fourth century, and before then Rome had little in the way of adequate defenses. Servius Tullius probably merely erected some form of rough-and-ready rampart).

The census number is problematic, too, and modern scholars propose a population of about 35,000 at the end of the sixth century B.C. Nevertheless, this would allow a force to take the field of more than 9,000 men of military age—in other words, one legion of 6,000 plus 2,400 light-armed troops and 600 cavalry. By the standards of the time, this was no mean army. So Rome had become a substantial power to deal with, and Servius is even reported as having conducted a war against the powerful Etruscans, including Veii, the richest city of the Etruscan federation.

ONCE AGAIN, THE offspring of a previous king stirred up trouble for the current ruler. As we have seen, Servius tried to ensure the loyalty of the sons of Tarquinius Priscus by marrying them to his two daughters. Both unions were unhappy. The eldest boy, Lucius, was a hothead, eager for the throne; his wife loved her father and did her best to calm her husband. By contrast, the second daughter despised her consort, Aruns, who was a peace-loving youth, and bitterly regretted that she had not been allotted Lucius.

A prototype of Lady Macbeth, this second daughter arranged secret meetings with Lucius at which she upbraided him for his lack of ambition and encouraged him to plot against her father. Their first step was to arrange their own affairs; the two did away with their respective spouses and, without any pretense of mourning and with the aged Servius's reluctant consent, they married.

The couple then proceeded to the main action. Lucius was in and out of the houses of the patrician families, reminding them of favors his father had done them and insinuating that now was the time to show their gratitude. Young men he swung to his side with money.

When he felt that the moment had come, he forced his way into the Forum with an armed guard, marched into the Senate House, sat himself down on the throne (this was the curule chair, or *sella curulis,* a sort of grand stool, ivory-veneered and with curved legs forming a wide X, with low arms and no back), and ordered a crier to summon the Senate to meet *King* Tarquin. He then delivered a tirade against Servius Tullius. The main charge, according to Livy, was that

> base-born himself, and basely crowned, he had made friends with the riff-raff of the gutter, where he belonged; hating the nobility to which he could not aspire, he had robbed the rich of their property and given it to vagabonds.

In other words, like Priscus, Servius was a Greek-style *turannos* and an enemy of the patricians. Just as he himself had every intention of becoming, he might have admitted to himself.

Tarquin was still in mid-flow when a report reached the king of what was afoot. Angry and alarmed, Servius hurried to the Forum and, standing in the antechamber of the Senate House, interrupted the speaker.

"What is the meaning of this, Tarquin? How dare you, while I am alive, to summon the Senate and sit in my chair?"

"It is my father's chair. A king's son is a better heir to the throne than a slave."

Confusion. Opposing cheers. A riotous mob rushed the Senate

House. Tarquin had gone too far to pull back now. A strongly built man, he lifted up the old king by his middle and flung him down the entrance steps into the Forum before turning back to the meeting. Meanwhile, Servius's retinue had fled, leaving him alone and unattended. Stunned, he was making his way back to the palace when some of Tarquin's men caught and killed him.

It was said that the murder was committed on his daughter Tullia's suggestion. She drove into the Forum in a carriage, called her husband out from the Senate House, and was the first to hail him as king. Tarquin advised her to go home, as the crowd might be dangerous. So she started off and, Livy writes:

> At the top of Cypress Street [*vicus Cuprius*], where the shrine of Diana stood until recently, her driver was turning to the right to climb Orbius Rise [*clivus Orbius*] on the way to the Esquiline, when he pulled up short in sudden terror and pointed to Servius's body lying mutilated on the road. There followed an act of bestial inhumanity—history preserves the memory of it in the name of the street, the Street of Crime [*vicus Sceleratus*]. The story goes that the crazed woman . . . drove the carriage over her father's body. Blood from the corpse stained her clothes and spattered the carriage.

MANY YEARS IN the mythical past, Apollo, beautiful god of the sun, music, and archery, was trying to persuade a young woman to have sex with him. He promised to grant her a wish. She grasped a handful of sand and asked to live for as many years as the grains in her hand. The wish was granted, but, like so many other mortals who attracted the lecherous attention of classical divinities, she forgot to include undying youthfulness in her request. As time passed, she gradually withered away. A prophetess, or Sibyl, she lived in a cave at Cumae. She predicted the future by writing on oak leaves, which she arranged at the entrance. According to the novelist Gaius Petronius Arbiter in the first century A.D., the Sibyl used to sit in a bottle suspended from the roof, and when someone asked what she wanted she replied, "I want to die." (The actual cave was discovered by a modern archaeologist, and in Cicero and Varro's day was used as a shrine tended by a priestess.)

The Sibyl was somewhat more mobile when Rome was young. One day she presented herself at court, looking like an old woman. She brought with her nine books filled with prophecies, and offered to sell them to King Tarquin for a certain sum. He refused, and the Sibyl went away and burned three of the books. Shortly afterward, she returned and offered Tarquin the six remaining books for the same price. Laughter greeted the offer. So off she went again, burned three more books, and came back, offering the final three—for the same price.

By now, the Sibyl had won the king's full attention. He asked the augurs to advise him. They warned him that his failure to purchase the complete set of books spelled disaster for Rome, and that he should at least secure those that were left. He paid up and stored the books in a cellar under the Temple of Jupiter on the Capitol, the construction of which he was superintending at the time. There they stayed, consulted during state emergencies, until the first century B.C., when the temple burned down and the books with it.

The story reveals contrasting dimensions of Tarquin's character—hastiness and arrogance, but also a realistic response to a check. Not surprisingly, he won the nickname of Superbus, the Proud. Cicero once remarked that the foundation of political wisdom is to understand "the regular curving path through which governments travel." In Superbus's case, the curve led inexorably from assassination to despotism. Cicero went on: "[He] did not begin his reign with a clear conscience and, as he feared suffering the death penalty for his crime, he wished to make himself feared by others."

Tarquin was no delegator, and he kept public business either in his hands or in those of his three sons, Titus, Aruns, and Sextus.

Access to his presence was strictly controlled, and he behaved with great haughtiness and brutality to all and sundry. He once, arbitrarily and against convention, had a number of Roman citizens stripped and bound to stakes in the Forum, where they were then beaten to death with rods.

In spite of his violent personality, Tarquin's reign was in many ways a successful one. Like previous kings, he conducted an expansionist foreign policy, deploying a combination of military force and guile. His main object was to establish Rome as the leader of the confederacy of the tribes of Latium, and he also moved farther down the peninsula to attack the Volsci, a tribe to the south of Latium. The city's territory now stretched to the sea, where the port of Ostia enhanced trade and, thanks to Superbus, was encroaching southward into the lands of its Latin neighbors. Here we see the beginnings of Rome's imperial career.

On one occasion Tarquin was besieging the town of Gabii, which refused to join the confederacy. Making little progress, he devised an ingenious stratagem. His son Sextus, pretending that he had been badly treated by his father, fled to Gabii, bearing on his back the marks of a heavy beating. He soon won the confidence of the inhabitants and was appointed the town's commander. He then sent for his father asking what he should do next. Tarquin, suspicious of the messenger's loyalty, said nothing but, seeing some poppies, simply walked up and down striking off the tallest heads.

The bemused messenger returned to Gabii and reported the king's curious behavior. Sextus immediately got the point. He was to rid himself of the town's leading citizens. Some were openly executed; others, who could not plausibly be charged with any offense, were put to death in secret. Still others were allowed to go into exile, forfeiting their property. Sextus distributed the profits of this exercise in liquidation. Livy neatly observes: "In the sweetness of private gain public calamity was forgotten." Without complaint or resistance, Gabii let itself be handed over to the Romans.

The king was a busy builder. He installed tiers of seating for the

Circus Maximus and completed the vast Temple of Jupiter Best and Greatest on the lower crest of the Capitol. (Priscus had, at most, laid only the foundations.) Standing on a massive platform fifty-three meters wide and sixty-two long, it was a proud assertion of the magnificence of the Rome of the Tarquins. Probably made from mud brick faced with stucco, it contained three *cellae* (inner chambers) dedicated, respectively, to Jupiter, his wife, Juno, and Minerva. (Here the goddesses were on their best behavior, the scandalous judgment of Paris a distant memory.) The cult image of Jupiter was made of terra-cotta and showed him brandishing a thunderbolt. He wore a tunic and a purple toga (as we have seen, the costume worn by generals celebrating a triumph, when they processed through the city to the Capitol). The roof was wooden, with bright, multicolored terra-cotta decorations, and on the peak of the triangular façade stood another terra-cotta statue of Jupiter riding a four-horsed chariot.

Before building began, the augurs investigated the opinions of deities who already had holy places on the site. They all agreed to be resettled elsewhere—except for Terminus, the god of boundaries, so a special shrine in his honor was incorporated into the temple. His lack of cooperation was regarded as a good omen, for it signified the permanence of Rome's borders.

The temple quickly became the center of Rome's religious life. It was the repository of treasures donated by victorious generals, dedications, and military trophies. The rooms got so cluttered that in 179 B.C. numerous statues and commemorative shields fastened to the columns were cleared out.

A development of more practical value was the transformation of the brook that crossed the Forum into the city's main drain, the Cloaca Maxima. Various smaller streams debouched into it. In Tarquin's day, it was an open sewer, crossed by a bridge that doubled as a shrine to Janus, the god of doorways and beginnings and endings. As a result, the Forum finally lost its marshiness, and large-scale building became possible.

A TERRIBLE PORTENT appeared. A snake was observed to glide out of a crack in a wooden pillar in the palace. Everyone ran away in a panic. Even Tarquin was alarmed, although in his case the emotion was not so much fright as foreboding. He decided to consult the oracle at Delphi, and ask for an authoritative explanation.

Delphi was a town in central Greece, occupying a series of terraces along the slopes of Mount Parnassus. In this precipitous location stood a shrine to Apollo. It was the home of an oracle, one of the sacred places scattered throughout the Mediterranean where a god would respond to inquiries about the future. The oracle at Delphi was world-famous and was consulted by states as well as individuals.

The king did not dare to entrust the oracle's reply to anyone but his closest relatives, so he commissioned two of his sons, Titus and Aruns, to journey to Greece, in Livy's words, "through country which Roman feet had seldom trod and over seas which Roman ships had never sailed." They were accompanied by the king's nephew, Lucius Junius Brutus, a descendant of one of Aeneas's companions. He was a strange young man, who deliberately assumed a "mask" to conceal his real personality. His family's great wealth had attracted the unwelcome interest of the king, who had had his elder brother killed. Brutus was well aware that Tarquin had no hesitation in putting aristocrats to death, and feared that his turn would be next. So he pretended to be a simpleton and allowed the king to seize his estate without protest. He even accepted the additional cognomen of Brutus, the Latin for "stupid."

Delphi was a spectacular destination. As the party neared the end of its journey, the road dwindled to a steep path and, according to Pausanias, the author of a celebrated guidebook to ancient Greece, became "difficult even for an active man." Once arrived in the town, the visitors walked up a processional avenue, the Sacred Way, to the Precinct of Apollo, a walled enclosure at the top of the city filled with monuments and dedications, gifts in return for favors received. There were twenty Treasuries, small buildings that resembled miniature Greek temples and contained splendid offerings to Apollo, often works of art, including the Bronze Charioteer, one of the greatest masterpieces of Greek sculpture to have survived to the present day, and a bronze version of the wooden horse of Troy. Everywhere were nude statues of victorious athletes.

The Tarquin boys made their way to the Temple of Apollo, which stood at the center of the Precinct. Carved on the temple's exterior were three famous maxims, epitomizing the Greek idea of the good life: "Know yourself" (γνῶθι σεαυτόν); "Nothing in excess" (μηδέν ἄγαν); and, somewhat mean-spiritedly, "Offer a guarantee and disaster threatens" (προφήτης ἐγγύα πάρα δ ἄτη). Here they paid a consultation fee and made a sacrificial offering. All having gone well, and the animal having behaved as it should when sprinkled with water, they went inside the temple and sacrificed again, placing the victim, or parts of it, on an offertory table. Hieratic spokesmen (the Greek word is προφήτης, from which we have our *prophet*) then ushered the Romans into a space where they could hear but not see the Pythia, a priestess who delivered her prophecies in an inner sanctum.

The Pythia was a local woman of a certain age, who served for life and was sworn to chastity. Before a séance, she purified herself by washing in the nearby Castalian Spring, and burned some laurel leaves (the laurel was Apollo's plant) and barley meal at a symbolic hearth inside the temple. She then sat on a tripod and, crowned with laurel and holding a dish of sacred spring water, became possessed by the god. In this probably self-induced trance, she "raved"—that is, spoke in some form of fragmentary and ecstatic speech.

The spokesmen translated the ravings into elegant hexameters. These oracular messages were often fork-tongued, and those who consulted the god needed to consider their meaning with great care before taking any consequential action. It does not follow that the

Pythia was hedging her bets. If she wished, she could speak clearly and authoritatively; she and the temple personnel were well-informed on international politics and, when it came to personal consultations, they doubtless built up experience of human psychology. However, the Greeks believed that divine messages were in the nature of things ambiguous. There was a limit to human beings' access to sure knowledge of the future.

Brutus knew how to get on the right side of the Pythia. He produced a wooden stick as an offering; Titus and Aruns had a good laugh at his expense for having made such a paltry gift. They did not realize that the stick had been hollowed out and that inside it Brutus had hidden a rod of gold. After the Tarquins had received an answer from the oracle (we are not told what it was), they decided to ask another question: Which of them would be the next king of Rome? The oracle's typically equivocal answer was "He who shall be first to kiss his mother shall have supreme authority in Rome."

Titus and Aruns made the obvious, literal interpretation. They decided that the prophecy should be kept a secret, so that at least their brother Sextus would be out of the running; they themselves would decide by lot which one would kiss his mother when they got back to Rome. But Brutus guessed that Apollo was being tricky. He pretended to stumble, and fell flat on his face, his lips touching the earth, the mother of all things.

This would by no means be the last time that senior Romans made their way up the steep path to the shrine of the god, in urgent need of his guidance.

IT WAS A sex scandal, not a political or military crisis, that brought the dynasty down. A long siege of the town of Ardea, the capital of a Latin tribe, the Rutuli, was loosening discipline in the Roman camp. Applications for leave from the front were rather easily granted, especially to officers. The young princes staged lavish entertainments in their tents. On one occasion, everyone was drinking heavily in the quarters of Sextus Tarquinius. Someone happened to raise the subject of wives, and each man praised his own in extravagant terms. A member of the royal family, Lucius Tarquinius Collatinus, broke in: "Stop! Why do we need words, when in a few hours we can prove beyond any doubt the superiority of my own Lucretia?"

He proposed that they all ride off to Rome, arrive at their houses without warning, and see what their wives were doing. They drunkenly agreed and galloped to the city, where they found the princes' wives thoroughly enjoying themselves with a group of young friends at an extravagant dinner party. They then journeyed on to Collatinus's house in his hometown some miles north of the city, Collatia. A very different sight greeted them. Although it was late at night, they found Lucretia, surrounded by busy maidservants, at work spinning. It was conceded by one and all that she had won the contest for female virtue hands down.

Collatinus asked the party to have supper with him. Nothing further occurred, and the men rode back to camp. It was at the meal, though, that Sextus was struck both by Lucretia's beauty and by the challenge of her chastity. He decided that he would bed her.

His plan was a simple one. A few days later, he rode back to Collatia with one attendant, without mentioning the expedition to Collatinus. Lucretia welcomed him and gave him supper. Afterward, Sextus was assigned a bedchamber and the household retired for the night. He waited eagerly till quiet had fallen and, as far as he could judge, everyone was fast asleep. Drawing his sword, he let himself into Lucretia's room. Holding her down with his left hand on her chest, he whispered, "Don't make a sound. I am Sextus Tarquinius. I have a weapon and if you say a word you will be dead."

Lucretia woke up with a start. Sextus did his best to persuade the terrified woman to consent to sex. She refused, even when threatened with death. Sextus then played his ace. If she would not let him sleep with her, he said, he would kill her and then his slave, whose naked body he would lay in her bed. He would then claim that he had caught her having sex with a servant, and put both of them to death. (An adulteress could be slain on the spot, without much danger of her killer's being convicted in a court of law.)

The thought of a posthumous reputation as a slut was too much for Lucretia, and she gave in. Sextus enjoyed her, and then rode exultantly back to camp. Meanwhile, the abused woman sent messages to her father in Rome and to her husband at Ardea, telling them that something terrible had happened and they must come to her at once, each bringing with him a trustworthy friend. Brutus happened to be with Collatinus when the messenger arrived, and agreed to be his companion on this mysterious mission.

Lucretia was found sitting sadly in her room. She burst into tears when Collatinus and Lucretius entered and told them all that had happened. She said, "My body only has been violated. My heart is innocent and death will be my witness. Give me your solemn promise that the adulterer shall be punished. He is Sextus Tarquinius."

They all gave their word, and then did what they could to comfort Lucretia. She replied, "I am free of guilt, but must take my punishment." She drew a knife that she had concealed in her dress, drove it into her heart and, bending forward over the wound, died as she fell.

A sudden and extraordinary transformation took place. Brutus withdrew the knife from Lucretia's body and, dropping his disguise of stupidity, spoke with intelligence, force, and feeling. His listeners were shocked.

Swearing a great oath on Lucretia's blood, he cried, "I will pursue Lucius Tarquinius Superbus, his wicked wife and all his children, and never again will they or any other man be king in Rome."

Lucretia's body was carried into the public square, where a crowd swiftly gathered. Brutus stirred them up to anger against the Tarquins and headed a march on Rome. He addressed the People's

Assembly in a packed Forum. He painted in vivid colors Sextus's crime and from there went on to attack the king's tyrannical behavior. He recalled the undeserved murder of the good king, Servius Tullius, and the cruelty of his daughter, Tarquin's wife, Tullia, who had ridden over Servius's corpse. The Assembly demanded the king's deposition and the exile of him and his family.

News of these events soon reached Tarquin, who immediately left camp at Ardea for the city to restore order. At the same time Brutus, with a force of armed volunteers, made for Ardea to incite the army to revolt. Learning of the king's whereabouts, he made a detour to avoid meeting him and arrived at the camp at about the same time that Tarquin reached Rome. They received very different welcomes. The troops greeted Brutus with great enthusiasm, while the authorities at Rome closed the city gates against the former despot. The king withdrew to Etruria with two of his sons; Sextus made for the town of Gabii, where he was quickly put to death by relatives of those he had massacred.

The year was 509 B.C., the kings were gone, history was about to take over from legend, and Rome was ready to embark on its great adventure.

4

So What Really Happened?

THE STORY SO FAR IS WHAT THE ROMANS WANTED TO be told, and how they believed it should be told. But to what extent is the account of Rome's foundation and the monarchy in the previous chapters true? It is hard to be quite sure, but the question seems to have two answers: on the one hand, very little and, on the other, quite a lot.

The Romans themselves recognized that some elements of the tradition were not to be trusted. Livy refers forgivingly to "old tales with more of the charm of poetry than of sound historical record" and goes on to say, "It is the privilege of antiquity to mingle divine things with human; it adds dignity to the past and if any nation deserves the right to a divine origin, it is our own."

The link with Troy was foisted on the Romans by Greek historians, who liked to bring interesting new foreign powers within their cultural net, but this was not an unwelcome gift. The Greeks saw the Trojans not as slippery Asiatics but as honorary Greeks. Indeed, some said that they were "a nation as truly Greek as any and formerly came from the Peloponnese." This meant that the Romans, much in awe of Hellenic culture and suffering from an inferiority complex regarding their own, could award themselves a Greek identity. Their admiration concealed envy and hostile emulation;

by associating themselves with the Trojans, they cast themselves as rivals who might one day conquer Greece and so avenge their ancestors.

It is possible that there was a war of some sort at Troy around the traditional date, 1184 B.C. The city certainly existed, and its remains have been uncovered by modern archaeologists. Even at this early stage, Greeks and Phoenicians sailed around the Mediterranean and eventually founded "colonies," independent city-states, but most of this happened four centuries or so later. Aeneas can hardly have called in at Carthage, for it did not then exist. (The Greek historian Timaeus believed that Dido founded the North African city in 814.) But then Aeneas did not exist, either. The panoply of gods and heroes whose adventures are described in Homer's *Iliad* is invented.

As for Romulus and Remus, they are equally fictional. In essence, *Romulus* means "founder of Rome" (the "-ulus" is Etruscan and denotes a founder), and *Remus* may be etymologically connected with the word *Rome.* Tales of exposed infants who rise to greatness are familiar features of ancient mythology (remember Moses, Oedipus, and, of course, Paris of Troy).

The real difficulty the Romans faced was that there were two contradictory foundation stories that ostensibly took place hundreds of years apart, the one about a wandering Trojan hero, and the other about local boys Romulus and Remus. They decided to accept both, and were then faced with reconciling them and knitting them together in a plausible narrative. Aeneas was limited to having discovered Italy and setting up house in Latium, so that Rome itself could be given to the twins. In order to fill the long time gap, a catalog of totally imaginary kings of Alba Longa was cooked up to link the two legends.

Roman historians in the last days of the Republic did not necessarily imagine things, but they tended to see remote and legendary events through the eyes of their own time. The fact that Romulus developed despotic tendencies and was assassinated in the Senate House may very well reflect a response to the traumas of their own day. Hence the uncanny pre-echoes in Livy of Caesar's death.

There was much discussion about the date of Rome's foundation. Most commentators favored a year sometime in the eighth century. As we have seen, 753 was the choice of Varro. It became the generally accepted date. This led to a second chronological conundrum. Only seven kings reigned between Romulus and the expulsion of the Tarquins. This meant an implausibly long average reign of thirty-five years apiece.

The Romans accepted this, but modern scholars have been more skeptical. Perhaps there were additional kings, of whom no record survives. Archaeologists seem to have settled the question: slight traces of primitive settlements have been found that go back many hundreds of years, but solid evidence of *city* as distinct from village life begins only in the middle of the seventh century. So the real foundation date was about one hundred years later than originally believed. This has helped, for although some monarchs may have slipped from view, the canonical number now fits comfortably into the time available. Also, bits of dug-up evidence begin to fall into place alongside the literary tradition. Thus, the Regia, or palace, in the Forum was constructed in the late seventh century, just where the new chronology places the reign of Numa Pompilius, who is credited with having commissioned it. Rome's first Senate House was attributed to Tullus Hostilius (hence its name, the Curia Hostilia): its remains have been identified, dating to the early sixth century, when we now suppose that Tullus ruled Rome.

It is a long time before we meet personalities who are (more or less) certain to have lived in history as distinct from myth. The first four kings seem to be largely if not entirely fictional, even if events in their reigns did actually take place. They were each given specialist tasks, which were in truth accomplished during the monarchy, but not necessarily by one particular king.

Romulus established an orderly social and political system with tribes and *curiae;* the un-warlike Numa was allocated everything concerning religion and (in Cicero's phrase) "the spirit of tranquillity"—cults, priestly colleges and a public calendar of sacred and secular days; the untranquil Tullius Hostilius and Ancus Marcius fought expansionist wars with an effective conscript army. Whether or not Ancus himself had anything to do with it, Ostia and the Pons Sublicius were certainly built. However, we can say with confidence that the two Tarquins and Servius Tullius lived real lives (although, because their recorded achievements are very similar, the Tarquins may have been only one person). The best estimate proposes that Priscus came to power between 570 and 550 B.C.

As we approach the end of the monarchy, the picture comes more and more sharply into focus. Although the story of Lucretia was "written up," its melodramatic trappings may conceal a true-life scandal. Even if we are suspicious of his antic disposition, Brutus is a major historical figure who helped establish the republican institutions that lasted for more than five hundred years.

Once we lift the mists of myth, we can make out a landscape of fact. Having comprehensively rubbished the traditional narratives, we have to concede that they do, after all, contain important ingredients of historical reality. During the monarchy, Rome did grow from being a small town beside a ford into a power in central Italy, extending its territory by countless miniature wars with local tribes in Latium. Political institutions such as the Senate and the People's Assembly were developed, and it is almost certainly the case that some method of linking wealth to political influence and military obligation was invented by the kings, and very probably by a ruler named Servius Tullius. (However, the details of the complicated centuriate system refer to a later period, for Romans tended toward a modernizing fallacy; namely, they supposed that the early Republic was identical to, if smaller than, its more elaborate incarnation in subsequent centuries.)

So a recognizable constitution evolved, as did an unresolved conflict between ordinary citizens and the lordly patricians. The later kings were indeed very like *turannoi,* who claimed a popular mandate, carried out aggressive foreign policies, and invested in the arts and architecture.

The grand public edifices that a thriving and ambitious city-state demanded were indeed built; the Forum was transformed from a muddy bog into a great public square. Some have argued that, for a time, Rome was forcibly enlisted as an Etruscan city, but recent scholars have demurred for lack of evidence. It seems that, although deeply influenced by the imperial Etruscan civilization to the north, where it obtained two of its kings, Rome retained a fierce independence.

It developed its own culture as a diverse community, welcoming to outsiders but proud of its own, traditional way of doing things. These two character traits were as old as the earliest stories about Rome. After all, it was Romulus who made a point of inviting foreigners to become citizens, and his successor Numa Pompilius, who, so Cicero claimed, introduced "religious ceremonial [and] laws which still remain on our records." Indeed, a cosmopolitan openness to the world and fidelity to the *mos maiorum,* the Latin term for "ancestral custom," may have been interrelated: if social cohesion was to be maintained, the one needed to be corrected by, or balanced with, the other. In any event, this was a tension that would mark Rome's subsequent history.

AS ROMANS OF the first century—Cicero and his friends, for instance—looked at themselves in the mirror of a distant, royal past, what did they see? First and foremost, they were a chosen people. It was their destiny to found the world's greatest empire. By their feats of arms, they would outdo the Mediterranean's dominant power, the Greeks, whose arts and culture and military successes were unparalleled. As Trojans, they were not barbarians beyond the pale of civilization but guest Hellenes. And, as Trojans, they would at last make good the fall of Troy.

Rome was not built in a day. In many foundation myths, cities suddenly appear from nowhere, fully grown and ready to go. Not so with Rome: Romulus, the official founder, was merely a milestone in an immensely long process that began in the embers of Troy and ended in Lucretia's bedroom. The story really gets going properly only with the expulsion of the Tarquins and the arrival of the Republic.

The Romans were deeply religious, but their religion, much influenced by the Etruscans, was little more than a complex web of superstitions. The gods were incalculable powers who had to be placated at every turn. Every aspect of life was governed by ritual procedures, whether it be the repair and maintenance of a bridge or the business of making a treaty.

This was a highly aggressive society, but one that understood a vital political truth: military victory can be secured only by reconciliation with the defeated. Although most empire-builders in the ancient world were cruel and unforgiving, this was not altogether an original insight. Thus, after his conquest of the Persian Empire in the fourth century, and much to the fury of his trusty Macedonians, Alexander the Great promoted leading Orientals to positions of power in his new administration and insisted on harmony between victor and vanquished. In a move that recalls the rape of the Sabine women, he even forced his soldiers to marry local women. What was remarkable about the Romans was the consistency, over many centuries, with which they pursued their policy. They could see that it enabled them not only to foster consent to their rule among their former enemies but also to constantly enlarge their population and, by the same token, the manpower available to their armies.

There was a difficulty, though. A war had to be just, a response to someone else's aggression. That was what religion and the law

said. Romans believed, self-righteously, in the sacredness of treaties. But it was obvious even to them that they did not always live
up to expectations; the rape of the Sabine women was a clear example of bad behavior (albeit redeemed by the women themselves).

By the same token, Rome's mixed constitution, a product of the
collective wisdom of generations, was an achievement to be very
proud of. It was a bitter paradox, then, that right from the outset
great men undermined it. Romulus was the city's founder, but he
also set a precedent for tyrannical behavior. The Romans were very
skilled at doing exactly what they wanted, while at the same time,
and with the straightest possible face, convincing themselves of the
propriety of their deeds.

Perhaps the most idiosyncratic quality of Roman life was the
way that it brought together three very different functions that are,
in most societies, kept apart. Political, legal, and religious activity
was completely fused: there was no separate priestly class, for the
priest and the politician were one and the same person. So were the
politician and the general, and the politician and the advocate.
Above all, political activity was inflected by, and embodied in, hal-
lowed ceremony. The Romans took very great care to ensure divine
endorsement.

II

STORY

5

The Land and Its People

Aside from Tarquin's hat, what else did the eagle see, on its unceasing search for prey, as it swooped and climbed, floated and dived in the humid air above Latium?

It was a countryside that for many ages had been unfit for human habitation. Until as late as 1000, volcanoes had spewed copious ash and lava over a coastal plain that was also prone to a contrasting peril, frequent floods. More than fifty craters can be found within twenty-five miles of Rome. When at last the eruptions fell silent (a shower of stones in the Alban Hills was recorded as late as the reign of Tullus Hostilius), a layer of ash rich in potash and phosphates covered the land. Forests spread quickly over the hills, and a rich surface soil was formed that contained nitrogenous matter. Farming, a new technology, was now possible, and here former nomads could settle, till the loamy earth, and flourish.

Today, cereal crops are harvested in June and during the summer months the sun is pitiless, the air parched, and the deforested hills and fields arid. The landscape is a nude, bony skeleton. Our eagle flew over a very different countryside—lush, fertile, and overgrown. Harvesttime was a month later, in July. Latium was well watered. Laurel, myrtle, beech, and oak grew on the plain, and evergreen pine and fir on the mountain slopes. Everywhere, dotted among the forests, were ponds, lakes, lagoons, and streams. The valley between hills that became the Roman Forum was typical of Latium, with its marshy soil and its transformation into a temporary creek when the Tiber regularly broke its bounds.

During its flight across Latium, the eagle could see fifty or more villages, probably protected by palisades, some of which were approaching the scale of small towns. They stood on cleared land where wheat, millet, and barley were planted. Domesticated animals were widespread—oxen, goats, sheep, and pigs. The fig was cultivated, as was the olive; the vine was new, having been introduced by the Etruscans. Demand for timber hastened the gradual process of deforestation. The geographer Strabo, writing in the first century A.D., observed: "All Latium is blessed with fertility and produces everything." Malarial marshes in southern Latium were the single black spot.

However, farmers were only too well aware that rainwater dripping down the hillsides would gradually sweep away the fertile volcanic soil, on which their livelihoods depended. They constructed tunnels and dams, partly to irrigate the fields but, of equal importance, to stabilize the thin layer of earth. The Tiber poured so much mud into the sea that the new port at Ostia, founded not long ago by the first Tarquin's predecessor on the throne at Rome, would soon begin silting up.

If our eagle spread its wings and ventured farther afield, it could patrol the narrow Italian peninsula, seven hundred miles long. The icebound Alps blocked it off from the European landmass; at their feet stretched a wide, flat plain through which the vast river Padus (today's Po) wended its leisurely way. Cut off from the rest of Italy by the mountain range of the Apennines, running almost due east and west, the Romans saw this plain as part of Celtic Gaul and nothing to do with Italy proper.

Then the mountains turned southward and became a long limestone spine, crossed and broken up by narrow gorges. Terraces, high valleys, and grassy uplands made these highlands eminently habitable, and easily defended, by hardy, pastoral hill folk, who specialized in breeding livestock and selling such by-products as wool, leather, and cheeses.

On the eastern seaboard, there was sometimes hardly space for a road to run between steep heights and the sea. There was little good land and few harbors. Finally, as our eagle approached Italy's boot and high heel, the chain widened out into the dry, windy prairies of Apulia.

The western coastline was a friendlier place. The beautiful hill country of Etruria, intersected and circumscribed by mountain ranges, contained few but extremely productive plains. Along with Varro, another first-century B.C. polymath, Posidonius, the Greek philosopher, politician, geographer, and historian, noted that the Etruscans' very high standard of living was due in large part to the fecundity of their land, which nourished all manner of fruits and vegetables: "In general, Etruria, being altogether abundant, consists of extended open fields and is traversed at intervals by areas which rise up like hills and yet are fit for ploughing; also, it enjoys moderate rainfall not only in the winter season but in the summer as well." To the south lay the broad, productive expanses of Latium and Campania. This is where Rome had the good fortune to be founded.

ITALY FACES WESTWARD. Its only disadvantage is that there are few navigable rivers and few good natural harbors along its littoral. Any great state to come into being there would have to be an agricultural land power rather than a nation of sailors.

This fact had a profound effect on a Roman's idea of himself, on his collective identity. The teeming countryside of Latium was close to his deepest feelings about place and about the good life. When in the city, he longed for an idealized smallholding. Describing the happy man, the poet Horace (properly Quintus Horatius

Flaccus), who flourished a little after Cicero's day, gave this nostalgia its classic formulation:

> [He] avoids the haughty portals of
> great men, and likewise the Forum;
> he weds his lofty poplar trees
> to nubile shoots of vine;
> in some secluded dale reviews
> his lowing, wandering herds;
> he prunes back barren shoots
> with his hook and grafts on fruitful;
> he stores pressed honey in clean jars;
> he shears the harmless sheep.

Elsewhere, such a man gratefully acknowledges his good fortune when he acquires a small farm:

> This is what I prayed for. A piece of land—not so very big,
> with a garden and, near the house, a spring that never fails,
> and a bit of wood to round it off. All this and more
> the gods have granted. So be it. I ask for nothing else.

This taste for rural simplicity went hand in hand with a belief that, originally, Romans were brave and frugal. The neighboring Sabines, a different group from those who were now Roman citizens, were famous for maintaining a severe, old-fashioned morality for many centuries and ignored the comforts of a later, decadent epoch. The city of Rome itself was more virtuous and more admirable when it had hardly become a city. Propertius, a younger contemporary of Cicero and Varro, evoked a remote, admirable past:

> The Curia, now standing high and resplendent
> with Senators' purple-fringed togas,

then housed skin-clad Fathers, rural hearts.
Horns gathered the old-time citizens to the moot:
a hundred of them in an enclosure in a meadow
formed the Senate.

In this golden age, there was little gold to be found. Politicians were poor and disinterested, and patriots. Only time would tell whether this ideal state of affairs would survive the growth of Roman wealth and power.

THE STONE AGE opened about two and a half million years ago, when early human beings began to use stone tools. An empty Italy, capable of supporting life, became a home for successive waves of incomers. Small bands, perhaps twenty-five to a hundred strong, roamed the peninsula, gathering edible plants and hunting, or scavenging, wild animals.

Around the year 10,000, the planet warmed markedly and sea levels rose. The conditions of life eased. Human beings learned to farm and began to give up their nomadic ways. They developed pottery, and ground and polished stone into sophisticated artifacts. Settled agricultural communities appeared here and there in the peninsula from about 5000. Evidence of their presence has been found in Liguria in the north, the foothills of the Apennines, and in the neighborhood of Rome. Immigrants from the east (perhaps crossing the Adriatic Sea) arrived in northern Apulia. They lived in villages surrounded by defensive ditches. A pastoral people, with goats, pigs, oxen, asses, and dogs, they moved on to new places when they had exhausted the land around their homesteads.

Sometime during the second millennium, stone tools and weapons gave way to bronze. Two predominant social groupings emerged; in the flatlands of the central Po Valley, the *terramare* (so named after the piles of black earth—*terra mara,* in modern local dialect—found in the low-lying villages of these Bronze Age communities), and to the south a less advanced Apennine culture. The population, though sparse, was growing.

Toward the end of the millennium, a series of tremendous convulsions shook the more advanced civilizations of the Eastern Mediterranean. At its largest extent, the great empire of the Hittites (properly, the Land of the City of Hattusa) controlled most of what is now Turkey and Syria. With a claim to have been the world's first constitutional monarchy, it boasted a sophisticated legal system. After about 1180, the Hittite state disintegrated thanks to civil war and an external threat of some kind, of which we know next to nothing.

In about the same period, Troy was sacked; we do not have to rely on Homer for this information, since the work of archaeologists has unearthed the ruins of a burned-out city which have been dated to between about 1270 and 1190 (not far from the traditional date of the ten-year siege, as described in the *Iliad*, and where Homer placed it) and might as well be called Troy as anything else.

In mainland Greece, the Mycenaean civilization was predominant. The colossal ruins at Mycenae, in the Peloponnese, still amaze modern visitors, and were the setting of one of Greek myth's tragic narratives, the fall of the house of Atreus. Atreus's sons Agamemnon and Menelaus led the campaign against Troy, and on his return Agamemnon was assassinated by his unfaithful wife and subsequently avenged by his matricidal children. In about 1100, the Mycenaeans disappeared in a storm of violence. Many of their cities were sacked, and a subsequent lack of inscriptions suggests the onset of a "dark age." It is not known who was responsible for the catastrophe, but it may have been invaders who were later called Dorians, one of the subgroups into which classical Greeks divided themselves.

Egyptian records report invasions by mysterious marauders, known as the Sea Peoples. Modern scholars are unsure who, exactly, they were, and it is possible that they played a part in the fall of the

Mycenaeans and the Hittites. Whatever their origin, they brought havoc with them.

WHETHER OR NOT there really was a dark age, we have to wait a couple of centuries before there is evidence of an economic revival. From the mid-700s, seafarers began voyages of exploration and trade, as a great increase in pottery finds across the Mediterranean goes to show. The general direction of travel was from the wealthier and more advanced East to the less developed West—that is, along the North African coast to Italy and Spain. The Phoenicians, with their great commercial entrepôts at Carthage and Gades, led the way. As already noted, Greece emerged as a patchwork of small city-states, many of which sent groups of citizens to found "colonies"— that is, similar independent city-states, usually with sentimental links only to their founders. Within a hundred and fifty years or so, almost every likely region in the classical world saw the arrival of Greek settlers.

Sicily and southern Italy were especially popular destinations, and so many large city-states were founded there—among them Parthenope, or Neapolis (today's Naples), and Cumae, both of them in Campania south of Latium, Tarentum (Taranto), Brundisium (Brindisi), and Syracuse—that the region was called Magna Graecia, or Greater Greece. As the name implies, the center of gravity for Hellenic culture shifted decisively westward—in much the same way that the growth of the United States in the nineteenth century came to overshadow the "old world" of Europe.

What the Greeks found in central and northern Italy when they arrived in the peninsula was what scholars today call the Villanovan culture (so named after an estate where an ancient cemetery was unearthed in 1853). All that we know about it is derived from grave goods. The Villanovans were not a people; rather, they were simply people who shared common cultural characteristics. Unlike other Italian communities, they cremated their dead. Most important, they learned the uses of iron. Their economy was based on hunting and stock-raising. By the eighth century, the high quality of their pottery and of bronze metalworking strongly implies that craft production was the specialized responsibility of professional artisans. The population continued to expand, and in some settlements could be numbered in the thousands.

THERE WERE VILLANOVANS in Etruria. Now what was it that transformed them into the sophisticated and unique civilization of the Etruscans, which came into flower from the eighth century? The ancient theory that the cause was a migration from Lydia, as set out in Chapter 3 [see page 31], or, alternatively, of Pelasgians (a legendary people displaced from Greece by their successors, among them the Dorians and the Ionians), seems to have been invented to give the Etruscans a proper Hellenic pedigree.

In fact, a plausible answer to the question is looking the inquirer in the face. The Etruscans disposed of large reserves of iron ore, which was much in demand as the Iron Age gained speed. They traded ore with the Greeks and, in return, amassed wealth and acquired many of the appurtenances of Hellenic culture, in terms of both goods (such as Athenian ceramics) and attitudes (such as a taste for sexy dinner parties). The economy and the arts thrived. (This leaves unaccounted for the enigmatic Etruscan language, but we may surmise that it was a chance survivor from an age before the arrival in Italy of all the peoples who spoke the dominant Indo-European tongues.)

Although the Etruscans were a loose federation of independent cities rather than a unitary state, they made territorial gains outside Tuscany, taking over much of Campania. They even allied themselves with the superpower of the Western Mediterranean, Carthage, fighting alongside it in a great victory at sea in 535 against Greek traders and founders of the city of Massilia (today's Marseille). The result was that the Carthaginians took control of Sardinia while they themselves claimed Corsica.

This glittering world on its doorstep was strongly attractive to provincial Rome at the very time that its villages were coalescing into a city. The notion that Rome was occupied by the Etruscans is unsubstantiated, but their influence was profound. They set an example in religious observance, agricultural improvement, large drainage works, metalwork, and the construction of public buildings. In Latium, the new cities of Etruria were an encouragement for villagers to join forces and create larger settlements. By the time of the expulsion of the Tarquins, in 509, the original fifty or so small communities had been transmuted into ten or twelve substantial towns. These dominated the region, and the most populous—Praeneste (today's Palestrina), Tibur (Tivoli), and Tusculum (today a ruin)—dealt with Rome on equal terms.

Economic growth brought with it social stratification—or, in plain terms, a class system. An aristocracy emerged in Latium, and princely chamber tombs have been excavated that contained jewelry and treasure—armor and chariots, brass cauldrons and tripods, gold and silver vessels, pottery from Corinth, and Phoenician amphorae.

The magicians who brought about these extraordinary transformations both in Etruria (as already noted) and, more slowly, in Latium were the Greeks. Their traders introduced the idea of the alphabet (so, too, we may suppose, did the Phoenicians), advanced technology, art and architecture, the Olympian gods and goddesses, myths and legends—including, of course, the story of Troy. Homer probably wrote his great epics, the *Iliad* and the *Odyssey,* a little earlier in the eighth century. They celebrate the virtues of aristocracy. Men such as Achilles had a pronounced sense of personal honor; in their eyes, they fought wars or engaged in politics in order to win glory, an imperishable name that was the nearest thing to immortality to which human beings could aspire. They were inordinately proud of their family trees (often fictional), and of their generous hospitality to strangers. They held that blood and bravery were qualities more desirable than the pursuit of wealth.

All of this the Romans digested and made their own. The patricians were Homeric in their pride and ambition for glory, in their hereditary claim to power in the state, and in their scorn for anything resembling a democratic form of government. In later ages, traditionalists liked to claim that Rome developed separately and only in its maturity discovered Hellenic civilization. Cicero has one of the speakers in his dialogue, *The Republic,* say, "We Romans got our culture, not from arts imported from overseas, but from the native excellence of our own people." That could not be more wrong. Greece was in the room at the birth of Rome, and was in truth her midwife.

WE MAY SMILE at the legendary adventures of Romulus and Remus, but when classical authors imagined the site of Rome at its earliest beginnings they did not go far wrong. They pictured wooded hills and ravines, occupied by different villages, whose inhabitants were herdsmen and shepherds, although it was not long before they also included farmers. Virgil wrote in his national epic, the *Aeneid,* that the inhabitants

> had no settled
> Way of life, no civilization: ploughing, the formation of
> Communal reserves, and economy were unknown then.
> They lived on the produce of trees and the hard-won fare of the
> hunter.

They were an "intractable folk." The Capitol, "golden today, [was] then a tangle of thicket. . . . Cattle were everywhere, lowing in what is now the Forum of Rome."

As already mentioned, the Romans believed that Romulus's fortified town was built on the Palatine and regarded the Casa Romuli, Romulus's house, on the western side of the hill, as a monument to those primal times. An assemblage of wattle and daub with a thatched roof, it survived for many centuries and often had to be

repaired, either because it burned down, thanks to careless priests
with their sacrificial fires, or to redress the ravages of weather and
time.

It is here that the foundations of a village have been excavated.
At the lowest strata, contemporary with the first huts, hearths have
been found with pottery of a kind common in the eighth century—
a happy coincidence with Varro's date for Rome's foundation, 753.
There have been other suggestive finds—graves, for example, that
contained pottery and bronze implements very similar to those of
contemporary cultures south of Rome among the Alban Hills.
Also, graves in the marshy land that was to become the Roman
Forum are of two types: ditches (*fossae*), in which the bodies of the
dead were buried in coffins; and pits (*pozzi*), in which after cremation their ashes were placed in urns. This tends to confirm the
tradition that different groups with different customs occupied different hills.

However, as we have seen, Varro was too early. Evidence from
under the ground has confirmed that a hundred years had to pass
before the villages among the seven hills were amalgamated into a
single settlement. It is only now, in the mid to late 600s, that
Rome comes into being as an urban community and, in all proba-
bility, a monarchy was established.

How do we know this? In the marshy valley beneath the Palatine
and the Capitol, there used to be a marketplace, doubtless consisting of little more than a few tables or carts. In about the middle of
the seventh century, some huts were demolished, infill was imported to level the ground, and a rough, beaten floor was laid—the
first public square, or Forum. Later, the pavement was extended to
take in the Comitium, an open-air space for the holding of Assemblies. In its earliest phase, the *Cloaca Maxima,* or Great Drain,
helped to dry out the land and make it usable for public meetings,
shops, and temples. A building dating from about 600 has been
identified as the Senate House.

At one end of the Forum, a small triangular edifice survives to the present day. Once larger than it is now, the structure was built on a site previously occupied by a group of ten or twelve huts, which were demolished to make way for it. This was Numa's Regia, and its name suggests that this was the king's official residence.

The foundations of a vast, archaic temple can still be seen on the Capitol. This was the Tarquins' Temple of Jupiter Best and Greatest. It testifies to the magnificence of the Rome they governed.

The eagle that stole Priscus's hat at the Janiculum saw across the river a patchwork of huts on the tops of wooded slopes. If the bird were to survive a normal span of thirty years and once again fly over the cluster of hills by the Tiber, it would be startled by the spectacle below—a busy market square, bright colored shrines and temples, shops and public buildings. A shiny, brand-new city.

6

□ □ □

Free at Last

HAVING DISPOSED OF THE TARQUINS, BRUTUS AND his fellow conspirators had to decide what to do next. In principle, each of them could very well have presented himself to the People as a successor king. That they did not do so, but instead established a republic, is a sign that this was not a revolt from "below" but a plot by resentful aristocrats, who wanted government by the élite.

We have already noticed that the last three kings were not patricians but outsiders, even foreigners; their power flowed from the People. According to the literary record, Superbus bullied the nobles mercilessly, and it looks very much as if they now took their revenge. That members of his family, Brutus and Collatinus, Lucretia's husband, headed the coup, shows that even his core support broke with him—quite possibly because of a sex scandal rather than because of political disagreement. The Lucretia story reads rather like the plot of a stage play, but, as we have surmised, there may have been more than a germ of truth in it.

Traditionally minded as they were, Romans disliked abolishing constitutional institutions, and although the monarchy had to go, they replaced it with something similar but cut up into different pieces. The object was not to remove royal power but to tame it.

The king's religious duties were passed to a priest, the *rex sacrorum,* or king of sacred things. His executive power, his *imperium,* which gave him command of the army and authority to interpret and execute the law, went to two officials called consuls. Rather like the president of the United States, the consuls were not accountable to a representative assembly. These "magistrates," as they were called, were elected, as the kings had been; they wore similar state robes, sat on the *sella curulis,* and were also attended by lictors. The first consuls took office in 509.

The nobility wanted to eliminate the risk that one ambitious man could restore the monarchy—hence the division of power between two officeholders. This has the appearance of being an eccentric decision, and one likely to foster inertia. But power-sharing of this kind was not unknown in the ancient world. Sparta, for example, the celebrated Greek city-state whose citizens had a well-justified name for self-discipline, boasted two kings, each from a different royal family.

Two other restraints were placed on the consuls. Their term of office lasted for only twelve months, and each could place a veto (*intercessio*) on the other's decisions. In Rome "No" always trumped "Yes." In alternating months, one consul took the lead. The lictors walked in front of him in single file, with their rods (and, when outside Rome, axes), while his colleague stepped back into second place. The designers of these new arrangements recognized that domestic or external crises might arise from time to time which demanded forceful emergency action. So they invented the post of dictator. He was to be appointed by the consuls and entrusted with supreme authority on his own. His term of office was limited to six months.

Under the monarchy, the Senate was probably only an ad hoc collection of patricians and other leading personalities. Members were selected by the king and, under the early Republic, by the consuls. This state of affairs may have lasted until the fourth century, after which the Senate became a permanent, standing committee. Senators were expected to behave with probity; they were not allowed to engage in banking or foreign trade and were excluded from public contracts. They were unpaid. Not surprisingly, ways and means were found of bending the rules.

Although its function was to advise the consuls, the Senate possessed that weighty thing, *auctoritas.* A difficult word to translate, it referred to the influence that came with experience and high position. Theodor Mommsen writes that the force of *auctoritas* "was more than advice and less than a command, an advice which one may not safely ignore." The Senate came to represent continuity, and its collective experience and expertise meant that its influence would only grow with the passage of time. There were no political parties and programs, but shifting networks of personal and collective alliances, often acting in the interest of aristocratic clans.

As we have seen, there existed a People's Assembly, supposedly shaped by King Servius Tullius, the *comitia centuriata.* During the early Republic, the Assembly held supreme authority in the sense that it was the only body entitled to elect officials and pass laws. In practice, though, its democratic impact was limited, because its structure was skewed in a way that gave the "centuries" of the well-to-do more voting power than was allocated to the poor.

A system of patrons and dependents, the *clientela,* also cut across the democratic process. Freemen became the "clients" (through circumstance or choice) of wealthier people who were higher up on the social, economic, and political scale. They did everything they could to advance their patrons' interests, and in return they received protection. When things went wrong, they could apply for assistance, usually financial or legal, in the sure knowledge that they would receive it. A patron's son could expect to inherit his father's list of clients. Like a feudal pyramid, the *clientela* brought signal benefits to the poor and financially insecure.

This web of interlocking obligations was tightly woven and

made change difficult. It was one of the reasons that Rome became a conservative society and, in its constitutional arrangements, fought shy of revolutionary upheavals.

BRUTUS, WHO WAS one of the first-ever pair of consuls, persuaded an Assembly to swear an oath never again to allow any man to be king in Rome. An early law of the Republic made it a capital offense for anyone to become a leading official without being elected. Forever after, until the days of Cicero and beyond, Rome's ruling élite were obsessed with a fear that one of their number would aim for royal power, *regnum,* and ruthlessly eliminate anyone suspected of meditating a coup. They liked to compete among themselves for a turn at the top, and although great families came and went through the centuries, a nobleman of any ability felt that public office was his birthright.

Brutus and his friends could not count on the People to support them, even if the Tarquins had lost popularity through high-handedness. If the fledgling Republic was to have a chance of surviving, they knew that something had to be done to reconcile them to the new order of things. When addressing the People, an early consul took the nervous precaution of ordering his lictors to lower their rods, as a gesture of submission, and had a law passed allowing the *comitia centuriata* to be the final court of appeal against a sentence of execution or whipping (if ordered inside the city's *pomerium*). It was uncertain that this concession would be enough, for in the long run ordinary citizens would notice that, as Cicero remarked, "though the People were free, few political acts were performed by them."

The crucial point to be made about this new constitution is that it would work only if there was give-and-take. To avert despotism, the forces in the state were almost too evenly balanced one against the other. A spirit of compromise and a refusal to resort to violence were essential to its success.

TARQUIN WAS NOT nicknamed Superbus for nothing. Pride had played a part in his and his sons' fall, but pride also goaded him to resist and regain his power. Three stories are told about this desperate period during which the fate of the new Republic was in doubt; they are (surely) fictions, but they express, in their sensational way, what Romans viewed as good and bad behavior.

Superbus sent an embassy to the city, which announced his abdication and promised not to use military force to stage a comeback. In a tone of sweet reasonableness, he merely asked for the return of his and his family's money and effects. His true purpose had nothing to do with his wealth but was meant to test public opinion and to identify supporters. At an assembly Collatinus, Lucretia's widower and Brutus's fellow consul, spoke in favor of granting Tarquin's request, but Brutus, uncompromising as ever, argued vehemently against this. However, the plea was allowed, evidence (it may be) of a degree of continuing affection for Tarquin among the lower classes.

The envoys, under cover of cataloguing, selling, or dispatching the former monarch's property, suborned some highly placed young men, nephews of Collatinus and, even more appallingly, two sons of Brutus. Treachery ate at the heart of the new state. The conspirators decided they should swear together a fearful oath and, after killing a man, pour a libation of his blood and lay hands on his entrails.

A slave happened to be in the room where the ceremony was to take place one night. He hid behind a chest in the dark when the young men entered and listened to their conversation. They agreed that they would kill the consuls and prepare letters, outlining their plan, for the envoys to take away with them when they went back to Tarquin. The slave reported what had been said and done to the authorities. After a struggle, the conspirators were arrested and the damning correspondence was discovered.

The question now was what to do with the culprits, coming as they did from such high and mighty families. At an Assembly, most people were embarrassed and silent, although a few, wanting to do Brutus a favor, suggested banishment as the most appropriate punishment.

The consul was having none of it. Having considered the evidence, he called each of his sons by name. "Come, Titus, come Tiberius, why don't you defend yourselves against the charges?" he asked. They did not answer, so he asked them the same question two more times. When they still held their tongues, Brutus turned to the lictors and said, "It is now for you to do the rest." They stripped the boys on the spot, tied their hands behind their backs, and beat them with their rods. Brutus watched the scene with a fixed, unflinching gaze, even when his sons were then flung to the ground and had their heads chopped off.

The case against the other conspirators was heard, and Collatinus, fearful for his nephews, called for a moderate punishment. When Brutus objected, he shouted sarcastically, "I have the same authority as you, and since you are so boorish and cruel, I order the lads to be released." Uproar followed, and it looked as though Collatinus would be unceremoniously removed from office then and there. To take the sting out of this constitutional crisis, he agreed to resign peaceably and went into exile.

This belief in the rule of law coupled with an almost inhuman severity were typically Roman qualities. Self-esteem was the gloomy reward for this kind of self-sacrifice. The pragmatic and puzzled Greeks found Brutus's behavior "cruel and incredible." Plutarch, whose biographies of Greek and Roman generals and politicians explore the ethics of public life, was taken aback, although he was too polite to moralize. Brutus, he wrote, had "performed an act which is difficult for one to praise or to blame too highly . . . [it] was either god-like or brutish."

———

SUPERBUS WAS DISMAYED by the turn of events. Halfheartedly, he led an army against Rome, fought an indecisive battle, and abandoned the enterprise. He took refuge at the court of Lars Porsenna, king, or *lauchme,* of the powerful Etruscan city of Clusium. Porsenna disapproved, as a matter of principle, of the expulsion of monarchs, felt solidarity with Tarquin, and feared a domino effect, for what had happened to Tarquin might one day happen to him. So in 507 he agreed to lead an expeditionary force against the new Republic.

When the enemy appeared on the far side of the Tiber, Romans in the fields withdrew into the city, which was soon surrounded. The river had been deemed a strong enough barrier in itself and no defenses had been built along its bank, so the Pons Sublicius, still Rome's only bridge, was a weak point. If Porsenna's men could cross it, the war would be lost and Superbus would be back in office.

The officer on guard at the bridge was a patrician, one Publius Horatius Cocles. He had lost an eye in battle—hence his last name, Cocles, which is Latin for "one-eyed." The enemy suddenly captured the Janiculum Hill and ran down toward the bridge. All the guards panicked and fled except for Horatius and two companions, Spurius Larcius and Titus Herminius, both of Etruscan extraction. They strode to the head of the bridge on the Janiculum bank of the river and prepared to mount a defense. Their aim was to buy time for the men behind them to dismantle the bridge. The bridge was far too narrow for more than a few of Porsenna's soldiers to advance across it at once, so the three men hoped they would be able to hold them up.

They had pluck and luck, and fought at close quarters, killing many Etruscans. Horatius ordered his companions to save themselves, and struggled on alone despite a spear having passed through one of his buttocks. At last, he heard the crash of the falling bridge behind him, and with a prayer to the god of the river he dived into the water and swam back to the Roman shore. The city was saved, at least for the time being.

In this second, less controversial instance of selflessness, Horatius's conspicuous courage summed up everything that Romans understood by *virtus*—a word whose nest of interrelated meanings embraced manliness, strength, capacity, moral excellence, and military talent (from it our softer term *virtue* is derived). A statue of Horatius was erected in the Comitium. Once, it was struck by lightning, a bad omen, and moved to a lower, sunless spot on the dishonest recommendation of some nationalistic Etruscan soothsayers. When this was discovered, the men were put to death (an overly severe punishment, one may judge, but it illustrates the sacredness of Horatius's memory). The statue was then moved up to the Volcanal; this terrace on the slope of the Capitol Hill, with an altar of the blacksmith god, Vulcan, was a prestige location where the consuls of the day conducted public business. It stood there for many years and its presence is attested to by the encyclopedia writer Pliny the Elder as late as the first century A.D.

Porsenna settled down to a long siege. Time passed. Food supplies were running low in the city, and the Etruscan king supposed that he would soon gain his objective by doing nothing. A young nobleman, Gaius Mucius, decided to take the initiative. Having obtained the Senate's permission to attempt to assassinate Porsenna, he slipped into the enemy camp, wearing Etruscan clothes and speaking Etruscan fluently. A sword was concealed on his person. Unfortunately, he did not know the king by sight and dared not risk his cover by asking someone to point him out. But he saw the royal dais and joined a large crowd surrounding it.

It was payday and a well-dressed man on the dais, sitting beside the king, was busy handing out money. This was because he was the treasurer. As most people addressed themselves to him, Mucius could not be certain which was the man and which the master. He made the wrong choice. He jumped up onto the platform and stabbed the treasurer. He tried to make his escape through the crowd, but was caught and brought back before a furious Porsenna.

Mucius betrayed no hint of fear. "I am a Roman," he said. "My name is Gaius Mucius. I can die as resolutely as I can kill. It is our Roman way to do and to suffer bravely." He then hinted that there were many other would-be assassins who would follow in his footsteps.

In rage and alarm, Porsenna ordered the prisoner to be burned alive unless he revealed full details of the plot to which he had alluded. Mucius cried out, "See how cheap men hold their bodies who fix their eyes on honor and glory!" He then put his right hand into a fire that had been lit for a sacrifice, and let it burn there as if he felt no pain. The king was deeply impressed and had his guards pull Mucius from the altar. He then set him free, as an honorable enemy.

But Mucius had no intention of letting Porsenna off the hook. Lying with conviction, he said, "I will tell you in gratitude what you could not extract from me with threats. There are three hundred young Romans in your camp, disguised as Etruscans, all of whom have sworn to attempt your life. I happened to draw the shortest straw!" The shaken king decided to abandon Tarquin, negotiate a peace, and go home. Mucius was given the additional name, or cognomen, of Scaevola, meaning "left-handed"—an indirect reference to the fact that his right hand was now unusable.

Like its predecessors, this third heroic anecdote promoted self-sacrifice, but with a curious twist. In principle, Romans disparaged trickery in war—ambushes and similar underhanded behavior. They were realists, though, and regularly practiced deceit without always acknowledging it. Here Mucius, although in agony from his charred hand, still had the presence of mind to lie about the number of Roman assassins lurking in the Etruscan camp—an unchivalrous response, one might think, to Porsenna's generosity in freeing him.

Scholars are unsure of the historicity of this tale. Perhaps it originated in a trial for perjury, for a hand placed in a fire was the established penalty for breaking an oath or a pledge. Entry into an enemy
camp in disguise recalls a Greek legend about an Athenian king
who dressed as a peasant in order to reach the camp of an invading
army. Part or all of the incident may well be a fabrication. However, its melodramatic quality does not disqualify its moral from
being taken seriously.

That said, the idea that Mucius's valor was enough to persuade
Porsenna to give up the war is inherently improbable. In fact, a few
clues suggest a completely different sequence of events. In a passing reference, a great Roman historian, probably using old Etruscan sources, reveals that the king did not abandon his siege but
actually captured Rome. Reporting the destruction by fire of the
Temple of Jupiter on the Capitol during a civil war six hundred
years later, he notes that even "Porsenna, when the city gave itself
up to him," did not harm the building. Also, Pliny the Elder, who
has something to say about everything, informs us: "In a treaty
granted by Porsenna to the Roman People after the expulsion of the
Kings, we find it specifically stated that iron shall be used only for
agriculture." This was a humiliating condition, for it meant that
the Romans had to disarm. Another report claims that the Romans
gave Porsenna a throne of ivory, a scepter, a crown of gold, and a
triumphal robe—in sum, the insignia of kingship. An act of hom-
age, if ever there was one. This is all we are told, but it is a reasonable deduction that, far from seeking to restore Superbus, Porsenna
was the agent of his expulsion.

It was Rome's great good fortune that soon afterward the king of
Clusium, continuing his aggression against neighbors, suffered a
decisive (and historical) defeat near the Latin town of Aricia at the
hands of the Latin League, a federation of Latin city-states, with
help from the powerful Greek foundation of Cumae, then under the
eccentric but highly effective rule of an effeminate despot who first

made his name as a male prostitute, Aristodemus the Queen. Porsenna was killed in the battle, and any threat he posed vanished with him.

Two echoes of these events can be detected in the city. Once the fighting was over, the Romans tended the Etruscan wounded and, in a rare gesture of altruism, brought them back to Rome, where they settled. They were given permission to build houses along a street that led from the Forum around the Palatine to the Circus Maximus; according to the common belief, it was named after them, *vicus Tuscus,* or Etruscan Street. Second, an old custom at public sales of captured booty survived into the first century B.C.; the auctioneer always included in a sale, as a formality, "the goods of king Porsenna." This must refer to property the captor of Rome left behind in his new base, before he marched out to meet his unexpected doom.

One way or another, though, the Roman Republic now no longer faced any challenge to its constitutional authority.

7

General Strike

I T WAS THE STRANGEST SPECTACLE SEEN SINCE THE foundation of Rome. A long stream of families could be observed leaving the city in what looked like a general evacuation. They walked southward and climbed a sparsely populated hill, the Aventine, which stands across a valley from the Palatine, the site of Romulus's first settlement. They were, broadly speaking, the poor and the disadvantaged—artisans and farmers, peasants and urban workers. They carried with them a few days' worth of food. On arrival they set up camp, building a stockade and a trench. There they stayed quietly, like a weaponless army, offering no provocation or violence. They waited, doing nothing.

This was a mass protest, one of the most remarkable and imaginative in world history. It was like a modern general strike, but with an added dimension. The workers were not simply withdrawing their labor; they were withdrawing themselves.

Of course, some people remained—the rich and those members of the lower classes who for one reason or another could not or would not join their fellows, but Rome was half deserted. The Senate was at its wits' end. What should, or could, be done if one of Rome's numerous enemies among its neighbors in central Italy seized the moment and launched an attack? Were the rabble planning violence after a pretense of passivity, and if so how should the Senate respond? Were those who had stayed put secretly mutinous or not, a fifth column? How could civil war be avoided?

As has been noted, all citizens had to buy their own military equipment. Only the wealthy could afford the heavy armor of the legionary soldier and everyone else served as light-armed troops and skirmishers. So, in a set-piece battle with the lower classes, affluent supporters of the status quo were likely to carry the day. But such a victory would be counterproductive. Rome could not survive on the strength of the rich alone. Every state needs its workers.

The ruling élite felt very alone. The decision was taken to send an embassy of older and more tolerant senators to parley with the protesters and persuade them to end their secession, as it was called, and come home. Their spokesman was a former consul, Gaius Menenius Agrippa, a man of moderate views.

He entered the temporary camp on the hill and addressed the crowd. According to ancient sources (as ever, prone to an amusing fiction), he issued no threats and made no concessions. In fact, he appeared to speak off the point, for he launched into a fable:

Once upon a time, the members of the human body did not agree together, as they do now, but each had its own thoughts and words to express itself. All the various parts resented the fact that they should have the worry and trouble and sheer hard work of providing everything for the belly, which remained idly among them, with nothing to do except enjoy the pleasant things they gave it.

The discontented members plotted together that the hand should carry no food to the mouth, that the mouth should accept nothing that was offered it and that the teeth should refuse to chew anything. Because of their anger they tried to subdue the belly by starvation only to find that they all and the entire body wasted away. From this it was that clear that the belly did indeed have a useful service to perform. Yes, it receives food, but, by the same token, it nourishes the other members and gives back to every part of the body, through its veins, the blood it has made by the process of digestion. On this blood we live and thrive.

Menenius Agrippa compared this intestine revolt of the body to the current political crisis and the People's rage against the state of things, and persuaded his hearers to change their minds. Negotiations opened to find a settlement that the secessionists would accept.

WHAT, THEN, WAS their complaint? These were no revolutionaries seeking to overthrow the constitution. In its first years of freedom, the Republic went through an economic crisis. What caused the slump is uncertain, but a series of military reverses may have had something to do with it. (See the following chapter.) There seem also to have been food shortages. Another long-standing problem was land hunger. Freehold properties for peasants were very small, although they had access to publicly owned land, *ager publicus,* for grazing or cultivation; however, the rich and powerful tended to control public land, ruthlessly crowding out the smallholder. Archaeologists tell us that fewer public buildings were put up at this time: a Temple of Mercury, the god of business, was a telling exception, but he was to be placated at a time of commercial failure.

But perhaps the itchiest cause of discontent was identified by Cicero. "The People, freed from the domination of kings, claimed a somewhat greater measure of rights," he noted, adding sourly, "Such a claim may have been unreasonable, but the essential nature of the Republic often defeats reason."

The poor were burdened with debt and arbitrary treatment by

those in authority; they sought redress. Many had reached a point where the only thing they owned with which to repay their debts was themselves—their labor, their bodies. In that case, they were able to enter into a system of debt bondage, known as *nexum,* literally an interlacing or binding together. In the presence of five witnesses, a lender weighed out the money or copper to be lent. The debtor could now settle what he owed. In return he handed himself over—his person and his services (although he retained his civic rights). The lender recited a formula: "For such and such a sum of money you are now *nexus,* my bondsman." He then chained the debtor, to dramatize his side of the bargain.

This brutal arrangement did not in itself attract disapproval, for it did provide a solution, however rough-and-ready, to extreme indebtedness. What really aroused anger was the oppressive or unfair treatment of a bonded slave. The creditor-owner even had the right to put him to death, at least in theory. Livy tells the story of a victim, an old man, who suddenly appeared one day in the Forum. Pale and emaciated, he wore soiled and threadbare clothes. His hair and beard were unkempt. Altogether, he was a pitiable sight. A crowd gathered, and learned that he had once been a soldier who commanded a company and served his country with distinction. How had he come to this pass? He replied:

> While I was on service during the Sabine war, my crops were ruined by enemy raids, and my cottage was burnt. Everything I had was taken, including my cattle. Then, when I was least able to do so, I was expected to pay taxes, and the result was I fell into debt. Interest on the borrowed money increased my burden; I lost the land which my father and grandfather had owned before me, and then my other possessions. Ruin spread like an infection through all I had. Even my body wasn't exempt, for I was finally seized by my creditor and reduced to slavery—no, worse, I was hauled away to prison and the torture chamber.

Uproar followed, and any senator who happened to be in the Forum quickly made himself scarce. Other bonded men identified themselves. When the mob surrounded the Senate House and demanded that the consuls convene the Senate, it began to look as if a popular insurrection was under way. The consuls complied, but it proved difficult to persuade enough nervous senators to turn up and make a quorum.

When the meeting eventually started, news arrived that a Volscian army was marching on the city. There was no alternative but to meet the mob's demands. One of the consuls issued an edict to the effect that it would be illegal to fetter or imprison a Roman citizen and so prevent him from enlisting for service and, second, to seize or sell the property of any soldier on active duty. This calmed opinion and the protesters willingly joined a military force that marched out of Rome to confront and defeat the invaders.

This did not end the matter, thanks to a contemptuous and choleric consul, Appius Claudius, founder of an immigrant Sabine family that won a name over the centuries for high-handedness. He insisted on pursuing debtors with the utmost rigor of the law, and gave no consideration to the riots that resulted. Leaders of the People began meeting secretly at night to plan their response.

This was the background of the general strike and the withdrawal to the Aventine, which took place in 494, a little more than ten years after the expulsion of Superbus. Those involved saw themselves as members of a gathering called the *plebs*. In later centuries, the word came to include everyone who was not a patrician or a nobleman—the common people as a whole. But, at this early stage, the evidence suggests that it signified a political or campaigning movement, recruited from the masses but not identical with them. It was not unlike a trade union, but representing all crafts and workplaces.

And, like a trade union, the plebs wasn't interested in the armed overthrow of the state or in a constitutional upheaval. It did not set itself in opposition to the dominant patrician class. It existed simply to protect and advance the interests of its members, the plebeians. This it did with extraordinary success. The consuls and the Senate had lost their nerve, at least for the time being.

The leadership understood the need to organize. A special assembly was created, the *concilium plebis,* or Plebeian Council, which voted on tribal lines. At this time, the Roman population was (probably) divided into twenty-one local tribes, to which citizens belonged by virtue of residence. The plebeians decided on resolutions by tribe, with each tribe exercising one vote (a fairer system than voting by centuries in the *comitia centuriata*). The council's enactments—*plebiscita,* whence our *plebiscite*—were not binding on the Republic itself but were difficult for the consuls and the Senate to ignore. As time passed, the plebs became a state within a state.

The negotiations with Menenius Agrippa and the other senatorial envoys saw a further strengthening of the influence of the plebs. It was agreed that the *concilium plebis* could elect extra-constitutional officials (probably two in the first instance), *tribuni plebis,* or tribunes of the plebeians. (By the middle of the fifth century, their number had risen to, and remained at, ten.) The first tribunes to take office were Lucius Sicinius Vellutus, the leader of the encampment on the Aventine, and Lucius Junius Brutus, a vain and pretentious man who so admired the Republic's first consul that he added the cognomen Brutus so that he could share the same name.

The tribunes' task was to defend the interests of plebeians within the city's *pomerium.* They drew their authority from a *lex sacrata,* a solemn oath taken by the plebs that they would obey their tribunes and defend them to the death. Anyone who harmed them would be *sacer.*

This rich and potent word has two definitions, one positive and the other negative. It can signify sacred or holy, consecrated to a deity; thus, the *via Sacra,* a street that led into the Forum, translates as the Sacred Way. Or it can mean consecrated to a deity for destruction. In this sense, the nearest synonym in English is the much weaker *accursed* or *impious.* The sentence *Sacer esto*—"Be accursed"—was pronounced on a man who by his actions harmed the gods. Such a person was forfeit to the gods, and when he died he fell under their unforgiving care. Anyone who killed him was fulfilling a holy task, committed no crime, and was free of blood-guilt. This was a fearful spell, and it enveloped the tribunes in the invisible but inviolable armor of sacrosanctity.

It was an armor that enabled them to defend plebeians from oppression by the rich and powerful and from arbitrary treatment by a magistrate by bringing them *auxilium,* assistance. This meant that a tribune could intervene in person and rescue a put-upon ordinary citizen. He enforced his will by coercion, *coercitio.* He could fine, imprison, or execute anyone who challenged his authority or, even, merely bad-mouthed him. If he was confronted with force, he could threaten the terrifying consequences of the *lex sacrata.* As one contemporary scholar has neatly put it, this was "lynch law disguised as divine justice."

At first, the authority of the tribunes was extralegal and formed no part of the Roman constitution. Many unreconciled patricians refused to recognize the new plebeian institutions, and it was not for another two decades that a law gave the plebs the official right to hold its own meetings and elect its own officers. In the middle of the century or later, the tribunes won their greatest and unparalleled power—the right to "intercede" in the business of government. *Intercessio,* as previously noted, was a polite word for "veto." A tribune could quite simply cancel any act by an elected official (except a dictator, until the year 300), any law, and any election. He had the authority, if he so wished, to bring the state to a standstill.

EVEN WHEN THE first secession was over (it is unreliably reported that there were to be more of them until a last one in about

287), the plebeians maintained their link with the Aventine. In fact, the hill became a memorial to the plebeian cause, a center for activism and a symbolic alternative city, an anti-Rome. In 493, a couple of years after the crisis, a temple to Ceres, the goddess of grain and fertility, was built. It had been vowed a few years earlier during a famine, and soon became a plebeian stronghold.

The shrine was a small but competitive copy of the Temple of Jupiter Best and Greatest, which could be seen in the distance. The resemblance can have been no accident. Like its counterpart on the Capitol, it was built in the old Etruscan manner, with deep eaves and colorful terra-cotta statues on the roof; there were chambers for three divinities, housing not only a statue of Ceres but also one of her daughter, Proserpina, and Father Liber, an Italian version of the Greek god of fertility and wine, Dionysus. It was a rich endowment where many works of art were assembled over the years. The walls were decorated with frescoes, and a famous painting of Dionysus, looted from Greece in the second century, was displayed there.

The plebs used the building for distributing food to the poor during times of shortage, and (along with the neighboring Temple of Diana, whose cult was especially popular with slaves) it was a safe sanctuary for runaways. Temple administrators were appointed, who reported to the tribunes; they were called aediles (after the Latin for *temple, aedes*).

The aediles soon had an addition to their job description. The consuls and the Senate understood that one way of preserving their power was to ban information about their activities. No reports of their proceedings were published, and the consuls suppressed or even falsified senatorial decrees. By the middle of the fifth century, pressure from the plebs opened up the proceedings of government to general scrutiny. The aediles were authorized to take charge of all the records of the plebs, of the People's Assemblies, and of the Senate, which they archived at the Aventine, "so that nothing that was transacted should escape their notice."

IN THE REPUBLIC'S early days, the surviving lists of consuls, the *fasti,* show that men who were not of the patrician class could be, and were, elected to the chief magistracy. But as time passed the consulship became in practice a patrician prerogative—a bitter response, perhaps, to the advances made by the plebs. The plebs reacted strongly, and what had begun as a campaign against unfair treatment gradually turned into a political struggle between the patrician aristocracy, with its inherited authority and control of the state religion, and the rest of society, spearheaded by the plebeians. It was at this point that *plebs* came to mean "the People."

This growing antagonism is well illustrated by an exemplary story of unbending pride and its consequences. Once again, it is an incident that tells a symbolic truth; we do not know how much, if any of it, actually took place. Gnaeus Marcius, a patrician, was a brave soldier and in his youth won the Civic Crown. This treasured honor, a garland of oak leaves, was awarded to anyone who saved the life of a fellow citizen in battle.

In the early fifth century, a war broke out with the Volsci in the south, constant as ever in their belligerence. The Romans laid siege to the enemy town of Corioli. All at once, a Volscian force appeared on the scene and, simultaneously, there was a sortie from the town. Marcius happened to be on guard at the time. He took a specially selected body of men and not only drove back the sally but managed to enter the town himself. He seized a firebrand and threw it into some houses overhanging the city wall. The flames and the wailing of women and children convinced the Volscians outside that Corioli was lost and they withdrew from the fray. The Roman army turned its attention back to the siege, and the town was soon theirs.

The consul in command showered praise on Marcius and, as a reward for his valor, offered him one-tenth of the captured booty—equipment, men, horses—before it was shared out, as was the practice, among the soldiers. He declined, saying fiercely that that would be a payment, not an honor. He accepted only a single horse, and asked that a prisoner, who was a Volscian guest-friend, be released. In response, the consul awarded him the cognomen of Coriolanus, to mark his leading role in the victory.

Back in Rome, Coriolanus stood for the consulship. His distinguished military service made it highly probable that he would be elected. He canvassed for votes in the Forum as candidates were expected to do, and made a good impression by showing off his battle scars. Unfortunately, on election day he made a pompous entry into the Forum accompanied by the Senate and crowds of patricians, and the popular mood swung against him.

Furious at having been rejected, Coriolanus decided to punish the voters. He surrounded himself with some arrogant and showy young patricians and did his best to annoy the tribunes, Brutus and Sicinius. He taunted them: "Unless you stop disturbing the Republic and stirring up the poor by your speeches, I'll not oppose you with words but with actions." There was a food shortage, and when a large delivery of grain arrived from Sicily the People assumed that it would be sold cheaply. Coriolanus spoke out against the proposition. "Any such measure on our part would be sheer madness," he said. "If we are wise, we shall take their right to have Tribunes away from the People, for it makes the Consulship null and void, and divides the city."

Wiser heads among the nobility felt that Coriolanus was going too far, but he was carried away by his hotheads. The tribunes impeached him at an Assembly, but he refused to come and answer the charges. When the aediles tried to arrest him, patricians drove them away. Evening put an end to the disturbances.

The next day, crowds again gathered in the Forum. The alarmed consuls gave reassurances about the price of market supplies, and the mood in the square lightened. Brutus and Sicinius, however, insisted that Coriolanus should answer accusations that he wanted to abrogate the powers of the People and had offered violence to the aediles. They calculated that either he would humiliate himself by apologizing or, more likely, he would do or say something unforgivable.

They knew their man, and his ungovernable temper. When Coriolanus appeared, he spoke with his habitual scorn and scuffles broke out. Once again, he was whisked away by patricians. It was agreed by all sides that there should be a proper trial. Coriolanus was indicted for planning to usurp the government and appeared before the popular Assembly, which acted as a jury. The prosecution was unable to prove its case and dropped the charge, but another last-minute allegation of wrongful distribution of campaign spoils was added. This threw the accused, who was not immediately ready with an answer. The Assembly voted its verdict by tribes, and Coriolanus was found guilty by a majority of three. He was sentenced to perpetual banishment.

Determined to avenge himself, he left Rome for the Volscian capital, where he volunteered his services. The Volsci were delighted and commissioned Coriolanus, with full powers, to lead an expedition against his former homeland. He carried all before him and soon appeared at the head of the Volscian army outside the gates of Rome. It seemed that the Republic was doomed.

Inside the city all was confusion. The plebs, unnerved, were eager to rescind their sentence, while the Senate, reluctant to pardon treason, rejected the proposal. An embassy was sent to the Volscian camp and a truce agreed, but Coriolanus insisted on harsh terms. The stalemate was broken when his mother, Volumnia, accompanied by his wife, Vergilia, with his children, unexpectedly appeared before him. She pleaded with him to spare the city and negotiate an equal settlement.

He stood stock-still and wordless for some time. "Why have you nothing to say?" asked Volumnia. "It would have been a mark of a son's respect for his mother to give me what I asked without the need for any pressure. Since I can't persuade you, I must use my last resource." With that, she and his wife and children flung themselves onto the ground at his feet, in a humiliating act of self-abasement.

"What have you done to me, mother?" he replied, lifting her up. "You have won. You've saved Rome, but you've finished me."

And so she had. As she requested, Coriolanus signed a peace and the Volsci returned home with their now discredited Roman commander. He began giving an account of his conduct of the war before a Volscian assembly, when some men, enraged by his betrayal, cut him down. Not a single person present came to his aid.

BY THE MIDDLE of the fifth century, the conflict between the patricians and the plebs was the major domestic political issue confronting the Republic. Livy has a conservative politician complain, "You were elected as Tribunes of the plebs, not enemies of the Senate." True enough, but the times were changing. The class of patricians began to react against the advances made by the plebs by transforming themselves into an exclusive hereditary caste with a monopoly on government. Richer non-patricians who had served as consuls in the early years of the Republic found themselves squeezed out. They, in turn, reacted to the patricians' reaction by joining with the plebs and forming a united front. This union of forces should not be allowed to conceal the fact that the two groups ultimately had different objectives—one sought access to fair treatment, and the other access to high office.

A leading statesman, three times a consul, Spurius Cassius, fell foul of the growing and mutual antipathy. An able negotiator, he brought about a durable peace with thirty Latin cities, the famous Foedus Cassianum (see the next chapter on page 114); its text could still be seen and read in Cicero's day, cut into a bronze column behind the speakers' platform in the Forum.

Cassius supported the plebeian cause and was the first to put forward a land-reform program. This was unforgivable to the nobles, in possession, as they were, of an unfairly large quantity of *ager publicus.* In 485, Cassius was accused of seeking to be king, in what looks like a thin case, but once his father had given evidence against him he was found guilty of this most heinous offense against the Republic and put to death. He was declared *sacer* to Ceres, patron saint of the plebs. It is rather odd that the plebeian leadership did not rescue him from patrician attack, but perhaps the tribunes weren't self-confident enough to defend him. His house was pulled down, and word has it that the land was never built on again. Livy writes that in his day the site was supposedly the open space in front of the Temple of Tellus, the goddess of Mother Earth. As luck would have it, it commanded a fine view of that populist hill, the Aventine.

For a while, the democratic process was stymied. Beneath the surface, though, pressure began to build toward another explosion. Having won a victory over the records of the Senate, the tribunes pursued their struggle for greater governmental transparency. One of the means by which oligarchies keep power in their hands is by controlling the legal system. In Rome, the laws were not published. They were in the care of the *pontifices,* who kept them under lock and key as sacred books, and only patricians were allowed to read them. In 462, a tribune launched an attempt to prevent the consuls from acting arbitrarily and demanded that legislation governing the powers of the consuls be fully disclosed. The campaign soon widened to embrace all the Republic's laws. Magistrates and the Senate mounted a spirited resistance, but in 451 both sides, exhausted by the long quarrel, came to a very remarkable agreement.

The constitution was suspended and the posts of consul and tribune were abolished—but for one year only. A new Board of Ten, the decemvirs, or *decemviri legibus scribundis* (that is, "ten men for writing the laws"), took charge of the state; they were given ple-

nary powers, and there was no right of appeal against their decisions. Their task was to review, codify, and then publish Rome's
laws. This they did, producing Ten Tables of laws. The next year,
the first slate of decemvirs, all of them patricians, retired and were
replaced by another, which included some plebeians. Only one man
was reappointed: Appius Claudius, grandson of the founding immigrant, with whom he shared the same high temper. The second
Decemvirate published two additional Tables and ran into a storm
of protest when it decided not to retire at the end of its year but to
remain in office for a third year.

This is all very mysterious. Why hand over the Republic and its
constitution to a group of people who are in effect a commission of
inquiry into one particular topic? They would have been able to get
on with their work much more easily if they were not at the same
time tasked with running the country. On the other hand, it may
be that the decemvirs were meant to be a permanent reform, presumably bringing the plebeians and their "state within a state"
inside the constitution. In that case, the election, after one year, of
a new college makes perfect sense (although one wonders why the
first decemvirs were all patricians). The main problem here is that
the literary sources insist that the new magistrates had a temporary
role and were to hand over power to consuls and tribunes when
their legal review was complete; according to them, the second college was elected only because the first one had not done its job to
everyone's satisfaction.

It is evident that the ancient historians were confused, and modern scholars have indulged themselves with ingenious speculations.
The most plausible solution of the riddle—that is, the account that
explains most of the data and is consistent with the realities of political life—is that the Decemvirate was intended as a permanent
new system of government and that the legal codification was the
first major item on its agenda.

One way or another, the reform failed. Livy writes: "The Decemvirate, after a flourishing start, soon proved itself a barren tree—all wood and no fruit—so that it did not last." His account of what happened next is one of the finest episodes in his long history, although (as ever) it is unclear how much of it is fact and how much fiction or imaginative reconstruction.

After elections were held for the second year, the new decemvirs, informally headed by Appius Claudius, took office. Once in place, they behaved brutally and irresponsibly, and it was whispered that they had bound themselves by oath to hold no more elections and to retain their power indefinitely. One of their two additional legal Tables included a ban on intermarriage between patricians and plebeians—tantamount to a declaration of war by the former against the latter.

The date for new elections in May 450 (then the beginning of Rome's political year) came and went. Technically, the decemvirs' term was over, but no new magistrates were nominated. Appius and his colleagues continued in power as if nothing untoward were happening.

A declaration of war by the Sabines and then the Aequi transformed the situation. The shaken decemvirs, well aware of their unpopularity, had no alternative but to consult the Senate. Lucius Valerius Potitus, a senior patrician who sympathized with the plebs, called for an open debate on the political situation, and an angry senator, Marcus Horatius Barbatus, said that the decemvirs were "ten Tarquins." A motion was put to take no action on Appius's proposal to raise troops, on the grounds that he held no official position. Eventually, though, after more hard words the Senate gave way and raised no objection to the holding of a levy.

THE WAR WENT badly, and disaffection spread among the soldiery. However, the final crisis, when it came, was neither military nor political in character. As with the fall of the kings, it apparently stemmed from a sex scandal. Appius fancied a beautiful young woman from a plebeian family. The daughter of Lucius Verginius, a serving centurion in the army, she was the fiancée of a former tribune, Lucius Icilius. Roman girls married young, and we may assume that she was in her early teens. She resisted Appius's blandishments, so he decided on an ingenious kind of compulsion.

He told a dependent or client of his to claim Verginia as his slave and seize her. One morning, the man laid hands on her in the Forum as she was on her way to school. He claimed that, like her mother before her, she was his slave and instructed her to follow him. The girl was dumbstruck with shock and fear, but her nurse had her wits about her and shouted for help. A crowd quickly gathered.

Appius, who was sitting on a nearby platform presiding over a law court, saw that abduction was now out of the question. He therefore summoned Verginia to appear before him and assured everyone that the affair was completely aboveboard. He had excellent evidence, he said, that she had been stolen from his house, where she was born, and palmed off on Verginius.

The mood in the Forum grew ugly, and Appius reluctantly agreed to postpone the hearing until Verginius could be recalled from the front. He insisted that in the meantime Verginia should be cared for by the claimant. By this time, Icilius had arrived and after angry exchanges Appius gave way again and surrendered the girl to her fiancé. The following morning, father and daughter appeared before the court. The proceedings had hardly begun when Appius interrupted and gave his judgment. Verginia was a slave and should be handed over to her rightful owner.

Supporters standing around the girl refused to let her go. An officer of the Decemvirate blew a trumpet for silence, and Appius spoke. "I have incontrovertible evidence," he said, "that throughout last night meetings were being held in the city for seditious purposes. I have therefore brought an armed escort with me to check disturbers of the peace. It will be wiser to keep quiet. Lictor, clear the crowd. Let the master through to take possession of his slave."

Until this point, Verginius had been loudly protesting, but he now changed tack. He apologized to the decemvir for his behavior. "Let me question the nurse here, in my child's presence," he said. "Then if I find I am not her father, I shall understand and be able to go away in a calmer frame of mind." Permission was granted, and he led the two women to a row of shops, called New Shops, near the shrine of Venus Cloacina, tutelary spirit of the Cloaca Maxima, the drain that crossed the Forum.

He then grabbed a knife from a butcher. "This is the only way to make you free," he said, stabbing his daughter to the heart. "Appius, may the curse of this blood rest on your head forever."

Undismayed, the decemvir summoned Icilius. The crowd was now at fever pitch. Valerius and Horatius joined the press around the young man and ordered the lictors to refuse service to Appius, as he had no official position. At this point, the decemvir's nerve failed him and, afraid for his life, he wrapped his head in his cloak and disappeared into a nearby house.

The decemvirs refused to resign, and the Senate could not make up its mind what to do. A Roman army in the field made it up for them. They returned to the city and encamped on the Aventine, where they were joined by much of the civilian population. This second secession did the trick. The decemvirs resigned, hoping not to be punished. Appius, though, remarked, "I know well enough what is coming to us."

He was right. The old constitution was restored. New consuls, Horatius and Valerius, who, in Cicero's words, "wisely favored popular measures to keep the peace," were elected, and so was a full roster of tribunes and aediles. Appius was summarily flung into jail. He appealed to the People and a trial was agreed. He kept up the typical haughty manner of a Claudian, but he could sense the rising anger in the city as the day of the hearing approached. He decided not to face his day in court and killed himself.

For a Roman, suicide was an appropriate act in the face of a hopeless situation—*nulla spes.* But a Claudian was expected to show contempt for circumstance, and Appius's family pretended that he had died a natural death. His son was in charge of the funeral arrangements, and asked the tribunes and the consuls to convene an Assembly in the Forum, as was the custom with the famous dead, at which he could deliver a eulogy. Permission was refused.

THE FATE OF the decemvirs had important consequences. First of all, it offered future generations a striking moral and human example. Verginius joined Brutus as another heroic killer of his own offspring—bloodshed as *virtus.* On this occasion, the lesson to be drawn is the high priority the Roman family placed on the purity of its daughters. Sex with an unmarried and freeborn young woman was absolutely prohibited, because it interfered with the hereditary bloodline. (By contrast, going to bed with a non-citizen, whether male or female, was acceptable, if not exactly admirable, behavior).

The collapse of the Decemvirate and the second secession marked a further triumphant phase in the advance of the plebs. The consuls had three important laws passed by the official, constitutional general assembly, the *comitia centuriata.* The first one endorsed the sacrosanctity of the tribunes of the People and perhaps their power of veto; until now, their status had been guaranteed only by an oath taken by the extraconstitutional *concilium plebis,* the Plebeian Council. In future, the Republic itself would stand guarantor of the tribunes' safety. The state within a state had at last joined the state.

The second law concerned citizens' right of appeal. The basic principle had been dealt with in 509, but the decemvirs had been created specifically without a right of appeal against their decisions. The loophole had to be plugged, and Valerius and Horatius prohibited the Republic from bringing into being any new magistrates not subject to appeal.

Finally, and most controversially, proposals approved by the Plebeian Council were given the force of law, although probably on condition of some kind of external validation. This was a significant advance, for it will be recalled that the council voted by tribes and not according to the unfair division into centuries, which heavily favored the voting power of the wealthy.

ALTHOUGH THE DECEMVIRS came to grief, they had a signal achievement of which they could be justly proud—the Twelve Tables (as the Ten plus the Two came to be called). These codified customary law into statutes, and opened the administration of justice to public scrutiny, at least in principle. Livy writes that they are "still today the fountainhead of public and private law, running clear under the immense and complicated superstructure of modern legislation." Cicero recalls having to learn them by heart when he was a schoolboy.

Curiously, for a document so highly valued and widely distributed, no text has come down to us. A number of quotations survive here and there in an archaic Latin, but one cannot be quite sure how accurately they have been remembered and how characteristic they are of the whole. The plebs quickly ensured the repeal of the offensive ban on marriage between noble and commoner, but the rest of the Twelve Tables were well received. A strengthening of the rights of wives moderated the domestic despotism of *patria potestas,* a father's authority over his family. Other rules facilitated the emancipation of slaves and regulated inheritance, debt, and *nexum,* interest on loans, contracts, and conveyancing. Extravagance was discouraged.

The emphasis was on day-to-day exchanges between individuals, and there is little concerning the relation of the individual and the community. Thus: "A man might gather up fruit that was falling down onto another man's farm," and "Let them keep the road in order. If they have not paved it, a man may drive his team where he likes."

The sheer strangeness of some of Rome's early laws puzzles the mind. Here is the grisliest: "Where a party is delivered up to several persons, on account of a debt, after he has been exposed in the Forum on three market days, they shall be permitted to divide their debtor into different parts, if they want to do so; and if anyone of them should, by the sharing out, receive more or less than he is entitled to, he shall not be responsible." This means, literally, what it says: if there was more than one creditor, they were entitled to cut a debtor's body into different bits, the shares reflecting the amounts of debt owed.

Shylock would have felt vindicated, with Portia straining for the quality of mercy.

THESE WERE FAMOUS victories for the People, but it was soon obvious that the game was not yet over. Within a few years, there was another dramatic but mysterious upheaval. In 444, the consuls were swept away and replaced by military tribunes with consular powers (*tribuni militum consulari potestate*). In any given year, there were not fewer than three of these new officials, and often as many as six.

The purpose of this reform is hidden in fog. Some sources say it was a compromise by the patricians, who refused to accept that a consul could be a plebeian but would not object in the case of a governing committee; unfortunately for this theory, plebeians were seldom elected to the new posts, at least at the outset. Others claim that Rome needed more than two army commanders; so why, as sometimes happened, were tribunes elected in years when there was no campaigning to be done? And why did the Republic switch unexpectedly from year to year between tribunes and consuls? The second explanation is perhaps the more convincing, if we add a probable increase in official domestic duties. We should also remember that the decision whether or not tribunes were to be elected, and if so how many, had to be taken in the year preceding the period of office. So guesswork, well-informed, doubtless, but sometimes off the mark, would have been the order of the day.

The struggle between the rich and the poor, the nobility and the People, the patricians and the plebs, called the Conflict of the Orders, had a century and more yet to run. But despite setbacks for the popular cause, most Romans could see that the pendulum of power was swinging irreversibly toward the plebs.

8

The Fall of Rome

L ATE IN THE AFTERNOON OF THE FIFTEENTH OF JULY
in the year 496 two tall, preternaturally handsome young
men, just growing their first beards, were spotted in the Forum at
Rome. They were washing their sweaty horses in the spring that
rose just by the Temple of Vesta and formed a small but deep pool.
They were dressed in armor, and it looked very much as if they had
just come from a battlefield. People gathered around them and
asked if there was any news, for Rome had dispatched an army
against the city's Latin neighbors.

The youths replied that, yes, there had been a great battle on this
day at Lake Regillus and that Rome had been the winner. Then
they left the Forum and, although a great search was made for
them, they were never seen again.

On the following day, letters arrived from the army reporting on
the victory. Old Tarquin Superbus had been present, fighting
alongside the Latins, and was wounded in the side. The enemy
camp was taken. Apparently, two young men on horseback had
suddenly appeared at the head of the Roman cavalry, spearing down
every Latin soldier they encountered and driving the enemy into
headlong retreat. Clearly they were gods, and the same ones who
had appeared a little later in the Forum. Everyone agreed that they

must have been the Heavenly Twins, Castor and Pollux, also known as the Dioscuri, or "sons of Zeus." Helen of Troy was their sister, and they were among Jason's Argonauts in the search for the Golden Fleece. They acted as helpers of mankind, typically intervening at times of crisis. They had an important shrine near Lake Regillus, so the battle had been fought on their doorstep.

The Roman commander vowed to found a temple in thanksgiving to the brothers and, although the story of their apparition is of course mythical, archaeologists have confirmed that it was built around this time in the Forum, near where they had been seen with their horses. The Romans revered the Heavenly Twins and the temple was twice rebuilt, each time more grandly. The massive ruins of the final version, commissioned by the emperor Tiberius in the first century A.D., can still be seen in the Forum today. The building stood on a high podium; the Senate frequently met inside it and its front steps were topped by a platform, much used for rabble-rousing open-air speeches during the riotous politics of the late Republic.

Every year on the date of the battle, a splendid ritual was conducted in honor of Castor and Pollux. Rome's official cavalry processed into the city as if coming fresh from a battle and marched past the temple. They were crowned with olive branches and dressed in purple robes with scarlet stripes, along with their military decorations. "It made a fine sight," wrote a witness of the ceremony in the first century, "and worthy of Roman power."

TWO HUNDRED YEARS of class struggle at home did not deter the Romans from fighting an almost continuous series of military campaigns abroad. Described in the ancient histories as if they were the wars of a great nation, these campaigns were in fact for the most part raids and counter-raids, state-sponsored brigandage. This was why, to Livy's "great astonishment," seemingly decisive victories apparently had no effect, and the Aequi and the Volsci returned fresh to the fray with every new campaigning season. However, in the long run the fighting was destructive and exhausting, for year after year harvests were trashed and buildings burned.

Under the kings, Rome had dominated Latium, but the arrival of the Republic coincided with a debilitating economic crisis. With their victory over Lars Porsenna, the Latins had removed Etruscan influence in the region and they were determined to cut the inexperienced regime at Rome down to size, too. However, the Republic's new rulers gave notice that they intended to maintain Superbus's expansionist foreign policy.

The first consuls negotiated a treaty with Carthage. It was a considerable achievement to obtain the recognition of such a great Mediterranean power. The text of the treaty sets out Carthage's sphere of influence, including Sicily, while also revealing Rome's (much more modest) pretensions in Latium:

> The Carthaginians shall do no injury to the peoples of Ardea, Antium, the Laurentes and the peoples of Circeii, Tarracina or any other city of those Latins who are subject to the Romans. As for those Latin peoples who are not subject to the Romans, the Carthaginians shall not interfere with any of these cities, and if they take any one of them, they shall deliver it up undamaged. They shall build no fort in Latin territory. If they enter the region carrying arms, they shall not spend a night there.

The Romans were exaggerating the extent of their influence. Antium, Circeii, and Tarracina were outside the boundaries of Latium at this epoch and fell squarely inside Volscian territory. But the treaty illustrated Rome's aggressive intentions, and by implication its desire to regain the ascendancy lost during the upheavals attendant on the fall of the monarchy. Adventures abroad would be a welcome diversion from poverty and indebtedness at home.

The Latins shared a mutual solidarity. Every spring they held a "national" festival, the Feriae Latinae, at which they celebrated their kinship. The central feature was a banquet. Each community brought to the party lambs, cheese, milk, or something similar; a white bull was sacrificed, and its meat was shared among all those attending. The Latin states formed a league from which Rome was excluded, and war soon broke out between them.

Hostilities were not long-lasting. For all the efforts of the Heavenly Twins, the Battle of Lake Regillus was not necessarily the success the Romans claimed it to be. And the opposing forces came to realize that they shared an important interest. They both faced a ring of hostile tribes and communities. Clockwise from the north, there were the Etruscans, especially the rich and powerful city of Veii. Then came the Sabines, the Aequi, the Hernici, and the irrepressible Volsci. Swaths of territory were being lost. Latium was in grave danger of being overrun unless Rome and the Latins reconciled their differences.

In 493, that is what they did. The consul Spurius Cassius (who, as we have seen, was later to be executed for aiming at *regnum*) negotiated a peace treaty, the Foedus Cassianum, named after him. Its terms were inscribed on a bronze pillar in the Forum, which was still there in Cicero's time. At its heart lay a commitment to mutual help:

> Let there be peace between the Romans and all the Latin cities as long as the heavens and the earth stay where they are. Let them neither make war upon one another themselves, nor bring in foreign enemies, nor give safe passage to those who shall make war upon either of them. Let them assist one another, when warred upon, with all their forces.

A few years later, the Hernici were brought into the entente. They and the Latins fought in separate contingents under a unified, Roman command. At last, sufficient military force had been assembled to meet the omnipresent threats of invasion from every quarter of the compass.

The background of these small-scale quarrels was a vast movement of peoples from the beginning of the fifth century into Italy and down the peninsula's Apennine spine. Facing overpopulation and, possibly, pressure from Celts who were beginning to cross the Alps into the Po Valley, Sabellians, mountain dwellers who spoke a language called Oscan, began to migrate southward from their habitat in the central Apennines in search of living space.

The migrations were governed, we are told, by a religious ritual called *ver sacrum,* the Sacred Spring. A year's generation of animals and humans was dedicated, or made *sacrati,* to the god Mars. The animals were sacrificed and the young people, when they had reached the age of twenty or twenty-one, were sent away from their community to look for somewhere else to live. Under a leader they followed an animal, such as a bull, a wolf, or a woodpecker. Where it stopped to rest, there they founded a new settlement or colony.

These bands of young shepherd fighters set off a chain reaction, knocking onto the toe of Italy and threatening the Hellenic cities of Magna Graecia. Oscan-speaking Samnites (a group of Sabellian tribes) flooded down from the hills and invaded fertile Campania. They took over the main cities and set themselves up as a new nation, giving up stock-keeping for farming. The Etruscan ruling class of Capua unwisely let the newcomers in and made them members of the community, only to be butchered en masse after a drunken festival one black night in 423.

For many years Rome only just held its own, much assisted by the Latins, against the Aequi and the Volsci, but in the second half of the fifth century the tide slowly began to turn. A decisive battle against the Aequi was fought on 19 June 431: the fact that the precise date stuck in the Republic's collective memory suggests how precious the victory was. Lost Latin cities were recovered, and Roman forces at last moved onto the offensive.

IT WAS DURING one of these scrappy campaigns, half skirmish, half full-dress battle, that the story of the staunchly anti-plebeian

Lucius Quinctius Cincinnatus is set. This elderly and distinguished patrician and politician had fallen on hard times and farmed a smallholding of four acres. One day, a delegation arrived from the city and found him at work on his land, perhaps digging a ditch or plowing a field. "Is everything all right?" he asked. No, it was not, but the formalities had to be observed. After a prayer for the gods' blessing on him and his country, he was invited to go and put on his toga, the uniform of the freeborn Roman.

It was no wonder that he was not wearing it, for it was among the most inconvenient garments ever devised by the mind of a tailor. A vast semicircle of heavy cloth, about ten by twenty feet in extent, it was draped over the body and worn without a fastening. Considerable skill was required to stop it from falling off, and it was drafty in winter and stifling in summer.

Cincinnatus returned duly garbed. Only then was he informed of a grave military crisis. A consular legion was besieged in its camp by an Aequian army. Cincinnatus was to serve as dictator and had been commissioned to march to its relief. He quickly accomplished the task. He made a lenient peace with the Aequi, but only after forcing a ritual humiliation on them; a yoke was set up, consisting of three spears under which the entire defeated enemy was obliged to pass, bowing down and so admitting defeat. Mission accomplished, Cincinnatus resigned the dictatorship a fortnight later and returned to his plow.

Although he is not a fully historical figure, Cincinnatus represented a combination of qualities that the Romans greatly admired, even if they were seldom honored in the observance. These were a simple life, commitment to country values, unquestioning patriotism, even-handedness, and disdain for riches. As usual, this admiration found a topographical expression: the old man's farm, which lay west of the Tiber and opposite the shipyards at the foot of the Palatine Hill, was preserved, at least in name, as the Quinctian Meadows.

As late as the eighteenth century A.D., Cincinnatus was still regarded as a moral model. The American city Cincinnati was so called as a compliment to George Washington, who was considered a latter-day Cincinnatus for his indifference to power. The example has been followed as frequently in recent times as it was in ancient Rome.

SOME TEN OR so miles north of Rome, at the confluence of two small rivers, a large grassy plateau stands on a tall rocky outcrop. Nearly five hundred acres in extent, it has been farming and grazing land for the past two millennia. Closer inspection points to a hidden, long-lost history. In the summertime, aerial or satellite photographs have revealed discolored markings on the fields, the ghostly patterns of lost edifices, and, here and there, ruined walls and the domes of tombs have broken through the earth.

Here once flourished the famous city of Veii, the southernmost outpost of the Etruscan federation (today bordering on the modern village of Isola Farnese). The plateau at the top of precipitous cliffs was probably covered with loosely scattered buildings. In the center, city blocks were arranged in a grid around a central square. Fine chamber-tombs have been excavated in the nearby hills. The city was easy to defend and amply supplied with water; it could sustain a lengthy siege.

Religion was important to the people of Veii. At its southern extremity a high citadel (today's Piazza d'Armi) contained a sanctuary in honor of the Queen of Heaven, Juno. A temple complex was built in a cutting on the western side of the Veii hill, where a wonderful terra-cotta statue of Apollo, or Apulu, in Etruscan, was discovered in the early twentieth century. The god, a little more than life size, sports a tunic and a short cloak. His hair is tightly plaited on the head and ends in what look very much like dreadlocks. He smiles the mysterious formal smile, each end of his lips pointing upward, of an archaic Greek statue. He was almost certainly made by the most famous of Etruscan sculptors, Vulca, whom the Tarquins commissioned to decorate the Temple of Jupiter on Rome's Capitol.

Evidently, Veii was a place of power and wealth, and Livy claimed that it was the "most opulent of all Etruria's cities." Well positioned strategically, it controlled wide and fertile lands, covering more than 340 square miles, most of which were kept under cultivation or used for grazing. A network of well-engineered roads linked the center to peripheral bases, facilitating the passage of trade, and a complex system of drainage tunnels (*cuniculi,* or "rabbit holes") fertilized a well-populated countryside. The tunnels collected surface water from marshy land and diverted it into another valley: one remarkable *cuniculus,* the Fosso degli Olmetti, extends for about three and a half miles. Within the city itself, conduits gathered, channelled, and stored water in cisterns. Here was an orderly, productive, and well-managed society.

Sited on the right bank of the Tiber, Veii had been a rival to Rome since the days of Romulus, competing for control of the salt industry and the trading routes up and down the peninsula. If it could cut its commercial links, the city threatened to strangle the newborn Republic. There was no way of avoiding a life-and-death struggle and, as well as routine raiding, serious hostilities broke out from time to time. Veii often had the best of the fighting; on one occasion, its forces reached Rome and alarmingly set up a fortified post on the Janiculum Hill across the Tiber.

One of Rome's leading clans, the Fabii, dominated the consulship. In the 480s, one Fabius or another was consul for eight successive years. They owned an estate on the border with Veii, and so had an interest in keeping the old enemy firmly in its place. A spokesman for the clan made the Senate a generous offer:

As you know, gentlemen, in our dealings with Veii what we need is a regular, permanent force, not necessarily a large one. Our suggestion therefore is that you put the task of confronting Veii into our hands, while you attend to wars elsewhere. We guarantee that the majesty of the Roman name will be safe in the keeping of our clan.

Senators, facing wars at the same time against the Aequi and the Volsci, felt unable to refuse. The clan marched proudly out of Rome and built a stronghold beside the river Cremera, near Veii. Their aim was to reduce Veian raids on Roman (and Fabian) territory. But two years later, in 479, the move misfired. Lured from the safety of their fortification by a tempting and cleverly placed herd of cattle, the tiny Fabian army was enticed into an ambush. The entire Fabii, one hundred and six of them (probably including dependants and hangers-on), were wiped out. Only one member of the clan, a youth, survived.

The story has about it a touch of the celebrated Battle of Thermopylae, in which three hundred Spartans fought to the death against the Persian king Xerxes. Nationalistic historians wanted to show the Greeks that Romans, too, could sacrifice themselves in a high but suicidal cause. Interestingly, though, the Fabii now vanish from the annual list of consuls for well over a decade, when the survivor of Cremera became old enough to hold the supreme office. So the disaster would appear to have some backing in circumstantial fact. Often enough, history throws up accidents that propagandists go on to exploit for their own purposes.

AS THE FIFTH century proceeded, Etruscan power began to wane. A fleet from the Sicilian city-state of Syracuse defeated the Etruscans in a sea battle and harried the Tyrrhenian coast. In the north Gauls crossed the Alps, settled in the Po Valley, and were pressing the once expansionist Etruscans back into their homeland. Veii's fellow cities failed to help it in its hour of need (perhaps because they had replaced their kings with elected officials, whereas Veii had restored its monarchy), and for much of the long struggle it stood alone against the Romans.

Veii's war plan was to establish itself on the left bank of the Tiber, threatening Rome and blocking the Via Salaria, the Salt Road. The small town of Fidenae commanded the road and changed hands more than once.

Battles were fiercely fought, and one remarkable act of valor still glitters across time. A consul, Aulus Cornelius Cossus, struck down the king of Veii and won the Republic's highest award for courage in the field—the *spolia opima*, "splendid spoils," awarded to an army commander who personally killed in hand-to-hand combat his opposite number in the field. Cossus struck and unhorsed the king, jumped on his body, and stabbed him repeatedly. Then he stripped the corpse of its armor, cut off its head, stuck it on a spear, and rushed at the enemy, who stepped backward in alarm and dismay.

Cossus carried the spoils in the triumphal procession that was later held in Rome. He then deposited them in the tiny Temple of Jupiter Feretrius, Subduer of Enemies, on the Capitol. The shrine had been dedicated by the legendary King Romulus, the only man previously to have won *spolia opima* (after Cossus, one final award was made in 222). There the Veian king's outfit remained on display for hundreds of years, until the end of the first century.

By this time the temple had fallen into disrepair. The roof had collapsed and the interior was open to the elements. Rome's first emperor, Augustus, was a religious traditionalist. He visited the temple and inspected what was left of the spoils, including a linen corselet on which Cossus's achievement was inscribed. He had the temple fully restored.

The year 426 saw the start of a twenty-year truce between Rome and Veii. In the last decades of the fifth century, military activity by the Aequi and the Volsci tailed off. It is not clear why. Maybe Roman endurance was at last winning through. Maybe the spread of malaria, plagues, and repeated food shortages took their toll.

Maybe fierce tribesmen were dwindling into pacific cultivators. One way or another, there was a breathing space and Rome was able to recoup her energy.

Once the truce had expired, Rome looked for an excuse to deal with Veii once and for all. An insulting remark happened to be made in the Veientine Senate. The reply was a demand for reparations. To no one's surprise, the ultimatum was refused and, on this slightest of pretexts, Rome declared war and proceeded to lay Veii under siege. To meet the demands of the coming struggle, the army was apparently expanded from four thousand to six thousand men.

At first, the campaign was a failure. The Veientines had stocked their city with military equipment, missiles, and plenty of grain; they had every reason to expect a fortunate outcome. The siege went on and on. The soldiers were accustomed to brief summer campaigns that ended before harvesttime. They were then able to go home and reap the produce of their fields. Stuck permanently in front of Veii's invulnerable cliffs year in and year out, they simply could not afford the war. Hitherto, every man had served at his own expense. The Senate was now forced to pay them for their service (and levy taxes to cover the cost). A citizens' militia was beginning the long journey to becoming a professional army.

AN EVENT TOOK place that caused great anxiety among the superstitious Romans. The water level of a lake, a small volcanic crater in the Alban wood, rose much above its normal height despite the fact that there had been no unusual rainfall. This was an alarming prodigy, and the Senate sent a delegation to ask the oracle at Delphi what the gods meant by it.

One day, Roman and Veientine soldiers were exchanging lighthearted insults from their respective guard posts when an old man from Veii unexpectedly appeared and burst into prophecy. Rome would never take Veii, he said, until the water of the Alban Lake had been drained. A Roman sentry said that he wanted to consult the old man on a private matter and persuaded him to come out and talk with him in confidence. Once they were together, the sentry picked up the aged soothsayer bodily and carried him to the guard post.

The old man was then taken to Rome, where he advised the Senate on how to drain the lake. Not surprisingly, he recommended the technology of his homeland—the exacavation of a *cuniculus*. This was confirmed by Delphi, where the Pythia was for once remarkably un-Delphic; the priestess straightforwardly suggested that the excess water from the lake be used to irrigate the fields. Once that was done, Veii would fall. The Romans swiftly complied and drained the lake down to its original level.

It is hard to know what to make of this tale. At first sight, it seems preposterous and obviously legendary; but, as so often with early Roman history, a substratum of fact can be detected. There is indeed an ancient outflow tunnel from the Alban Lake that can be seen to this day, although exactly when it was originally constructed is uncertain. (It is not far from Castel Gandolfo, the Pope's summer residence.) If there was a rationale for the drain, apart from the musings of an antique seer, it may have been designed to prevent seepage into a malaria-generating bog. In other words, it was a health and safety project that, for some unguessable reason, imaginative Roman authors translated into a prediction of Veii's doom.

We have not heard the last of *cuniculi*. One of Rome's most celebrated heroes was elected to the emergency post of dictator and entrusted with the task of bringing the siege to a successful conclusion. This was Marcus Furius Camillus, who, during a long career, was the holder of every senior office in the Republic and five times a dictator. He arranged for the digging of a tunnel underneath Veii's central fortress, no easy task, as Livy describes it:

This work was now begun, and to keep it going without intermission the men engaged on it were divided into six parties, working six hours each in rotation—as continuous labor underground would have broken them up. The orders were that the digging should go on day and night until the tunnel was complete and a way opened into the enemy citadel.

The crisis of the campaign was approaching. Like most of his compatriots, Camillus was plagued by superstitious fears. For him, it was crucial that he win over to his cause the gods of Veii and, in particular, the city's divine protectress (and his own favorite in the Olympian canon), Juno, known in Veii as the Etruscan Great Goddess, Uni Teran. Her shrine in the citadel housed an archaic wooden statue of her, a highly prized object of reverence. The Romans had a ceremony for every occasion, and at this crucial juncture Camillus conducted an *evocatio*—a calling out of the deity from her home at Veii. At an army parade, he called on Juno to "leave this town where you now dwell and follow our victorious arms into our city of Rome, your future home, which will receive you in a temple worthy of your greatness."

The tunnel was a great success. It was said that the ruler of Veii was offering a sacrifice, and a priest declared that he who carved up the victim's entrails would be victorious in the war. The diggers overheard the remark and immediately broke through the floor into the fortress, snatched the entrails, and took them at once to Camillus. Even Livy's credulity was stretched. He wrote that this tale was "too much like a romantic stage play to be taken seriously. I feel it is hardly worth attention either for affirmation or denial."

However, once again, archaeologists have found a pea of fact beneath a mattress of invention. Excavations at the spot on the Veian peninsula where the Romans must have encamped have shown that the rampart ran over some earlier drainage *cuniculi.* They had been filled in with tightly packed shards, stone, and earth, presumably with defense in mind. It is hard to resist the conjecture that the Romans discovered one or more of these tunnels, emptied them out, and went on to storm the city.

Whatever the case, Veii fell to a determined assault. There was

much slaughter, but Camillus ordered his men to spare everyone
not bearing arms. He was not sentimental, though, and Veii was
emptied and destroyed. On the following day, all movable goods
were taken from the city and the surviving townsfolk were offered
for sale as slaves. (In fact, it would seem that the market could not
absorb such a large number of people. Now that the Veientine state
had been abolished, there was nothing else that could be done with
the unsold remainder but to give them the only civic status available, Roman citizenship.)

Then it was time to transport Juno and the temple treasures to
Rome. Young soldiers were detailed to lift the statue from its ped-
estal, an act that seemed to them like sacrilege. For a lark, one of
the boys shouted, "Juno, do you want to go to Rome?" The statue
nodded its head in awe-inspiring reply. Livy was having none of
this, either:

> We are told, too, that words were uttered, signifying assent. In
> any case—fables apart—she was moved from her place with only
> the slightest application of mechanical power, and was light and
> easy to move—almost as if she came of her own free will—and
> was taken undamaged to her eternal dwelling place on the Aven-
> tine, whither the dictator had called her in his prayer.

Juno was given a temporary base, probably the plebeian sanctuary
of Diana, while Camillus lived up to his word and built a new
temple nearby, which he dedicated to the Queen of Heaven a few
years after the destruction of Veii. We can only presume that, for
the time being, the goddess had set aside her long enmity of Rome,
mollified by an attractive new home.

The city became completely uninhabited, as a first-century poet
lamented: "How sad, ancient Veii! You were once a mighty kingdom and a throne of gold was set in your market place. Now inside
your walls the shepherd loiters and sounds his horn. Men reap corn-
fields above your graves."

The Romans were hugely proud of their victory. Claiming that the siege had lasted ten years, they presented the long campaign against Veii as their version of the Trojan War. And, strategically, it was indeed a great achievement. It signaled the weakening of Etruscan power and the emergence of Rome as the leading state in central Italy. There was also a large domestic benefit. Allotments of the *ager Veientanus* were distributed to Roman citizens, alleviating plebeian claims of poverty and perhaps helping, at least for now, to mitigate the problem of indebtedness.

But, as so often happens, pride was followed by a fall—in fact, not to put too fine a point on it, the fall of Rome itself. Even Livy, who loyally took the edge off every Roman misfortune, admitted, "Calamity of unprecedented magnitude was drawing near."

IN 390, A rumor spread that a vast horde of barbarians was moving down Italy—with what purpose in mind nobody knew, but everyone agreed that they posed a terrible threat. For two centuries and more, Celtic tribes had overflowed from their heartlands in central Europe and Asia, crossed the Alps, and (as already noted) poured down into northern Italy, where they settled, and looked covetously at the lands of their southern neighbor, the Etruscan Empire.

The civilized world—that is to say, the Greeks and their admirers the Romans—did not know what to make of these rough, unpredictable tribesmen. The usually reliable Polybius, a Greek who spent much of his life in Rome, wrote:

> [They] had no knowledge of the refinements of civilization. They lived in unwalled villages, without any unnecessary furniture. They slept on straw and leaves, ate meat and practised no other pursuits but war and agriculture, so their lives were very simple and they were completely unacquainted with any art or science. Their possessions consisted of cattle and gold, since these were the only objects which they could easily take with them what-

ever their circumstances and transport wherever they chose.
They placed a high value on comradeship, and the man who was
believed to have the greatest number of dependants and companions about him was the most feared and the most powerful member of the tribe.

The Celts, or (as the Romans liked to call them) the Gauls, were
usually tall, well-built, and blond. They wore their hair long, whit-
ening and stiffening it by frequent washing in limewater. They
then pulled it back over the head so that the general effect was of a
horse's mane. They let their mustaches grow over their lips so that
"when drinking the beverage passes, as it were, through a kind of
strainer." It is reported that male homosexuality was very common,
and that men particularly liked to have two boys at a time in bed
with them: "Young men offer themselves to strangers and are in-
sulted if the offer is refused." Women, too, enjoyed considerable
sexual freedom, and were entitled to divorce husbands who failed
to perform their marital duties. Unlike Greek or Roman women,
they played a respected part in public life, acting as ambassadors
and, on occasion, fighting in battles.

The Celts were undisciplined, gorged themselves on food and
drink, and were always quarreling with one another. Politically
they seemed to be fickle and inconsistent; they found it difficult to
take a long-term view and stick to it.

It is hard to know how much weight to place on these accounts,
for we have no counterbalancing records from the Celts themselves.
Taken as a whole, the portrait of a race of noble savages is coherent,
but we must not forget that it reflects the fears of the observer as
much as it does the quality of life as experienced by a Celt. It is
telling that the Greco-Roman authors pay no attention whatsoever
to the extraordinary skill and beauty of Celtic metalwork and crafts.

What is certainly the case is that the Celts were fine warriors and
knew how to frighten an enemy army out of its wits. Completely

fearless, they rushed naked into battle, with their long hair stream-
ing and strange war cries, accompanied by harsh trumpet blasts.
Their cavalry rode with iron horseshoes, a military innovation, and
the infantry carried finely tempered slashing broadswords. The
Celts were able to muster very large forces and were hard to defeat.
The news of their imminent arrival in central Italy was seen, rightly,
as an emergency order.

Myriad warriors and even greater numbers of women and children arrived before Clusium, an important Etruscan city and once
Lars Porsenna's base. A foolish story is told that they were tempted
there with a promise of Clusium's large supplies of wine, and that,
responding to an appeal from the city, the Romans sent some ambassadors, who met and remonstrated unsuccessfully with the
Celtic king, Brennus. The ambassadors then fought alongside the
army of Clusium in a vain attempt to repulse the Celts. This broke
the principle of diplomatic neutrality, and infuriated Brennus, who
ordered a retaliatory march on Rome, only eighty miles away.

What really seems to have happened is that Brennus led a band
of marauders intent on plunder, not a people in search of Lebens-
raum. It is very possible that they were in the pay of the *turannos* of
Syracuse, Dionysius, whose principal aim in these years was to un-
dermine Rome's ally, the Etruscan trading entrepôt of Caere, and
the Greek cities of Magna Graecia. If that was so, the Celts were
passing through on their way to southern Italy.

The Romans may have sent an advance force north to discover
the truth behind the reports of a Celtic advance, but what is certain
is that a hastily assembled Roman army confronted the invaders in
a great battle at the little river Allia, a tributary of the Tiber. The
numbers on each side are uncertain, but perhaps two legions, or
about ten thousand Romans faced thirty thousand Celts. To avoid
being outflanked, the Roman commander stretched his line out,
but too thinly. Presumably, the well-to-do heavily armed legionaries were posted in the center, with the poorer citizens as light-

armed troops on each wing. The center could not hold, fractured, and gave way.

It should have been a rout with high casualties, but Brennus had expected a larger enemy army. Suspecting an ambush, he held his men back. Many Romans were able to get away, and a good number escaped to nearby Veii, whose citadel was eminently defensible.

However, the way to Rome lay open.

LIVY DESCRIBES WHAT happened next in one of his great set pieces. It was a mark either of overconfidence or carelessness or both that Rome was not encircled by a protective wall. Earthen ramparts and hills were deemed a sufficient defense. Even worse, most of the army was either dead or cowering in the ruins of Veii. The city was undefended. There was nothing to stop Brennus from marching in and giving the Romans the treatment they had meted out to the people of Veii.

The Celts could hardly believe their eyes and, once again, feared a trap. They watched and waited until evening fell. Inside the beleaguered city, the most was made of a night's reprieve. The handful of remaining troops took up position on the Capitol, where they should be able to hold out indefinitely. Civilians were allowed to take refuge there, too, but many others, especially of the poorer sort, poured out of the city gates across the wooden bridge, the Pons Sublicius, to the Janiculum Hill and vanished into the countryside. Vesta was goddess of the civic hearth and guarantor of Rome's permanence. Her priestesses, who were vowed to chastity, the Vestal Virgins, debated what to do with the sacred emblems. It was decided to bury those that could not be moved and to travel with the remainder to the friendly Etruscan city of Caere. The Vestal Virgins' main task was to tend the goddess's eternal flame, and presumably they took it with them in the shape of a torch or a brazier. Abandoning their native land, they set off on foot but were given a lift by a patriotic carter. Rome was dead.

With morning came the Celts. The citadel was now safe, but, rather than hide away, senators decided to consecrate themselves to the underworld and death in a strange ritual called *devotio* (whence, in passing, our word *devotion*). The sacrifice of their lives would bring the same *devotio* onto the heads of their enemies—in other words, it would consecrate the Celts to *their* destruction, too. Only a current holder of state authority (a consul, say) could devote himself, but a former public official could regain his *imperium* by the ritual gesture of clasping his chin. The senators went home and dressed themselves in their old robes of office. They sat quietly, awaiting their fate in the courtyards of their houses.

The *porta Collina,* the Colline Gate, at the northern tip of the city, had been left open, and it was here that the Celtic invaders made their entry. They proceeded coolly and calmly down the long, straight street that led from the gate to the foot of the Capitol and then the Forum. They wandered around the square, gazing at the temples and the citadel. After sightseeing, they fanned out through the city in search of booty. To their surprise, they found that while the dwellings of the poor were locked and barred, the mansions of the rich lay unprotected.

They were startled by the senators, sitting stock-still, and one Celt touched the beard of a certain Marcus Papirius, thus interrupting the ritual *devotio* gesture. The offended Papirius at once hit the man on the head with his ivory staff. The furious Celt butchered him on the spot, and the other senators soon met the same fate. The *devotio* was complete.

Looting now began in earnest. Houses were ransacked and set on fire. Many public and private records were consumed in the conflagration, greatly hindering the work of Roman historians like Livy. But the citadel held out. The Celts settled down for a siege.

CAMILLUS WAS NURSING mixed feelings. The victor of Veii had been sent into exile because of a disagreement over distribution of the booty. Sensing that he had become old and useless, he seethed with resentment at his lot. He lodged in a small town not far from Rome and watched events from an impotent distance.

Some lucky star brought Celtic raiders to his vicinity, for it aroused his patriotic wrath and he led the townsfolk in a successful sortie. News of this small victory spread quickly. At Veii, the site of his most famous exploit, the Roman soldiery were coming to regret Camillus's absence, and after consultation with the Senate he was recalled to become dictator for the second time, the Republic's *fatalis dux* (its predestined leader), and resume command of the army.

He was lucky not to have arrived too late, for the Capitol very nearly fell to the invaders. What happened was one of the most delightful stories of Roman history. The Celts noticed that the rocky ascent up the hill from where the Temple of Carmenta, the goddess of childbirth, stood could be easily climbed. One starlit night, an unarmed man was sent to reconnoiter the route and a scaling party followed after him. Although it was a scramble, they made it to the top of the cliff not far from the huge Temple of Jupiter Best and Greatest. The Roman guards heard nothing, and sleeping dogs lay undisturbed.

Livy continues the narrative:

It was the geese that saved them—Juno's sacred geese, which in spite of the dearth of provisions had not been killed. The cackling of the birds and the clapping of their wings awoke Marcus Manlius—a distinguished officer who had been Consul three years before—and he, seizing his sword and giving the alarm, hurried, without waiting for the support of his bewildered colleagues, straight to the point of danger. One Celt was already up, but Manlius with a blow from the boss of his shield toppled him headlong down the cliff. The falling body carried others with it: many more who dropped their weapons to get a better grip of the rocks were killed by Manlius, and soon more Roman troops were on the scene, tumbling the climbers down with javelins and stones, until every man of them was dislodged and sent hurtling to the bottom of the cliff.

Time passed slowly in the heat of summer. Good hygiene was always difficult to maintain in an ancient army, and an infection spread through the Celtic camp. The invaders lost the energy to burn corpses separately at individual funerals and piled them up in heaps for mass cremation in the Forum Boarium, near the city end of the Pons Sublicius. As late as Livy's day, the spot was still known as Busta Gallica, or the Celtic Pyres.

As for the defenders on the Capitol, time was no less an enemy. In their case, the challenge was hunger rather than disease. They disguised their shortage of supplies by flinging loaves of bread down into the Celtic outposts. But hope as well as food was beginning to fail. Men were hardly strong enough for guard duty. If only Camillus would arrive soon and relieve the city. But although he was believed to be near at hand, there was neither sight nor sound of him.

Brennus let it be known that he and his horde would abandon Rome for no very great sum of money. So the Senate met and authorized the military tribunes to arrange the terms. A price—a thousand pounds of gold—was agreed. Livy writes:

> Insult was added to what was already sufficiently disgraceful, for the weights which the Celts brought for weighing the metal were heavier than standard, and when the Roman commander objected the insolent barbarian flung his sword onto the scale, uttering words intolerable to Roman ears: "Woe to the vanquished"—*vae victis.*

At the eleventh hour, Camillus turned up at the head of his army. He ordered the gold to be removed and the Celts to leave. As he was dictator, the military tribunes had lost their *imperium* and their entente with Brennus was null and void. A confused engagement followed, and the surprised Celts withdrew from Rome. A more regular battle was fought eight miles or so east of Rome, on the road to the town of Praeneste. The Celts had had time to reorganize themselves, but for all that the omnicompetent Camillus was again victorious. The Gallic camp was captured and the army annihilated. The greatest danger in which the Republic had ever found itself had passed.

THIS EXCITING NARRATIVE is a blend of fact and fiction. The basic theme, the sack of Rome by the Celts, is indisputable. The humiliation was never forgotten, and Brennus's proud taunt, *vae victis,* was an indelible affront. Worse, the barbarians may have gone, but not forever.

For many generations, they remained just beyond the range of peripheral vision, their possible return an abiding nightmare. And, as we shall see, from time to time throughout the history of the Republic the Celts *did* march down again into the peaceful Italian peninsula. During the prolonged death throes of the Roman Empire many hundreds of years later, successive waves of barbarians followed one after another, and in the fifth century A.D. the much feared calamity occurred. Rome was sacked for a second time, at the hands of a new Brennus—king of the Visigoths, the fearsome Alaric. It would not be long thereafter before the Western Empire itself collapsed.

Elements of the story are not to be trusted, though. The exile of Camillus was probably an invention, to give him an alibi during the sack. His final victory over the Celts and the saving of the gold sound very much like false excuses. We may guess that in fact the invaders left at their leisure, with the classical equivalent of Danegeld in their pockets. Polybius says that "at that moment an invasion of their own territory by the Veneti [a tribe in the area where today's Venice is located] diverted their attention, and so they made a treaty with the Romans, handed back the city and returned home."

It took a surprisingly short time for Rome to recover. Having your city looted and burned is obviously a cataclysm. It is reported that some traditional enemies—the Etruscans, the Aequi, and the Volsci—tried their luck and attacked Rome when it was down, but to little effect. Some members of the Latin League suspended or abandoned their alliance with Rome, which dominated the federation. The fact that the city still had most of its army intact, and that Veii and its territory remained in the Republic's hands, was of far greater importance. New grants of citizenship were awarded to people in the Veii region and in two neighboring towns. Land was distributed to Roman citizens, and in 387 four new tribes were created in the newly conquered territory. None of these measures sound like the actions of a state in crisis.

As for the Celts, they had not disappeared, but it was thirty years before they returned. By that time Rome had fully reestablished its power. The city was quickly, although haphazardly, rebuilt. According to Livy:

All work was hurried and nobody bothered to see that the streets were straight. Individual property rights were ignored and buildings went up wherever there was room for them. This explains why the ancient sewers, which originally followed the line of the streets, now run in many places under private houses, and the general layout of Rome is more like a squatter's settlement than a properly planned city.

Greater efficiency marked the building of a wall around the city's perimeter to insure against another invasion. Its circuit ran for about seven miles, longer than the earlier earthworks. In later times, as we have seen, it was attributed to King Servius Tullius, but in fact work began in 378. Up to twenty-four feet high and twelve feet wide, the wall consisted of large rectangular blocks of tufa from the annexed quarries of Veii. On a plateau running south-ward behind three of the city's hills—the Quirinal, the Viminal, and the Esquiline—the wall gave way to a vast earthen rampart, revetted with stone, which stood behind a ditch 100 feet wide and 30 feet deep. This ambitious and costly enterprise was funded by an unpopular tax, which bore down heavily on the poor, but once complete Rome was as good as impregnable.

These great Servian fortifications survive in part to this day, but they long ago lost their defensive importance. By the first century, suburbs extended far beyond them, "giving the beholder the im-pression of a city stretching out indefinitely." The walls themselves, smothered by buildings, became almost invisible.

9

Under the Yoke

HALF A CENTURY AFTER THE CELTIC INVASION CAME another disaster, as humiliating and apparently as complete as the first. An entire Roman army surrendered, en masse, to the enemy, Samnite hill-tribesmen from the central Apennines. This was a more serious threat to Rome's existence than the fact that the city had been without walls when the barbarians came.

In 321, both consuls led their legions, one each probably, southward along the route of what in a few years' time would be Rome's first great road, the Appian Way. The Samnites had recently suffered a heavy defeat and disconsolately sued for peace. The Senate had refused to negotiate, and the Samnites were so furious that they recovered their morale. They laid a trap for the approaching Romans at a place called the Caudine Forks (*furculae Caudinae*).

According to Livy, this was a small, grassy, and well-watered plain surrounded by steep wooded hills. Two narrow defiles at its western and eastern ends were the only means of entry. The very able Samnite leader, Gaius Pontius, advanced his army in the greatest possible secrecy and set up camp nearby. He sent out ten soldiers disguised as shepherds, with orders to scatter and graze their flocks not far from Roman outposts. Whenever they came across enemy raiding parties, they were all to tell the same story—that the Samnite army was campaigning miles away to the south, in

Apulia. A rumor had already been spread to this effect, and the shepherds' reports would be convincing confirmation.

The ruse worked, and the consuls decided to make their way to the Samnite legions by the shortest route, even though it meant marching, via the Caudine Forks, straight across the middle of enemy territory. They entered the first, western gorge and were shocked to find the second obstructed by a barricade of felled trees and huge boulders. Samnite troops were seen at the head of the pass.

The Romans turned back, only to realize that the road by which they had arrived at the Forks was now blocked with its own barricade and armed men. They were trapped. The consuls ordered their legionaries to set up a full Roman camp, with trenches, ramparts, and palisades, although this seemed a pointless exercise.

Meanwhile, the Samnites could not believe their luck, and were unsure what to do next. Pontius sent a letter to his father, Herennius Pontius, elderly and astute, asking for guidance. Herennius replied, "My advice is that you should let all the Romans go away free." His opinion was brusquely rejected and he was asked to think again. In that case, he said, "they should all be put to death, down to the last man."

Pontius feared that his father's once acute mind was softening, but he gave way to a general wish that the old man be brought to the camp for a consultation in person. He declined to change his opinion, but gave his reasons. Livy writes:

> "My first advice," he said, "which I thought the best, would establish lasting peace with a very powerful people by conferring on them an immense benefit. The second would postpone war for many generations during which the Romans would not easily recover their strength. . . . There was no third option."

But what if the Samnites took a middle course, letting the Romans go unhurt but imposing terms on them as defeated men according to the laws of war? Herennius would have none of it. "Your idea will neither win friends nor remove enemies," he said. "The Roman People does not know how to lie down under defeat." His advice was rejected for a third and final time, and he went home.

The Romans made a number of unsuccessful attempts to break out. Food stocks began to run very low, and the consuls sent a delegation to Pontius to seek terms. If they failed to win a peace, they would challenge the enemy to fight. "You Romans never admit catastrophe even when conquered and taken captive," the Samnite leader responded. "So I will send you under the yoke unarmed, with a single item of clothing each." (By "yoke," he meant the arch made of three spears beneath which defeated and captured soldiers were obliged to walk in return for their freedom.) He added that the Romans should immediately evacuate Samnite territory and withdraw its two forward colonies at Cales and Fregellae.

It was self-evidently a disgraceful settlement, but, thought the consuls, better than the alternative—the complete destruction of their army. However, Livy assures us, they were only in a position to offer a personal guarantee that Rome accepted the terms (a *sponsio*). A final treaty (or *foedus*) would have to await approval by the Assembly at Rome. The trusting Pontius took the point and allowed the legions to depart in return for a *sponsio,* to which the consuls and senior officers subscribed. However, he demanded six hundred Roman cavalry as hostages. A dramatic scene ensued:

> The Consuls, pretty much half-naked, were the first to be sent under the yoke, then their officers were humiliated, each in order of rank; then the legions, one by one in turn. The enemy stood round, taunting and jeering at them; many were threatened with swords, and some were wounded or killed if the expressions on their faces showed too much resentment at their intolerable position.

Once the troops were back in Rome, the public mood darkened. Many people went into mourning, feasts and marriages were canceled, shops closed, and official business in the Forum suspended. New consuls were elected, and the Senate held a debate on whether or not to endorse the *sponsio*. One of the defeated commanders advised his colleagues, self-sacrificially, to reject it on the bare-faced excuse that he and his fellow consul had not acted of their own free will but from necessity, thanks to the enemy's treacherous ambush. But as a matter of honor, he went on, he and all the other army officers involved should be handed over to the Samnites.

This was agreed, but, on their arrival at the Samnite camp, Pontius refused to accept their surrender. He argued that if the treaty was refused everything should revert to the status quo ante. In other words, the legions should go back to the Caudine Forks. "You are never without a reason for not keeping your word in defeat?" he asked. "You agreed with us on a peace, so that we should return you the legions we had captured. Now you have nullified that peace. And you always give your fraud some semblance of legality."

It is hard to disagree with this judgment, which is remarkable in that it is Livy, the most patriotic of authors, who put these words into the mouth of the Samnite commander. The Romans placed a very high value on fair dealing. On this occasion, they claimed to be keeping to the letter of the law, but one has the impression that they sensed, guiltily, that they were not keeping to its spirit. According to one report, the Romans, far from being grateful to the Samnites for letting their soldiers go, "actually behaved as if they had been the victims of some outrage."

In any event, war resumed and the Romans allegedly won a resounding victory, after which they compelled Pontius and his fellow captives to submit to the yoke themselves, a remarkable example of instant and mirror-imaged retribution that probably never took place.

In fact, we have good grounds for supposing that the official version of the affair does not square with what actually occurred. Some ancient writers asserted that the agreement between the warring parties was in fact a *foedus,* not a *sponsio,* and that Roman apologists tried to hide the fact. Cicero, for example, an intelligent and thoughtful voice, twice speaks of a *foedus*.

What happened to the six hundred hostages? These are the dogs not barking in the night. Were they killed, or released? A suspicious silence hangs over their fate. They are needed to back up a *sponsio,* but once a *foedus* was in place they would become superfluous and be handed back. But if the *sponsio* was rejected, the presumed consequence would be their execution. From the fact that nothing is said about them, we may infer that a treaty *was* approved by the Roman Assembly. It looks very much as if the aborted *sponsio* was a later invention designed to excuse Roman bad faith.

A further problem muddies the narrative. The description of the Caudine Forks is only very roughly right. We are not absolutely certain where they are, but the only plausible candidate is a pass in Campania between the two modern Italian towns of Arienzo and Arpaia, which was helpfully known in ancient times as Furculae or Furcae—namely, "forks." Here there were two entrances leading into an area surrounded by mountains and steep hills, as Livy says. However, while the eastern gorge was narrow enough to be easily blocked, the western defile was two miles wide—far too long for the Samnites to have erected barricades capable of bottling in a Roman army. There must have been a battle of some sort that led to a surrender. Why the inaccuracy? Perhaps because it was less shameful to capitulate to deceit and trickery than to do so after a straightforward defeat in the field.

It is certain that the Romans suffered a devastating military setback at the Caudine Forks. It is now too late to establish the details of what took place beyond doubt, but a plausible scenario might run as follows: The Samnites forced a battle by blocking the eastern defile of the Caudine Forks and then turning up en masse at the western entrance. A battle ensued and the Romans were routed but had nowhere they could escape to, so they surrendered. A *sponsio* was agreed while Rome was informed and approved a *foedus*.

It is likely that the terms of the *foedus* were abrogated and hostilities resumed. This was a dishonorable thing to do (and something, as far as possible, to be hidden from posterity), but there is evidence of continued fighting (in 319, a Roman general is recorded as celebrating a triumph *de Samnitibus*). Alternatively, it has been contended that Rome in fact abided by the treaty it had accepted and that hostilities ceased for a few years. But if that was the case it is difficult to explain why some ancient authors should concoct a canceled *sponsio* and others a broken *foedus,* for both of these acts are more to Rome's discredit than a perfectly respectable truth.

The debacle of the Caudine Forks and its aftermath is a useful reminder, if that were needed, that, whatever their high principles, the Romans were more than capable of cynical and self-interested behavior. They criticized Pontius for outmaneuvering an army by a trick, but throughout their history many of their own generals acted just as deceitfully. Cassius Dio judged that the Samnites were unfairly treated, and his assessment is not far off the mark: "It is not inevitable that those who are wronged should conquer; instead, war, in its absolute sway, adjusts everything to the advantage of the victor, often causing something that is the reverse of justice to go under that name."

THE FIFTY-YEAR INTERVAL between Rome's two massive setbacks illustrates its capacity to regenerate after failure. The Republic, battered but unbowed, pressed ahead with its program of reconciliation at home and expansion abroad.

The Conflict of the Orders had not gone away. Once the dust had settled after the Celtic invasion, domestic hostilities resumed, with a vengeance. Debt remained a crushing burden for the poor, whose landholdings were too small to make even basic subsistence easy, and wealthy plebeians were still finding it hard to gain access to high office. In effect, the patricians maintained their monopoly on power.

Some fifty-three patrician clans, or *gentes,* are known to have existed during the early Republic, making a closed community of not more than a thousand families. There was a small inner ring of especially powerful clans—in particular the Aemilii, the Cornelii, and the Fabii. To them can be added the immigrant Claudii. In total, the patricians amounted to one-tenth of the citizen population of Rome and possibly not more than one-fourteenth.

A revolutionary moment seemed to be approaching, but once again the Romans found their way to a workable compromise. Plebeians wanted the state to release plots of *ager publicus,* public land, to individual farmers rather than hold it as common land. We do not know how much of Veii's land was expropriated by the Republic, but it may have been half or even two-thirds. Two tribunes of the plebs, Gaius Licinius and Lucius Sextius, got themselves reelected year after year and argued for root-and-branch reform. In 376, they put forward three bills, the Licinio-Sextian Rogations (a *rogation* is a proposal placed before the People's Assembly for its decision), aimed at breaking the dominance of the patricians. The first one dealt with debt: interest already paid should be subtracted from the original debt, and what remained should be paid in three equal annual installments. The second forbade anyone to own more than five hundred *iugera* (one *juger* was about two-thirds of an acre) of public land. The third abolished the post of military tribune and brought back the system of two consuls. The real innovation here was that, in future, one consul was always to be a plebeian.

As Livy tells the story, the tribunes repeatedly called an assembly, but a body of armed patricians refused to allow the voting to go ahead. "Very well," shouted Sextius. "As you are determined that a veto shall be so powerful, we will use that very weapon to protect the People. Come on, Senators, call an assembly for the election of Military Tribunes. I'll see that you get no joy out of that word 'veto,' which now so delights your ears." This was not an idle threat, for the tribunes aborted the elections, at least for a year.

The crisis trundled on angrily for a decade. In 368, the number of commissioners who looked after the Sibylline Books and organized the annual Games of Apollo was increased from two patricians to ten men, five of whom had to be plebeians; these were the *decemviri sacris faciundis*. It was clear which way the wind was blowing, and the following year the aged Camillus presided over a historic compromise. The Licinio-Sextian Rogations were finally passed and, as a concession to the opposition, the post of praetor was created as a junior colleague for the consuls to be reserved for patricians. The praetor became the acting chief magistrate in Rome when the consuls were away on military business, as they often were, and came to specialize in running the law courts.

It is perhaps no accident that in this year Camillus promised a Temple of Concord, for the new legislation went a long way toward pacifying the plebeian movement. The poet Ovid wrote:

> Camillus, conqueror of the Veian people,
>   vowed the old temple and kept his vow.
> The cause: the mob's armed secession from the Fathers,
>   and Rome itself, fearful of its power.

A small mystery adheres to this gift: the grateful People absolved the old dictator from his pledge and said they would fulfill it in his place, but for some reason failed to do so. Its site, in the Forum just below the Capitol, was designated for the temple and kept as an open space. The temple was finally built in the second century, following the violent death, at the hands of senators, of a turbulent tribune—a bitter irony.

The Rogations did not finally settle the great quarrel between patricians and plebs, and further measures of social appeasement were undertaken. Above all, the problem of indebtedness remained despite the lawgivers' best intentions. In 326, a scandal led to the reform of debt bondage, the *nexum*. An attractive youth sold himself into bondage to a creditor of his father. The creditor regarded the youth's charms as an additional bonus to sweeten the loan and tried to seduce his new acquisition. Meeting resistance, he had the boy stripped naked and flogged. Bleeding from the lash, the boy rushed out into the street. An angry crowd gathered and marched on the Senate House for general redress.

The consuls, taken aback, conceded the point. They won the People's approval of a law limiting the *nexum* to extreme cases, which, in addition, had to be adjudicated by a court. As a rule, to repay money lent him, a debtor's property could be seized, but not his person. This was tantamount to abolition, and, in Livy's slightly overheated opinion, "the liberty of the Roman People had, as it were, a second birth."

IT IS AT this point that we meet the first truly historical, truly alive personality in Rome's story so far. This was Appius Claudius Caecus, or the Blind (he lost his sight toward the end of a long life). He was as arrogant and awkward as most of his clan. An individualist to the core, he wrote a series of sharply turned moral sayings in verse. The most famous asserts, "Every man is the maker of his own luck."

A wealthy patrician, Appius Claudius served twice as consul and once as dictator. A radical populist who aimed to win a following among the masses, he was a ferocious partisan for the plebs, as he made clear during his famous censorship of 312. Every four years or so, two censors were elected to hold office for eighteen months. They were usually former consuls, and although they did not have *imperium,* they wielded great influence. The post was regarded as the pinnacle of a Roman's career.

Censors had two main tasks. Their primary function was to make up and maintain a comprehensive list of Roman citizens. They were also charged with the supervision of morals; if they agreed that a citizen deserved censure, they set out their reason and marked his name on the list. This had the effect of disqualifying him from his tribe and removing his voting rights. Sometime in the second, third, or the fourth century, the censors took over from the consuls the responsibility for appointing senators, who served for life. (Over time, membership became ex officio for present and former public officials.) They also reviewed the behavior of senators and excluded those they deemed guilty of serious misconduct.

Appius Claudius seized the hour. His basic aim was to bring plebeians into public life, and he particularly wanted to further the interests of the lowest of the low, the landless urban population. These were the *capite censi,* the "head count"; they were so poor that they did not have any property to be assessed in the census and so were disqualified from military service. No reformer had ever tried to help this group before.

Some were not necessarily without funds but owned no land or property—for example, freedmen and their sons. With astute generosity, the Romans often liberated their slaves (although they remained in the owner's *clientela*), and so, in effect, gave them citizenship. However, they were not allowed to run for elective office. Scandalously, the radical new censor enrolled some sons of freedmen in the Senate. His colleague as censor resigned in disgust, but Claudius obstinately stayed in office and, indeed, did not step down until well after the eighteen-month limit had expired. The concession was quickly revoked by the following year's consuls, and for centuries afterward it remained only a revolutionary idea.

Appius Claudius also distributed landless city dwellers among all Rome's thirty-one tribes, not simply the four urban ones. This was a most ingenious move, for they would then have an advantage over their rural fellow tribesmen because they were on the spot and some of the latter would be unlikely to bother traveling to Rome to cast their votes (despite the impact of the Via Appia—see below). The reform significantly enhanced the power of the urban proletariat.

Censors had other duties—certain kinds of tax collection and the letting of contracts for public works. Appius Claudius commissioned two vastly expensive building projects that emptied the treasury—Rome's first aqueduct (*aqua Appia*) and the Appian Way (*via Appia*). The aqueduct is evidence of the growing size of Rome and the probable overuse of the city's wells. For most of its ten-mile course, it ran underground, partly because of the layout of the land and partly to protect the water supply from enemies. The builders may have borrowed the tunneling techniques of Veii's irrigation experts. The aqueduct dropped only 30 feet over its entire length and delivered 240,000 cubic feet of water every day—a remarkable feat of engineeering.

The Roman road was the outcome of military necessity. At the time of Appius's censorship, the Republic was absorbed in a life-and-death struggle with the Samnites. The Via Appia led south to Capua, in Campania, and was an invaluable communications link, facilitating resupply and reinforcement of Rome's armies in the field, its bases, and *coloniae* (settlements of Roman citizens or Latins in former enemy territory); the road also made it easier for voters living in outlying areas to get to Rome for Assembly meetings and elections. Over the years, it was extended across the Apennines to the Greek seaport of Tarentum. It finally reached Brundisium, today's Brindisi, the customary port of departure for sea voyages to the Eastern Mediterranean. Originally surfaced with gravel, its first few miles from the city were paved and became an ideal place for wealthy families to memorialize their dead. By Cicero and Varro's day, two long lines of grand marble tombs and mausoleums bordered the road and stretched far into the distance. They can still be visited today.

Appius Claudius had not finished. Despite the publication of the Twelve Tables, the system of law and government was still infuriatingly opaque, and the Senate was unwilling to go to the trouble of cleaning its windows. So some years after the censorship, a secretary of his, a freedman's son who had become a state official, leaked a confidential manual of legal procedures, the *legis actiones.* He also posted in the Forum a list of the days on which official business could be conducted, whether the courts could sit, and when the Senate and the Assembly could meet. These things were decided behind closed doors by the patrician college of *pontifices.* The disclosures, no doubt inspired by Claudius, created a furor, but once out the cat could not be put back into the bag. The secretary was pleased with himself and marked his achievement by erecting a shrine, not altogether appropriately, to the spirit of Concord in the Comitium, the assembly area in the Forum. Respectable opinion disliked being teased in this way, and a law was quickly passed forbidding anyone in future to dedicate a temple or an altar without the Senate's permission or that of a majority of the tribunes of the plebs.

The great censor was a man of contradictions. Despite his political beliefs, he remained a noble snob at heart. He vigorously opposed the admission of plebeians into the two senior religious colleges, the *pontifices* and the *augurs,* and on two separate occasions he tried to exclude plebeians from the consulship. It is this inconsistency that allows us to detect in Appius Claudius a genuine human being, warts and all.

His career was spectacular, but it ended in failure. The reforms of his high-handed censorship were unpicked by his opponents in the Senate. His attempts to empower the Assembly turned out to be fruitless, and until the end of its days the Republic was never anything more than a partial democracy. However, his two astonishing construction projects are a lasting monument to one of Rome's most remarkable characters.

ROMANS WERE FINE builders and engineers, and much of their work still survives (in particular, structures dating from the imperial period—i.e., the first century A.D. onward). Dionysius of Halicarnassus was not far wrong when he wrote:

In my opinion, the three most magnificent works of Rome, in which the greatness of her empire is best seen, are the aqueducts, the paved roads and the construction of the sewers. I say this with respect not only to the usefulness of the work, but also to the magnitude of the cost.

The Aqua Appia was the first of eleven aqueducts that were constructed over the centuries, channeling water into an ever more thirsty Rome. They provided drinking water and supplied the city's many public baths and elaborate fountains. They complemented the complex sewage system, which (as we have seen) originated in the sixth century, when the first Tarquin built the Cloaca Maxima to drain the marshy Forum. By the first century A.D., "gray," or used, water was being channeled into the sewers, clearing out wastes and emptying into the Tiber.

Fresh running water became a symbol of civilized urban living. Among Rome's greatest accomplishments, especially in western Europe, was the promotion of the pleasures and uses of towns and cities. Wherever the legions marched and conquered, temples, amphitheaters, forums, triumphal columns, and arches sprang up, and, of course, as the necessary precondition for health and happiness in crowded conurbations, aqueducts and drains. From the second century, vast utilitarian edifices—warehouses, basilicas, and apartment blocks—also became routine features of the built landscape. Such large-scale developments were made possible by technical advances, especially the introduction of concrete during the third century, which allowed architects to cover wide spaces with domes and vaults.

None of this was done purely from kindness of heart but from imperial self-interest. Monumental architecture became a powerful and persuasive tool of Romanization.

The Via Appia opened the way to the construction of a web of roads, throughout Italy and later farther afield. Their purpose was primarily military, but they also linked communities and facilitated trade. They were punctuated by milestones, which enabled a more accurate measurement of distance and of the size of Rome's territory than had been possible in the past.

Wherever feasible, the engineers who built roads made them run showily straight, bullying and overriding the landscape through which they passed rather than working cooperatively with its hills and valleys. A Roman road was well designed, and typically consisted of two parallel trenches and a well-drained core. Packed stones allowing water to run away formed the foundation. These were covered with layers of concrete and concrete gravel, and topped off by gravel, packed stones, or sometimes paving stones. Roads were made to last, and some of them have, to the admiration of the modern tourist.

When searching for the origins of Rome's power, we should not forget its engineering record, evidence as it is (alongside its commitment to legal process) of an energetic, practical orderliness.

THE CONFLICT OF the Orders was at last nearing its conclusion. Long years of war meant that farms and smallholdings had fallen into decay, and their owners into debt. In 287, the plebs seceded again, this time to the Janiculum Hill across the Tiber. A dictator, one Quintus Hortensius, took some economic measures to ease the crisis. What these were we do not know, but he also passed a remarkable constitutional law. This gave the resolutions of the Plebeian Council—that institutional symbol of estrangement and revolt, of the state within the state—the full force of law. At last, a right that had been claimed for one and a half centuries was conceded. The long bipolar episode was over, and Rome's fragmented persona re-formed into an integrated whole.

Not that the results were neat. The Romans were no theorists and, constitutionally speaking, they hated throwing anything away. So, for example, they now had four popular assemblies: the *comitia curiata,* from the days of the kings (by the first century, its duties had dwindled to confirmation of official appointments and the authorization of adoptions and wills); the loaded-against-the-poor *comitia centuriata,* which decided elections of senior officials; the *concilium plebis;* and, a new institution, the *comitia tributa,* which imitated the *concilium* but was convened by consuls and praetors, incorporated the entire male adult population, patricians as well as plebeians, and approved bills.

However, the fruits of victory were not exactly what might have been expected. It became clear that the different components of the plebeian movement did not share the same fundamental interests. The poor were concerned to improve their financial situation by means of the assembled People. The wealthy plebeians had now achieved their goal, access to public office, and gradually made common cause with their old enemies, the patricians. A new mixed nobility came into being, and the tribunes of the plebs were absorbed into the official processes of the state, cooperating with the Senate and introducing agreed legislation.

There are two ways of looking at this development. On the one hand, it was a betrayal of the head count, of the oppressed and the dispossessed. Ordinary people could vote on legislation and elected officials, but the rules of procedure forbade debate and access to the levers of executive power was denied them. The confident senatorial oligarchy adjusted itself to the new political situation and remained in charge. One step back, two steps forward.

On the other hand, there was no denying that reconciliation of warring interests had taken place, and without bloodshed. Greeks, who were beginning to be aware of this new aggressive state in central Italy, looked on with a certain jealousy, for the popular and aristocratic factions in Hellenic city-states had a habit of butchering one another, whereas the Romans solved their political difficulties by painful give-and-take.

Writing in the first century B.C., Cicero has one of the speakers in his fine dialogue, *The Republic,* make the explicit comparison: "Our own commonwealth was based upon the genius not of *one* man [*sc.,* as often in Greece], but of many; it was founded, not in one generation, but in a long period of several centuries and many ages of men." A well-informed Greek observer commented that the Romans arrived at their form of government "not by abstract reasoning, but rather through the lessons learned from many struggles and difficulties." They were the complete pragmatists.

THE LATINS HAD jumped at the chance to free themselves from Roman dominance after the Celtic invasion. The Latin League was broken up. It took some time for its members to be brought to heel, but by 358 the Republic had reasserted its authority. The confederacy was reconvened, but with a difference. The post of commander-in-chief no longer alternated yearly between Rome and the Latins. Now it was controlled by two praetors who were accountable to the consuls in Rome.

The Latins deeply resented being treated as subjects rather than as partners, and in 341 their simmering feelings boiled over into open revolt. Four years of bitter campaigning followed. The consuls for 340 were remarkable men. The first of them, Titus Manlius, acquired the cognomen of Torquatus after having killed in battle an enormous Celt and stripped him of his torque. He sent some cavalry off to reconnoiter in all directions, but strictly enjoined them not to take part in any fighting. Among the squadron leaders was his son Titus. The young man managed to ride with his men beyond the enemy camp until he was hardly a spear's throw from their nearest outpost. Here he was jeered at by some enemy horse from Tusculum and its commander challenged him to a duel. He shouted, "The outcome will show how much better a Latin cavalryman is than a Roman."

Titus's blood was up and, forgetting his father's orders, he threw himself into a fight that had little tactical point. The rest of the cavalry were made to stand back as if to watch a riding display. The two men rode at each other, spears leveled. Manlius's spear glanced off the helmet of his opponent, whose own missed the mark altogether. As they wheeled for a second encounter, Titus pricked with his spearpoint the forehead of the Tusculan's horse, which reared up and threw its rider. As the man struggled to his feet, Titus ran through his throat, so that the spear came out between his ribs and pinned him to the ground. The brief fight was over.

Titus rode back to camp, surrounded by his cheering men. He proudly presented the dead man's armor. The consul abruptly turned away from his son and gave orders for a trumpet to summon an assembly. "Titus Manlius, you have respected neither Consular authority nor your father's dignity," he said. "I believe that you yourself, if you have any drop of my blood in you, would agree that the military discipline you undermined by your error must be restored by your punishment. Go, lictor, bind him to the stake."

The ax struck and blood gushed from the severed neck. The army was horror-struck, but it was noticed that from then on better attention was given everywhere to guard duties, night watches, and picket-stationing. The execution of Titus Manlius on his father's orders was one of the most celebrated morality tales in Rome's history, matching the examples set by Brutus and Verginius. It was a reminder that a father had the power of life and death over his children, and that *virtus* trumped parental love.

Soon afterward, another never-to-be-forgotten case of self-sacrifice took place. It so happened that both consuls, Manlius and his colleague Publius Decius Mus, dreamed that a man of superhuman size told them that, if either army's general should "devote" to death the enemy's army and himself, his side would win the coming battle. Shortly afterward, an engagement was fought near the foot of Mount Vesuvius. As usual, before the opening of a battle an animal was sacrificed in the name of each consul. An Etruscan diviner scrutinized their livers for any abnormality that might reveal the displeasure of the gods. He gave Manlius a clean bill of health; however, he pointed out that the head of Decius's liver had been cut in the wrong place. Otherwise, the victim was acceptable to the gods.

Decius replied coolly, "If my colleague's sacrifice went well, then that should be all right." The army advanced, with Manlius on the right wing and Decius on the left. The lines clashed and the Romans were pushed back. In this moment of crisis, Decius called to a priest from the college of *pontifices,* who presided over the army's religious rituals, "We need the gods' help. Come on now, you are a state pontiff of the Roman People. Dictate to me the form of words by which I may 'devote' myself to the legions."

The priest told him to put on his purple-edged toga, veil his head, and, with one hand protruding from the toga, touch his chin, stand on a spear laid under his feet, and repeat the following words:

Janus, Jupiter, father Mars, Quirinus [a name for the deified Romulus], Bellona [goddess of war], Lares [household gods], New Gods, Native Gods, divinities who have power over us and our enemies, and gods of the Underworld: I supplicate and revere you, I seek your favor and beseech you, that you prosper the might and victory of the Roman People, the Quirites, and afflict the enemies of the Roman People, the Quirites, with terror, dread and death. As I have pronounced the words, even so on behalf of the Republic of the Roman nation of Quirites, and of the army, legions and auxiliaries of the Roman nation of the Quirites, do I devote myself and with me the legions and auxiliaries of our enemies to the gods of the Underworld and to Earth.

Decius then sent a message to his colleague telling him what he had done. He reorganized his toga so that his arms were free, leaped on a horse, and rode directly into the enemy's ranks. He fell under a hail of missiles.

In due course, the battle was won and the Latins fled. The spell had worked. Decius was found under a pile of corpses and given a hero's funeral (if he had survived, the rules of *devotio* dictated that an effigy of him would have been buried instead, for the gods of the Underworld could not be cheated of their dead man). Did these episodes take place? We cannot be absolutely sure, but they probably have a basis in fact. The ancient accounts of events in the fourth century that have come down to us are on the cusp of genuine historical memory.

HARD FIGHTING CONTINUED, but by 338 the war was over and the Latins had definitively and permanently been defeated. The League was dissolved forever. The settlement that followed was of historic importance, for the Romans established a system of governance that gave them security but was also acceptable to the Latins. Rather than echo the Celtic leader Brennus's vindictive cry of triumph, *vae victis,* they devised ways and means of binding conquered peoples to them. They invited their victims to join them in their enterprise of territorial expansion. The prudence of this policy is borne out by the fact that never again would the Latins rebel.

Just as in the distant mythical past Romulus granted citizenship to the Sabines, so now the Republic offered the Latins civic rights. In this way, it enlarged the pool of potential military recruits to the legions. A human reservoir was created that gave Rome a unique staying power in times of war. Defeat could follow defeat, if the Fates willed it, and still there would be new conscripts to replace lost armies.

In place of a federation in which each member was connected to one another, Rome set up bilateral relations with individual communities, which were forbidden to undertake treaties among themselves. They were also compelled to surrender substantial tracts of land. The Latins and some others were divided into three different constitutional and legal classes. First of all, some defeated statelets were incorporated as *municipia,* or free towns, in the Republic and their inhabitants given full Roman citizenship. One example was Antium (today's Anzio), the onetime Volscian capital, but not before it was obliged to surrender its fleet after a sea battle. Some ships' prows or "beaks" (*rostra,* in Latin) were displayed in the Roman Forum on the main speakers' platform, thereafter known as the Rostra.

The second category consisted of communities that kept their independence—at least in theory, for they forfeited the power to conduct their own foreign policy. These "allies" had rights of *connubium* and *commercium*—that is, their citizens were allowed to marry Romans and enter into contracts with them, according to Roman law. When asked, they had to supply troops.

Finally, for those more distant communities in the new Roman "commonwealth" that lay beyond the borders of Latium, such as the Campanian cities of Capua and Cumae, partial enfranchisement was granted: *civitas sine suffragio,* or citizenship without the vote. This included the rights of *connubium* and *commercium,* and liability to the obligations of full Roman citizenship, especially military service. They were entitled to move to Rome, if they so wished, and in that case could acquire full Roman citizenship. The duty to fight alongside the legions sounds more punitive than it actually was, for, as when Rome won its wars, these compulsory comrades would have their share of the spoils of victory.

Another innovative device helped the Romans not only to secure their conquests, but to unify them with their conquerors. This was the foundation of *coloniae,* "colonies," by which small groups of Latin, Campanian, and Roman settlers established their own townships on annexed enemy territory; sometimes these were new foundations, but on occasion they were attached to existing settlements. They were useful watch posts that could detect early signs of trouble in the surrounding population; they also alleviated economic pressures at Rome by providing farms and jobs for the landless poor. Coastal *coloniae* relieved the Republic of the need to build a fleet to defend home waters. Above all, this colonial system, as it developed over time, contributed powerfully to the cultural Romanization of Italy.

It took some time for the settlement to bed down. Many Latin communities resented the loss of their age-old freedoms, and Rome took care to leave them free to run their own local affairs. Their city walls were not leveled but left standing—clever and persuasive symbolism.

It has been estimated that the extent of territory now occupied by Roman citizens of every kind, the *ager Romanus,* was 3,400 square miles, and that of the larger Roman commonwealth as a whole 5,300 square miles. According to a modern calculation, the total population of the *ager Romanus* was 347,300 free persons and that of the commonwealth 484,000 free persons.

Rome had become a substantial state, by Greco-Roman standards; it was a token of its growing power that a second treaty of friendship with Carthage was negotiated in 348. Its conquests meant, among other things, that the problem of poverty and indebtedness that beset the young Republic was alleviated, although it never vanished. As we have seen, an indigent Roman would be paid a salary if he fought in the army. He might be allocated a smallholding in freshly conquered territory and, if he was willing to leave the city, he could join a *colonia* and make a new life for himself.

IF EVER A landscape made its people, it was Samnium.

This is a mountainous, landlocked plateau in central Italy. Here the Apennines are not so much mountains as a tangled maze of massifs, spurs, and reentrants. The region is roughly rectangular and is cut through by steep valleys often ending in culs-de-sac, down which rivers or seasonal torrents cascade. Here and there gray limestone mountains push up toward the sky, and are covered in snow for most of the year. Much of the usable land is suitable only for grazing, but there are many fertile pockets where earth can be tilled and crops grown. Rich, narrow fields lie alongside streams. Winters were wild and austere, summers arid and baking hot. Earthquakes racked and eroded the hills.

As we have seen, the Samnites were among the infiltration southward, propelled by Sacred Springs, of Oscan speakers in previous centuries. By 500, if not earlier, they had settled in their new rugged homeland. They coveted the flat, fertile earth of Campania and its cultured cities. Some of them descended from their aeries, conquered the inhabitants, and took over the territory. They soon learned to enjoy an easier way of life and forgot their highland ancestry.

The Samnites were fierce and hardy mountaineers. Excavated skeletons show that they were ethnically homogeneous and dolichocephalic (that is, their heads were unusually long from front to back), from which we can infer that, isolated among their peaks, they did not intermarry with their Latin neighbors. Pre-urban, they lived in scattered villages and built many small stone forts on remote hilltops (about ninety of which have been located by archaeologists); most were not for living in but were a temporary refuge in times of trouble.

There were four Samnite tribal groups, each forming a community called a *touto.* The Hirpini lived in the south, the Caudini in the west, the Carracini in the northeast, and the largest, the Pentri, occupied the center and east of Samnium. The total number of inhabitants was surprisingly high for a remote rural area and is estimated at about 450,000 persons.

In general, the Samnites were poor and relatively unsophisticated, with no coinage and little trade. There seems to have been an aristocracy with large landholdings, but their politics were democratic and simply organized. One or more villages made up a *pagus,* an economically self-sufficient and independent-minded canton. It elected a governing official called a *meddis.* A group of *pagi* made up the tribal *touto,* whose annually elected chief magistrate was a *meddis tovtiks.* There appears to have been a council that magistrates were obliged to consult. Despite their decentralized political system, Samnites possessed a powerful sense of cultural identity.

The economy—landlocked as it was, and lacking in raw materials for industries—was centered on animal husbandry and peasant farming. The Samnites raised horses, poultry, pigs, and goats. Above all, they were sheep breeders. In the summer, their animals grazed on high ground; for the winter months, they were taken down to the plains along wide drovers' trails, which doubled as the main means of human communication in Samnium. Among the region's specialties were fine wines and sweet Sabellian cabbages.

Only glimpses of daily life have come down to us. Oscans, such as the Samnites, were known for their barbaric and uncouth ways, although their addiction to obscenity may, as often happens, have been a jokey stereotype attributed to them by their neighbors and based on an ecccentric etymological derivation of *obscenus,* from *O(b)scan.* They appear to have had some odd habits. They had their pubic hair shaved off in barbershops, in full view of passersby, for example. According to Strabo the geographer:

> The Samnites have a splendid law, well designed to foster excellence. Every year ten virgins and ten young men are chosen as the best of their sex. And the best young woman is given to the best youth, the second to the second and so on. If the youth who wins the prize changes and turns out bad, they dishonor him and take away the woman he has been awarded.

Little is recorded of the place of women in Samnite society, but the first-century poet Horace, who came from the southern Samnite town of Venusia and was in a position to know, implies that they exercised authority in the household; they brought up the children and had a reputation for severity.

In their scant leisure time, Samnites hunted, as much for food as

for amusement. They were very fond of the theater, with a pronounced taste for farce, satire, and crude invective. A fresco of dancing girls has survived, and perhaps folk dancing was among their
entertainments. It is said that the bloodstained diversions of the
arena were invented by Oscans. It cannot be proved that gladiators
derive from Samnium itself, but their emergence in Campania coincided suspiciously with the Samnite invasion in the fifth century.
It may be no accident that, in later times, the most popular type of
gladiator, equipped with a short sword, a rectangular shield, a
greave, and a helmet, was called a Samnite.

THESE WERE THE people with whom Rome found itself in a
long life-and-death duel in the latter part of the fourth century. To
begin with, the two nations were friends, signing a treaty in 354.
However, Rome wished to expand, and the Samnites were compelled to do so as well. Their growing population spilled out in all
directions of the compass, into adjoining lands. Rome's new dominance in Campania was a particular affront. A collision was inevitable.

A short first war only temporarily interrupted the alliance. Then,
in 328, the Romans planted a *colonia,* Fregellae, in the western valley of the river Liris, a provocative act because this territory was
claimed by the Samnites and led up into their heartland. Then, in
the following year, the Samnites could not resist taking advantage
of internal dissension at the port of Neapolis, in Campania, and occupying it. The Romans reacted strongly to this challenge to their
authority; they drove out the occupiers and thus precipitated the
Second Samnite War.

This was a long and bitter struggle that lasted on and off for
more than twenty years. Samnium was a vast natural fortress, with
few points of access. Any army determined enough to enter it was
confronted by a labyrinth of narrow valleys and tight gorges—ideal
terrain for the layer of ambushes. Not unnaturally, the Romans

fought shy of a direct assault and much of the fighting occurred on or near the Samnite borders. The Caudine catastrophe of 321 was an example of this, taking place as it did on one of the two main routes that led from Samnium and Campania to Latium. Although it was a grave setback, recovery was swift.

Rather than seek to invade Samnium itself, with all the risks that entailed, Rome's strategy was to surround the Samnites with enemies. Alliances were struck with communities in Apulia, on the eastern seaboard, and Lucania in the foot of Italy, thus opening up a second front. In 315, a Roman consul captured the key town of Luceria on the far side of Samnium, near the Adriatic coast, a potential third front. The enemy counterattacked in the west, threatening Latium. They successfully pushed down the river Liris valley—and took Fregellae, the cause of all the trouble. They reached the coast, where they inflicted a heavy defeat on the Romans near the seaside city of Tarracina. The road to Rome lay open, and it may be that only the new walls dissuaded the Samnites from marching up to it.

The important city of Capua revolted, and other Campanian towns wavered. The Republic was shaken but unbowed. The wisdom of its generous Latin settlement now became clear, for no Latin community changed sides. They remained loyal to their conqueror. In the following year, the legions regrouped and doggedly went on the offensive. A second hard-fought battle was waged near Tarracina. One Roman wing was nearly put to flight but was rescued by the prompt arrival of the other. This time the Romans gained a famous victory and, according to tradition, thirty thousand Samnites were killed or captured—almost certainly an exaggeration, but a sign of the importance of the engagement.

The first stretch of Appius Claudius's great strategic road, 132 miles long, from Rome to the gates of Capua, was completed; rapid communication was now ensured between the capital and any recrudescence of trouble in Campania.

The Samnite moment had come, and now it had gone. Capua was brought to heel, and Fregellae resettled. Perhaps inspired by their new Greek friends in Naples, the Romans created a small sea squadron, but they did not really understand ships and fighting at sea, so little came of the experiment. Nevertheless, all things considered they had seized back the initiative.

For many years, little had been heard from the Etruscans, now in a condition of decay. Veii, of course, had been lost and the Celts were harrying the northern outposts of their empire. They had contentedly watched the conflict between Rome and Samnium from the sidelines. They had little sympathy with the latter, who had, after all, driven them out of Campania a hundred years earlier. However, the apparently irresistible growth of Roman power was alarming. Taking advantage of the fact that a forty-year truce between Rome and the Etruscan city of Tarquinii had expired, they threw in their lot with the Samnites.

To dampen down this fire, in 310 a Roman consul boldly forced his way through the unbroken, primeval Ciminian Forest into central Etruria. A natural barrier between the two nations, this trackless wilderness was believed to be impassable, and the news alarmed public opinion at home. Another Caudine Forks was predicted. In fact, the consul won a battle, Etruscan towns made peace, and the treaty with Tarquinii was renewed.

The struggle with the Samnites dragged interminably on. In 305, they launched an attack on the wine-rich *ager Falernus,* in northern Campania. They were repulsed and a relieving army was defeated. By the next year, after further setbacks, the Samnites had had enough and accepted not ungenerous terms. They were made to withdraw into their own territory. Their onetime allies were to transfer their allegiance to Rome, and would lose some of their land. Rome made solid but not spectacular gains, winning a number of frontier towns and completing its hold over Campania. But one thing was clear beyond any doubt. The Republic was now the first state in Italy and, it followed, a power to be reckoned with on the Mediterranean political stage.

At the beginning of the war, Livy had made a Samnite ambassador tell his Roman counterparts, "Let us pitch camp facing each other, and determine whether the Samnite or the Roman shall govern Italy." That question had now been settled, except for the awkward fact that it was not in the former's character to accept the decision of history. When he said *pax,* he plotted war.

In 298, Roman attention was distracted by a new Celtic incursion, probably only marauding bands and mercenaries but dangerous nonetheless. The Samnites indulged themselves with one last throw of the dice. They attacked a new Roman ally, the Lucani, on their southern border. During this third war, the legions did not linger on the edges of Samnium but marched directly into enemy territory.

Nothing daunted, the Samnite commander-in-chief, Gellius Egnatius, assembled a remarkable pact. Its members had little in common, apart from fear and hatred of Rome and a sense that this would be their last chance to destroy the monster before it grew too great ever again to be suppressed. Egnatius's bold plan was to join forces with the Etruscans, the Umbrians (a long-standing enemy), and the Celts in the north and launch a combined attack against the irrepressible Republic.

The existence of this alliance became a matter of common knowledge in 296 and caused a panic at Rome. One of the consuls, the democratic reformer Appius Claudius Caecus, was in command of an army commissioned to keep a watch on the Etruscans, and he warned the Senate to take the threat posed very seriously. Every category of men was called up, even former slaves, and special cohorts of older citizens were formed. The two consuls for the following year commanded an army of four legions, and a special force of two legions guarded Campania from Samnite incursions. If they were at full strength, that added up to 25,200 legionaries, as well as a strong contingent of cavalry. Also, two legions were dispatched to ravage the Etruscan countryside, to discourage the Etruscans from marching to Egnatius. This wasn't all. The citizen legions were accompanied by a greater number of troops contributed by the allies and the Latins—further witness, if it were needed, of the success of the Latin settlement. In total, this was the largest force Rome had ever assembled.

The consuls hurried to prevent the Celts from joining up with the Samnites. But they arrived too late and their advance guard was badly mauled. However, the Etruscans and the Umbrians were absent and, when the two armies met for a full-scale battle at Sentinum (near the modern town of Sassoferrato, in the Marche), they were probably evenly matched.

The hour of reckoning had arrived and, to mark it, a portent occurred. A female deer was chased by a wolf across the open space between the front lines. Then the animals veered off in opposite directions. The wolf ran toward the Romans, who opened a pathway for it to pass through. The deer rushed into the arms of the Celts, who struck it down. A Roman front ranker made the obvious connection. "On that side lies flight and slaughter," he shouted. "The deer, the goddess Diana's beast, is dead, but here on this side the wolf is the winner, whole and untouched. He reminds us of our descent from Mars, god of war, and of Romulus our founder."

It does not matter much whether or not this incident is a historical event, for, one way or another, it is evidence that the Romans saw this day as a turning point in their history. The battle at Sentinum, like Waterloo, was the "nearest run thing." The Roman left, commanded by Publius Decius Mus, the son of the commander who had "devoted" himself during the Latin war, was hard-pressed by the Celts and their chariots. In a bid to redeem the situation, Mus followed his father's example. After saying the ritual prayers, he galloped on his horse into the Celtic lines, to his death. The army's priest cried out that the Romans had won the day, now that they were freed by the consul's fate. Meanwhile, the Roman right wore down and eventually routed the Samnites. They then turned back and smashed the Celts from the rear.

Victory was complete, but it came at a cost. According to Livy, 25,000 of the enemy were killed and 8,000 taken prisoner, while the Romans lost 8,700 men. The decision of Sentinum was permanent: Egnatius's grand alliance was broken for good, and its inventor lay dead on the field of battle.

The Samnites still would not give up. Even the ultra-patriotic Livy acknowledged their stamina. He wrote:

> They could carry on no longer, either with their own resources or with outside support, yet they would not abstain from war—so far were they from tiring of freedom even though they had not succeeded in defending it, preferring to be defeated rather than not to try for victory.

Fighting continued for a few years, and finally Samnium was penetrated by Roman forces and ravaged from one end to the other. Resistance was no longer possible. To judge by the amount of loot seized and the number of captives enslaved, little mercy was shown: auctions of booty and prisoners raised more than three million pounds of bronze—a windfall that funded the Republic's first ever issue of coinage. For the fourth time, the Samnites signed a treaty with their conqueror. They became "allies" of the Republic—in other words, a vassal nation liable to send its young men not to fight its conqueror but to help it win its future wars.

The struggle had lasted half a century. The Samnites were down, but even now they refused to be counted out. Sullen, resentful, and subjugated, they nursed their grievance against Rome and awaited an opportunity for revenge.

FOR AN INDIVIDUAL Roman soldier, a battlefield was a narrow and constricted place, electric with fear and tension. As most fighting took place in the summer, the air would be filled with dust raised by thousands of tramping feet, the ancient equivalent of von Clausewitz's fog of war. Rain brought no relief, for an army soon turned wet ground into a quagmire. Sharp and repulsive smells spread through the armies—caused by sweaty unwashed men, the panicked loosening of sphincters and bladders, and, in due course, the cutting open of guts. There was a tremendous noise of metal on metal, of war cries and screams, of regimental trumpet blasts. The soldier was surrounded by comrades but could not see anything that was going on beyond them, nor easily hear orders. He had no idea how the battle as a whole was going. At best, he might glimpse his general riding past, himself hardly able to descry events. In the middle of a crowd, our Roman was fearfully on his own.

In modern warfare, combatants are often more or less remote from their opponents, and so are insulated from the terrors of hand-to-hand fighting. For the Roman, a javelin could perhaps be thrown thirty meters, but once two armies collided he was in touching reach of his enemy. His duty was to try to kill or disable him with his trusty *gladius,* a short cut-and-thrust sword, and to avoid getting killed by use of his shield, or *scutum,* two and a half feet in width and four feet in height.

In the fourth century, military reforms improved the effectiveness of Roman arms but probably made the battlefield a more frightening place than it had previously been. Originally, a legion fought as a phalanx. A phalanx was a tight infantry formation, eight and, later, twelve or sixteen ranks deep. It was a Greek invention that the Romans copied. As if they were a single invincible organism, soldiers marched close together shield to shield. They carried long spears thirteen to eighteen feet in length that, like a lethal porcupine, presented an impenetrable thicket of shafts. The phalanx crashed into the enemy line and usually prevailed by virtue of its sheer momentum and perfect drill. Not for nothing is the word *phalanx* the Greek for "roller," or heavy tree trunk.

However, the phalanx had weaknesses. It was vulnerable to attack from the sides and men found it hard to stay in formation on rough ground. Once broken up, this monument of human solidarity disintegrated into a collection of individual soldiers, easily picked off and put to flight. Except in the Po Valley, Italy is not a land of flat plains, and during the fourth century Rome found that the phalanx was at a disadvantage when confronting the loose, open tactics of the Celts, with their terrifying chariots, or the guerrilla tricks of Samnite mountaineers.

So the Romans abandoned the phalanx for a more flexible arrangement. Rather than form a single deep rectangle, a legion's heavy infantry was divided into three successive lines. The first consisted of *hastati,* young soldiers; the second, *principes,* men in their prime; and, finally, the *triarii,* mature veterans in reserve. The *hastati* and the *principes* carried two throwing javelins a man, six feet long and made from wood and iron, and the *triarii* one long thrusting pike. Each line was broken down into ten subunits, or maniples (from the Latin *manipulus,* or "handful") of about 120 men. Maniples were separated from one another by intervals equal to their own frontage. The gaps in the front line were protected by the maniples of the second, and those in the second line by the third.

The formation resembled a checkerboard and allowed fighters in the first line to withdraw and be replaced by fresh troops. The task of the *triarii* was defensive. If both the *hastati* and the *principes* had been forced to retreat, they were the last obstacle before an ignominious defeat. They knelt down beneath their banners, held up their shields, and pointed their pikes into the air, a kind of human barbed-wire entanglement. The phrase "to have come to the *triarii*" was a common expression that things were going badly.

Severity was essential if men were to be serious about fighting. We have no eye-witness testimonials to the experience of battle in classical times, but research into modern warfare offers findings that doubtless have a general application. It seems that comparatively few soldiers put their heart into fighting. Battles often have a rhythm, with waves of men pushing forward, feinting, and then rushing back. Men are usually capable of facing the danger they are in, but only a quarter of them actually attack with a will to kill. A paralysis of terror overtakes some soldiers; they are unable even to surrender, much less fight back, and are killed where they stand or lie.

Joy in combat and the taking of an almost sexual pleasure in killing occurs but is rare. In a modern survey, about one-third of combatant soldiers show strong or mild fear, another third are "in the middle ground of tension and concentration," and about one quarter are "calm and neutral": these last may be presumed to be the effective combatants. A small number are stunned or incapacitated.

According to a recent sociological study of violence, "in ancient and mediaeval warfare, there appears to have been a high degree of incompetence in the use of . . . weapons." As is usually the case, most wounding and killing took place when the opposing forces were unequal—for example, during a rout or an ambush. "Forward panic" is a kind of fever that maddens advancing troops, who may then commit atrocities. Likewise, after victory in the field or the capture of a besieged city, soldiers allow themselves a temporary moral holiday. Individuals feel protected by the crowd and behave with great cruelty to the vanquished. When normal social controls have resumed, the same men may share their rations with surviving victims.

One way of reducing fear and tension has been to put troops into massed formations, such as the phalanx, where they must act in concert and there is little or no room for individual initiative. Rome's new manipular formation offered more scope for individual initiative but also (it follows) for cowardice or, at least, ineffectiveness in the face of the enemy.

So it is no surprise that, to maximize fighting efficiency, discipline had to be fierce. Two centurions stood at either end of a maniple's front row, each commanding one half of the unit, while a third officer, an *optio,* kept watch in the rear. Great care was taken in appointing men to these crucial positions. According to Polybius:

> The Romans look not so much for the daring or fire-eating type, but rather for men who are natural leaders and possess a stable and imperturbable temperament, not men who will open the battle and launch attacks, but those who will stand their ground even when worsted or hard-pressed, and will die in defense of their posts.

It was an understood right of war for the winner to take as booty anything of value that could be found. A Roman soldier, both citizen and ally, could count on a fair share of the spoils. But the most persuasive encouragement to valor was the fact that Rome established a habit of winning its wars. Yes, there could be terrible setbacks and high casualties, but the Roman Republic now controlled most of central Italy; its territory had grown to more than 6,000 square kilometers at the turn of the century and ballooned to more than 15,000 square kilometers by the 280s. There was an unparalleled increase both in public and private wealth.

The wars of the fourth century made Rome into a warrior state. Campaigns took place more or less every year. The regular annual levy rose from two to four legions during the Samnite Wars—that is, about eighteen thousand men—and during the Sentinum crisis six legions were under arms, perhaps twenty-five percent of all adult male citizens. However nerve-racking the experience of battle, warfare paid, and there was now no other power in the peninsula that dared challenge Rome's supremacy.

SO WHAT WAS it like to be a Roman, as the Republic found itself on the threshold of history and greatness? And how did he or she see the world? It is hard to be certain in the light of an unreliable written record that later imaginative historians tampered with and "improved," but a recognizable personality begins to emerge into the light of day.

The vast majority of people were poor and scratched a hard living from the land. Although Latium was fertile, hostile marauders trashed crops and burned down huts and houses. Smallholders were often absent on service with the legions. Women and children presumably worked the fields when not forced to make their escape to nearby strongpoints. However, with the expansion of Rome's territories, fighting increasingly took place on the territory of others.

The problem of indebtedness remained endemic, and it was many years before the humiliation of debt bondage, the *nexum,* was outlawed. Economic hardship was never totally dispelled, but foreign conquests relieved its worst symptoms. As the Republic became wealthier, rural austerity, exemplified by the experience of Cincinnatus, came to be regarded with a certain nostalgia.

With migrants moving about the peninsula and rising populations, war was a way of life in central Italy. The Romans learned to be extraordinarily aggressive. There were few periods in their early centuries when the Republic was not invading its neighbors or resisting invasion by them. Little wonder that a constitution was devised which intermingled the military with the political.

A fierce culture of self-sacrifice developed, at least in the ruling class, illustrated not only by such legends as Brutus's execution of his delinquent sons but also by the (apparently historical) deaths of Decius Mus *père et fils*—suicide for the greater good, negation of the individual for the deliverance of the collective.

Two factors kept the Roman's instinct for aggression under control: religion and the law. Both were systems of regulation. Spiritual experience was regarded with deep suspicion; what was required was a ritual formula for ascertaining the will of the gods and averting their displeasure. Likewise, the Twelve Tables set out in grinding detail rules for managing relations between citizens.

These two systems helped to ensure good behavior, dutifulness, trust, *fides*. Bad faith brought with it divine disappproval and legal sanctions. But the Roman was crafty and, while very free with his condemnation of others, was willing enough to favor the letter rather than the spirit of the law in his own affairs; on occasion, he might even rewrite the letter.

Prescription is insufficient by itself; goodwill has to be added to the mixture. The remarkable story of how Rome's class struggle was resolved is evidence that generation after generation of pragmatists were willing to compromise, to make do and mend, to strike deals with their political opponents.

THESE WERE THE people who were about to encounter, for the first time, the armed might of Greece.

III

HISTORY

10

The Adventurer

A YOUNG KING LAY DYING ON HIS BED IN BABYLON. On 29 May, he had given a splendid banquet in honor of one of his commanders and taken a bath, as he was accustomed to do. Then, uncharacteristically, for he enjoyed late-night drinking sessions, he wanted to go to bed. Perhaps he was feeling out of sorts. However, a friend of his invited him to a party and he changed his mind. He went on drinking all through the next day, at the end of which he felt feverish.

That night he slept in the palace bathhouse, for its coolness. The following morning, he returned to his bedroom and spent the day playing dice. By the night of 1 June, he was back in the bathhouse, and the following morning he discussed a projected military expedition with his senior officers. The fever intensified, and two days later it became clear that he was seriously ill. What, exactly, was the matter is unknown, but he had recently returned from a boating trip on the river Euphrates and may have contracted malaria; also, he had not fully recovered from a serious battle wound to his chest.

The king continued to fulfill his royal duties, leading the daily sacrifice, but by 5 June he was forced to recognize the gravity of his condition and issued orders for high officials to stay within reach of his bedside. Not many hours passed before he began to lose the power of speech and, in a bleak symbolic gesture, he handed his signet ring to his senior marshal. Authority was transferred.

The city was seething with rumors, and anxious soldiers gathered outside the palace, threatening to break down the doors. Eventually, they were allowed in and passed in an endless file one by one through the king's bedroom. The king could not say a word and, as the men took their leave, he sometimes painfully raised his head a little and gestured to them with his right hand. Otherwise, only his eyes expressed awareness.

At some point during his illness, while he was still able to converse, the king was asked to whom he left his kingdom. He gasped, "To the strongest." His last words reveal a cynical prediction that his generals would soon be at one another's throats as they fought for their share of his empire. He added, "There will be funeral 'games' in good earnest when I have gone."

So died Alexander the Great on 10 or 11 June 334, at the early age of thirty-two. While Rome was engaged in its long, slow struggle with the Samnites for control of central Italy, this boy-king of Macedon had spent ten years in a whirlwind of triumphant campaigning against the vast Persian Empire; although he claimed to be leading a Hellenic crusade, he expropriated it for himself. One of the world's great field commanders, he seems to have seen war as an end in itself. Homer's *Iliad* was his bible, and he agreed with the indomitable warrior Achilles that the only reasonable purpose of life was the pursuit of personal glory. The cost in lives was of little concern to Alexander and hecatombs of men, women, and children were sacrificed to his vaulting ambition.

In his final months, he was planning new campaigns. According to his biographer Arrian, there were reports that he meant to make for Sicily and southern Italy in order to check the Romans, whose growing reputation was already causing him concern.

He would never have remained idle in the enjoyment of any of his conquests, even had he extended his empire from Asia to Europe and from Europe to the British Isles. On the contrary, he would have continued to seek beyond them for unknown lands, as it was ever his nature, if he had no rival, to strive to better his own best.

Alexander personified a human type, the legendary seeker for the world's end, whose purpose, in Tennyson's unforgettable phrase, is always "to strive, to seek, to find, and not to yield."

The Macedonian king's cynical view of a future without him was more than justified by the event. His empire was divided up among his generals and members of his family. Nicknamed the *Diadochoi,* or Successors, they immediately started squabbling among themselves and war succeeded war. Like players in a murderous game of musical chairs, almost every one of them came to a violent end. Alexander's half-witted half brother and nominal successor as king; his formidable mother, Olympias; his wife, Roxana, and their posthumous son—all were eventually executed as the wheel of fortune whirled round.

THE GLAMOUR OF Alexander's personality and the blinding afterglow of his achievements caught the imagination of many ambitious young men of the time and, indeed, later throughout the classical period. His example energized famous Greeks and Romans in their own pursuit of glory. (Not everyone was an admirer, it is worth noting. Cicero saw Alexander as a global menace and told of his encounter with a captured pirate. The king asked the man what wickedness drove him to terrorize the seas. He replied, "The same wickedness that drives you to terrorize the entire world.")

One of the earliest emulators was Pyrrhus, king of the disputed throne of the Molossians. The Molossians were one of the tribes that made up the federation of Epirus (a territory in what is today northern Greece and southern Albania, which looks across a narrow stretch of the Ionian Sea to the island of Corfu); their monarch was the federation's hereditary *hegemon,* or leader.

A rugged and mountainous region, Epirus is dominated by the high Pindus range and lay on the edge of the Hellenic world. The Greeks looked down on its inhabitants, as they did on the Macedonians, as being semi-barbarous. Epirotes spoke a sort of Greek but lived in scattered villages rather than cities, or *poleis,* like Athens, Thebes, and Sparta. Of course, after Alexander, northern outlanders were no longer beyond the pale.

Pyrrhus boasted a remarkable pedigree, for he was believed to be a descendant of Achilles, and bore the name of the hero's son. As so often in this story, the elaborate tapestry of the Trojan War forms the backdrop of contemporary events and personalities. To us it may be legend, but to the Greeks and Romans it was reality. Achilles had been the invincible fighter on the Greek side (and, as a point of interest, had defeated Rome's originator, Aeneas, in single combat), but in the last year of the war he fell victim to an arrow shot by Paris, whose love for Helen had set in motion the whole long, tragic saga. The original Pyrrhus (he was also known as Neoptolemus) was one of the stowaways in the wooden horse. He led the charge during the fall of the city and killed its aged king, Priam. On his return to Greece, he settled in Epirus and founded the Molossian dynasty.

The infancy of his descendant and namesake was disturbed. Born in 319, Pyrrhus was a baby when his father was forcibly removed from the throne and replaced by a relative, and he had a hair-raising escape from pursuers. He was in the care of three sturdy young men and a nurse. They had nearly reached a place of safety, but just as the sun was setting they came to a river swollen by rains. They could not cross it in the dark without help. They saw some local people standing on the far bank and shouted for help, but the noise of the torrent made them inaudible.

One of the youths had the bright idea to strip some bark from a tree and scratch a message on it with a buckle pin. He wrapped the bark around a stone and flung it across the river. Those on the other side read the message and quickly cut down some trees, lashed them together, and improvized a rough-and-ready rail that Pyrrhus's party could grasp as they crossed the turbulent water.

The child's final destination was a tribe in Illyria, to the north. This was a lawless land, and the Illyrians had a deserved reputation for sea piracy. The tribe's ruler, a certain Glaucias, gave him asylum and resisted large bribes to hand him over to his enemies. This was where Pyrrhus grew up—in a wild world of heroic bandits who set a premium on physical bravery and personal honor.

He was only thirteen when he was restored to the Molossian throne under a regency, but a few years later he was ousted once again, this time by the ruthless and ambitious king of Macedonia, Cassander, who was one of the Diadochoi and had cast a covetous eye on northwestern Greece.

Now adult, Pyrrhus dreamed of winning or creating an empire somewhere in the world, but he had no choice but to lead the life of an adventurer. He served in the army of one of the Successors and received his first taste of large-scale warfare at the Battle of Ipsus, where his patron lost his life at the hands of a grand coalition. One more athlete in Alexander's funeral games was removed from competition.

The only Successor to die comfortably in his bed after many years in power and to found a long-lived dynasty was Ptolemy, who had known Alexander as a boy and had been one of his most trusted companions. He seized Egypt and made himself pharaoh. Less ambitious than his rivals, he contented himself with this corner of the empire and aimed for no more than dominance of the Aegean. Pyrrhus spent some time in Egypt and so impressed Ptolemy that he married the young man to his stepdaughter (a political polygamist, he collected five wives during his career). The pharaoh also gave him substantial military and financial support, which enabled Pyrrhus once more to regain the Molossian throne.

The charms of his small kingdom soon palled. Pyrrhus devoted time and energy to expanding the territory he controlled, but he was a marginal player in the great game of international politics. He nursed his hopes. A second cousin of Alexander the Great through Olympias, who had been a Molossian princess, he went so far as to claim a special relationship with the dead conqueror. He once reported that Alexander called to him in a dream. He answered the summons and found the king lying on a couch. Alexander promised him his help. "But your majesty," said Pyrrhus, never backward in coming forward, "how will you be able to help me, seeing that you are unwell?" The king replied, "My name will be enough," and, mounting a pedigree horse, led the way into the future.

And so it was. Pyrrhus did not hesitate to use Alexander's name, and he made the most of the family connection when, in 287, he persuaded the Macedonian army to proclaim him king of Macedon. However, a rival pretender soon drove him out, and back into his Molossian backwater.

Pyrrhus was a chivalrous and charismatic figure, although Plutarch writes that his appearance "conveyed terror rather than majesty." As with the King's Evil, practiced by medieval and early modern European monarchs, sufferers from depression believed the king could cure their condition by pressing his right foot against their spleen. No beauty, Pyrrhus had few teeth and, oddly, it is said that his upper jaw was a continuous line of bone on which the usual intervals between the teeth were indicated by slight depressions. (There is no plausible condition known to modern dentists that matches this description; the most likely explanation is that the king wore a bone or ivory denture.) He was discreet and polite in his personal life, but tended to be aloof with social inferiors. He was widely acknowledged to be naturally brilliant, well-educated, and experienced in public affairs—an opinion of himself that he shared.

As the years passed, though, Pyrrhus remained a man of promise rather than of accomplishment. Like his ancestor Achilles, he could not stand idleness, and, as Homer writes,

> ate his heart away
> remaining there, and pined for war-cry and battle.

He was in his late thirties when, not a moment too soon, the opportunity of his lifetime finally presented itself. An embassy from the city of Tarentum (today's Taranto), a Greek foundation on the heel of Italy, traveled to Epirus and laid before the king an extremely interesting proposition.

TARENTUM WAS ONE of the wealthiest cities of the Greek world. Founded in 706 in Apulia, on the instep of the Italian boot, it stood on an island between a large inland lagoon and a bay, which was itself protected from the open sea by another island and a spit of land. The city was "leafy" and the climate delightful, with "mild winters and long lingering springs." To the poet Horace, the surrounding countryside was:

> To me the bonniest square miles
> In all the world, a coast of smiles,
> Where bees make honeycombs so sweet
> Hymettus has to own defeat,
> And even the olives vie with those
> That silvery-green Venafrum grows.

Tarentum enjoyed a thriving cultural life; it was a center for the philosophy of Pythagoras and manufactured high-quality decorated pottery and a beautiful silver coinage. The city was especially famous for the purple dye it made from the murex, a marine mollusk. It also had a thriving wool industry and sold figs and salt. Politically, it was a democracy and was dominated for thirty years in the middle of the fourth century by a certain Archytas, whom we would call today a Renaissance man. He is believed to have been the founder of mathematical mechanics, and designed a bird-shaped flying machine, probably propelled by steam power. Archytas had known Plato personally and attempted to rescue him from his difficulties with the tyrant of Syracuse Dionysius II. The Athenian philosopher may have seen in him a model of the philosopher king he recommended in his *Republic* as the ideal ruler of a state.

Archytas was also a successful field commander against continual incursions by the Sabellian tribes that ringed the city from their mountain fastnesses. The Tarentines could field an army of more than thirty thousand men and deployed a powerful fleet. However, in more recent times they seemed to have lost their edge. According to the geographer Strabo:

> Later, because of their prosperity, luxury prevailed to such an extent that the public festivals celebrated every year were more in number than the days of the year; and in consequence of this they were poorly governed. One evidence of their bad policies is the fact that they employed foreign generals . . . to lead them in their war[s].

The Sabellians were not the only threat. For a long time, the Tarentines watched the growth of Roman power with concern, and then alarm. They had no *locus* in the Second Samnite War and at one point offered their services as neutral mediators between the warring parties, but in truth they were pro-Samnite nonbelligerents. They could see that sooner rather than later the expanding Republic would interest itself in the affairs of southern Italy. This was particularly worrying for the democratic government of Tarentum, for Roman practice with its defeated "allies" was to support the local aristocrats, who tended to welcome external support in order to maintain their rule.

It was not that the Romans were actively looking for trouble. As already noted, they believed in the principle of a just war, at least in theory, and wished to avoid the displeasure of the gods brought on by acting aggressively without due cause. However, a due cause duly presented itself in 285, when Thurii, another port in the Gulf of Tarentum, appealed to Rome for protection against Sabellian attacks, and some help was apparently provided. One might have thought Thurii would apply to its bigger neighbor Tarentum, but Thurii was an oligarchy and there was little love lost between the two of them. A curse of the political culture on the Greek mainland was the inability of small city-states, such as Athens, Sparta, and Thebes, to get on with one another. Those colonists who migrated to Italy brought the bad habit with them.

Three years later, another request came from Thurii. From the Republic's point of view, the timing was extremely inconvenient. The Romans had recently been defeated by a Celtic force from the north, and the Samnites had risen once more against their overlords. However, it was decided to respond favorably and a consular army was sent south to beat back the Sabellians and to garrison Thurii. Some other Greco-Italian, or Italiote, cities came into alliance with Rome. The Senate was coming to understand that, as Italy's dominant power, it would be unwise not to develop a rational policy for Magna Graecia.

The Tarentines were furious, and a chance opportunity of displaying their displeasure soon arose. In breach of an old treaty agreement not to sail in the Gulf of Tarentum, a squadron of ten Roman warships unexpectedly appeared in the harbor, hoping to anchor there. One tradition suggests that it was merely on a sightseeing expedition, but not surprisingly, the Tarentines guessed at a more sinister intention. They feared a plot to overthrow their democracy or, at least, some kind of hostile naval reconnaissance.

As luck would have it, a festival in honor of the god Dionysus was being held that day and a large, inebriated audience sat in the city's open-air theater watching a show. Soon there was news of the squadron's arrival, tempers rose, and an enraged mob rushed out to the quayside. An attack was launched on the intruders. Four Roman vessels were sunk, the commander was killed, and a fifth was captured with its crew; the others were hard put to make their escape.

As far as Thurii was concerned, Tarentum acted quickly and decisively. Its army marched on the city and expelled not only the ruling élite but also the Roman garrison. In its view, Thurii was doubly to be damned: it had preferred Rome to fellow Greeks, and an oligarchic form of government to a democracy.

These were serious provocations, but the Senate responded with a cool head and merely dispatched an embassy led by a former consul, Lucius Postumius Megellus, to seek an explanation. It probably calculated that Rome did not need another declared enemy at this point and could turn a blind eye if Tarentum agreed to maintain its ostensible neutrality. However, if the delegation expected anything approaching an apology it was to be disappointed.

Tarentum being a Greek-style direct democracy, all important decisions were taken by its citizens in full assembly. Postumius was invited to attend a meeting in the theater. The Tarentines happened to be celebrating another festival and, doubtless fueled by alcohol again, were in high good humor. They looked on the envoys as figures of fun, ridiculing their heavy and elaborate togas and slips Postumius made when speaking Greek. The Romans were unamused, which only made the Tarentines laugh the louder.

Postumius demanded the release of their sailors and ship, and required the Tarentines to surrender Thurii, pay compensation, and hand over for punishment those who had ordered the attack on the Roman fleet. When their presentation was over, the former consul and his colleagues made their way out of the theater, pursued by catcalls. At the exit, a well-known local drunk planted himself in Postumius's way, turned his back on him, bent over, lifted his tunic, and evacuated his bowels over the Roman's toga. This feat was greeted with laughter and applause.

"Laugh while you can," shouted Postumius. "You will soon be weeping for a very long while." Noticing that his threat infuriated some in the crowd, he went on, "Just to make you even angrier, let me say this. This toga will be washed clean with much blood."

Romans regarded ambassadors as sacrosanct and did not expect this kind of treatment. Taken by surprise, Postumius had handled the incident maladroitly, but he understood how to exploit the humiliation and inflame opinion in Rome. He kept the soiled toga just as it was and, once he was back home, put it on display as evidence of the insults he had endured. Although Rome's armies were fully stretched elsewhere, the Senate voted for war at once, and the Assembly ratified the decision.

This incident may have been somewhat enhanced in the telling, but it exposed an important truth. At this stage in its history, Rome was regarded by civilized opinion in the Greek world as a provincial semi-barbarous backwater; its representatives were good for a laugh and hardly to be taken seriously.

THE SMILES WERE wiped from their faces when the Tarentines witnessed the rapid arrival of a Roman army outside their walls, which proceeded methodically to ravage their delightful countryside, before withdrawing for the winter of 281/80 to a *colonia* at Venusia, where it could keep an eye on the Samnites and on the southern Sabellian tribes. They cautiously appointed a pro-Roman general who might be able to negotiate an early peace.

The commanding consul offered the Tarentines the same terms as Postumius had, or all-out war if they were rejected. As the historian Appian puts it, "This time they did not laugh." At a rowdy public meeting, the debate on what to do next was evenly balanced, but eventually it was agreed to send for the Molossian king to come over from Epirus with an expeditionary force and make war on the Romans. The idea of recruiting a foreign general was not a new one. In the past, feeling themselves too weak to fight on their own, the Tarentines had invited a succession of condottieri to provide military support against Sabellian incursions, albeit without great success: one of them had been Pyrrhus's uncle Alexander the Molossian, Olympias's brother and a previous occupant of the Molossian throne. He had died campaigning for the city. The present crisis provoked a surprising entente with Tarentum's aggressive neighbors, who found that they disliked Rome even more than they did Italiotes.

When the embassy arrived at Pyrrhus's court, it presented the king with gifts and assured him of a military coalition of the Sabellians, the Tarentines, and—a great prize, this—the Samnites. The envoys gave him a ludicrously inflated estimate of the number of troops that would be awaiting his arrival, but they were good judges of their man. A potential opportunity was opening up for Pyrrhus to regain the Macedonian throne, but he took the bait without hesitation, although his senior adviser, a Thessalian intellectual named Cineas, tried to dissuade him.

According to a famous anecdote of Plutarch's, Cineas asked the king, "What will you do when you have beaten the Romans?" We would take Italy was the reply. "What then?" Sicily would be a rich prize, the king opined, not seeing the trap. "And then?" Carthage and Libya would be too tempting to resist. Cineas concluded his interrogation: "After that, it's obvious that we will have no trouble taking back Macedonia and Greece."

Pyrrhus said, smiling, "Why then, we will be able to live a life of leisure and spend our days drinking and in private conversation." "What is stopping us from doing that *now*?" Cineas inquired.

The king was somewhat cast down, for he could see that he was inviting a world of trouble, but he was unable to renounce his high hopes. The Elysian shades of Alexander and Achilles expected nothing less of him.

THE VALLEY WAS remote, cold, and barren, with a craggy backdrop of snow-capped mountains. At the foot of a hill stood an oak tree inside a walled enclosure. There was a small, very basic stone temple. This was Dodona, the most ancient of Hellenic oracles and sacred to the king of the gods, Zeus, and his consort, Dione, usually called Hera (Rome's Jupiter and Juno). Three priestesses, known as "doves," interpreted the rustlings of the oak tree's leaves in the breeze for those with questions about their future.

Despite its great age, Dodona was not as well known as the sanctuary at Delphi and was used mainly by ordinary people to help them solve the difficulties of daily life, rather as today we seek the advice of a lawyer or a doctor. Anyone who consulted the oracle was required to submit his or her questions to the two gods in writing, scratched onto lead tablets. These were then put into a pot and studied by one of the priestesses. Archaeologists have discovered some of the tablets (ranging from throughout the oracle's long history): suppliants included not only local peasants but travelers from across the Mediterranean world.

Among them are Eubandros and his wife, who ask to what god, hero, or spirit (*daimon*) they must pray and sacrifice if they and their household are to be prosperous "for all time." A man named Socrates wants to know how he can trade most profitably for himself and his family. Agis inquires about his mattresses and pillows, which have been lost: Has some foreigner stolen them?

From time to time, celebrities consulted the divinities of Dodona. Homer has Achilles pray to "Lord Zeus, Dodonean, Pelasgian Zeus, you that live far away and rule over wintry Dodona" that his lover, Patroclus, come back victorious and alive from battle with the Greeks on the plain of Troy. Typically, the god gives with one hand and takes with the other. Homer adds, "Zeus the Counselor heard Achilles' prayer and granted him half of it but not the rest." Patroclus drives back the Trojans but is killed.

The oracle was perfectly capable of unscrupulous subterfuge. During the great war between Athens and Sparta in the fifth century, the Athenians were advised to colonize Sicily. Without considering what the oracle really meant, they felt encouraged to mount their disastrous Sicilian invasion. In fact, what the doves were referring to was a hillock of that name near Athens.

As the Molossian king, Pyrrhus was ex officio the patron of the oracle at Dodona. He was an enthusiastic supporter and made it the religious center of his kingdom. At considerable expense, he upgraded its facilities. The Temple of Zeus was rebuilt on a grand scale, and an arts and athletics festival launched, with plays performed in a new open-air theater.

When the king was planning his Italian expedition, he consulted the oracle about his prospects of success. With his close connection to the oracle, he would be forgiven for expecting the king of the gods and his queen to allow him an auspicious outcome. However, the doves listened to the rustling leaves and offered an ambiguous interpretation. In the Greek, their words could be read two ways—either "If you cross into Italy, you will be victorious over the Romans" or "The Romans will be victorious over you."

Pyrrhus was no fool and must have recognized the double meaning, but, as Cassius Dio put it, he chose to "construe the advice according to his wishes, for desire is very apt to deceive." He refused to countenance the slightest delay and would not even wait for the arrival of spring before setting off on his grand enterprise.

BEING ONLY A constitutional monarch in Epirus, Pyrrhus could not simply do as he pleased. His first step was to win the federation's backing and, more particularly, an agreement to supply troops. He made full use of his descent from Achilles: if the Romans claimed to be inheritors of the Trojan name, an invasion led by the Molossian king should be seen as a return match. Troy redivivus had to be cast down for a second time. Inheritor of the mantle of Alexander, Pyrrhus presented himself as the leader of a Hellenic crusade against barbarians. He was also the avenger of his uncle Alexander the Molossian.

Coins had a wide distribution throughout the Mediterranean, and for rulers with an instinct for public relations they were an invaluable means of communicating their message. Those issued under Pyrrhus's aegis at Tarentum could hardly have been more explicit. On some of them, the image of Zeus and Dione of Dodona appear, guaranteeing Pyrrhus's optimistic expectation of their divine blessing. Others imitated the gold staters of Alexander the Great, and showed Athena Promachos, champion against the barbarians, and a personified Nike, or Victory, bearing a trophy. On one coin we see Achilles, possibly with Pyrrhus's features. On another, Achilles' mother, Thetis, is depicted, as Homer described in the *Iliad,* bringing a shield and new weapons to rearm her son after the death of Patroclus.

Pyrrhus got his way, winning the support not only of his Epirote tribes but also of other Hellenistic monarchs, Diadochoi, or their heirs, who were delighted to see this military and militant nuisance sail away and annoy other people elsewhere. The king recruited an army of up to 22,500 infantry, including 2,000 archers and 500 men with slings (both of them little used by the Romans but lethal at a distance). He also disposed of 2,000 cavalry and 20 elephants.

Elephants were something of a novelty. The Greeks first came across them when Darius III, the Persian King of Kings, fielded them, unsuccessfully, against Alexander the Great at the Battle of Gaugamela in 331. Alexander never used elephants himself, but they became a favorite weapon of his successors. They were imported from India and, unlike African bush elephants, were large enough to carry a howdah, with a mahout and a few soldiers armed with missiles.

Their main advantage was that they terrified the enemy; horses would not face them, especially if they had not encountered them before. On the debit side, they could do serious damage to their own forces if they were wounded or for some other reason panicked and ran amok.

Arrian gives a vivid account of what can happen in those circumstances, when describing another of Alexander's battles, on this occasion against an Indian king:

By this time the elephants were boxed up, with no room to maneuver, by troops all around them, and as they blundered about, wheeling and shoving this way and that, they trampled to death as many of their friends as of their enemies. The result was that the Indian cavalry, jammed in around the elephants and with no more space to maneuver than they had, suffered severely; most of the elephant-drivers had been shot; many of the animals had themselves been wounded, while others, riderless and bewildered, ceased altogether to play their expected part, and, maddened by pain and fear, set indiscriminately upon friend and foe, thrusting, trampling, and spreading death before them.

In early 280, Pyrrhus wisely sent Cineas ahead with an advance guard of three thousand troops. Only when they had arrived safely at Tarentum and received their expected welcome did he follow with the main body of his army. They traveled in a fleet of transport ships that the Tarentines had sent across the Adriatic to Epirus. The king soon had cause to rue his insistence on sailing before the winter was over. His fleet was scattered far and wide by a storm. Some ships, including the flagship, which carried Pyrrhus, were unable to round the Iapygian promontory (the heel of the Italian boot) into the Bay of Tarentum. Night fell and a heavy sea drove them onto a bare and harborless coast, where many ships broke up on the rocks. An exception was the royal galley, which was saved because of its great size and sturdy build.

Saved only for the moment, though. The wind unexpectedly veered round and began to blow from the shore. The ship was likely to founder if it met the wind head-on, but to sail out to sea and

allow it to bounce about in the boiling swell was equally dangerous. The king took a bold decision, as Plutarch reports:

> Pyrrhus jumped up and threw himself into the sea, and his
> friends and bodyguards, eager to help him, immediately fol-
> lowed suit. But night and the waves with their heavy crashing
> and violent recoil made assistance difficult. It was not until day
> had already come and the wind was dying away that he managed
> to reach the shore. He had lost all his physical strength, but with
> boldness and a refusal to give in he mastered his distress.

The king made his way to Tarentum, where he lay low for a
time. Although immediately appointed commander-in-chief with
unlimited powers, he did nothing that might alarm his hosts,
until his damaged fleet limped into port and disgorged the Epirote
army. Surprisingly, all his elephants survived the passage, although how a nervous animal weighing five tons was kept calm
on board a twenty-meter-long galley in stormy seas must remain
a mystery. Then Pyrrhus ran up his true colors. He believed, so
Plutarch puts it, that "the mass of people were incapable, unless
under strict discipline, of either saving themselves or saving anyone
else, but were inclined to let him do their fighting for them while
they remained at home in the enjoyment of their baths and social
festivities."

This was not his idea of how to run a war. He occupied the acrop-
olis, or citadel, with his own troops and billeted his officers in citizens' houses. Military conscription was introduced for the Tarentine
youth. All theatrical performances were banned, the gymnasiums
were closed (people met there not only for exercise but also for conversation during which "they fought out their country's battles"),
and the men's communal messes (an institution peculiar to the
communal lifestyle of Sparta, Tarentum's founder) were prohibited.
The city's loungers and layabouts were shocked, and some of them

managed to evade Pyrrhus's guards and left town. The king's popularity fell, and opponents of the ruling democracy tried to stir up trouble. They were quickly rounded up and sent to Epirus or simply put to death. Tarentum was no longer its own master.

THE NEWS OF Pyrrhus's arrival on Italian soil caused consternation in Rome. A joint Celtic and Etruscan army had only recently been defeated in the north, and what the Republic needed was a period of recuperation. The heavy casualties in the third and last Samnite War were still a painful memory. However, there was nothing for it; another immense effort was required if the threat posed by Pyrrhus was to be met. Fresh troops were levied, even (apparently) from those citizens, the *proletarii,* who owned no property and so were usually exempt from military service. Such a step was taken only when there was a *tumultus maximus,* an extreme military emergency. Rome was garrisoned and an army in the north was tasked to prevent the Molossian king from making common cause with the Etruscans.

One of the consuls for 280, Publius Valerius Laevinus, marched a force of about thirty thousand men southward toward Tarentum. At this point, Pyrrhus intervened with a peace proposal. Although his highest value was prowess on the battlefield, he was not a warmonger. Throughout his career, he would always deploy diplomacy to win an argument before resorting to arms, and he recommended this policy in his well-known (but now lost) book on military tactics. If we can trust Cassius Dio, he wrote to the consul in the following terms:

> King Pyrrhus to Laevinus, Greeting. I understand that you are leading an army against Tarentum. Send it away and come to me yourself with a few attendants. For I will judge between you, if you have any charge to bring against each other, and I will compel the party at fault, however unwilling, to deal justly.

This was the first direct dealing the king had had with representatives of the Republic, so it is hard to assess whether he expected a favorable reply. He certainly did not receive one. The consul asked, "What use have I got for trash and rubbish, when I can stand trial in the court of Mars, our forefather?"

Pyrrhus was slightly outnumbered by the Romans, for he had to leave a garrison behind in Tarentum. He was encamped on one side of a river near Heraclea, a town a little inland from the Gulf of Tarentum. The consul approached and made his camp on the other. He captured one of the king's scouts and, rather than execute him, Laevinus drew up his army in battle formation and showed the man around. He asked him to report faithfully to his master what he had seen. Pyrrhus himself rode up to the river to get a view of them. When he had observed their good order, impressive drill, and the efficient arrangement of their camp, he remarked, "The discipline of these barbarians is not barbarous."

He was now less confident of victory and tried to avoid being forced into battle until reinforcements arrived. He prevented the Romans from crossing the river. Laevinus, in the light of his numerical superiority, was eager for a fight. The consul took a leaf out of Alexander's book at Granicus and sent his cavalry off to ride along the river and cross where they were unopposed. When the legions appeared unexpectedly in their rear, the Greeks guarding the riverbank pulled back and Laevinus's infantry was able to begin crossing the river.

It is difficult to make sense of the surviving accounts of the battle, which opened messily. What exactly happened was probably confusing to those taking part. But it appears that Pyrrhus, much alarmed, rode with three thousand Epirote horsemen to meet the Roman cavalry and hold them up, giving time for his phalanx and the rest of his army to form themselves into order of battle. Unfortunately, he was unhorsed and severely shaken.

In an echo of the Achilles and Patroclus story, and presumably to give him a breathing space in which to recover, the king handed over his richly ornamented armor and purple cloak shot through with gold to one of his companions, a certain Megacles, to wear in his place, for his disappearance would be fatal for his soldiers' morale. For the time being, he stayed in the rear. Unfortunately, Megacles was killed. Pyrrhus mounted another horse and rode along the line with his head bare to show that he was alive, both by his appearance and his voice.

The king's tactics were similar to those of Alexander, who combined an unbreakable phalanx with a flanking cavalry charge. The Epirote phalanx, with its bristling pikes, was to hold or push back the Roman infantry. Elephants were usually deployed about fifteen to thirty meters apart along the front of an army, but Pyrrhus had too few of them to do this. So he placed his band of twenty as a reserve to be brought forward at an appropriate moment in the battle. His cavalry were on the wings, with instructions to rout the enemy's horse and attack its infantry from the flanks. Although the legions, armed with short swords and throwing javelins, had some difficulty engaging with the phalanx, they stood their ground. The battle became a stalemate.

Pyrrhus decided to bring on his elephants, which thoroughly unnerved the Roman cavalry. Horses bolted and threw their riders. Men in the howdahs shot down many foot soldiers, and others were trampled. Disheartened, the legions pulled back and left the field. They managed to cross the river and retreated to Venusia (joining the Roman force that had originally appeared before Tarentum and ravaged the city's territory). More than seven thousand men had fallen and eighteen hundred been captured.

But success was sour, for Pyrrhus had lost about four thousand men, including friends and officers whom he knew well and trusted. As we have seen, Rome commanded a very substantial reservoir of men of fighting age, and had no difficulty in quickly reinforcing the consul. However, the king would struggle to raise more troops.

THE WOLF

If ancient Rome were to have a logo, it would be this bronze wolf, ferocious and tender, that suckled the babies Romulus and Remus, who as young men went on to found the city of Rome. The wolf is traditionally believed to be of Etruscan make, dating from the fifth century (although some scholars argue that it is medieval). The infants were added by the Renaissance artist Antonio Pollaiuolo.

Capitoline Museums, Rome

THE GREAT DAYS OF OLD

There are no original images of Rome's early history. The French revolutionary painter Jacques-Louis David admired the legendary stories of austere patriotism and created his own versions, which are close in spirit to a Republican Roman's worldview.

In his *Rape of the Sabine Women*, Hersilia, Romulus's wife and daughter of his enemy Titus Tatius, rushes between the two men and halts a battle in the Forum between Romans and Sabines. She proposes that the Sabine women, whom the Romans have kidnapped, be given the chance to accept their forced marriages. This agreed, the union of the two peoples soon follows. *Louvre, Paris*

In *The Oath of Horatii*, three brothers swear, in the presence of their father, to sacrifice their lives, if need be, in Rome's war with the city of Alba Longa. With their unflinching gaze and taut limbs, they are the embodiment of noble valor. They go on to fight a ritual duel with three Alban counterparts, the brothers Curiatii, whom they kill. The women on the right remind us that one of their sisters is in love with a Curiatius. A brother puts her to death as punishment for her treasonable grief. *Louvre, Paris*

THE RIVALS

Hannibal was Rome's greatest enemy and for a time brought it to its knees. This marble bust is reputed to be of the Carthaginian general and was found at the ancient city of Capua. If genuinely classical, it must surely have been carved after the defeat of his cause at the battle of Zama, for fierceness and focus are softened by melancholy and resignation.
Museo Archeologico Nazionale, Naples

It took Rome more than a generation to produce a commander capable of beating Hannibal. The young Scipio Africanus learned from his opponent, and outdid him. This bust of the mature Scipio was discovered in the Villa dei Papyri in Herculaneum.
Museo Archeologico Nazionale, Naples (Photo: Massimo Finizio)

Hannibal's greatest victory was at Cannae, a town near the river Aufidus in Apulia. Eighty thousand Roman soldiers lost their lives. A solitary, commemorative column stands above the flat, dusty plain where the battle was fought. *(Photo: Jörg Schulz)*

THE ROMAN ROAD

Everywhere they went, Romans built roads. These linked distant settlements to the capital, enabled the legions to march swiftly to trouble spots, and asserted power over the mountainous Italian landscape. In 312 Appius Claudius Caecus built the opening stretch of the Republic's first major highway, the Via Appia, and parts of it can still be seen to this day.

DESTROYERS OF THE REPUBLIC

As the first century got under way, Marius spoke for the People and Sulla for the aristocracy. One after the other, each man hijacked the state and massacred his opponents. During their time, the ruling class lost its tolerance of opposition, without which the finely balanced Roman constitution could not function.
Both busts, Munich Glyptothek

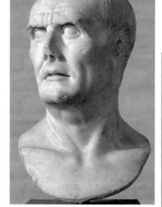

LIBERATOR

In 196 Titus Quinctius Flamininus proclaimed the freedom of the Greeks, a gesture that won him immense popularity. He was the first Roman whose portrait head appeared on a Greek or Macedonian coin, in this case a gold stater in the style of Alexander the Great's money.

EMPIRE BUILDER

In 63 Pompey the Great defeated Mithridates, king of Pontus. With his long-lasting settlement of the provinces and kingdoms of the Middle East, Rome became the unchallenged superpower of the classical world, and remained so for centuries. *Ny Carlsberg Glyptotek*

DEFENDER OF THE REPUBLIC

The great orator Cicero believed that the Roman constitution was nearly perfect, despite all the evidence that it was in a state of terminal decay. He looked back with pride to a glorious past. He was put to death for defending the Republic he loved by those who worked to destroy it and replace it with an autocracy.
Capitoline Museums, Rome

THE FORUM ROMANUM

The Forum Romanum was the public square in the heart of ancient Rome. Here were the Senate House, the Comitium, or place of public assembly, the law courts (held in the open air), shops, and temples. As this panoramic view shows, all that remains are pillaged ruins. In the center stands the columned frontage of the temple of Saturn behind which can be seen the arch of the emperor Septimius Severus and, beyond, the plain brick wall and pediment of the Curia Julia, the Senate House. On the right are the foundations of a shopping mall and business center, the Basilica Julia, in the distance three tall columns of the temple of Castor and Pollux and on their left the white fragment of the circular temple of Vesta, where the city's sacred flame was kept. *(Photo: Arnold Dekker)*

DAILY LIVING

Roman authors say little of the life of the people, but structures, objects, and carvings have survived that throw light on everyday pursuits. The rich lived in spacious luxury, as can be seen in first-century A.D. Pompeii *(Photo: S. H. O'Leary),* but most urban Romans made do with one or two rooms in apartment blocks, or *insulae,* like this one (restored) in Ostia.

There were few facilities for cooking at home in an *insula* and eating out was popular, as at this bistro with a heated bar for keeping food warm *(Photo: Daniele Florio).* It is backed by a fresco that shows the spirit of the house flanked by the household gods, with Mercury, god of business and commerce, on the far left and Bacchus, god of wine, on the far right.

Sex was widely available, and often for sale; this bedroom fresco gave stimulation and guidance to its occupants. Brothels thrived. So too did old-fashioned male attitudes, as a Pompeiian wall graffito indicated. "If Venus can break my tender heart, why can't I hit her over the head?"
(Photo: Heinrich Stürzl)

When congratulations were offered him, he replied gloomily, "Another victory like this, and I am done for!" (Hence the modern phrase a "Pyrrhic victory.")

Nevertheless, he made the most of a good public-relations opportunity. Captured enemy weapons were sent to Dodona as a votive trophy. A small bronze tablet marking the gift has survived: "King Pyrrhus and the Epirotes and the Tarentines to Zeus Naios from the Romans and their allies." The Tarentines sent offerings to Athens to celebrate this triumph over barbarians, and the armor the king wore during the battle, or at least part of it, was sent to a Temple of Athena on the island of Rhodes. The underlying message was simple and clear: the Hellenic world would soon be hearing no more of the upstart Italian Republic.

The Samnites and the Sabellian tribes now declared openly for Pyrrhus, as did a number of Italiote cities that had been waiting on events before deciding whom to back. However, the king seems to have been unsure of his next military move. One of his rivals for the throne of Macedonia once said of him, "He is like a player with dice, who makes many fine throws, but does not know how to exploit them when they are made."

What appears to have been a weakness may in part have been a certain reasonableness of disposition. His war aim was not Rome's unconditional surrender, something he must have known he could not achieve with the army at his disposal. Instead, he wanted to force the Republic to withdraw from Greater Greece and revert to its status as a middling power in central Italy. This could be done, he hoped, by demonstrating his military superiority so convincingly that the Republic would be persuaded to accept a negotiated peace.

ONE FURTHER THROW of the dice was worth risking. Pyrrhus tested the loyalty of Rome's Latin allies by marching his army north through Campania and along the Via Latina toward Rome. He may also have hoped to entice Etruria into revolt. But central Italy was unimpressed, and if the king expected defections he was disappointed. The cities of Naples and Capua refused to capitulate. He advanced to within a few miles of Rome, but the threat to the city, with its high walls and garrison, was not serious.

Laevinus, having gathered together his scattered forces and added to them the reinforcements sent by the Senate, chased after Pyrrhus, harassing his army. The king was astonished and compared the Roman army to the Hydra, a poisonous water serpent with many heads; if one was chopped off, others grew in its place. "After being cut to pieces the legions grow whole again!" he remarked admiringly. The consular army that had been keeping watch over the Etruscans began to move south, and the king, fearful of being trapped in a pincer, turned around and went back to Tarentum, where he spent the winter of 280.

The time had come for diplomacy, and the Romans delivered another shock. A delegation of three senior politicians, headed by Gaius Fabricius Luscinus, arrived to treat with Pyrrhus. Much to his surprise, the only topic they wished to raise was the ransoming of Roman prisoners of war. He had assumed that, as was customary in the Hellenistic world, they would accept the fact that they had been defeated and seek terms. Uncertain what to do, he consulted his advisers. He followed Cineas's recommendation that he free the captives without price and send envoys and money to Rome.

Before the embassy left Tarentum, he took Fabricius on one side, offered him generous gifts, and asked for his cooperation in securing peace. The Roman declined the gifts on the grounds that he already had enough possessions, and said coolly, "I commend you, Pyrrhus, for wanting peace and I will secure it for you, always providing that it proves to be to our advantage."

Fabricius was not offended by these advances, for sometime later he very decently passed intelligence to Pyrrhus that his personal physician was planning to assassinate him. The king was not put off by the Roman's rebuff, either, and commissioned Cineas to go to Rome and induce the Senate to come to an agreement. Reputed to be the most eloquent public speaker of his day, Cineas reminded his hearers of the famous fourth-century orator Demosthenes. Pyrrhus rated his persuasive powers so highly that he used to say, "His words have won me more cities than my own military campaigns."

Just in case words were not enough, Cineas brought with him a large amount of gold and, we are informed, every kind of fashionable women's dress. If the men could not be won over, he thought, then their wives, corrupted by the allure of classical haute couture, would charm them into changing their minds. Hellenistic monarchs were expected to be magnificently openhanded, but to Romans this was bribery, even if many pocketed what was on offer.

Although he did not quite understand this cultural difference, Pyrrhus's adviser was no fool. Once he had arrived in Rome, he delayed seeking an audience with the Senate. Alleging one reason or another, he hung around the city, getting the feel of the place and making the acquaintance of all the best people. A charming conversationalist and a generous giver, Cineas was soon a popular figure on the social scene. By the time he met the Senate, many of its members knew him well and had been persuaded to back his peace plan.

The terms he proposed were tough. Tarentum and the other Greek cities in southern Italy were to be fully independent. All lands taken from the Samnites and other Sabellian tribes were to be returned to their original owners. Finally, an alliance would be offered with Pyrrhus (not, interestingly enough, with Tarentum or Epirus). The total effect of this pact would have been to reduce Rome's sphere of influence to Latium only. It is evidence either of Cineas's golden tongue (and gold specie) or of the Republic's exhaustion and demoralization, or something of both, that it appeared that the Senate would accept the proposals.

This was to reckon without Appius Claudius Caecus. Old, ill, and completely blind, he had retired from public life. When he learned that a vote for a cessation of hostilities was about to be passed, he could not hold himself back. He ordered his servants to lift him up and had himself carried in a litter to the Senate House. At the door, his sons and sons-in-law took him in their arms and helped him inside.

He addressed the Senate in the strongest terms. According to Plutarch, he said, "Up to this time, I have regarded the misfortune to my eyes as an affliction. But when I hear your shameful resolutions and decrees, I am only sorry I am not deaf as well as blind."

He insisted that Pyrrhus must first leave Italy before there was any talk of friendship and alliance. The Senate performed a rapid volte-face and voted unanimously to accept his opinion. Cineas was sent back to his master empty-handed, except for a greater understanding of the Roman character. He told Pyrrhus ruefully that the Senate was a "council of many kings."

Claudius's speech must have been a powerful and persuasive composition. It was still read in the first century and, although now lost, was believed to be the oldest text of its kind to have been preserved. Cicero judged the aged radical to have been a "ready speaker."

IN PYRRHUS'S OPINION, the Romans had been defeated and the war should have been over, but only now did the monarch from Epirus understand the depth of Rome's resources and its stamina. To keep his army fed and paid in a foreign land was prohibitively expensive, even more so now that he had recruited new mercenaries, mainly from southern Italy. Large sums of money had to be raised if he was to stay in the game. The Italiote cities on whose behalf the campaign was being fought were requested (in a tone of voice that signified "required") to finance operations.

The wealth of these cities and the extent of the demands made of them was startlingly revealed in the late 1950s, when archaeologists unearthed a stone box containing thirty-eight bronze tablets with writing incised on them from the Temple of Olympian Zeus at Locri, a port on the toe of Italy. Seven can be dated to between 281 and 275, the years of Pyrrhus's Italian adventure. During that time, no less than 11,240 silver talents (about six hundred and forty thousand modern pounds of silver) were paid to the king from the temple income as a "contribution to the common cause." With this huge sum, a force of between twenty thousand and twenty-four thousand mercenaries could be paid their customary salary of one drachma a day each for six years. The revenue of temples derived from taxes, collections, and gifts, from the sale of wheat, barley, and olive oil grown on temple lands, the sale of homemade tiles and bricks and, last but not least, from temple prostitution, a custom at Locri in times of crisis. One of the city's largest payments was made after the Battle of Heraclea. We can safely assume that its neighbors in the region made similar contributions.

Seeing that the Senate refused to make peace, Pyrrhus had no option but to resume hostilities. In the spring of 279, he marched his army, forty thousand strong, slowly north through Apulia and encamped near the town of Asculum beside a bridge over the river Aufidus, then in full flood. The Romans faced them across the river. In the days before the battle, Pyrrhus's troops became obsessed with the fact that one of the Roman consuls was Publius Decius Mus, whose father and grandfather had both "devoted" their lives to the gods of the underworld and fought suicidally to the death in the field. This had won Rome divine favor and victory.

The rumor (inaccurate, as it turned out) spread that this latest Decius Mus was planning the same religious act. The king was obliged to encourage his superstitious soldiers by saying that incantations and magic could not defeat arms and men. He added that if anyone saw a man wearing a toga pulled over his head, the prescribed costume for a *devotio,* they should make sure *not* to kill him but to take him alive. A message was sent to the consul forbidding him to try to devote himself.

Yet again, the surviving accounts of an ancient battle are confused and contradictory. It appears that the fighting took place over two days. To enable an engagement, the Romans were allowed to cross the river, but Pyrrhus found himself on rough ground unsuitable for both his cavalry and his phalanx. Inconclusive and scrappy fighting lasted until nightfall. At first light, the king sent skirmishers to occupy the battlefield and so deny it to the Romans. He then drew up his main forces for battle on a level plain where they would be able to operate with greater ease. His cavalry was placed on the wings, with the elephants once again held in reserve. The Greek army faced four Roman legions with roughly the same number of auxiliary troops.

Since Heraclea, the Romans had thought hard about how to deal with the elephant problem. This time they fielded wagons equipped with movable poles tipped with scythes, three-pronged spikes, grappling irons, or flaming devices wrapped in tow and pitch. These were swung into the elephants' faces and had some success in disturbing the animals, at least to start with.

The Greek cavalry on the left wing retreated, and Pyrrhus extended his center to fill the gap they left behind them. Meanwhile, some Roman allies arriving late for the battle saw that the enemy camp was poorly defended and seized the opportunity to capture and loot it. Eventually, Pyrrhus, with his cavalry and elephants, succeeded in breaking up the front lines of two Roman legions. The fighting was fierce, and the king was seriously wounded in the arm by a javelin, but the day was his.

However, the consuls managed to extricate their forces and withdrew to their camp across the river. They had lost six thousand men, but, as had happened at Heraclea, the winners also suffered losses. According to the king's war commentaries (no longer extant), three and a half thousand of his soldiers were killed. Because his camp had been fired and destroyed, he had lost all his tents, pack animals, and slaves. His army was compelled to sleep under the open sky. Many of the wounded died from lack of food and medical supplies.

The Battle of Asculum was as disastrous a victory as could be imagined. Plutarch summed up the king's predicament:

> He had lost a great part of the forces with which he came, and most of his friends and generals. He had run out of reinforcements he could summon from home, and he could see that his allies in Italy were losing their keenness. Meanwhile the Roman army was like a gushing fountain, easily and speedily refilled when emptied.

LUCK STRUCK again for the restless monarch. Just when his Italian campaign was losing steam, two new and enticing opportunities presented themselves. The inexperienced young king of Macedonia had gone down to defeat and death in a great battle with an invading Celtic horde. Pyrrhus had always yearned for the Macedonian throne and Alexander's realm. If he could only find a way out of his obligations to Tarentum, he could cross back into Greece and drive the barbarians away. Epirus would certainly support the move, for it worried that the Celts might turn their gaze in its direction. Pyrrhus could hardly imagine a more glorious goal than to be the acknowledged savior of the Hellenes.

Then messengers arrived at Tarentum from the rich Sicilian city-state of Syracuse. Once more than capable of looking after itself, Syracuse was now riven by internal disputes. The numerous other Greek communities on the island were also politically unstable, veering wildly between rule by a despot and a rowdy democracy. For many years, the Carthaginians had controlled western Sicily. Always fearful that the Greeks would, if left to themselves, threaten their trade routes in the Western Mediterranean, they saw in their present confusion a chance to take control of the entire island. Hence the desperate Syracusan appeal to Pyrrhus to cross over from Tarentum, become the city's supreme commander, and combat Carthaginian aggression.

There is no evidence, but we can safely guess that the king had long meditated as a career option not to stop at Italy but to press on westward to the invasion of Carthage, a sail of only 130 miles from Sicily. Indeed, his late father-in-law, Agathocles, who had been the ruler of Syracuse until his death in 289 (surprisingly, in his bed, despite the most colorful of careers), had anticipated him by leading an expedition against the North African merchant-state. Admittedly it had failed, but it was not in Pyrrhus's nature to be disheartened by the difficulty of an enterprise, rather the opposite. The future was always bright.

The king's weakness was not uncertainty or excessive caution but, rather, a short attention span for the matter at hand. Rome, a tougher prey to engorge than he had expected, was already beginning to recede from the front of his mind. He decided to accept the invitation from Syracuse, rather than the Celtic challenge. He never explained his choice, but we may suppose that the West offered new, untrodden lands and an Alexandrine vista of unending conquest, whereas the East was tediously familiar and crowded with powerful competitors and fellow claimants.

Not unnaturally, the Tarentines were extremely upset by Pyrrhus's demarche, but he promised to return in due course and resume his campaign. He also took the precaution of installing garrisons in all the Italiote cities, although this augmented his already rising unpopularity in Greater Greece.

Carthage was also angered. Just when its dream of taking all Sicily under its control was about to be realized, the last thing it wanted was for a general of Pyrrhus's ability to champion the Sicilian Greeks. It immediately sought an alliance with Rome against the king. This would keep the Republic in the war and so make it unsafe for Pyrrhus to leave Italy.

After a brief demurral, the Senate agreed to a third treaty with Carthage, the terms of which survive in the Greek translation of Polybius. The previous accords had in large part been designed to protect Carthage's trading interests and had set down the parties' respective zones of influence and exclusion, with Rome mostly as the junior partner. These restrictions were now overridden in the current emergency. The key clauses read:

> Whichever party may need help, the Carthaginians shall provide the ships both for transport and for operations, but each shall provide the pay for its own men.
>
> The Carthaginians shall also give help to the Romans by sea if the need arises, but no one shall compel the crew to disembark against their will.

The Republic knew little of the sea and had few warships. The treaty was weighted in its favor, for it brought into play the resources of the Mediterranean's naval superpower; so it would now be easy to blockade Tarentum by sea and reduce the likelihood of any new reinforcements coming in from Epirus. By contrast, Rome was under no obligation to go to Carthage's aid in Sicily.

PYRRHUS'S ADVENTURES IN Sicily followed a familiar pattern. Before his own arrival there, he sent Cineas ahead to prepare the ground diplomatically. Then, in the summer of 278, he set sail, this time with a comparatively small army of eight thousand infantry and some cavalry and elephants. He lifted the Punic siege of Syracuse and entered the city to a hero's welcome. He marched triumphally across the island, liberating city after city, and besieged the port of Lilybaeum (today's Marsala) at Sicily's far western end, the only stronghold not under new Greek management.

The Carthaginians changed their tune and proposed peace terms, which included a large indemnity and the provision of ships. Clearly, they were tempting Pyrrhus to return to Italy (despite the treaty with Rome), and he *was* tempted. In his absence, consular armies were regaining their dominance in Greater Greece and the situation needed to be retrieved before it was too late. Unfortunately, the royal council, which included Sicilian representatives, rejected the offer. No deals were to be struck until the last Carthaginian had been chased from the island.

The shine was rubbing off the Molossian king. Lilybaeum proved to be impregnable by land and would fall only to a sea blockade, but unfortunately the Greeks did not have enough ships for the purpose. So Pyrrhus, who had been behaving despotically, decided to play double or quits. He would invade Carthage on its home territory. To transport the war to Africa meant commissioning a new fleet, and that, in turn, meant taxing his Sicilian allies and demanding oarsmen and sailors. The plan aroused furious opposition.

Carthage spied a chance to turn its fortunes around and dispatched a powerful new army to the island. Meanwhile, the Samnites and Sabellian tribes in Lucania and Bruttium sent an embassy to Syracuse begging the king to return as quickly as possible, for Rome was forcing them into submission. In other words, his overland link to Tarentum was under threat and unless he acted now his entire position in Sicily and southern Italy might collapse.

So in the late summer of 276, Pyrrhus set sail from Syracuse with 110 warships and many transports. On his way north up the Sicilian coast, he was surprised by a Punic fleet that sank 70 ships and severely damaged others. Luckily, the transports escaped and his army landed safely at Locri. It was an ignominious end to a high undertaking.

Before marching to Tarentum, the king tried to capture the strategically important city of Rhegium, which was garrisoned by the Romans and some Italian mercenaries. The attempt failed and the mercenaries mauled his army as it made off. Pyrrhus himself was badly wounded on the head. A huge enemy soldier in splendid armor challenged him to a duel "if he is still alive." With typical chutzpah, the new Achilles accepted. Plutarch writes, if we are to believe him:

Wheeling round he pushed through his guards—enraged, smeared with blood and with a terrifying expression on his face. Before the man could make a move he struck him such a blow on the head that, what with the strength of his arm and the fine temper of the blade, his sword cut down through the body and the two halves fell apart.

The king managed to extricate his forces from the fight and made his way back to Locri. He had under his command twenty thousand infantry and three thousand cavalry, and was in urgent need of funds with which to pay them. He again required a substantial sum from the Temple of Zeus. He also foolishly plundered another temple for its treasures, which, he had to acknowledge, was an act of sacrilege. The ships transporting the stolen goods ran into a storm, and Pyrrhus superstitiously gave back most of what he had taken.

All sides in the war were tiring. Plague at Rome depressed public opinion and Livy reports that the number of citizens fell from 287,222 in 280 to 271,224 in 275. The Samnites and other Italian allies of Pyrrhus had been weakened by heavy losses during five long years of war. Nevertheless, in the spring of 275 two consular armies marched south and took up positions designed to prevent an advance on Rome. Meanwhile, Pyrrhus, in order to help the hard-pressed Samnites, moved northward with a force of about twenty thousand men. He meant to meet the consuls singly and found one of them at the Samnite town of Malventum (later Beneventum).

He detached part of his army to intercept the other consul in case he came up to help his colleague. With the remainder, he was now outnumbered by the Roman legions, and decided on a bold night operation. His idea was, under cover of darkness, to find high ground from which he could make a surprise attack on the enemy camp. He set out after sunset, with his best troops and his fiercest elephants. He marched on a wide circuit through dense woods, but his soldiers lost their way and straggled. This created delay, their torches failed, and daybreak revealed them to the Romans as they descended the heights. The consul led his forces out and routed the Epirotes. Some of the elephants were captured. This engagement was followed by a conventional battle on the plain. Showers of burning arrows stampeded the remaining elephants, which ran in panic among their own men. Pyrrhus's camp was captured and his army driven from the field.

The king did not entirely give up his dream of a western empire, but this was, to be realistic, the end of the expedition. As token of a hopeful return, he left a strong garrison at Tarentum under his son Helenus's command, but with the rest of his troops—about eight thousand infantry and five hundred cavalry, less than half the number he had brought with him six years earlier—he set sail for Epirus. Despite his optimism, Italy had seen the last of him.

The Romans spent the next three years subduing the Samnites and their Sabellian cousins. Then they turned their attention to Tarentum, forcing out the Epirote garrison in 272 and compelling the Tarentines to hand over their fleet and pull down their walls. Tears in plenty rather than laughter now. Eventually, all the Greek cities in southern Italy came under Roman control.

As for Pyrrhus himself, his career went from good to worse. He defeated the existing king of Macedon, Antigonus Gonatas, and, to great applause, won back his throne. However, he had learned nothing from past experience and almost immediately alienated the Macedonians by occupying their towns with his troops and allowing some Celtic mercenaries to plunder the royal tombs at Aegae (archaeologists rediscovered them in 1976).

Unable to keep still, he suddenly turned up at the head of an army in the Peloponnese, with a mission to restore the ancestral rights of a Spartan general in his employ. Bogged down by a fierce Spartan defense, he then announced his intention to expel Antigonus from Greece and marched to Argos to do battle with him. Maddened by the killing of one of his sons, he challenged the Macedonian ruler to come down from the hills where he was encamped and fight for his kingdom. "Many roads to death lie open to Pyrrhus if he is tired of life," came the dismissive response.

Argos begged the king to go away and leave them to their neutrality, but Pyrrhus was having none of it. An Argive friend of his let him and his soldiers into the city at dead of night. The alarm was raised, and Antigonus sent in some troops to help repel the Epirotes. Pyrrhus was in the marketplace and saw he was in trouble, so sounded a retreat. He sent a message to troops outside the walls, asking them to create a diversion. Due to a mishearing, reinforcements were sent into Argos through the same gate by which Pyrrhus was trying to leave. The result was that he was immobilized in a traffic jam. He attacked a local man, whose mother happened to be looking down from a rooftop. Seeing that her son was in danger, she flung a roof tile at Pyrrhus, which struck him in the base of the neck. His sight blurred and he fell off his horse. The man pulled him into a doorway. He decided to chop Pyrrhus's head off but, made nervous by the recovering king's glare, slashed him across the mouth and chin. It was some time before he finished the job.

PYRRHUS ACHIEVED NOTHING that lasted. Achilles and Alexander were his evil angels, but in his case the pursuit of glory was not accompanied by the necessary unswerving obsessiveness. Unlike his cousin, the conqueror of the Persian Empire, Pyrrhus's cult of himself was not conducted within a broader framework of policy but was undiluted egoism.

He certainly had good qualities. He had a charismatic personality, a generous nature, and, on the battlefield, he led from the front. He enthusiastically flung himself into hand-to-hand combat, taking wounds and risking death. Famous for his chivalry, he was a courteous paladin of the ancient world. He was much admired for his genius as a field commander. Contemporaries said that other successor kings resembled Alexander,

> with their purple costumes, their bodyguards, the way they copied the poise of his neck which was tilted slightly to the left, and their loud voices in conversation, but Pyrrhus, and Pyrrhus alone, in arms and action.

From our perspective thousands of years later, it is hard to understand his military reputation. This may not be his fault so much as that of our literary sources, whose accounts of his battles are confused and maddeningly vague just when precision is most needed.

For all the brilliance, energy, and charm, a cloud of pointlessness hangs over Pyrrhus's career. He was an opportunist who failed to make anything of his opportunities. The danger the Molossian king posed to Rome was serious but never life-threatening. One senses that he failed to research his projects sufficiently. He did not understand until it was too late the extent of the Republic's human reserves. The rapid Hydra-like rebirth of Laevinus's mangled army came as a severe shock, but by then he was committed to Tarentum and war.

However, the failure of his Italian expedition had one major consequence. The Greeks now recognized that a new player had joined the international table. They were hypnotized by the steely stare of this warlike state that now dominated the Italian peninsula. For their part, having bloodied Pyrrhus's nose, the Romans hoped they had persuaded the quarrelsome Hellenic world to mind its own business and leave them free to conduct theirs without interruption.

Now that they had won responsibility for the city-states of southern Italy, they wondered whether they might have to keep an eye open for trouble in Sicily, just across the narrow strip of water between Rhegium and Messana (today's Messina). Instability there would act like an airborne infection capable of blowing across seas to an exhausted peninsula, which more than anything needed a period of peace and quiet.

After all, Pyrrhus had warned them. On his final departure from Tarentum, he discussed with his entourage the consequences of his failure in Sicily: "My friends, what a wrestling ring we are leaving behind for the Carthaginians and the Romans."

11

All at Sea

ON ITS MISSION OF EXPLORATION, THE FLEET sailed out of the Mediterranean, through the Pillars of Hercules, and into the unnerving swell of the Atlantic Ocean. It turned south and set its course along the generous bulge of western Africa.

The Pillars are on either side of the narrow stretch of water we call the Strait of Gibraltar, and for most well-informed people of the fifth century they marked the western limits of the known world. The name was a reminder that the demigod once passed this way while undertaking his labors. So, too, did Greek explorers and traders, but their heyday was over. Massilia and some settlements in northern Spain were the only Hellenic outposts left. These Occidental waters had become the monopoly of Phoenician merchants, especially those from the great North African city of Carthage.

Sixty galleys with fifty oars apiece were commanded by Hanno, a member of a leading Carthaginian family. His orders, issued sometime about or after the year 500, were to found trading outposts on the African coast. Two days from Gibraltar, the explorers set up their first mini-colony and then arrived at an inland lagoon that was covered with reeds. Elephants and other animals were feeding there. They continued sailing and established some more settlements along the way, which in due course probably became the source of pickled and salted fish that Carthage exported to Greece; perhaps also Tyrian purple dye was extracted from sea snails harvested on this coast.

Carthage was interested in what is called "dumb barter" with African tribes south of the Sahara, as Herodotus, the Greek "father of history," explained in the fifth century:

> They unload their goods, lay them out neatly on the beach and return to their boats, whereupon they send up a smoke signal. As soon as they see the smoke, the natives come down to the beach and place on the ground a certain amount of gold in exchange for the goods. They then withdraw to a distance. The Carthaginians come ashore again and examine the gold. If they believe it represents a fair price for the articles on offer, they pick them up and sail off. If not, they go on board once more and wait. The natives come and add more gold until the Carthaginians are satisfied. There is complete honesty on both sides: The Carthaginians never touch the gold until it equals the value of the goods and the natives never touch the goods until the gold has been removed.

In the dispatch he wrote about his expedition, which was displayed as an inscription in the Temple of Baal Hammon, in Carthage, Hanno made no mention of the gold trade, doubtless to avoid alerting competition.

The basic purpose of the enterprise had now been achieved and, despite the fact that they suffered from a lack of water and blazingly hot weather, the flotilla sailed on, presumably motivated now by curiosity and a taste for excitement. At one point, the ships tried to make landfall, but savages clothed in animal skins made it clear they were unwelcome by throwing stones at the visitors. On another occasion, some black men ran away from them.

A number of days later, they arrived at the Niger Delta, where they encamped on an island. Hanno wrote:

> Landing on it we saw nothing but forest and at night many fires being kindled; we heard the noise of pipes, cymbals, and drums, and the shouts of a great crowd. We were seized with fear, and the interpreters advised us to leave the island. We sailed away quickly and coasted along a region with a fragrant smell of burning timber, from which streams of fire plunged into the sea. We could not approach the land because of the heat. We therefore sailed quickly on in some fear, and in four days' time we saw the land ablaze at night; in the middle of this area one fire towered above the others and appeared to touch the stars; this was the highest mountain which we saw and was called the Chariot of the Gods.

The Carthaginians were not sure how to interpret all this, although we recognize that they had encountered an erupting volcano.

Some time later, as they continued sailing south, they arrived at another island in a lake, where they came across some mysterious beings:

> It was full of savages; by far the greater number were women with hairy bodies, called by our interpreters "gorillas." We gave chase to the men but could not catch any, for they climbed up steep rocks and pelted us with stones. However, we captured three women, who bit and scratched their captors. We killed and flayed them and brought their skins back to Carthage.

Another puzzling encounter, then, this time between *homo sapiens* and some primate cousins.

Thirty-five days had elapsed since Hanno left Carthage and, running short of provisions, he ordered his ships back to the familiar Mediterranean and safety.

THE CARTHAGINIANS IN particular and the Phoenicians in general were intrepid explorers and traders. They usually acted for commercial reasons, although as early as the seventh century an Egyptian pharaoh with a penchant for grandiose schemes commissioned some Phoenicians to circumnavigate Africa. Their fate is uncertain, but if they succeeded—and it was claimed that they did, after a journey lasting two years—it was to little purpose, for the continent's landmass was unexpectedly large and the sea route was too long to be of practical use to denizens of the Mediterranean.

Himilco, a contemporary of Hanno and perhaps his brother, made another daring trading voyage and published a report of his adventures (now lost, although quoted by a fourth-century A.D. Latin author). He, too, sailed to the Pillars of Heracles, but turned northward. His aim was to reconnoiter the Atlantic coast of Spain, Portugal, and France. This time there was no question of searching for gold but for control of the trade in tin for making bronze and in lead, the two newly exploited metals of the age.

He reached Brittany, rich in ore, and perhaps even Heligoland (a source of amber), but seems not to have stopped off at Britain. In his dispatch, he made his journey sound as difficult and unpleasant as he could. He reported marine monsters, dangerous sandbars, and carpets of thick, clogging seaweed. The ocean was terrifyingly vast, if only one could see it through the fog. One senses that Himilco was talking up the dangers to discourage any rivals from following in his wake.

The Carthaginians were ambitious, energetic, and clever. They kept in touch with their mother city, Tyre, but in the sixth century Nebuchadnezzar laid siege to it for thirteen years. According to the Bible, an excited Ezekiel crowed on behalf of his single god, "I will stop the music of your songs. No more will the sound of harps be heard among your people. I will make your island a bare rock, a place for fishermen to spread their nets." The prophet spoke too soon. The city held out, but eventually agreed to recognize Babylonian suzerainty. In later centuries, Egyptian and Persian invaders took their toll, and finally, in 332, Alexander the Great captured Tyre after another bitter siege. Furious at having been held up, he had two thousand citizens crucified on the beach and thirty thousand sold into slavery.

It was evident that an independent future for Phoenicians did not lie in the East. The balance of power shifted toward Carthage, whose location and excellent harbor in the Bay of Tunis suited it well for the development of trade in the Western Mediterranean. With time, its citizens were "transformed from Tyrians into Africans" and became leaders of an informal empire of Phoenician colonies, usually small mercantile outposts, throughout the region. The Atlantic port of Gades, an island stronghold separated from the mainland by a narrow arm of the sea, fell under its control around the year 500.

The Carthaginians were congenital seafarers and had little interest in acquiring land. However, to protect their "pond" and to exclude other traders, they occupied western Sicily, Sardinia and Corsica, and southern Spain. They also acquired footholds along the North African coast, although there were no good harbors between the Atlantic and Carthage itself. This was their backyard, and woe betide any wandering Greeks whose ship strayed into their waters. Drowning was the best that could be expected.

IN ORDER TO lower their reliance on food imports, the Carthaginians annexed the fertile hinterland that lay to the south of their capital. They became expert farmers, and were guided by a celebrated writer on agriculture named Mago. He disliked urban living: "If you have bought land, you should sell your town house so that you won't be tempted to worship the city's household gods instead of those of the country."

Although his book is lost, it was often cited by Greek and Latin authors. Mago advised on planting and pruning vines, on the management of olive trees and fruit trees, on growing marsh plants, on beekeeping (including the lost art of "getting bees from the carcass of a bullock or ox," once known to Samson), and on preserving pomegranates, known to the Romans as *malum Punicum,* or the Punic apple. One of his recipes was for a sweet raisin wine, or *passum* (still drunk today in Italy as *passito*). Carthaginian amphorae have been found all over the Mediterranean, evidence of a thriving export trade.

The city of Carthage itself, which consumed these provisions, stood on a triangular peninsula connected to the mainland by an isthmus about two miles wide at its narrowest point. On one side lay a lagoon and on the other the sea. Any visitor walking in from the countryside was confronted by a massive battlemented wall that ran across the isthmus. It was more than forty feet high and thirty feet wide, with four-story towers every fifty or sixty yards. Inside, stables housed elephants and horses. In front were two ramparts and a wide ditch. The wall was said to have continued for twenty miles, on a less gargantuan scale, around the entire city. (By comparison, Rome's walls ran for a little more than thirteen miles.) It was a bold general who imagined that he could capture Carthage.

In his historical novel about Carthage, *Salammbo,* Gustave Flaubert vividly evokes the urban panorama:

Beyond [the wall], the city rose in tiers like an amphitheater. There were tall, flat-roofed houses built of every type of material—stone, wood, reeds, shells, and beaten earth. The trees in the temple gardens made green pools in this mass of multicolored blocks, which was honeycombed with public squares and intersected by countless narrow streets. The walls of some of the old quarters of the city presented huge blank surfaces relieved only by climbing plants and streaked with the sewage thrown over them. Streets passed through yawning openings in the walls like rivers under bridges.

One of these internal walls surrounded the city's heart, a hill called Byrsa and the two harbors, forming a citadel. Here also was a public square, or forum, and a council chamber outside which justice was administered in the open air. Three narrow winding streets, lined with six-story houses, led up to the top of Byrsa.

The first or outer harbor catered to merchant vessels. It was rectangular, measuring about 1,600 by 1,000 feet, and opened to the sea through a single entrance that could, if necessary, be barred with iron chains. Outside this entrance, a massive quay was built where merchant ships could load and unload goods. At the other end of the rectangle, a narrow channel led into the inner naval harbor. This was a circle of water about 1,000 feet in diameter, with a small island in the middle. Appian writes:

On the island was built the admiral's house, from which the trumpeter gave signals, the herald delivered orders, and the admiral himself overlooked everything. The island lay near the entrance to the harbor and rose to a considerable height, so that the admiral could observe what was going on at sea, while those who were approaching by water could not get any clear view of what took place inside.

Around both the island and the circumference of the circle were quays and sheds to accommodate two hundred and twenty warships, as well as arsenals and shipbuilding yards. Two Ionic columns stood in front of each shed and gave the impression of continuous porticoes running around the island and the harbor's edge. All these state-of-the-art facilities, probably completed in the late fourth century, were a state secret. They were surrounded by a high double wall and were invisible even from the mercantile harbor.

This was the city that, legend had it, Dido had built and her treacherous lover, Aeneas, had abandoned. Her dying curse of unceasing enmity between Carthage and Rome was approaching its fulfillment.

THE CARTHAGINIANS RECEIVED a bad press from ancient historians. There was sarcastic talk of *Punica fides,* "Punic good faith," meaning sharp dealing and betrayal. Plutarch, writing in the second century A.D. but following some much older source, claims:

[They] are a hard and gloomy people, submissive to their rulers and harsh to their subjects, running to extremes of cowardice in times of fear and of cruelty in times of anger; they keep obstinately to their decisions, are austere, and care little for amusement or the graces of life.

There is hardly any surviving evidence for this harsh judgment— with one colossal exception, their religious practices, to which (like other Semitic peoples) they were fiercely attached. There were many temples, shrines, and sacred enclosures, or *tophets,* in Carthage. The city's most popular deities in a numerous pantheon were Baal Hammon, Lord of the Altars of Incense, and his wife, Tanit, Face of Baal. Tanit's name suggests that she was subordinate to her husband, but in fact she was more than his equal. Once the Carthaginians had acquired their North African lands, they felt the need for a guarantor of life and fertility and looked to Tanit, as their mother goddess, to fill that role.

Various ancient texts report a dark side to Punic worship. The Bible has it that the Phoenicians sacrificed small children. A king of Judah desecrated one of their holy places "so that no one could sacrifice his son or daughter as a burnt offering," and the prophet Jeremiah quotes the Jewish God as saying, "They have built altars for Baal in order to burn their children in the fire as sacrifices. I never commanded them to do this; it never even entered my mind."

The Greek Diodorus Siculus, not the most reliable of historians,

has left a celebrated description of a Carthaginian attempt to placate an angry Baal. He equated Baal not with the chief Greek god,
Zeus, but with his terrifying father, Cronos, who ate up his own
progeny:

> In their anxiety to make amends for their omission, [the Car-
> thaginians] chose two hundred of the noblest children and sacri-
> ficed them publicly. . . . In the city there was a bronze statue of
> Cronos, extending its hands, palms up and sloping toward the
> ground. Each child was placed on it, rolled down and fell into a
> sort of gaping pit filled with fire.

According to Plutarch, parents saved their own infants by replacing them with street children, whom they purchased, and loud
music was played at the place of sacrifice to drown out the victims'
screams.

Modern scholars were unsure what to make of these exotic holo-
causts. Were they invented by hostile propagandists? If there was
any truth in the stories, perhaps animal sacrifices were substituted
at some point for human beings (as in the legend of Abraham and
Isaac). Then, in the 1920s, a *tophet* was unearthed containing the
burned remains of young children. For a time, it was argued that
this was merely a cemetery for dead newborn and stillborn infants,
offered postmortem to appease the gods. Further investigation,
however, revealed the remains of children up to four years old, and
inscriptions made the nature of the sacrifice explicit. Thus, one father wrote: "It was to the lady Tanit and to Baal Hammon that
Bomilcar son of Hanno, grandson of Milkiathon, vowed this son of
his own flesh. Bless him you!"

A NATION WITH a small territory will necessarily have a small
population, and so it proved with Carthage. The geographer Strabo
claimed a total number of 700,000 inhabitants, but that is conceiv-

able only if it encompassed the entire countryside and the other townships that made up the Carthaginian estate. There were surely never more than 200,000 people of pure Phoenician descent living outside the city walls. At the time of its greatest prosperity in the early third century, the city probably housed about 400,000 souls, including slaves and resident aliens.

For a nation with international and imperial responsibilities, Carthage did not have enough citizens to stock its armies. To fight its wars, it routinely recruited mercenaries, from among African tribesmen and, farther afield, from Spain and Gaul. This practice brought with it certain dangers, for mercenaries are motivated by pay rather than by patriotism and have been known to turn on their defenseless employers if they have a grievance. Sea, not land, being the Punic element, citizens, perhaps of the poorer sort, apparently helped to man its ships.

It was unusual for non-Greek states to have an established constitution, but Carthage and Rome were exceptions to the rule. To the Hellenic mind, this meant they were not altogether barbarians— that is to say, incomprehensible foreigners whose speech was pilloried as sounding like "bar bar"—and, at least in this regard, were allowed to become honorary members of the club of civilized nations. The philosopher Aristotle was a connoisseur of constitutions and found that the Carthaginians had "an excellent form of government." He went on, "The superiority of their constitution is proved by the fact that the common people remain loyal to it. They have never had any revolution worth speaking of, and have never been under the rule of a popular dictator"—unlike many if not most Hellenic states, he might have added.

The Punic and Roman constitutions were in some ways similar, for they were both "mixed"—that is, they contained elements of monarchy, oligarchy, and democracy. It is unlikely that Carthage (pace Dido) was ever ruled by a king or queen, but at various times one leading family or clan dominated the government. In the third century, there were two chief officials, the *sufets;* this is the same word as the Hebrew *shophet,* usually translated as "judge," as in the Book of Judges. So we may infer that *sufets* exercised a judicial as well as an executive role. Like Roman consuls, they were elected by an assembly of the People, held office for only a year, and probably shared power with one other colleague. Candidates for office had to be wellborn and wealthy.

A Council of Elders drawn from the upper class advised the *sufets* on the full range of political and administrative issues; there were several hundred members, and a standing committee of thirty dealt with pressing business and, as is the way with such groups, probably managed the council's agenda. If council and *sufets* agreed on a course of action, there was no need for it to be submitted to the assembly. So far, so conventional. More constitutionally innovative was a special panel of 104 members of the Council of Elders. Called the Court of the Hundred and Four Judges, it controlled justice and the law courts and, like the Spartan *ephors,* looked after state security and supervised the activities of officials. It had something in common with a Ministry of the Interior in a police state.

Unlike Roman consuls, the *sufets* had no military duties. There was a separate post of general to which anybody could be elected. Carthage's characteristic mode was one of peaceful commerce. When wars did occur, they were usually fought a long way from home and regarded as short-term upheavals best handled by short-term appointees. In times of peace, *sufets* could simultaneously serve as generals, too, but if Carthage was at war the door was opened wider to attract proven military ability.

Self-confidence was an essential qualification for Punic generals, for theirs was a dangerous job. Failure on the battlefield was completely unacceptable to the authorities, and often led to instant crucifixion. Success also brought negative consequences, for the home government feared that victorious commanders would return to Carthage with their mercenaries and seize power.

Of the three elements of the Punic constitution, there is no doubt that oligarchy had the upper hand. The Carthaginians' main occupation was making money, and few objected to the wealthy being in charge of government. The mass of people failed to develop the solidarity and capacity for collective action that marked the Roman *populus*. In our terms today, Carthage was more of an international corporation than a nation-state.

Whatever reservations we may have about Punic politics and society, it is worth recalling Cicero's remark: "Carthage would not have maintained an empire for six hundred years had it not been ruled with statesmanship and professionalism."

THE GREEKS HAD largely been driven out of the western seas, but they had no intention of letting go of Sicily. With intermittent hostilities between them and Carthage for three hundred years, the island was still the flash point between the two halves of the Mediterranean world. And now a newcomer had arrived on the scene, Rome. A spark presented itself.

If ever evidence were required of the danger posed by mercenaries, the story of what happened to the city of Messana, guardian of the straits between Sicily and Italy, stood as a terrible example. A band of daredevils from Campania was hired by the ruler of Syracuse. On his death in 289, they found themselves unexpectedly out of work. They liked Sicily and the soldier's life away from home, but what were they to do? Reluctantly en route back to Italy, they came upon wealthy, beautiful, pacific but gullible Messana. This was the mercenaries' last chance to stay on the island, and they had a smart idea. They insinuated themselves into the city as friends and, betraying their unsuspecting hosts, one night took possession of it. According to Polybius:

They followed up this action by expelling some of the citizens, massacring others and taking prisoner the wives and families of their dispossessed victims, each man keeping those whom he happened to have found at the moment of the outrage. Lastly they divided among themselves the ownership of the land and all the remaining property.

This hijacking of a city went unpunished. The mercenaries, who named themselves Mamertines—after Mamers, the Sabellian version of the war god Mars—transformed Messana from a quiet trading emporium into a raiding base. They applied the only skills they were able to command: they made a living from plundering nearby towns, capturing unwary merchant ships, holding people they abducted for ransom, and generally disseminating mayhem. They impartially damaged Carthaginian and Greek interests.

Eventually, the greatest power in western Sicily, Syracuse, decided that enough was enough. In about 270, its young despot, Hiero, defeated the Mamertines in a pitched battle and arrested their leaders. This halted their depredations, although they still held Messana. A few years later, Hiero felt it was time to put an end to the Mamertines altogether and besieged Messana.

These superannuated and ageing hirelings made a fateful decision, or, rather, two decisions. Some of them appealed for help to a passing Carthaginian fleet, which accepted the commission and garrisoned the citadel. When he saw Punic ships in the harbor, Hiero did not want more trouble than he could handle and tactfully retired to Syracuse. Then another faction called on the Romans for support.

The Senate was at a loss. The Mamertines were the most disreputable of victims. Across the narrow water from Messana some other Campanians, this time serving in the Roman army, had been sent to Rhegium as a garrison during the war against Pyrrhus. Inspired by the Mamertines, they had committed a copycat massacre of its citizens and taken over the town. Rome refused to tolerate such a scandalous breach of faith and sent an army to take the city. This it did, killing most of the renegades. Three hundred survivors were sent to Rome, where they were marched into the Forum, flogged, and beheaded.

How could the Senate conceivably go to the rescue of men who had committed exactly the same crime? But this was what happened, and the explanation was reason of state. The undeceived Hiero observed that the Romans were using "pity for those at risk as a cloak for their own advantage." The Carthaginians already dominated much of Sicily, and might very well cast a predatory eye northward across the narrow straits if they won Messana.

From the Senate's point of view, as Polybius noted, "they would prove the most vexatious and dangerous of neighbors, since they would hem Italy in on all sides and threaten every part of the country. This was a prospect that Rome dreaded. It was obvious that they would soon be masters in Sicily, if the Mamertines were not helped." The anxiety was not misplaced, for Sardinia and Corsica were already Punic possessions and the Etruscan port of Caere was so full of Carthaginian traders that it had been nicknamed Punicum. What was more, the cities of Greater Greece would expect their new master to consult their interests; the loss of Sicily to the "barbarian" African power would be a terrible symbolic blow to the Hellenic cause.

Opinion in the Senate was finely balanced and, most unusually, the matter was referred to a popular Assembly without a recommendation. Despite the fact that the Republic was worn down by years of nonstop fighting, a resolution in favor of sending help was carried. A consul was sent to Messana at the head of an army. He managed to slip through a sea blockade. The Carthaginian commander, lacking instructions, was finessed into withdrawing his troops from the city. The authorities in Carthage promptly had him crucified "for want of judgment and courage."

Both the Carthaginians and the Syracusans were shocked by the turn of events and, despite their long enmity, entered into an im-

probable *mariage de convenance* with the common aim of expelling
the Romans. However, the consul picked off each of their armies in
separate engagements before they could join forces. The astute
Hiero had second thoughts; judging that it was in Syracuse's long-
term interest to switch sides, he agreed to an alliance with Rome,
from which he never strayed during the rest of a long life. In the
coming years he remained an invaluable friend, offering the legions
a base and local supplies.

The parties had slipped into war without altogether intending to
do so or being fully conscious of the consequences. But once full-
scale hostilities had opened, the true reasons for the conflict emerged
like a mountain out of mist. Dio explains that Messana was no
more than a pretext:

> The truth is otherwise. As a matter of fact, the Carthaginians,
> who had long been a great power, and the Romans, who were
> now growing rapidly stronger, looked on each other with jeal-
> ousy. They were drawn into war partly by the desire of continu-
> ally acquiring more possessions—in accordance with the
> principle that people are most active when they are most
> successful—and partly by fear. Both sides alike thought that the
> one sure salvation for their own possessions lay in also obtaining
> those of the others.

Messana and the Mamertines faded into the background. (In fact,
we never learn what was the Mamertines' final fate; they simply
vanish and one can only hope they came to a bad end.)

The Senate cannot have had firm war aims. To secure Messana as
a Rome-friendly outpost may have been enough at the outset. But
once Hiero's friendship had been won and Syracuse became, in effect, a client kingdom, it was possible to be a little more ambitious
and attempt to push the Carthaginians back eastward into their
traditional zone of influence. Rome could then gather the Greek

settlements in central Sicily under its security umbrella. It soon became clear, though, that Carthage would not tolerate a Roman presence in Sicily, and it followed that conquest of the entire island was the only rational response.

Campaigning went well for the Romans, who captured Acragas, an important Greek city and the Punic headquarters. Nevertheless, the Senate realized that however well the war went on land, it would be impossible to expel the Carthaginians as long as they commanded the seas, transporting reinforcements, blockading harbors, and raiding Italy. Rome, which had never been much interested in maritime matters, would have to build a fleet.

THE SEA WAS busy but perilous. For hundreds of years sailors, Phoenicians and Greeks especially, had crisscrossed the Mediterranean, ferrying wheat from the Black Sea, boat timber from Berytus, woolen fabrics from Miletus. Heavy goods such as oil and wine were much more easily transported by ship than on carts lumbering along unmetaled roads. Merchant vessels could carry from one hundred tons of cargo to a maximum of about five hundred tons. Their hulls were broad and well rounded, and they were equipped with a single low, rectangular sail (sometimes with additional triangular sails). They had no rudders, and one or two steering oars fastened to the stern were used instead.

Warships were very different creatures—sleek, fast death machines. They were galleys with rows of oars to supplement sails. By the third century, the quinqereme was the craft of choice. It carried a crew of some three hundred oarsmen. It might be about forty meters long and, at sea level, five wide. The deck stood about three meters above the water. A metal beak was attached to the keel and projected from the bow, and the main tactic of attack was to ram an enemy midships and sink or, at least, swamp it. A quinquereme at action stations could attain more than ten knots an hour, but only in spurts. Five knots was a more likely average.

The word *quinquereme* derives from the Latin for "five oars." This is misleading, for it seems it was oarsmen not oars that were arranged in groups of five. They controlled three oars set one above another. Two men rowed with each of the top two oars and one with the bottom oar. The team occupied a wooden box, or frame, that jutted out of the ship's side.

Ships of every kind were vulnerable to bad weather and tended to hug the coast for safety. Few ventured out in the winter months. This was not only to avoid storms but also because of the increased cloudiness. In the daytime, mariners navigated by the sun and landmarks, and by the stars at night. Without clear skies, they were lost.

The Carthaginians had the most technically advanced navy, and for Rome to create a fleet from a standing start that could compete with them was a bold, some must have said foolhardy, enterprise. But just as the serendipitous capture of an Enigma code machine helped the British win the Battle of the Atlantic in the Second World War, so chance came to the Republic's rescue. Apparently, quinqueremes were unknown in Italy and Roman shipbuilders were completely inexperienced at building them. Polybius observes:

> It was not a question of having adequate resources for the project, for they in fact had none whatsoever, nor had they ever given a thought to the sea before this. But once they had conceived the idea, they embarked on it so boldly that without waiting to gain any experience in naval warfare they immediately engaged the Carthaginians, who had for generations enjoyed an unchallenged supremacy at sea.

At the beginning of the war, Rome had no warships of any kind and borrowed some small secondhand vessels from Tarentum and other Italiote cities to guard the transport of troops to Messana.

Luckily, all went well, and, even more luckily, a Punic quinquereme ventured too close to shore, ran aground, and fell into Roman hands.

We know from the discovery of the remains of a third-century military craft off the port of Lilybaeum that each part of it was marked with different letters, enabling speedy "flat pack" assembly. So it cannot have been a difficult or lengthy task to produce copycat versions of the captured ship. Within two months, despite the inexperience of their shipwrights, the Romans were the proud owners of a brand-new fleet, comprising one hundred quinqeremes and twenty triremes (galleys rowed by oarsmen in groups of three).

While the ships were being built, sailors—more than thirty thousand of them—were recruited. Their training had to be undertaken on dry land, however foolish those taking part must have felt. Polybius records what happened:

> [The trainers] placed the men along the rowers' benches on dry
> land, seating them in the arrangement as if they were on those of
> an actual vessel, and then stationing the keleustes [time-caller]
> in the middle, they trained them to swing back their bodies in
> unison bringing their hands up to them, then to move forward
> again thrusting their hands in front of them, and to begin and
> end these movements at the keleustes' word of command.

As soon as the ships were completed, they were launched and the crews went aboard for some "real-life" practice. Under the command of a consul-admiral, they then set sail for the high seas.

To have established a maritime arm in so short a space of time was an extraordinary achievement. In its wars with the Samnites and the campaigns against Pyrrhus, Rome had shown a capacity to hang on, to bear disaster, and to return grimly to the fray. Here was evidence now of a less reactive, more purely aggressive energy. The creation of a new fleet almost out of thin air revealed Rome's unremitting enthusiasm for new challenges. It had learned how to upgrade itself into a more expansive, more irresistible state of being.

WOULD THIS UNTESTED fleet win victories against the marine superpower of the age? An instant setback and the consul's humiliating capture by the enemy gave pause for thought. However hard the shipbuilders tried, the fact was that the Roman ships were heavier and clumsier than their Punic counterparts. The Carthaginians were masters of maneuver. They knew how to sink their opponents by ramming, and they avoided having to fight hand to hand.

Some creative but now anonymous Roman came up with a very clever idea that restored the balance of advantage. He invented a device called a *corvus,* or "raven." This was a wooden bridge with low railings attached to a vertical pole. Probably fixed near a ship's bow, it could swivel around and be raised or lowered by a system of pulleys. A spike was attached to its underside. A Roman warship would approach an enemy quinquereme and drop the bridge down onto its deck. The spike pierced the deck and held the bridge in place. Then a team of between seventy and a hundred marines, experienced soldiers all, crossed over to the other vessel and captured it.

In effect, the *corvus* transformed a sea battle into a land battle on water, and took the Carthaginians completely by surprise. In the summer of 260, the Romans received intelligence that the enemy was ravaging the countryside near Mylae (today's Milazzo), not far from Sicily's northeastern tip, and sent their entire fleet there. As soon as the Carthaginians sighted them, they sailed ahead without hesitation. They were full of scorn for these Italian amateurs and did not trouble to keep any formation. They were puzzled by the ravens but rowed on regardless.

To their dismay, the first thirty ships to engage were grappled and boarded. The rest of the Punic fleet saw what was happening and sheered off to encircle and ram the Romans. But they simply swung their gangways around to meet attacks from any direction. The Carthaginians, unnerved, turned and fled, having lost 50 ships out of a total of 130.

The Punic commander avoided execution because he had pro-phylactically sought and won advance permission from the authorities in Carthage to fight the battle. But when the cock-a-hoop Romans successfully extended their field of operations to Corsica and Sardinia his men mutinied and put him to death, perhaps by stoning.

An odd reversal of reputations was taking place. On the one hand, the Republic was ruling the waves, launching successful raids and scoring a devastating second victory over the enemy fleet; on the other, the Carthaginians were doing well on land in Sicily. They practiced a policy of attrition, avoiding open battle and forc-ing the Romans to undertake siege after lengthy siege of fortified hill town after hill town.

The Senate engaged in another strategic review. It was decided to exploit Rome's new superiority at sea, bypass Sicily, and send an expeditionary force to attack Carthage itself. In 256, the two con-suls and an armada of 330 ships set sail for North Africa; 120 foot soldiers joined each boat, making a total army strength of 120,000 in addition to the regular 100,000 oarsmen. This was a hugely am-bitious project, with an unprecedented number of lives at risk.

The Carthaginians saw that this was a crisis point and assembled an even larger fleet of 350 galleys. The two sides met at Cape Ecno-mus (today's Poggio di Sant'Angelo, in Licata), on Sicily's southern coast, and once again the Romans routed the enemy, sinking or capturing more than ninety ships. The way lay clear to the Punic capital.

The consuls disembarked safely to the east of Cape Bon, a prom-ontory at the opposite end of the Gulf of Tunis from Carthage, and set about plundering the countryside, ravaging fertile estates and capturing twenty thousand slaves. The campaign could not have gotten off to a better start. But summer was wearing on, and the Senate recalled one of the consuls, who sailed back to Italy with much of the army, loot, and captives. His colleague, Marcus Atilius Regulus, was left behind to winter in Africa with fifteen thousand infantry, five thousand cavalry, and forty ships. The Carthaginians realized, as they were meant to do, that this was no brief raid but an invasion. The legions intended to stay.

The Punic army came to the relief of a fort only twenty or so miles from the town of Tunes (today's Tunis). Nervous of the Roman infantry, its commanders did their best to avoid a set-piece battle but still managed to get dislodged, with heavy losses, from their safe position on high ground. Tunes then fell to Regulus. Refugees from the hinterland crowded into Carthage and food supplies fell dangerously low. The endgame was at hand.

The Carthaginians opened peace talks. Regulus was an unimaginative man with too high an opinion of himself. He wanted the campaign over during his year of office, and then the satisfaction of a triumph. He was in a hurry. Virtually master of the city, he felt that all he needed to do was state his terms for them to be accepted. These were unrealistically harsh and had the opposite of the intended effect. The Carthaginians were to withdraw from Sicily and Sardinia; all Roman prisoners of war were to be released, while Punic captives were to be ransomed. Rome's war costs were to be paid and an annual tribute levied. Carthage would be allowed to go to war only with Rome's permission. These conditions were tantamount to unconditional surrender, but while the situation of the Punic state was critical, it was by no means terminal. The talks foundered.

Meanwhile, the Carthaginian high command recognized that its generals were incompetent and, in the spring of 255, sought advice from a Spartan military expert on the best way of dealing with the invaders. Firm discipline and training were introduced, and the soldiers' morale rose. The Punic army marched out and trounced the complacent Romans. The victory was won by cavalry outflanking the legions and destroying them. Regulus and five hundred others were captured, and of the rest of his force only two thousand made their escape from the field of slaughter.

Regulus's fate is uncertain. He most probably died of natural causes in captivity. A tradition grew that he was released on his honor to negotiate a treaty at Rome. He advised the Senate to reject the Punic proposals and, keeping his word, returned to Carthage. According to a first-century historian, an acquaintance of Cicero:

> They locked him in a dark and deep dungeon, and a long time later brought him out into the bright light of the sun, held him in its direct rays and forced him to look up at the sky. They even pulled his eyelids apart up and down and sewed them fast, so that he could not close his eyes.

Others report that he died from sleep deprivation.

The disaster put an end to the invasion, but it was not yet complete. The Senate had intended to send out a fleet to blockade Carthage while Regulus attacked from the city's landward side. News of the debacle arrived before the fleet set out, but some 210 vessels were dispatched to rescue what was left of the expeditionary force. This they accomplished, brushing off a Carthaginian fleet and raiding the countryside for provisions. On their way home, though, they sailed into a tremendous storm. Hampered by their *corvi,* most ships were driven onto the rocks off the southeastern corner of Sicily. About 25,000 soldiers and 70,000 oarsmen drowned. In no previous war had Rome lost so many men at a single blow. The fleet was soon rebuilt, but in 253 it, too, was destroyed in a storm after raiding the African coast. This time, 150 ships were lost.

It is hard to know how much these catastrophes owed to bad luck. No doubt, something, but it seems that Rome's admirals understood fighting better than they did seamanship. Whatever the explanation, the public in Italy was shocked by the losses at sea and even Rome could not stand this human hemorrhage. The decision to fight Carthage by sea had failed. The Carthaginians were exhausted, too, not only by the struggle with Rome but also by a long-standing insurgency by the Numidians, their African neighbors. The war had reached a stalemate. For the next two years, there was a lull in hostilities.

A NEW CLAUDIUS now arrived on the political scene at Rome. Grandson of Claudius Caecus, the Blind, Publius possessed a full share of the clan's awkward, arrogant genes (or else was typecast by later disobliging historians). He was given the cognomen of Pulcher, meaning beautiful or pretty, so good looks can be inferred— or perhaps merely vanity about his looks.

The campaign in Sicily remained a long, hard slog, but Rome made some progress, capturing the Punic city of Panormus (today's Palermo). Lilybaeum, on the island's western tip, was one of Carthage's last two strongholds. In 250, it was decided that a further effort should be made to clear Sicily of Carthaginians. A consular army and a new fleet of two hundred ships was sent out from Italy and invested the highly defensible port.

Consul for the following year, Claudius decided to launch a surprise attack on nearby Drepana (close to modern Trapani), the only other Punic base. Before battle commenced, he took the auspices in his capacity as admiral. An auspice was an omen as revealed through the observed behavior of birds—how they flew, sang, or ate. On this occasion, some sacred chickens were given food. They refused to touch it, a very bad sign, and Claudius ought to have aborted his enterprise, at least for that day. Instead, he lost his temper and threw the fowls into the sea, with the words "Let them drink, if they won't eat!"

The raid was an embarrassing failure. Apparently the Roman ships were not equipped with the *corvus,* allowing the enemy full scope for maneuver and ramming. Claudius lost more than 90 galleys (out of 120), although many of the crew made it to shore and rejoined the army outside Lilybaeum.

But a fresh disaster quickly followed. A consular fleet of 120 ships accompanying 800 transports sailed from Syracuse to resupply the army outside Lilybaeum. It was outsmarted by the enemy and driven without a battle onto the rocky coastline of southern Sicily. The Carthaginian admiral, an experienced sailor, detected a change in the weather and withdrew behind a promontory, Cape Pachynus (today's Cape Passero), leaving the Romans to face a tempest that blew unforgivingly at the shore. The entire fleet was wrecked, except for twenty ships.

Claudius was recalled and put on trial. He was accused of impiety as well as of commanding without due care and attention. A thunderstorm, a bad omen, halted the trial, but he was impeached a second time and found guilty. He was heavily fined and only just escaped the death penalty. He did not long survive his disgrace and may have killed himself. Not long after his death, one of his sisters, another chip off the old block, was returning home from the Games in her litter and was held up by large numbers of people in the street. "If only my brother were alive," she exclaimed, "he might lose another fleet and thin out these crowds!"

ROME WAS NOW without a navy and was too exhausted to raise another one. Carthage also was content to let sleeping dogs lie. It was running out of money and had to debase its coinage. It was reduced to asking its North African neighbor Ptolemy II of Egypt for a large loan. The king was too wily to intervene in a quarrel between two states, both of which he wanted to be on good terms. He explained, dryly, "It is perfectly proper to assist one's friends against one's enemies, but not against one's friends." Meanwhile, the Senate had relatively few financial worries, for Hiero was minting large quantities of silver and bronze coinage and helped finance his ally's war effort.

Although nothing much was happening to relieve the Sicilian

stalemate, the Romans were in much the stronger position, for the enemy had only a toehold on the island. Lilybaeum and Drepana remained under siege. In 247, an energetic young Punic commander, Hamilcar Barca, arrived in Sicily after raiding southern Italy. He was probably too much of a realist to suppose he could win the war, but he aimed to at least wear the enemy down. He mostly avoided pitched battles and adopted guerrilla tactics. He made a permanent camp on a mountain not far from Panormus and later at the high-altitude city of Eryx, although the temple sacred to Astarte, the Phoenician goddess of fertility and sexual relations, which was perched on a mountaintop above Eryx, remained in Roman hands. From these bases, he launched hit-and-run attacks. He scored many successes, although they were more spectacular than of strategic importance.

The weary years passed. Both sides were being driven to despair by the strain of an unbroken succession of hard-fought Sicilian campaigns. Polybius writes:

> In the end the contest was left drawn; . . . but they left the field like two champions, still unbroken and unconquered. What happened was that before either side could overcome the other . . . the war was decided by other means and in another place.

This was because Hamilcar's efforts did achieve something, for they persuaded Rome, not for the first time, that it would not win the war on land.

So the Senate braced itself for one last life-and-death effort. It would launch another fleet and, for the third time, try its fortunes at sea. It raised a loan, repayable in the event of victory, and no doubt the wealthy and the well-to-do were pressed for "voluntary" patriotic contributions. Individuals and syndicates each promised to pay for a quinquereme. Two hundred warships were built and fitted out in short order, on the more technically advanced and lighter model of a Punic galley captured off Lilybaeum. These vessels were not equipped with *corvi,* in the belief that their crews were expert enough now to outdo the enemy at its own combat methods.

The arrival of a new Roman fleet in Sicilian waters in the summer of 242 astonished the enemy. The Carthaginians' own ships were laid up at home, for the crews were needed for continuing wars in Africa. By March of the following year, they managed to man about 170 ships, recruiting sailors mostly from citizens. The plan was to resupply Hamilcar's forces, take on board some of his best mercenaries as marines, and return to the open sea to face the Romans. Because of a lack of transports, the warships were weighed down with freight.

Unluckily for the Carthaginians, the commanding consul, Gaius Lutatius Catulus, learned that they were approaching and lay in wait for them at the island of Aegusa off Lilybaeum. He warned his crews that a battle would probably take place the following day. With dawn, though, the weather deteriorated. A strong breeze blew and it would be difficult for the Romans to beat up against the wind. However, they dared not wait and risk the Carthaginian fleet's linking with Hamilcar's land forces, so an attack was decided. The fleet was marshaled in a single row facing the enemy.

The Carthaginians stowed their masts and, cheering one another on, advanced toward the enemy. Their confidence was ill-placed: the heavily laden ships were clumsy to maneuver; the new crews were poorly trained; and such marines as there were were raw recruits. They were swiftly put to flight. Fifty ships were sunk outright and seventy captured. The poor remainder raised their sails and ran before the wind, which had swung to an easterly, to make their escape. The victorious Roman consul sailed to the army at Lilybaeum and busied himself with disposing of the men and ships he had captured. This was a considerable task, for he had in his possession nearly ten thousand prisoners.

Carthage had shot its bolt. No longer in control of the seas, it could not supply its forces in Sicily and had none at home with which to continue the war. Hamilcar was given full powers to take what steps he deemed necessary. All his instincts were to continue the fight, but he was too prudent a commander not to see that this was impossible. He sued for peace.

Catulus's opening position was that he would not agree to a cease-fire until Hamilcar's army handed over its arms and left Sicily. Hamilcar replied, "Even though my country submits, I would rather perish on the spot than go back home under such disgraceful conditions." The Romans conceded the point and, in the event, agreed to fairly lenient terms. The two warring states were to be friends and allies; Carthage should evacuate Sicily and not make war on Hiero, return all prisoners without ransom, and pay substantial reparations in annual installments over twenty years.

The authorities in Rome took a sterner view and refused to ratify the draft treaty. Ten commissioners were sent to Sicily to renegotiate it. They raised the indemnity and reduced the repayment period to ten years. Perhaps as a compensating concession to Hamilcar, a new clause stated that the allies of both parties should be secure from attacks by the other.

SUDDENLY, THE WAR was over. It had lasted twenty-three years and cost hundreds of thousands of lives (most of them Romans or their allies). As Polybius wrote in the second century, it was "the longest, the most continuous and the greatest conflict of which we have knowledge." Nevertheless, it had not been a struggle *à outrance*. As in a boxing match, the decision had been given on points, not by a knockout.

In essence, the quarrel had been over who was to control Sicily. That question was now settled, for the island was to become Rome's first province. A *provincia* usually signified an elected official's sphere of activity (for example, a campaign against a particular enemy), but from now it began to take on its conventional meaning as a territory outside Italy under Rome's direct rule. This was a novelty, for in Italy the Republic usually imposed its will by treaty or by absorption. It preferred to allow local administrations to govern themselves. But Sicily was rather too large and too far away to be left safely to its own devices. A governor was appointed, probably a former praetor.

The loss of Sicily was a setback, a bad one, but not a mortal blow. In fact, it seems that Carthage had already been contemplating expansion elsewhere. For some time it had been fighting on two fronts, battling with local tribes to enlarge its lands in Africa while simultaneously trying to fend off the Romans.

Rome showed that, in addition to stamina, it had a killer instinct, and was beginning to imagine for itself an imperial destiny. By contrast, its Punic opponents were willing enough to endure but they did not have a hunger for victory, nor did they ever come close to achieving it. They did not want the war, they did not choose the war, and if only the war would go away they could concentrate on their peaceful habit of wealth creation.

And, in spite of defeat, that was what the peace allowed them to do. Carthage remained a great mercantile power and still dominated the trade routes of the Western Mediterranean. The voyages of Hanno and Himilco had pointed the way long ago to a prosperous future in corners of the world free from the aggressive interference of their new "friends and allies."

12

"Hannibal at the Gates!"

THE ELDERLY GENERAL WAS A VISITOR AT COURT. NO
longer in command of any armies, he was a wandering exile.
He was hoping to be military adviser to Antiochus the Great, lord
of many of the Asian lands conquered a century before by Alexander the Great. The king was pondering a war with that annoying
new Mediterranean power, Rome, and was uncertain of his guest's
loyalty.

In response, the old man told a story to prove his bona fides:

I was nine years old and my father was about to set off on a military expedition to Spain. I was standing beside him in the temple of Baal Hammon where he was conducting a sacrifice. The
omens proved favorable, and my father poured a libation to the
gods and performed the usual ceremonies. He then ordered all
present to stand back a little way from the altar and called me to
him. He asked me affectionately if I would like to come on the
expedition. I was thrilled to accept and, like a boy, begged to be
allowed to go. My father took me by the hand, led me up to the
altar and made me place my hand on the victim that had been
sacrificed and swear that I would never become a friend to the
Romans.

The king was convinced and put the old man on his payroll.

For the little boy, the oath he swore that day was a defining, emotionally purifying moment. It remained a vivid memory and guided his actions all his life. He was Hannibal the Carthaginian—a military genius and, in all its long history, the Roman Republic's most formidable enemy.

When, as commander of a great army, he camped outside Rome's walls, it was a monstrous, never-to-be-forgotten image of nightmare; in future, if Roman children were boisterous their parents would calm them by uttering the worst threat imaginable: *"Hannibal ad portas"* ("Hannibal's outside the city gates").

HANNIBAL'S FATHER WAS the energetic Hamilcar Barca, who had commanded Carthage's armed forces in Sicily during the final years of the First Punic War. His arrival on the island in 247 coincided with his son's birth. Barca was not a family or clan name but a nickname meaning "lightning" or "sword flash" (the word is related to the Hebrew *barak*), which conveys a reputation for liveliness and drive.

This was a quality Hamilcar appears to have asserted in his private as well as his public life. As well as siring three sons and at least one daughter, he became besotted with an attractive young male aristocrat, Hasdrubal (nicknamed the Handsome). Since Hamilcar was a leading politician and general, this gave rise to much critical comment (indeed, his rivals may have invented the story) and the authorities charged with oversight of morals banned the two men from seeing each other. Nothing daunted, Hamilcar married his lover to a daughter of his, on the grounds that it would be illegal to prevent a father-in-law and his son-in-law from meeting.

Once Hamilcar had negotiated the peace that brought the war in Sicily to a close, he sailed back to Carthage, leaving to others the thankless task of repatriating the multiethnic Punic mercenary army. Being an agile tactician, he wanted to distance himself as far as possible from the humiliating capitulation to Rome and the problem of how a bankrupt state could pay off its soldiery. He also had to deal with charges of maladministration brought by his political enemies.

The return of twenty thousand mercenaries proved to be a mistake of truly disastrous proportions and nearly led to the destruction of Carthage. They were not Punic citizens, and their first loyalty was, very naturally, to themselves, not to their employers. The cash-strapped authorities paid them only a small proportion of the money owed, and the men promptly revolted. It was a mortal crisis, for the rebels *were* the national army and there was no other soldiery with which to resist them. The Carthaginians were obliged to recruit in short order a citizen force and, with the small amount of cash in its coffers, hire some new mercenaries.

To begin with, an incompetent commander was appointed and the war went very badly. So Hamilcar was given a small force to try his hand at defeating the insurgents. Both sides perpetrated disgusting acts of cruelty. Hamilcar trapped the mercenary army and eventually the revolt collapsed. Anyone luckless enough to fall into his hands was crucified. One of the main leaders, an African named Matho, endured a parody of a triumphal procession through the streets of Carthage. He was led along by young men who, Polybius writes, "inflicted on him all kinds of torture." What this may have meant in practice was imagined by Flaubert in his novel *Salammbo:*

> A child tore his ear; a young girl, with the point of a spindle hidden in her sleeve, split his cheek. They tore out handfuls of hair and strips of flesh; some had sponges steeped in excrement on the end of sticks and rammed these into his face. Blood was streaming from his throat and the sight of it excited the crowd to a frenzy. To them this man, the last of the barbarians, symbolized the entire barbarian army; they were avenging themselves on him for all their disasters, their terror and their shame.

One final twist in the story deepened the rancor against Rome among leading Carthaginians. Mercenaries on the Punic island of Sardinia revolted in solidarity with their comrades in Africa. They came under pressure from native inhabitants and appealed to Rome for help. In 238/7, the Senate decided to send an expedition to take over the island. When the Carthaginians learned of this, they reminded the Senate that Sardinia was still regarded as their possession and they intended to recover it. The response was both surprising and cynical. Despite the fact that they had not a shred of justification, the Romans claimed that Carthage's preparations were a hostile act and delivered an ultimatum demanding an abdication of all its rights to the island and an indemnity of twelve hundred talents. These new conditions were added to the treaty of 241. Rome took possession of Sardinia and, with it, Corsica, which became a single province, like Sicily.

This was grand larceny. The historian Polybius was a great admirer of Rome, but even he condemned the annexation out of hand. He observed, "It is impossible to discover any reasonable ground or pretext for the Romans' action," and noted that men like Hamilcar neither forgot nor forgave the injustice.

IMMEDIATELY AFTER THE war ended, Hamilcar set off for Spain. Carthage was no place at present for a child, and it was little wonder that he took young Hannibal with him. But the motive for his departure was not personal; it was nothing less than to reverse the misfortunes of his motherland.

Little is known of internal Carthaginian politics, but there appear to have been two factions—one representing the landed interest, which much preferred expansion in Africa and the development of agriculture to risky foreign escapades, and the other consisting of merchants and traders who sought military protection for their activities in international waters. The former represented the governing oligarchy, and the latter advocated democratic reform.

Hamilcar was a leading figure in the second group. Although he was respected as a prudent statesman, the defeat in Sicily and the agony of the Mercenary War appear to have radicalized him. According to Diodorus:

> Later on after the conclusion of the Mercenary War, he formed a political power base among the lower classes, and from this source, as well as from the spoils of war, amassed wealth. Perceiving that his successes were bringing him increased power, he gave himself over to demagoguery and to currying favor with the People. In this way, he induced them to put into his hands for an indefinite period the military command over all Spain.

Hamilcar was behaving very much like a common Hellenic political type—the *turranos,* whose one-man rule was backed by the ordinary citizen. However, as it turned out, he had no ambitions to stage a coup d'état at Carthage. He merely wanted a free hand in Spain.

Two basic and interlinked challenges faced Carthage. How was it to rebuild its ruined economy? Both trade abroad and agricultural production at home had been gravely damaged by the recent military struggles, and the huge indemnity was an annual financial hemorrhage. And, taking the longer view, how was Carthage ever to get its own back on the Romans?

For Hamilcar, the answer to both questions lay in the Iberian Peninsula, which boasted a large human reservoir of potential military recruits and a seemingly inexhaustible supply of silver, iron, and other metals. He accepted that the loss of Sicily was permanent. Like all Carthaginians, he was humiliated by Rome's decision to annex the Punic islands of Corsica and Sardinia, a clear and scandalous breach of the peace treaty. The Phoenicians had long had mercantile outposts in Spain, and Gades was a great city and port. Hamilcar now decided to create a large and powerful Carthaginian province in the peninsula. Predictably, even those tribes which were accustomed to a Phoenician coastal presence put up resistance. Hamilcar applied the combination of clemency and cruelty that had served him when dealing with the rebellious mercenaries.

He brought with him his son-in-law-cum-lover, the beautiful Hasdrubal, who turned out to be as persuasive a diplomat as he was an aggressive and resourceful commander. Hasdrubal tactfully chose a Spanish princess as a second wife. During the next decade, the two leaders conquered most of southern and southeastern Spain. The Carthaginians also reorganized the silver-mining industry, massively increasing its productivity. It has been calculated that in later centuries a labor force of forty thousand slaves worked the mines and created a hundred thousand sesterces of profit every day. There is no reason to suppose that the Carthaginians in Hamilcar's day were any less efficient.

Having no strategic interest in Spain or assets to protect, the Romans paid little attention to these developments, but after a time decided to look into reports of Punic expansion (not that this meant Carthage had in any way breached an agreement). They sent an embassy to Hamilcar to ask for a briefing. It was received with carefully controlled courtesy. The Carthaginian general replied to its inquiries with a plausible explanation. "I have to make war on the Spaniards," he asserted, "to find the money to pay our indemnity to Rome." This very effectively silenced the envoys.

In 229, Hamilcar suffered a rare military setback at the hands of a Spanish chieftain. Hannibal and another son were with him, but he saved their lives by turning off onto a different road, the enemy following after him rather than the rest of his force. He was overtaken by the chieftain. To escape from him, he plunged on horseback into a river and drowned. Hamilcar's death did not dent Punic dominance in the peninsula, and a successor was swiftly appointed. At eighteen, his son Hannibal, though popular and able, was too

young to be considered. So the Council of Elders in Carthage confirmed Hasdrubal, who had shown himself to be far more than a
pretty face.

The new commander-in-chief continued his predecessor's good
work, achieving as much by negotiation as by force of arms. This
included a treaty with Rome: the Senate realized it had been "fast
asleep" and let Carthage recruit and equip a large army. It sent a
second embassy to Spain, and Hasdrubal agreed not to cross the
river Hiberus (the present-day Ebro). This was some way north of
territory then controlled by Carthage and was an easy concession;
and, from Rome's point of view, the accord satisfactorily protected
the interests of its anxious ally, Massilia, and its colonies on the
coast of northeastern Spain. The larger issue of the unwelcome
Punic revival remained unsettled, and, indeed, even the most ob-
durate senatorial envoy could hardly expect Carthage to renounce
its acquisitions simply on request.

Even if Rome had wanted to issue any threats at this time, it
would not have been able to follow them up, for the Republic was
facing a major crisis in northern Italy. The Celtic tribes that formed
the population of the Po Valley were infuriated by Roman en-
croachments and had mobilized a vast horde of warriors. In 225,
they were defeated at the Battle of Telamon but remained discontented and ungoverned neighbors.

Hasdrubal's enduring accomplishment was the foundation of a
new port, one of the best harbors in the Western Mediterranean,
which he called Carthago Nova (New Carthage, today's Cartagena).
The name was appropriate, for, like the mother city, it was built
on a promontory between a shallow lagoon and a bay. An island
at the mouth of the bay broke the waves of the sea. Occasionally,
a southwest breeze raised a slight swell, but otherwise few winds
ruffled the surface of the water inside. It was an ideal spot, not
merely for fishermen and merchants but as an up-to-the-minute
export facility for the growing silver trade. On the city's highest
eminence, Hasdrubal erected a magnificent palace, which stood as

a gleaming symbol of the new empire he and his father-in-law had created.

The message to the world was unmistakable: Carthage was back.

HASDRUBAL'S PACIFIC POLICIES did not save him from a violent end. One night in 221, he was killed in his lodgings by a Celtic slave, whose master he had had executed. The assassin was seized by bystanders but showed no sign of fear or remorse. Under torture, the expression on his face never changed.

Hannibal was now twenty-five years old, popular with his men, daring, with a quick and fertile brain and, though still young, experienced; he had, after all, spent the past fifteen years at the center of affairs while his father pursued his self-ordained mission of conquest. As a member of a leading democratic family, the rank and file acclaimed him as the new commander-in-chief, as did the popular Assembly at Carthage. Despite some opposition in the Council of Elders, Hannibal's appointment was confirmed.

He was soon to win Rome's complete attention and his personality became of absorbing interest. Livy summed up the general perception:

Reckless in courting danger, he showed superb tactical ability once he was at risk. Physically and mentally tireless, he could endure with equanimity excessive heat or excessive cold. He ate and drank according to need rather than for enjoyment. His hours for waking, like his hours for sleeping, were never determined by daylight or darkness: when his work was done, then and only then, he went to sleep, without needing silence or a comfortable bed. Often he was seen lying in his cloak on the bare ground among ordinary soldiers on sentry or picket duty. . . . He was the first to go into battle, and the last to leave the field.

On the negative side, he was notorious among his fellow citizens for his love of money and among Romans for his cruelty. This, at least, was the general impression. The accuracy of these criticisms is obscured by the murk of hostile propaganda. Also, in Polybius's wise words, pressure of circumstances made it exceptionally difficult "to pass judgement on Hannibal's real nature."

At this point, the young general's thinking was unknown. For two years, he maintained the Carthaginian policy of expansion but reverted to his father's aggressive military approach. He, too, took care to marry a local princess, as his brother-in-law had done. Soon Punic territory reached as far as the Hiberus. Did he have a long-term plan?

If he did not, events soon prompted him to create one. Saguntum was a small coastal town well south of the Hiberus, of no great military or commercial importance. It was on friendly but not formal terms with Rome, which at the town's request had acted as arbiter in an internal political dispute. It is not known exactly when this entente with Rome was agreed, but if it was before Hasdrubal's Hiberus treaty, then that, it might be supposed, superseded the entente. If afterward, Rome had incontestably breached the treaty, for Hasdrubal's commitment not to march his forces beyond the Hiberus could only mean that territory south of the river lay inside Carthage's sphere of influence. Either way, Hannibal had grounds for irritation with Roman meddling.

Then Saguntum became involved in a quarrel with a local, pro-Punic tribe, which appealed to Hannibal for assistance. For the Punic general, this was the last straw. However, he acted with caution, not wanting to give the Romans any pretext for war until he had completed his conquest of all territory south of the Hiberus, and fully secured his gains. This he achieved in 220, after a decisive victory over enemy tribes. He now controlled about half of the Iberian Peninsula, some 230,000 square kilometers.

Only Saguntum refused to recognize Punic dominance, but feared Hannibal's anger. The townsfolk could feel the noose tightening around their neck and sent embassy after embassy to Rome asking for urgent assistance. The Senate, busy with other matters, took a long time to respond but eventually dispatched envoys to warn Hannibal against taking action against Saguntum.

The Carthaginian general found them at the palace at Carthago Nova, where he was to spend the winter after the end of the campaigning season. He launched into a critique of Rome for intervening in Saguntum's internal affairs. He said, "We will not overlook this breach of good faith."

The Roman delegation concluded that war was inevitable and sailed to Carthage to repeat their protests, to no avail. Hannibal reported to the home authorities that Saguntum, confident in its Roman support, had attacked a tribe under Punic protection and asked for instructions. There was some token opposition, but the Council of Elders hesitated to take a stand against a well-liked and successful general in command of a large army and with support among the People. Hannibal was given a free hand, if without great enthusiasm.

In early 219, he lay siege to Saguntum. The inhabitants put up a stiff resistance, believing that the Romans would come and save them. They were to be disappointed, for the Republic had just finished one war, against the Celts of northern Italy, and was now busy with another, against the piratical Illyrians on the far side of the Adriatic Sea. The Senate never liked to fight on two fronts, so Saguntum went to the wall. It fell to Hannibal in the autumn after eight long, desperate months.

The defenders were driven by starvation to cannibalism. Once they had despaired of Rome, they gathered together all their gold and melted it with lead and brass to make it unusable. Believing it best to die fighting, the men sortied from the town and battled bravely but futilely against the besiegers. Appian writes:

> When the women watched the slaughter of their husbands from the walls, some threw themselves from housetops, others hanged themselves and others killed their children and then themselves.

Hannibal, whose temper had not been improved by a javelin wound, was so cross over the loss of the gold that he put all surviving adults to death by torture.

Everything now went into slow motion. Rome was of two minds what to do. The clan of the Fabii, led by a respected Senator, Quintus Fabius Maximus (to which was added the descriptive cognomen Verrucosus, or Warty, for he had a wart above his lip), opposed war, whereas the Cornelii Scipiones argued for it. It was not until early or late spring of 218 that, after a lively debate, the Senate sent some senior politicians to Carthage to deliver an ultimatum. They told the Council of Elders that either Hannibal was to be handed over to Rome or there would be war. A Punic spokesman pointed out that the annexation of Sardinia had been a Roman breach of the peace treaty of 241, and that Saguntum had not been listed in that treaty as a Roman ally and so was not protected by its terms from Carthaginian attack. The Romans did not like being seen to have acted illegally, and declined to reply to what had been said. Polybius reports what happened next:

> The senior member of the delegation pointed to the bosom of his toga and declared to the Council of Elders that in its folds he carried both peace and war and that he would let fall from it whichever of the two they chose. The Carthaginian sufet answered that he should bring out whichever he thought best. When the envoy replied that it would be war, many of the Elders shouted at once, "We accept it."

The Romans went home and, for a time, very little seemed to happen. It was assumed that the war would be fought out in Spain and in Africa. So the two consuls, Publius Cornelius Scipio and Titus Sempronius Longus, raised armies for that purpose. Sometime in the summer, they set off from Italy in different directions. Scipio took ship for Massilia, after which he was to march to the

Pyrenees. Meanwhile, his colleague established himself in Sicily and laid his invasion plans.

HANNIBAL HAD OTHER ideas. Although no record survives of his having said so, he must have thought long and hard about his next step, which was nothing less than the invasion of Italy.

He did not acccept the verdict of the First Punic War as final, and we may strongly suspect that his dead father, Hamilcar, had been of the same mind. This is not to say that either of them intended war from the outset. Twenty years had passed since the loss of Sicily, and many of these were spent on the arduous, absorbing, and ambitious task of reasserting the greatness of Carthage and building a Spanish empire. An eventual second round with Rome would have seemed to them a possibility rather than a realistic objective. However, now that it had arrived, the energetic young commander relished the prospect.

For Hannibal, the unfair and illegal annexation of Sardinia and the massive reparations still rankled. In his eyes, the Saguntum affair was yet another example of Rome playing fast and loose with freely negotiated agreements. Romans liked to sneer at *Punica fides,* Carthaginian "good faith"; what price now *Romana fides?* Perhaps the most important factor in persuading Hannibal to make war was his belief that he was able to do so with a good prospect of success. The conquest of half the Iberian Peninsula gave him two huge advantages—for all practical purposes, an inexhaustible flow of cash, thanks to the silver mines, and of manpower, thanks to the fierce Spanish tribesmen whom he now governed. There would never be a more favorable opportunity for a return match.

He had no intention of destroying Rome altogether; rather, he would cut it down to size. This would mean unpicking its web of Italian "allies." If he could give them back their freedom, he would remove from Rome what *he* had just won in Spain—the money and men that a minor regional player needed if it was to become a great power. This political objective determined his military strategy. He had to take the war to Italy.

He laid his preparations carefully and secretly. He dispatched a large contingent of Spanish troops to protect North Africa and of African troops to garrison Spain; in this way, he insured himself against disloyalty by separating soldiers from their home communities. He entrusted the defense of the peninsula to his younger brother, another Hasdrubal. He would also, and crucially, depend on him for reinforcement as and when required, and for supplies of ready money. Messages were sent to forewarn the Gallic tribes whose territory in southern France he would have to traverse and to make logistical arrangements for the upkeep of a large army.

Hannibal went to Gades and sacrificed at the famous Temple of Melqart-Hercules, with its eight columns of brass on which the money-minded Phoenicians had inscribed the cost of its construction, before proceeding to his capital, Carthago Nova. In May or thereabouts he set out northward with an army of about ninety thousand infantry and twelve thousand cavalry. He crossed the contentious river Hiberus and, after conducting a quick blitzkrieg in northern Spain, sent a number of troops home to stand ready as a reserve for future deployment. He crossed the Pyrenees and advanced into Gaul with a force of fifty thousand infantry, nine thousand cavalry, and thirty-seven war elephants. He forced a crossing of the river Rhodanus (the Rhône), with difficulty persuading his nervous elephants to be drawn across the water on large earth-surfaced rafts.

A LEGENDARY PERSONALITY from the early years of Rome's story (see pages 12 and 13) now puts in a reappearance.

Hannibal took care to promote his image as a great commander, and as a practitioner of moral and social virtues. Like Alexander the Great (as ever a model for would-be conquerors), he gathered round him a group of trusted Greek intellectuals. One was his old teacher, a certain Sosylus of Sparta, who had taught him Greek, a language in which he was fluent, and another the distinguished historian Silenus, the author of a four-volume study of Sicily, whom Cicero praised as a "thoroughly reliable authority on Hannibal's life and achievements."

Their task was not simply to record the events of the campaign but to put the best possible gloss on them and even to tell symbolic stories (invented or enhanced) about their hero. It was Silenus who first recounted a dream Hannibal was supposed to have had after taking Saguntum. He was summoned by Jupiter to a council of the Olympian gods and ordered to invade Italy. One of those at the assembly was produced as his guide. After he and his army began their march, the guide told him not to look back. He could not resist doing so. But unlike Orpheus, who yielded to a similar temptation when leaving the underworld ahead of his wife, Hannibal was not punished but given a vision of the horrors to come. According to Cicero:

> He saw a vast monstrous wild beast, intertwined with snakes, destroying all of the trees and shrubs and buildings wherever it went. Staggered, he asked the god what such a terrible occurrence could mean. "It is the devastation of Italy," answered the god. "Go forward and do not worry about what is happening behind your back."

The beast sounds very much like the Hydra, a many-headed serpent whom Hercules killed during one of his labors. In the dream it stands for Rome, and Hannibal is cast as the brave demigod.

This was no casual identification. The Punic commander presented himself as a new Melqart-Hercules who restaged the demigod's original journey from west to east, which began at Gades, proceeded up Spain, along southern Gaul, and as far as Italy. (In the original legend, of course, Hercules then crossed over into Greece.)

He issued silver shekels to pay his troops, some showing Hercules with (almost certainly) the features of a bearded Hamilcar and others of his clean-shaven son. A reconciler of different cultures, especially the Greek and the Phoenician, an upholder of law, a dauntless fulfiller of labors, Hannibal was to be a standard-bearer for civilization, sent by heaven to defeat the cruel, barbaric power that was Rome. It was these qualities which helped him unite his disparate army and would, he hoped, persuade the peoples of Italy to switch their allegiance to him.

Hannibal also seems to have appealed to one of Rome's most implacable enemies on Mount Olympus, the goddess Juno. She may have reconciled herself to the fall of her city of Veii, but she forgot nothing and forgave nothing—especially her humiliation at the hands of Paris, prince of Troy, and Aeneas's rejection of her favorite, Dido, the lovelorn queen of Carthage.

MEANWHILE, THE UNKNOWING Consul Scipio arrived in Gaul on his way to Spain at about the same time as the Carthaginians, coming in the opposite direction. The armies brushed against each other, Hannibal avoiding an engagement and slipping away toward the Alps and Italy. It was only now that, with a shock of dismay, the Romans realized what Hannibal's destination was. The consul chose not to chase after him; instead, he sent most of his force onward to Spain as planned, and he himself returned to Italy, where he would confront Hannibal with new troops. It was the single most important strategic decision of the war, for if Roman legions were active in Spain they should be able to remove or, at least, severely limit Hasdrubal's opportunities to reinforce his brother.

In October or early November, Hannibal crossed the Alps. He would probably have taken Hercules' route by the relatively straightforward Montgenèvre Pass, but he had to avoid Scipio and so marched north away from the sea. We do not know which pass the Carthaginians actually chose (it was a matter of dispute even in ancient times), but wherever it was they were confronted by aggressive mountain tribesmen and unseasonable snow. Both men and animals made heavy going of it. The descent was just as hazardous as the ascent. The track down the mountainside was narrow and steep. New snow lying on top of old made surfaces treacherous. At one point an earlier landslide had removed part of the pathway, and the army looked fearfully over the edge of a brand-new precipice. Going back was out of the question—but how to go on? The pass had become an impasse.

Hannibal refused to admit defeat at the hands of nature. He had the snow cleared off a ridge and made camp. Livy writes:

> It was necessary to cut through rock, a problem they solved by the ingenious application of heat and moisture; large trees were felled and lopped, and a huge pile of timber erected; this, with the opportune help of a strong wind, was set on fire, and when the rock was sufficiently heated the men's rations of sour wine were flung upon it, to render it friable. They then got to work with picks on the heated rock, and opened a sort of zigzag track, to minimize the steepness of the descent, and were able, in consequence, to get the pack animals, and even the elephants, down it.

And then, all at once, the ordeal was over. The soldiers, freezing, filthy, unkempt, and starving, found themselves strolling amid sunny Alpine pastures with woods and flowing streams. Hannibal gave them three days' rest to recover and clean themselves up, and then they continued their descent into the plains—in Livy's words, "a kindlier region with kindlier inhabitants."

The news of Hannibal's arrival on Italian soil at the head of a large army stupefied public opinion, for at Rome the last that had been heard of him was his capture of Saguntum. Although Celts regularly went to and fro across the Alps, there was widespread amazement at his achievement in taking a large army across the mountains in wintry weather. Rather than a campaign in Spain, the Senate now had to contemplate a struggle in its backyard: It canceled the invasion of Africa and instructed Sempronius to rush north. Worse, in place of the usual incompetent generals of the First Punic War, it faced in Hannibal a commander of daring, stamina, and élan.

However, this public-relations triumph came at a high price. Since leaving Spain five months previously, Hannibal had lost more than half his army. As we saw, the Carthaginians had begun their journey with 50,000 foot and 9,000 horse. By the passage across the Rhodanus, these numbers had dwindled to 38,000 and 8,000, respectively. Only 20,000 infantry and 6,000 cavalry, plus a handful of elephants, made it to the valley of the mighty river Padus. The greater part of Hannibal's supplies had been lost, along with many pack animals. Undaunted, he immediately launched a recruitment drive among the discontented Celtic tribes of northern Italy, who regarded him as a liberator from their Roman conqueror, and soon 14,000 fresh volunteers had joined his ranks. A successful cavalry engagement near the river Ticinus convinced the Celts that they were backing a winner. The careful Scipio was in command, and nearly lost his life. Luckily, his seventeen-year-old son Publius was close at hand, as Polybius describes:

> Scipio had put his son in command of a picked troop of horse to ensure the boy's safety, but when the latter caught sight of his father in the thick of the action surrounded by the enemy, dangerously wounded and with only two or three horsemen near him, he at first tried to urge the rest of his troop to ride to the rescue. Then, when he found that they were hanging back because of the overwhelming number of the enemy around them, he is said to have charged by himself with reckless daring against the encircling cavalry.

This shamed his comrades, who followed him into the fray and saved his father. Scipio's wound incapacitated him (although it did not kill him), and he stepped down as commander.

Effective control of the legions was handed to his colleague, the incautious and overconfident Sempronius. Hannibal was lucky.

IT WAS A bitterly cold December morning with gusts of snow, on or around the winter solstice. The night before, there had been a downpour and the river Trebia, together with its accompanying web of streams running beside it, was in full spate. Hannibal decided to make the weather work for him.

The two armies, Carthaginian and Roman, both perhaps forty thousand strong, were encamped on either side of the river. The land was flat and treeless and suitable for a set-piece battle, but the Punic commander noticed that it was crossed by a watercourse with high banks that were densely overgrown with thorns and brambles. There was room here for quite a substantial special-service unit to hide away out of sight. Hannibal arranged for a body of a thousand cavalry and the same number of foot soldiers to be assembled and placed his younger brother Mago in charge of them.

After dark on the evening before the battle, once the army had eaten its evening meal, this force made its way through rain to its place of ambush. First thing in the morning, some Numidian horsemen galloped across the river and threw javelins at the Roman camp. Their instructions were to lure the consul Sempronius to lead out his army before the men had had breakfast, ford the Trebia, and offer battle. Sempronius, eager to fight before his term of office expired at the end of the year, was only too happy to oblige.

The legions struggled across the rushing river and formed up in battle order. The whole process must have taken several hours and the men were soaking wet, cold, and hungry. In contrast, before deploying, the Carthaginian rank and file had time to warm themselves by large fires in front of their tents. They breakfasted at leisure and groomed their horses. They were given portions of olive oil so that they could rub themselves down to keep their bodies supple.

After all this, the outcome of the battle itself was a foregone conclusion. The foot soldiers faced one another in the center and were
evenly matched, but the Punic cavalry on the wings soon drove
back their Roman counterparts. This exposed the legions' flanks to
attack. Then Mago's hidden force suddenly emerged and fell on
them from behind. Despite the fact that ten thousand Roman legionaries pushed their way through the enemy line out of the battle
and quit the field in good order, the day was lost. Well over half of
the Roman army was slaughtered.

On the Carthaginian side, the Spaniards and Africans were more
or less unscathed, but the newly recruited Celts suffered heavy
losses. Unluckily, the winter continued harsh and, in the coming
days, more rain, snow, and intolerable cold took their toll. Men and
horses perished. In this weather, Hannibal, riding the only surviving elephant, marched south through marshy terrain on the way to
Etruria. He suffered intense pain from a bout of ophthalmia and
lost the use of one eye.

For all that, it was the Romans who had been defeated. The Senate was not so much alarmed as energized. A hundred thousand
men were conscripted, and Sicily, Sardinia, and Rome garrisoned
against possible attack. The losses sustained by the four consular
legions at the Trebia were made good. Nevertheless, it was a dark
time. Many portents were reported to bode ill for Rome. A spring
sacred to Hercules at the Etruscan city of Caere was found to have
flecks of blood in it, and a propitiatory *lectisternium* was held—
a banquet at which an image of the demigod reclined on a couch,
with the food spread around him. Expensive gifts were donated to
shrines of hostile Juno—evidence, perhaps, that Hannibal's public-
relations campaign was working.

LAKE TRASIMENE, IN Etruria, was shallow, muddy, and humid,
a breeding ground of pike, carp, tench—and malarial mosquitoes.
Its northern shore was guarded by a line of steep hills. Approached

from the west, some high ground gently sloped down to the lakeside (near today's Borghetto, in the *comune* of Tuoro). It opened out onto a small plain that extended for a mile or so before closing in again and ending at almost but not altogether impassable heights. Beyond lay the way to the south.

In the spring of 217, the Punic army, well rested after its winter trials, marched down through Etruria, laying waste to the countryside as it went. It bypassed a Roman army led by a new consul, Gaius Flaminius, who immediately set off in hot pursuit. Hannibal reached the lake and turned east into the defile. An idea struck him; here was the ideal spot for an ambush, if only the consul was foolhardy enough to walk into the obvious trap. One of the habits of the Carthaginian was to seek out intelligence on enemy commanders and to tailor his tactics to what he knew of their personality. Flaminius, he discovered, was not without military experience, but as a plebeian he seems to have had a chip on his shoulder and was an impatient leader. He would have felt humiliated by having to take his legions through a devastated landscape, and now be eager for revenge.

This was a correct judgment. Flaminius saw the Punic army enter the defile and followed straight after, setting up camp on the plain. Hannibal's camp could be seen in open view right at the far end of the lake, but he had stationed most of his troops unseen in the hills, where the ground narrowed and there was no room for maneuver.

In the early dawn of 21 June, Flaminius formed up his troops into column of route and they proceeded along the lakeside. He did not trouble to send out scouts. Visibility was poor, for a heavy mist hung over the water and the shore. So when the Carthaginians charged down from the high ground, the surprise was complete. The Romans hardly knew what had hit them and there was little they could do to defend themselves. Nevertheless, the battle, or perhaps more accurately the bloodbath, lasted for three hours. Flaminius fought bravely, but at last was struck down by a Celtic lance. Livy takes up the narrative:

> The Consul's death was the beginning of the end. Panic ensued, and neither lake nor mountain could stop the wild rush for safety. Men tried blindly to escape by any possible way, however steep, however narrow; weapons were flung away, men fell and others fell on top of them. Many, finding nowhere to turn to save their skins, plunged into the lake until the water was up to their necks, while a few in desperation tried to swim for it—a forlorn hope indeed over that broad lake, and they were either drowned or, struggling back exhausted into shallow water, were butchered wholesale by the mounted troops who rode in to meet them.

A vanguard managed to push through the Carthaginian line and escape into the hills, but fifteen thousand Romans perished, while Hannibal lost only fifteen hundred men. When the news reached Rome, there was no attempt to hide the magnitude of the catastrophe. A praetor went to the Forum and announced, with becoming brevity, *"Magna pugna victi sumus"* ("We have been defeated in a great battle").

A YEAR PASSED, and the date was now 2 August 216. The scene was a windy, dusty plain in Apulia a few miles from the Adriatic coast. High summer in southern Italy brought fierce heat and a permanent chorus of cicadas. Within a space of five square miles, two armies, consisting in total of about 150,000 men, confronted each other. One of the great battles of the world was about to be fought, and has inspired generals down the ages. It is a rare military training college today whose curriculum does not include it.

After the Battle of Lake Trasimene and two routs in a row, the Romans had lost heart. A dictator was appointed for a six-month term of office, the warty Fabius Maximus. He seems to have attracted nicknames; as well as Verrucosus, he was called Ovicula, or "lambkin." According to Plutarch, this was

> because of his gentle and solemn personality when he was still a child. In fact, his calm, quiet manner, the great caution with which he took part in childish pleasures, the slowness and difficulty with which he learned his lessons, and his contented submissiveness in dealing with his comrades, led those who knew him superficially to suspect him of something like foolishness and stupidity . . . but his seeming lack of energy was only lack of emotion, his caution was prudence, and his never being quick nor even easy to move made him always resolute and reliable.

According to Cicero, he had read a lot "for a Roman."

Fabius raised two new legions and, adding them to existing Roman and allied troops, commanded an army of forty thousand men. He pursued a wise, but extremely unpopular, policy of tailing Hannibal but never offering battle. His idea was to wear down the enemy in the hope that eventually he would make a bad mistake and expose himself to defeat. The policy nearly brought a quick success, for Fabius bottled up the Carthaginians in mountainous territory. On the following night, Hannibal, never at a loss, tied burning brands to the horns of two thousand cattle and set the terrified animals to run around on the high ground. This bizarre ruse worked. The Romans thought they were about to be attacked and the Carthaginians crept away through the concealing dark.

The policy of delay also enabled the elderly dictator to train his new troops and allowed time to heal the Republic's wounded morale. But public opinion very soon swung against Fabius, who duly retired after his six-month term. A huge army of eighty-seven thousand men was assembled—that is, eight legions plus roughly the same number of allied troops. This would give them the edge over Hannibal, who disposed of only about fifty thousand soldiers.

The two consuls who succeeded Fabius held very different views of the plan of campaign. Lucius Aemilius Paullus, a member of one of the most ancient patrician clans, was a Fabian and believed Hannibal should be starved out of his winter quarters in southern Italy; but Gaius Terentius Varro, a plebeian parvenu much disliked by the *gratin,* argued that Rome should make the most of its advantage in numbers and provoke a full-scale battle as soon as possible.

They tracked Hannibal down to the neighborhood of a small town in Apulia called Cannae, amid the dust and the cicadas. As was the practice, they alternated command daily. Paullus was in charge when Hannibal led his army out and offered battle; he declined the invitation. The next day, Varro accepted the challenge. Immediately after sunrise, he sported the red flag, or *vexillum,* outside his tent, the traditional signal for battle. He formed up his army, with cavalry on the wings and a mass of infantry in the center; the right wing abutted against a river and the left against rising ground.

Hannibal looked carefully at the enemy and noticed that the foot soldiers were short of space, and as a result were in deep formation and rather squashed together. They would find it hard to maneuver. The Carthaginian general formed his troops in a way that would exploit that potential weakness. He lined his Celtic and Spanish infantry in a convex curve opposite the Roman center. Behind them, at either end and out of sight, he placed two substantial detachments of his best troops—Libyan infantry, well-trained and reliable. On his wings, his cavalry faced the Roman horse.

When the fighting started, the Roman center pushed back the Celts and the Spaniards, so that their line changed from convex to concave. Pleased to find more space to fight in, they unwisely continued to press forward until the Libyans suddenly came into view on either side and turned inward to attack them on their flanks.

Meanwhile, Hannibal's cavalry on his left wing routed their Roman counterparts, commanded by Consul Paullus. With great self-discipline, the victorious Celtic and Spanish horsemen then disengaged and crossed behind the Roman army to attack the enemy cavalry on the far wing, which fled in panic. For a second time, they pulled away and proceeded to attack the rear of the Roman infantry, which now found itself boxed in on all sides.

The rest of the battle consisted of exhausting hours of blood-slippery butchery. Gradually, the packed mass of Roman legionaries and allies was cut down. Paullus, felled by a stone from a slingshot, fought bravely to his last breath, but Varro escaped with seventy horsemen. He rounded up stragglers and took general charge of the grim aftermath. When he returned to Rome, crowds turned out to greet him "because he had not despaired of the Republic." He continued to receive public appointments, although he was never to lead a consular army again. This was Rome at its magnanimous best.

A larger group also managed to extricate itself from the hecatomb, among whom was Publius Scipio, now nineteen years old. He threatened to kill some young noblemen who chattered disloyally of fleeing abroad, and forced them to swear that they would never abandon their homeland.

Seventy thousand Romans lay dead on the battlefield. Twenty-nine senior commanders and eighty senators lost their lives. Cannae was the worst military disaster in Rome's history. Immediately, the Greek *poleis* and the local tribes of southern Italy switched their loyalty to Carthage. The famous city of Capua and other towns in Campania defected. After the death of the aged Hiero, Syracuse abandoned its long-standing alliance with Rome. Tarentum was captured by a clever trick (although the Roman garrison retained the citadel and control of the harbor).

Rome was inflamed by religious panic, stoked by portents and prodigies. In some inexplicable way, the gods were gravely offended. An embassy was sent to Delphi for advice, and two Greeks and two Gauls were buried alive in the city in a bid to regain divine favor. This extreme gesture was a sign of the despair and hysteria of the time, for human sacrifice was almost unknown in Roman religious practice.

Everyone could see that the Republic was staring total defeat in the face.

13

The Bird Without a Tail

CANNAE APPEARED TO BE THE END OF THE ROAD for Rome, but although nobody knew it at the time and many years would pass before peace came, the war was already won. This was because Hannibal depended for victory on two factors, and both failed him. These were the expected defection of Rome's Italian allies and the arrival of reinforcements from Spain.

First, the Republic's fair-minded concordat with the peoples it had conquered in central Italy more or less held good. The Republic could still draw on its large supply of men of fighting age to serve in its armies. Second, for seven years the former consul Scipio and his brother Gnaeus campaigned tirelessly in Spain, dismantling Hamilcar Barca's hard-won empire and preventing Hannibal's brother Hasdrubal from sending any troops to Italy. The Punic reservoir was drained.

But perhaps the most important factor of all was the Republic's sheer bloody-mindedness. After his brilliant sequence of victories, Hannibal (like Pyrrhus before him) expected the Romans to do the sensible thing and negotiate a peace. He did not understand that they were at their most obstinate in defeat. When knocked down, they would not lie down. The Carthaginian general offered to ransom the prisoners of Cannae, but the Senate refused to discuss anything whatever with the enemy, even though this meant consigning many Roman and allied citizens to slavery or execution.

By 211, much of the lost ground had been recovered. Fabius Maximus came into fashion again and set-piece battles were avoided. A new cognomen, Cunctator, or Delayer, was a badge of pride, as was recognized by the second-century epic poet Ennius. He famously wrote of Fabius that one man's procrastination saved the state:

Unus homo nobis cunctando restituit rem.

New legions were recruited, but they were divided into small forces rather than large armies, encircling the enemy like dogs and biting as opportunity offered. In an (unsuccessful) attempt to make the Romans break off their siege to regain Capua, Hannibal marched on Rome itself. He encamped three miles from the city and then rode up to the Colline Gate with a cavalry escort. He threw a spear over the wall; as he knew very well, the gesture was symbolic of wish rather than fulfillment. There were a number of temples near the gate, one of them dedicated to Fortuna. The Carthaginian left that undependable goddess to herself, but he paid his respects at a shrine to Hercules, whose metaphorical reincarnation he remained. This was evidently felt to be something of a propaganda coup, for a couple of years later the temple was removed to the safety of the Capitol. With its massive walls, Rome was in no danger of capture, but the visit was a terrifying event.

Cities that resisted Rome's military might were treated with merciless ferocity. Capua fell. Most of its citizens were dispersed without hope of return, its wealth was confiscated, and its leaders were beaten with rods and beheaded. What had been a rich and famous city was reduced to a dim agricultural market town, directly administered by a Roman official.

After a siege, Marcus Claudius Marcellus, an able if hotheaded commander, took Syracuse. Apparently, on the eve of its fall he looked down on the city from a hill and (not unlike Lewis Carroll's Walrus and Carpenter, we may think) wept at the havoc he intended to wreak. In the event, he looted so many paintings and statues that he boasted that he had taught the ignorant Romans to appreciate Greek art. During the sack, Marcellus was embarrassed by the unintended death of a brilliant but absentminded scientist and mathematician, Archimedes. He was absorbed by a diagram he had drawn in the sand and was oblivious of the rape and pillage going on around him. A passing soldier killed him.

In 209 Tarentum, betrayed to Hannibal, was betrayed again to Fabius. The city was sacked and a vast amount of war booty captured. Fabius showed less interest than Marcellus in art. When asked what he wanted done with some statues of the city's divine guardians, he replied, "The Tarentines can keep their gods, who are obviously angry with them."

Tellingly, Hannibal now spent his winters after the campaigning season in Italy's southern toe, a silent acknowledgment that he was no longer free to roam where he wished.

But then Carthaginian prospects in Spain took a sharp turn for the better. Within a few days of each other, the Scipio brothers were defeated and killed in two successive battles. Everything they had gained south of the river Hiberus was lost. Had the Punic generals the slightest aptitude for cooperating with one another, the Romans would very probably have been driven out of the peninsula altogether.

IN ROME, PEOPLE went into mourning for the two dead heroes and had no clear idea of the next step to take. They were tired of the war, and some exhausted allied communities said they were unable to send their due contingents to join the legions. The burning question of the hour was who could replace the Scipios. According to Livy, the Senate was unable to make up its mind whom to appoint to the Spanish command, and referred the question to the People. This self-denial was out of character and it is much more likely that public opinion favored a candidate of whom the political class disapproved, and that in some way the Senate was circumvented.

And there was indeed a rogue applicant for the job. This was Publius, the promising young son of the former consul Scipio. At a public election meeting for senior government appointments no name was put forward, and Publius suddenly announced that he wanted the commission. He was famous for his bravery at Trebia and Cannae, but he was only twenty-four years old. According to the rules, he was much too young for the job. But he brushed aside such quibbles, as he had done a few years previously when elected to the post of aedile. Objections were raised because of his youth, but he replied, rather pompously, "If the People want to make me aedile, then I am old enough."

The young man made a powerful speech to the Assembly. He was the only Scipio left to avenge his father and uncle, he said, and he promised not merely to win back Spain but to conquer North Africa and Carthage, too. This sounded boastful, but it cheered up his listeners and he won the command as a *privatus cum imperio* (a private citizen with the public authority of a proconsul) by a unanimous vote. Grumblings among senior politicians gave him pause, however, and he saw it could be argued that the People had acted impulsively. So he arranged for another session, at which he agreed to stand down if any older and more experienced candidate put himself forward. This took the wind out of the opposition. As he had anticipated, nobody wanted to risk the fury of the assembled citizenry. Silence fell, and his election was confirmed.

Scipio was a new type of Roman—dashing, attractive, humane, and proud to be a man of culture. Even at this early stage in his career, all could see that he was exceptionally gifted. Having been given a Greek education, he was impatient with Rome's traditions.

He had a pronounced sense of his own destiny and claimed always to consult the gods before making any important decision. Where, for the ordinary Roman, religion was a set of superstitious rules designed to placate volatile deities, he seems to have had, or claimed to have had, a more Hellenic, more mystical sense of the numinous. If he was in Rome on serious business he would go up to the Capitol, where he would sit alone and commune with supernatural powers. The temple dogs, it was said, never barked at him. He liked to convey the impression that there was a touch of the divine about him, and the story was bruited about that a snake slithered over the infant Scipio but did not harm him (echoing a legend about the childhood of Alexander the Great).

The historian Polybius was a friend of the Scipios, but he was a rationalist and believed that Scipio acted with calculation, perhaps even a degree of cynicism. There is something to this, for Scipio placed as much value on imaginative propaganda as did Hannibal. However, the most effective propaganda has a basis in truth. It is likely that this talented and arrogant young patrician believed his own publicity.

He turned out to be a brilliant field commander. When he arrived in Spain, he learned that there were three Carthaginian armies in different parts of the peninsula, and none of them were less than ten days' march from the Punic capital, Carthago Nova. In a bold move, the new commander led his legions several hundred miles at top speed from the river Hiberus to the city and laid siege to it. He threw up earthworks on its eastern, or landward, side, and launched assaults from that direction.

These were in fact diversions, for he had learned from local fishermen that the lagoon north of the promontory on which the city was built was shallow enough to be forded, especially in the early evening, when water ebbed from it through a channel into the bay south of the city. (This was perhaps the result of a regular breeze blowing up at that time of year.) Scipio ordered a specially picked unit with scaling ladders to wade through the lagoon and take the defenders by surprise. He promised money to the first soldiers to scale the walls and, typically, told them that the sea god Neptune had suggested the plan of attack to him. All went well: the water ebbed as predicted, the men entered the city, opened a gate, and let the legions in.

Scipio showed his lack of conventional *Romanitas* by not doing to Carthago Nova what had been meted out to the citizens of Capua, Syracuse, and Tarentum. The killing of civilians stopped as soon as the garrison surrendered. The legionaries were given leave to pillage for a short, fixed period, but were then withdrawn. The citizens were not massacred but allowed to return to their homes (albeit probably now empty of valuables). The Roman commander released all the hostages whom the Carthaginians had interned to ensure the Spanish tribes' good behavior. This intelligent clemency won him high praise, and most of the Iberian tribes lost no time in changing sides.

In 208, to stem the flood of defections, the Punic commander-in-chief, Hasdrubal, accepted battle at Baecula (probably present-day Bailén, Jaén). Seeing himself about to be outflanked, he disengaged and led what he could of his troops—not much more than half of the original twenty-five thousand men—on the long march to join his brother in Italy. At last he could bring Hannibal the reinforcements he had sought for so many years, even if this meant leaving affairs in Spain in dangerous disarray. Scipio did not chase after him but turned his attention to the two Carthaginian armies that remained in the field.

After the victory all the tribes hailed Scipio as king, a dangerous title for a Roman to accept. He paid no obvious notice at the time, but summoned their chieftains to a meeting. He told them, "I am happy to be spoken of as kingly, and to act in a kingly manner, but I do not want to be king nor to receive this title from anyone." In other words, they could treat him as a king even if they could not call him one. A pattern was beginning to emerge of a man who saw himself as rising above the constitutional rules of the game. Scipio had the potential to become a Greek-style *turannos*. This set a dangerous precedent for less scrupulous men in future years.

A relief force from Africa was quickly disposed of, and in 208 Scipio met the Carthaginians at Ilipa (near today's Seville). Outnumbered, he planned an encirclement, borrowing from Hannibal's tactics at Cannae. Several days passed and each morning the opposing armies formed up but did not engage. Every time, Scipio placed his crack legionaries in the center and his weaker Spaniards on his wings facing Punic Spaniards. Then one day he emerged from his camp at first light, but on this occasion his Spaniards were in the center and the Roman infantry on the wings (with cavalry on the far wings). Obviously, he had in mind an outflanking movement with his more disciplined, well-drilled, and experienced troops.

The Punic general (confusingly, yet another Hasdrubal) deployed as usual, and didn't notice Scipio's new dispositions until it was too late for him to make any changes. The Roman commander now forced a battle: his cavalry and legions wheeled quickly to the left and right in column of route curving away from and then toward the Carthaginian wings. The cavalry drove off its opponents and the legions maneuvered back from column into line and attacked the Punic Spaniards on their flanks, who broke and fled. They proceeded to cut into the flanks of the Punic center, which also had to fight off a frontal attack by Scipio's Spanish infantry. What had been an army became a rabble in headlong flight.

Spain now belonged to Rome. His task completed, Scipio set sail for home. His performance at Ilipa showed that he possessed the triple qualities of a great field commander: a daring conception, meticulous preparation, and commitment to intensive training. At last, Rome had produced a match for Hannibal.

HASDRUBAL MADE GOOD progress to Italy, where he arrived in 207. He recruited Gauls in the Po Valley, raising his total numbers to about thirty thousand. He sent six horsemen to ride south with a letter to his brother specifying that their two armies should meet in Umbria. They lost their way and were picked up by a Roman foraging party outside Tarentum. Having read the letter, the consul, who was keeping an eye on Hannibal, detached part of his army without the Carthaginian commander's noticing. He marched north to join his colleague, who was facing Hasdrubal at the river Metaurus (today's Metauro, in the Marche). He arrived at night unobserved, but the following day Hasdrubal sensed that something was wrong. According to Livy:

> Hasdrubal's army was already drawn up in front of his camp. Fighting may have begun sooner but for the fact that Hasdrubal, riding forward with a small cavalry escort, noticed some old shields he had not seen before in the enemy's ranks, and some horses that looked unusually stringy. Their numbers too seemed larger than usual. This led him to suspect the truth, so he hurriedly had the retreat sounded.

Hasdrubal confirmed his fears by checking how many ceremonial consular trumpet calls had sounded that morning in the enemy camp; when he was told that, surprisingly, two had been heard, he realized that both consuls were now present. He presumed, correctly, that one had arrived secretly with his army from the south. He was tortured by the fear that his brother had suffered defeat and might be dead.

Now heavily outnumbered, the Carthaginian commander had no choice but to extricate himself as best he could. He withdrew after nightfall, having ordered his men to pack their gear in silence. His guides ran off and the army strayed from the correct route. The Romans soon caught up, and in the ensuing battle routed the Carthaginians. Hasdrubal acted with great gallantry and, according to Livy, refused to survive the destruction of his army. He set spurs to his horse and galloped straight into the middle of an enemy cohort. Polybius paid him a generous tribute:

> When Fortune had deprived him of all hope for the future and driven him to the last extremity, then, while he used every re-source which might bring him victory both in his preparations for the battle and on the field itself, he gave equal thought as to how in the event of total defeat he should face that eventuality and suffer nothing unworthy of his past career.

Hasdrubal's head was mummified and taken south. It was flung down in front of one of Hannibal's outposts. Two Punic prisoners of war were released and sent to Hannibal to tell him all that had happened. The story is that he groaned, "Now, at last, I see plainly the fate of Carthage."

In Hannibal's final stronghold, in Bruttium, stood a famous shrine to Juno, Rome's old foe and so, as we have seen, a favorite of the Punic publicity machine. Livy reports that "it had an enclosure surrounded by dense woodland, with lofty firs, and, in the center, rich grassland where cattle of all kinds, sacred to the goddess, grazed without any shepherd to attend them." Here in 205 the Punic general, assiduous self-promoter that he was, erected an altar on which he inscribed at some length, in Greek as well as Carthaginian, his achievements, his res gestae. Perhaps this was less a brag than an epitaph for lost hopes.

If we can believe Cicero, he nearly committed an act of divine lèse-majesté. Inside the temple there was a golden column. Hannibal was curious to find out if it was merely plate, and bored a hole in it. Finding it to be solid gold, he decided to take it away. The enraged goddess appeared to the Carthaginian commander in a dream and warned him that unless he left her column alone she would make him lose the sight in his good eye. He complied. With the gold shavings from his drilling, he had a little heifer made which he apologetically affixed to the top of the column.

What are we to make of this story? It comes from a pro-Carthaginian original source. In one sense, it redounds to Hannibal's credit; he behaved well and gave way to Juno's wishes. But, with the defeat of Carthage looming, the anecdote also reflects a coolness between them.

The Romans knew it was in their interest to be equally energetic champions of Juno. Two years previously, her famous temple on the Aventine Hill was struck by lightning. To propitiate the goddess, an elaborate ceremony was staged: a couple of white cows led a procession in which two ancient statues of Juno were carried through the streets and twenty-seven virgins sang a hymn in her praise. The cows were sacrificed. The goddess accepted the best offer still on the table, and finally set aside her anger with the descendants of Troy. The bad-tempered consequences of the Judgment of Paris and of Aeneas's betrayal of Queen Dido had finally arrived at a harmonious conclusion.

For, in truth, Hannibal was right to be pessimistic. Continuing attempts to reinforce his army failed. He no longer held the initiative and was condemned to enforced inactivity. The once all-conquering general had played his last card.

At the time, Cannae appeared to mark a turning point in world history, but it is the battle at the Metaurus that deserves the accolade. It was now obvious to all, including the Queen of Heaven, that Carthage was entering a bleak endgame.

THE END OF the saga is swiftly told. Back in Rome, the *privatus cum imperio* was not allowed a triumph, because he was not and had not been a praetor or a consul. However, it was some recompense that he was easily elected consul for 205. He was assigned Sicily as his *provincia,* or theater of activity, with permission to invade Africa if he saw fit. The permission was reluctantly given, for the old Delayer, Fabius Maximus, took a dim view of harebrained gambles. Better by far, he argued, to concentrate on removing Hannibal from Italy.

Scipio completely disagreed, for once the Punic army had left, a war-weary people would surely press for a quick peace, leaving Carthage more or less where it had been at the end of the First Punic War—still a substantial and independent power. Scipio envisaged Rome as master of the Western Mediterranean, and that meant demoting Carthage to the status of a permanent dependent. This would be accomplished only by a decisive victory in Africa.

In the spring of 204, Scipio landed an army of thirty-five thousand men in the Punic heartland and laid siege to the important town of Utica. In these early days, his weakness was cavalry, although a new ally, the young Numidian chieftain Masinissa, supplied some horsemen, and little progress was made until the following year. Peace discussions were held, inconclusively, but they had a surprising by-product. Roman officers were able to visit the two enemy camps and learned about their construction (timber and reeds) and layout. One night, in a remarkable commando operation, Roman troops set fire to them and caused heavy casualties. Many victims did not even realize that the conflagration had been arson, rather than misadventure. If Hannibal had engaged in such a stratagem, it would have been denounced as typical underhand Punic treachery.

Later in the year, Scipio won a full-dress battle. Although he had fewer troops, he pushed back the enemy's wings and encircled the infantry in the center, in fine Hannibalic style. Peace terms were agreed to end the war. Carthage was to surrender all prisoners, evacuate Italy and Gaul, abandon Spain and all islands between Italy and Carthage, hand over its entire navy (bar twenty ships), and pay a large indemnity of five thousand talents. However, the Council of Elders crossed its collective fingers behind its back and sent word to Hannibal, recalling him and his army to Carthage. He angrily obeyed, but blamed the home authorities for not having supported him wholeheartedly in the past. If they had, Carthage would not be in its present state.

Still determined to win the public-relations battle for Juno's goodwill, the Romans put about a story that some Italian soldiers in the Punic army refused to go to Africa. Hannibal invited them to an assembly in the goddess's peaceful and hitherto inviolate precinct in Bruttium, where he had them surrounded by other troops and slaughtered. Another black mark in the goddess's book.

With between fifteen thousand and twenty thousand men safely back in North Africa, the Council of Elders was ready to abandon its peace treaty and renew hostilities. In a deliberate provocation, a convoy of Roman supply ships was attacked. A coldly furious Scipio, who had probably suspected all along that the enemy was playing for time, summoned Masinissa, who was now able to supply a substantial cavalry force, and set about compelling Hannibal to offer battle. This he did, by launching a ruthless campaign of massacre and destruction in the fertile Punic countryside. Towns were taken, laid waste, and their populations sold into slavery.

The policy worked. In late October 202, the Carthaginian and Roman armies met near Zama, a town five days' march from the sea. Eager to meet his young rival, Hannibal asked for a personal conference à deux with Scipio. Halfway between the opposing lines, each attended by an interpreter, the generals met. Nothing came of this remarkable encounter. The Carthaginian proposed peace, but Scipio was confident of victory and refused.

The following morning, battle was joined. In one sense, the outcome did not much matter. If fate insisted, Rome could afford yet another defeat, and would simply come back with yet another army. Carthage, however, was at its last gasp. Hannibal commanded the larger number of men, but for once he had few cavalry and much of his infantry was untested. His battle plan took account of these weaknesses. He knew that Scipio's cavalry would scatter his own and gallop away in pursuit; his task was to rout the legions in the Roman center and win the day before the horsemen had time to return and take his infantry in the rear. Eighty war elephants were drawn up in front. Behind them, the Carthaginian commander arranged his foot soldiers in three lines, with the less experienced in the first two and his seasoned veterans from the Italian years at the back.

The course of the battle went more or less as Hannibal guessed it would, but not with a happy outcome for him. The Romans quickly drove his cavalry from the field. Unfortunately, the elephants were a disaster, some hurtling down lanes or gaps in the line that Scipio specially created for them (the beasts were then dealt with at leisure in the rear) and others stampeding back into their own forces. Hannibal's first two lines of foot soldiers were swept away. Then the Roman legionaries paused methodically to regroup from their loose maniples into a dense phalanx, before engaging with his third line. For a while there was an evenly balanced slogging match, until, crucially, Scipio's cavalry rode back and, as Hannibal had gloomily foreseen, attacked them from behind. He had done his best under the circumstances, but it had not been good enough. The game was up, and sixteen years of blood and victories had gone for nothing.

Further resistance by Carthage was futile, and risked bringing on the annihilation of the city itself. The fates of Capua, Tarentum, and Syracuse were fresh in the mind. The final peace terms were more severe than those previously negotiated. The indemnity rose to ten thousand talents, payable in fifty annual installments. Carthage was to remain independent but within boundaries, as it was before the war (a territory about the size of modern Tunisia); formerly Numidian lands claimed by Masinissa were to be returned. The city was not allowed to make war outside Africa, and only with Rome's permission within Africa. The entire fleet was to be burned, except for ten triremes, the maximum now permitted. This was the end of Carthage as a Mediterranean power.

When the draft treaty was laid before the Council of Elders, a member stood up and began to oppose acceptance. Hannibal forcibly pulled him down from the speakers' platform. Censured for breeching the conventions of the house, he apologized. According to Polybius, he said:

> You must pardon me, for you know I left Carthage when I was only nine and have now only returned when I am past forty-five. . . . It seems to me amazing and quite beyond my comprehension that anyone who is a citizen of Carthage . . . should not thank his lucky stars that now we are at [Rome's] mercy we have obtained such lenient terms. . . . So now I beg you not even to debate the question, but declare your acceptance of the proposals unanimously.

The council followed Hannibal's advice and passed a resolution to conclude the treaty on the conditions set out.

TWO ROMAN LEGIONS are on the march, commanded by one of the consuls. It is late afternoon and twilight will soon set in. The long column comes to a halt, and the men break up into an extraordinary daily routine. In a few hours, they build a complete military camp.

The pattern is always the same. First an officer goes forward to find a suitable site. When that is done, the spot where the consul's tent, or *praetorium,* is to be erected is decided and, in front of it, a forum or marketplace. Nearby will be the tent of the quaestor, the logistics manager, and those of the tribunes, or staff officers. Every other component falls into a predetermined place. The camp is square, with four gates and a grid of streets laid out with flags planted in the ground. All the distances are regulated and familiar.

The site quickly becomes a busy anthill. Each legionary has a specific task to fulfill. Some dig a ditch and a low rampart, with stakes (every soldier carries one) hammered into it to form a defensive palisade. Others put up tents in orderly rows. Watchwords are set, and sentries posted, and officers prepare to do their rounds. Night falls on what looks like a small city.

The whole process is a fine example of discipline under pressure. When Pyrrhus of Epirus witnessed the Roman legions encamp for the night, he was daunted by the spectacle, realizing for the first time that, when fighting Rome, he might have issued a challenge he could not win. Another Greek, the historian Polybius, has left a detailed and admiring description of the Republic's military dispositions as it emerged from the struggle with Hannibal, from which this account is taken. He wanted to understand the legions' remarkable record of success in war after war.

When the need arose for recruiting an army, the consuls announced the day for a levy when all men of military age, between seventeen and forty-six, and with property valued at more than four hundred denarii, were to assemble on the Capitol. The denarius was a small silver coin, the value of which in today's terms is hard to compute because of widely differing economic conditions, but a legionary in this period received a daily allowance of one-third of a denarius. Each man was allocated the legion with which he would serve and the fighting category—whether he was to join the light-armed *velites,* the youthful *hastati,* the mature *principes,* or the veteran *triarii.* Meanwhile, messengers went out to the allied communities throughout the peninsula, requiring the provision of a requisite number of troops.

Much of a Roman's life on and off through his twenties and thirties was spent in the army. The maximum length of service was sixteen years for an infantryman (twenty in a national emergency) and ten for an *eques.* Normally, he would serve for a continuous period of six years, after which, as an *evocatus,* he could be called back to the colors as and when required. Conscription was compulsory, and no one could stand for public office before completing a decade of national service.

Punishments were ferocious. A man on nighttime guard duty

who was found to be asleep or absent without leave could expect to suffer a *fustuarium.* A military tribune touched him lightly with a cudgel, whereupon his fellow soldiers fell upon him with clubs and stones and beat him to death. Other capital offenses included theft, perjury, homosexual acts committed by a mature adult on a teenager, and cowardice in the field (for example, throwing away one's weapons in fear). A "third strike and you're dead" policy was applied to convictions for noncapital crimes.

If a group of soldiers—for example, a maniple—broke and ran under pressure and deserted their posts, no mercy was shown. The legion was paraded and those found guilty were brought to the front and reprimanded. Then one out of every ten of them was selected by lot and beaten to death. The remainder were put on iron rations and expelled from the camp; they were forced to quarter themselves in a place without any defenses.

Carrots accompanied sticks. When soldiers distinguished themselves in battle, the commander would summon a general assembly of the troops and call forward those whom he considered to have shown exceptional courage. When a city was stormed, the first man to scale the wall was awarded a crown of gold. Anyone who had shielded or saved a comrade's life was honored with gifts from the consul—a spear or a cup or horse trappings. A man whose life had been saved was obliged to treat his rescuer as if he were a parent, a *paterfamilias,* for the rest of his life.

Polybius was much impressed by this system of discipline and decorations: "When we consider this people's almost obsessive concern with military rewards and punishments, and the immense importance which they attach to both, it is not surprising that they emerge with brilliant success from every war in which they engage."

The Greek historian has a point, but, as the Punic Wars showed, other factors also need to be taken into account if we are to give a complete explanation of Rome's talent for making war. The way the state fused civilian politics and military activity meant that many members of the ruling class could expect to command an army at some point in their careers. They received long and intensive military training and so were equipped, in principle at least, to get the best from the legions.

The fact that senior politicians usually held office only for a year led to a rapid throughput of distinctly variable talent. Disasters in the field occurred with surprising frequency. It took a generation before a general was identified who was capable of worsting Hannibal. However, this disadvantage was amply compensated by Rome's access to abundant human capital.

Both Pyrrhus and Hannibal were astounded by the legions' capacity for self-renewal. An army could be destroyed and within a very short space of time a brand-new fighting force took its place. Being a militarized society with long experience, Roman leaders developed a culture of invincibility, a powerful will to victory, and a bloody-minded refusal to accept defeat. They also had the self-confidence to innovate when their backs were to the wall; there is no more striking example of this than the Senate's decision to build fleets during the First Punic War despite its almost complete inexperience of naval matters.

HANNIBAL WAS IN early middle age. What was he to do with the rest of his life? He decided to stay on in Carthage and play an active part in the city's recovery. He seems to have encouraged the further development of agriculture as compensation for the loss of the Punic trading empire and employed the army (what remained of it) to plant a huge number of olive trees.

He also had a score to settle with the ruling oligarchy, for failing to back his Italian campaign. For the first time, he entered domestic politics and emerged as a radical reformer, as energetic in the council chamber as he had been on the battlefield. In 196 he was elected *sufet,* one of the city's two chief magistrates, and set in motion a review of public finances. He ordered a treasury official to appear before him, but the man refused, relying on the fact that he was about to join the Hundred and Four—the "supreme court," which had the right of scrutiny of public administrators, and in which membership was for life.

A furious Hannibal had the official arrested and hauled before the People's Assembly, where he launched an attack on the committee for its arrogance and its overbearing use of power. He immediately proposed and carried a law whereby committee members could hold office for only one year and never for two years in a row. Having conducted his review, he returned to the Assembly and reported widespread embezzlement of public funds and tax evasion. If property and harbor duties were properly collected, the war indemnity could be paid off, he claimed, without the necessity of levying higher taxes.

The great and the good of Carthage were much put out. They wrote letter after letter to the Senate in Rome, alleging that Hannibal was in secret and seditious communication with Antiochus the Great, who was then engaged in a diplomatic confrontation with the Romans. There appears to have been no good evidence to back this up, and Hannibal's generous onetime adversary, Scipio, advised his colleagues that it would be undignified to intervene in what was obviously an internal dispute. "We should be satisfied with having defeated him in the field without then taking him to court!" he declared.

The Senate disagreed and sent delegates to Carthage to charge Hannibal with conspiracy before the Council of Elders. In order to avoid arousing his suspicions, they put it about that they were coming to arbitrate in a dispute between Carthage and Masinissa, the Numidian ruler. Hannibal was too wily to be taken in and quietly slipped abroad to avoid arrest. His first stop was Carthage's mother city, Tyre, but he ended up at Antiochus's court. Whether or not he had been in contact with the king previously is unknown, but the maladroit Senate had driven Hannibal into his arms, the precise opposite of what it wanted.

The two men did not get on very well. Hannibal thought little of Antiochus's military abilities. From the king's point of view, the advice his guest dispensed was always a variation on the same theme: war with Rome should be taken to Italy. It was as if Hannibal wanted to rerun his career. The king paid no attention and gave him only second-ranking jobs.

The ancient historians report that in 193 Scipio, now called Africanus in honor of Zama, was among an embassy the Romans sent to Antiochus. He and Hannibal met at Ephesus and had a conversation on the subject of generalship. Scipio asked the Carthaginian who in his opinion was the greatest commander of all time. Hannibal chose Alexander and placed Pyrrhus second. And the third? inquired Scipio, rather nettled but expecting that he would at least be given third place. Hannibal unhesitatingly chose himself:

> Scipio laughed and asked, "Where would you place yourself, Hannibal, if you had not been defeated by me?" Hannibal, now perceiving his jealousy, replied, "In that case I should have put myself before Alexander." In this way, Hannibal continued his self-praise, but delicately flattered Scipio by suggesting that he had conquered one who was the superior of Alexander.

It is a good story, but (probably) too good to be true. Scipio seems to have been in Carthage at the time that he was supposed to be in Ephesus.

As we shall see in Chapter 15, Antiochus lost his contest with Rome, and Hannibal was obliged to set off on his travels again. He sought refuge in various corners of the Middle East, eventually ending up at the court of Prusias, king of Bithynia, on the Black Sea coast. Rome had a long memory. When a former consul came calling, he criticized Prusias for sheltering Rome's great enemy. The king took the hint and made some necessary dispositions.

Hannibal knew that he would always be on the run, and had ar-

ranged for his house by the sea in Bithynia to have seven underground exits; if necessary, he should be able to make a swift and
secret getaway. The arrival of a Roman envoy meant that it was
time to escape, but he had left matters too late. He found the king's
guards in all the passageways. His only remaining option was suicide if he was not to fall into the hands of his lifelong foe. He
wound his cloak around his neck and ordered a slave to plant his
knee in the small of his back and simultaneously twist and tug at
the cloak as if it were a rope. In this way, he choked to death. According to another account, he took poison; but most poisons
known at that time were slow-acting, and Hannibal would have
needed something that killed quickly.

Plutarch gives the Carthaginian some famous last words: "The
Romans have found it too tedious and difficult a business to wait
for a hated old man's death. Let us now at last put them out of their
misery." Whether or not this is what he actually said, it is surely
what he would have liked to say. When the news of Hannibal's
suicide reached the Senate, many thought the former consul's behavior had been odious and officious, for Hannibal was "like a bird
who is too old to fly and has lost his tail, and who is allowed to live
on tamely and harmlessly." Others took the view that the Carthaginian's hatred of Rome was ingrained and that, if ever he were
given the chance, he would be as dangerous as ever.

One thing was certain: the little boy had been true to the oath he
swore in the temple at Carthage nearly half a century earlier, although it cost him a failed life and a lonely death.

14

Change and Decay

THE BOY WAS IN HIS LATE TEENS AND ENJOYING HIS first serious love affair. Then a small cloud appeared on the horizon. One day in 186, he lightheartedly told his girlfriend that they would be unable to have sex for a week or so.

He was Publius Aebutius and she, somewhat older than he, was Hispala Faecenia, a high-class prostitute and former slave. An archetypal good-time girl with a heart of gold, she adored her young lover. He had not started the affair, for, uncharacteristically in a man's world, *she* had picked *him* up. In fact, rather than make money from the relationship, as she would with an ordinary client, she subsidized him.

This was because Aebutius had trouble at home. He came from an affluent, upper-class family, but his father died when he was small and he was brought up by his mother and a stepfather. They embezzled his fortune and made as little provision for his daily needs as possible. He was able to get by only thanks to Hispala's generosity.

After Aebutius had recovered from an illness, his mother told him that she wanted to initiate him into a secret cult devoted to Bacchus, the Latin name for Dionysus, the god of intoxication and ritual madness. She had vowed to do this on his behalf, she claimed, once he had got better. He agreed to fall in with her wish, and she warned that he would have to be sexually continent for ten days before the ceremony.

This was the reason, Aebutius explained to Hispala, for staying away from her bed. Her reaction astonished him. "Heaven forbid!" she exclaimed. "Better for both of us to die than you should do that!" He protested that he was only following his mother's request.

"This means that your stepfather—I suppose it would be offensive to mention your mother—is in a hurry to destroy your virtue, your good name, your prospects and your life."

Swearing her lover to the strictest secrecy, Hispala said that she had been initiated while still a slave, and the cult was a cover for the grossest immorality and even murder. As Livy describes them, the rites were

> a workshop of corruptions of every kind; and it was common knowledge that for the past two years no one had been initiated who was over the age of twenty. As each one was introduced, he became a kind of sacrificial victim for the priests. They led the initiate to a place that resounded with shrieks, with the chanting of a choir, the clashing of cymbals and the beating of drums, so that the victim's cries for help, when violence was offered to his chastity, might not be heard.

Aebutius went home and announced that he would have nothing to do with the Bacchic cult. This enraged his mother and his stepfather, and they drove him out of the house. He took refuge with an aunt, who advised him to go and tell all to the consul Spurius Postumius Albinus. After checking that Aebutius was a reliable witness, Postumius made some discreet inquiries. He arranged for his mother-in-law to ask Hispala to pay her a visit. Mystified by the fact that this well-known and eminently respectable lady should want to see her, Hispala obeyed.

Puzzlement turned to terror when she saw the consul's lictors and entourage in the hall, and then the consul himself. Eventually, she calmed down and told her story. Apparently, the rites had originally been all-female and had taken place only three times a year, but then a Campanian priestess had introduced reforms. Now men were allowed to take part, the ceremonies were held at night, and their frequency had risen to five times a month. According to Livy:

> There were more obscenities practiced between men than between men and women. Anyone refusing to submit to outrage or reluctant to commit crimes was slaughtered as a sacrificial victim. To regard nothing as forbidden was among these people the summit of religious achievement. Men, apparently out of their wits, would shout prophecies with frenzied bodily convulsions: married women, dressed as Bacchantes, with their hair disheveled and carrying blazing torches, would run down to the Tiber, plunge their torches into the water and bring them out still alight—because they contained a mixture of live sulfur and calcium.

Anyone unwilling to take part was whisked away by, or in, some sort of mechanical device and done away with in hidden caves.

Postumius made a full report to a shocked Senate. Although the immoral goings-on were to be deprecated in themselves, what really worried members was that a secret society could recruit adherents from across the classes and plan heaven knows what clandestine mischief, political as well as sexual. Dionysus was associated with breaches of social control and the dissolution of gender, age, and class distinctions. It may be no accident that the orgies took place in a grove on the Aventine, the traditional center of popular agitation, and that Aebutius and Hispala both lived on the hill, too.

An inscription has survived communicating the Senate's decision on the cult to communities across the peninsula. It ordered:

No man is to be a priest; no one, either man or woman, is to be
an officer (to manage the temporal affairs of the organization);
nor is anyone of them to have charge of a common treasury; no
one shall appoint either man or woman to be master or to act as
master; henceforth they shall not form conspiracies among themselves, stir up any disorder, make mutual promises or agreements, or exchange pledges.

Care was taken not to offend the god needlessly. Bacchic rituals
could still be performed, but only with official permission and in
the presence of no more than five people.

As for the lovers, they were handsomely rewarded. Aebutius was
forgiven his military service and Hispala was allowed to marry a
freeborn Roman, and, it was decreed, "no slur or disgrace on account of the marriage should attach to the man who married her."
History does not relate what happened to them next.

With this permission granted, the couple were entitled to become husband and wife, in theory. But the boy was young and, like
many who have their first sexual experience with a knowledgeable
and kindly older woman, he probably moved on. After all, he and
his girlfriend were from radically different social classes. Whatever
the Senate said, prejudice against former slaves and prostitutes was
fierce. The integrity of the family line had to be protected at all
costs.

We may hope for, but doubt, a happy ending.

THE REAL IMPORTANCE of the scandal was the light it threw on
Rome's contradictory attitudes toward Greece. From the Republic's earliest years, the Hellenic world had been a major influence,
but now that they were emerging as the dominant Mediterranean
state, Romans were coming into direct contact with this culture for
the first time. They admired the deathless achievements of a glorious past—the works of the great tragedians Aeschylus, Sophocles,

and Euripides; the philosophy of Socrates, Plato, and Aristotle; the sculpture of Pheidias; the architecture of Ictinus and so forth—and knew they could not compete with them.

The decadent descendants of these great men looked down their noses on the provincial newcomers from Italy. They "would jeer at their habits and customs, others at Roman achievements, others at the appearance of the city itself, which was not yet beautified in either its public places or private districts." For his part, the average Roman harbored a healthy distrust of contemporary Greeks (they were the classical equivalent of cheese-eating surrender monkeys). Livy makes this clear when, with a sneer, he attributes the Bacchanalia as a "method of infecting people's minds with error" to a "Greek of humble origin, a man possessed of none of those numerous accomplishments which the Greek people, the most highly educated and civilized of nations, has introduced among us for the cultivation of mind and body."

While the Senate disliked and discouraged foreign cults from the Orient, it was by no means consistent in practice. In 293, an outbreak of plague led to a consultation of the Sibylline Books and the importation from Epidaurus, in Greece, of a snake sacred to the god of medicine, Asklepios (Latinized into Aesculapius), for whom a shrine and a healing center were built on Tiber Island. In 206, a prophecy was discovered which stated that if ever a foreign enemy were to invade Italy he would be driven out only if Cybele, or the Great Mother, was brought to Rome (in the shape of a holy black stone).

Desperate to see an end to Hannibal's occupation of the peninsula, the goddess was welcomed into the city and a new temple was built for her on the Palatine. Cybele and her youthful consort, Attis, expressed the annual cycle of the fertility of the land in a manner that a Roman traditionalist would find distinctly unappealing. Her spring festivities, during which self-castrated eunuchs danced to cymbals and drums, were no less exotic than those dedi-

cated to Dionysus. Attis had set the precedent. As the first-century
poet Catullus writes, he,

> moved by madness, bemused in his mind,
> Lopped off the load of his loins with a sharp flint.
> Woman now, and aware of her wasted manhood,
> Still bleeding, the blood bedaubing the ground still,
> With feminine fingers she fetched the light drum
> That makes the music, Great Mother, at your mysteries.

This was all most un-Roman, and care was taken to limit the
impact of the new cult. The goddess's priests were and remained
foreigners, and their numbers and activities were strictly limited.

Meanwhile, the ruling élite maintained, with its usual attention
to detail, the superstitious, placatory rituals of Rome's official religion. Change was unwelcome, and loyalty to the *mos maiorum* was
essential to the Republic's well-being. This was sometimes taken to
absurd lengths. One example may speak for all. Every year the senior outgoing consul proclaimed his successors in office. In 163,
the officeholder of the day, Tiberius Sempronius Gracchus, conducted the ceremony as usual. But after the new magistrates had
taken command in their respective spheres of activity Gracchus
came across an ancient book of religious practices, in which he
found a regulation he knew nothing about. Plutarch explains it:

> Whenever a magistrate, sitting in a hired house or tent outside
> the city to take auspices from the flight of birds, is compelled for
> any reason to return to the city before sure signs have appeared,
> he must give up the house first hired and take another, and from
> this he must take his observations anew.

Tiberius had innocently twice used the same house for his observa-
tions before making his consular proclamations. Horrified, he re-

ferred the matter to the Senate, which recalled the consuls and made them resign their offices. They were then reappointed after the liturgy had been repeated in proper form.

The *mos maiorum* received its symbolic incarnation in the funerals of noblemen. The corpse was carried into the Forum and displayed in an upright position, as if the dead man were still alive, on the Rostra. His son or some other relative delivered a eulogy, listing the facts of his career, as both a history lesson and an assertion of Republican virtue. Polybius, the observant foreigner who spent much of a lifetime observing Romans, describes the most extraordinary aspect of the ceremony. He reports that an image of the deceased was present alongside those of his famous forebears and, after the burial, was put on permanent show in a wooden shrine in his house:

> The image consists of a mask, which is fashioned with extraordinary fidelity both in its modeling and its complexion to represent the features of the dead man. . . . And when any distinguished member of the family dies, the masks [of his predecessors] are taken to the funeral, and are there worn by men who are considered to bear the closest resemblance to the original, both in height and in their general appearance and bearing. These substitutes [they were usually family members] are dressed according to the rank of the deceased: a toga with a purple border for a consul or praetor, a completely purple garment for a censor, and one embroidered with gold for a man who had celebrated a triumph or performed some similar exploit. They all ride in chariots with the fasces, axes, and other insignia carried before them . . . and when they arrive at the Rostra they all seat themselves in a row upon chairs of ivory.

What a spectacle this must have been. The dead had reawakened— perhaps they had never fallen asleep—and were now listening attentively to the life story of their freshly deceased posterity. Today's generation could see, with all the sharpened focus of a waking dream, that it was on trial before its ancestors.

THERE WERE OTHER ways in the city of Rome by which the sanctified past kept company with the present. On every corner were shrines, temples, and holy groves, sacred to one divinity or another. Temples were storehouses of old trophies, bronze tablets with the texts of laws and treaties, votive offerings, and other obsolete odds and ends. In the Forum and elsewhere, paintings of famous military exploits, originally made for triumphs, were on display. Masterpieces of Greek art, captured in the sack of such cities as Syracuse and Tarentum, transformed Rome into an open-air museum. Here was a treasury of clutter, awaiting the explanations of both the historian and the antiquarian, although these were often inaccurate or imaginative.

On the Sacred Way, Romulus and his Sabine counterpart, Titus Tatius, kept watch, in sculptural form, over the Forum below. In the middle of the square itself, the fig tree beneath which the founding brothers were suckled by the she-wolf still flourished. Nearby was a pool, now dried up, called the Lacus Curtius. Here a chasm had once split open; it was said that it would never close until Rome's most valued possession had been deposited in it. Gold and jewelry were thrown in, to no effect. At last, a young cavalryman realized that the answer to the riddle was the Roman soldier. He galloped into the abyss and the earth closed above his head.

Not far away, next to the Temple of Castor, with its lofty podium, was the spring of Iuturna, where the divine twins watered their horses after the Battle of Lake Regillus. At the other end of the Forum was the speakers' platform, the Rostra. Orators addressing the populace had to compete for attention with a throng of half-life-size statues of ambassadors who had perished while on missions for the state.

The hill of the Capitol was also littered with statues of famous Romans, kings, and that expeller of the kings, Marcus Brutus. Among them stood two colossi of the hero Hercules and another of Jupiter himself, erected in the fourth century. There were so many representations of the great men of old that visitors must have had the eerie impression that they were walking through a crowd turned into stone by some passing Medusa.

Subterranean chambers beneath the temple of Jupiter Best and Greatest were packed not only with old dedications but also with sculptures that had fallen from the temple roof and a variety of superfluous gifts. Walls were covered with bronze tablets on which the terms of treaties and the texts of laws were inscribed. Victory trophies and votive monuments occupied every spare corner.

OF COURSE, ROME was more than a space for memory, a cemetery field of relics; it was also a living city, expanding all the time and well on its way to becoming an early megalopolis. The Forum was the city's center, part shopping center, part law courts, and part political arena. Human life in all its variety pushed its way up among the statues, the shrines, the temples.

We are lucky to have a direct account of daily life from someone who lived and thrived in Rome during and after the wars with Carthage. He was the comedy playwright Titus Maccius Plautus. In one of his pieces, a character conducts a tour of the Forum, a locale where the best and worst of human nature can be found. "From virtue down to trash," he says, "here is god's plenty." The lower or southern part of the piazza was the preserve of the respectable or, in Plautus's words, "the good men and the opulent." He comments, "For perjurers, you can apply to the courts of law," which were held in the open air near the circular Comitium, where public assemblies were convened (there was room, at a squeeze, for perhaps five thousand citizens to attend and for ten thousand in the Forum as a whole). Liars and dishonest salesmen congregated at the little shrine of Venus Cloacina, or Venus of the Drain. A statue of Venus was said once to have fallen into the open drain here, hence her cognomen. The shrine was a low circular platform with two statues of the goddess, a pleasant enough place to loiter.

"Rich and errant husbands" frequented the Basilica, a business hall where bankers set up their tables and entrepreneurs sold shares in enterprises. Across the square a line of retail outlets, the *tabernae veteres,* or Old Shops, was largely peopled with moneylenders, and behind the Temple of Castor and Pollux "conmen extract loans from the unwary." Near the Vicus Tuscus (Etruscan Street), was the rent boys' cruising ground. The street led to the Velabrum, a saddle of land between the Palatine and Capitoline hills, where "you'll find bakers, butchers and fortune-tellers."

Unlike Alexandria, the gleaming white, checkered capital of the Ptolemies, Rome was unplanned. Buildings grew up ad hoc along ancient pathways that led to the Palatine and Capitoline hills, until the city became a maze of gloomy, narrow alleys and little squares. The principles of hygiene were little understood and infectious diseases were rife. Some (not altogether successful) efforts were made to collect sewage for use as agricultural fertilizer, and it was recognized that a copious supply of clean water was essential. Two aqueducts, mainly running underground, were built in 312 (by Appius Claudius Caecus, see pages 145 and 147) and in 272. By the middle of the second century, a rising population had led to the construction of the Aqua Marcia, an astonishing feat of engineering that brought water to the top of the Capitol. Few people could afford baths at home, and by about 100 public baths had become a universal feature of daily life.

Most thoroughfares in the city were unpaved, although they might have raised sidewalks; people dumped rubbish and sewage in them, as well as dead animals and the occasional unwanted corpse. Slops from pots often fell on the heads of unwary passersby (Laws were passed regulating claims for damages.) Unsanitary conditions were not the only danger, for wheeled traffic took up much of the available space and accidents were common.

The urban unit was the *vicus,* a street that functioned as an artery for pedestrians and wheeled traffic and served the neighborhood around it. Each *vicus* had a central point of reference—a crossroads, a sacred grove, a shrine. To qualify officially for the title of street, or *via,* the Twelve Tables specified that a roadway should be eight feet wide when straight and sixteen at bends; only two roadways merited the title—the Via Sacra and the Via Nova (New Street), which ran between the Forum and the Palatine.

A snatch of dialogue from the comic playwright Publius Terentius Afer (or Terence) from the middle of the second century, conveys the flavor of a well-to-do part of town. A slave is giving someone directions in a city that has no street signs.

"Do you know that arcade by the market?"

"Of course I do."

"Go uphill past it, straight along the road. When you get to the top, there's a slope downward. Rattle your way down that. Next there's a little shrine on this side, and there's an alleyway thereabouts."

"Which one?"

"There's also a big fig tree."

"But you can't get through that alleyway."

"You're absolutely right! Really! . . . I made a mistake: go back to the arcade; yes, you'll get there much more directly this way, and there isn't so far to walk. Do you know the house of old Cratinus?"

"I do."

"When you've passed that, go left straight along that road; when you come to the temple of Diana, go to the right. Before you reach the gate, just by the pond, there's a bakery, and a workshop opposite: that's where he is."

On main streets, one- or two-room shops or poky apartments for the poor faced one another along either side. These were usually open to the passersby and could be secured by wooden shutters. All sorts of goods were sold—food, cloth, kitchenware, jewelry, and books. Bars served wine mixed with water and flavored with herbs, honey, or resin (the ancestor of today's Greek retsina). Soup with bread, stews, diced roasted meat, sausages, pies, fruit, and filled buns were also on offer, even a kind of proto-pizza. Restaurants with seating catered to the more affluent customer.

THE ROWS OF shops and apartments protected the houses of the well-to-do, which lay behind them, from the noises and stinks of the street. They were laid out according to a basic pattern on which those with money and space could expand. A front door led through a narrow vestibule to a semi-public waiting room or hallway; this was the *atrium,* with an opening to the sky, and lined on three sides by small dark bedrooms. The side facing the visitor was occupied by a raised space, the *tablinum,* originally the master bedroom but now the owner's study, with rich frescoes on the walls and the masks of the family's ancestors on pedestals. Nearby, the *triclinium* was a formal dining room where guests ate elaborate meals lying on couches. The back of the house was the family's living quarters, dominated by a columned garden courtyard or peristyle. In the bigger houses there was a first floor and a summer *triclinium* by the peristyle.

As always, some parts of town were more fashionable—and costly—than others. The most expensive houses could be found on the Palatine and the Velia, a ridge of ground running down alongside the Sacred Way into the Forum, the hub of élite transactions. The land surrounding the city was taken up with market gardens that produced flowers and vegetables. During the second century, many of these *horti* were purchased by the rich and powerful, who built villas in them: calm, green retreats where they could escape the din and anger of city life. This was *rus in urbe,* an urban countryside.

There was too little space inside the city walls to meet Rome's requirements, and buildings began to appear on the Campus Martius, the Field of Mars. This was an open area beyond the Capitol that was used for pasturage and military exercises. Scipio Africanus built a villa and garden there. The Circus Flaminius, a public square, was commissioned in 221 for the Plebeian Games by Gaius Flaminius, the populist leader who fell at Lake Trasimene a few years later. It also served as a marketplace and a display area for triumphal booty. There were government structures on the Campus, too; the Ovile was an enclosure rather like a sheep pen where the *comitia centuriata* held its votes; the adjoining Villa Publica, rebuilt and enlarged in 194, was a headquarters for state officials in which the census was taken and troops were levied.

Rome's increasing wealth in the second century led to civic improvements. The rich and famous built triumphal arches (Scipio among them), porticoes, and basilicas as public amenities. More streets were paved and the drainage system was improved. Concrete, *opus caementicium,* was widely used and new temples were constructed, in the Greek manner, from marble or travertine. But the city's largest entertainment venue, the Circus Maximus, remained a less than glamorous construction of painted wood.

Rome had a long way to go before it could match the magnificence of the Hellenic cities of the East.

AS EVER, THE poor had a hard time of it. There were plenty of jobs in service industries such as food supplies (grain, meat, fish), in construction, in retail and crafts of various kinds (ceramics, glassware, metalwork). But Rome's population was growing rapidly and slaves soaked up much available work. We can assume high levels of unemployment or part-time employment, at least periodically.

Space was at a premium. As in modern cities, developers began to look skyward and built apartment blocks as many as eight stories high. At first, these were rickety wood-framed structures that had an alarming tendency to catch fire. With the introduction of concrete, something rather more solid was created; the Romans called it an *insula,* or island. This solidity was more apparent than real, however, for *insulae* often collapsed without warning.

Many people joined associations (*collegia, sodalicia, corpora,* or *curiae*), which would give their lives some stability beyond the family. There was little in the way of local government, and no regular police force or fire service. However, the four aediles (two were originally deputies to the tribunes and were joined in 387 by another pair elected by patricians only) were responsible for the upkeep of the city's fabric, presentation of the Games, the supply of grain and water, and oversight of the markets. Membership in a trade guild, a professional association, or a cult group provided some protection against the vicissitudes and injustice of life. Members of these organizations met regularly (say, once a month), held a sacrifice, and ate a meal together. There were neighborhood societies, which took part in the annual festival of the Compitalia, a celebration in honor of the Lares Compitales, the gods of local crossroads. Some *collegia* were burial clubs, to which members made small, regular financial contributions to pay for their funeral costs.

The state was uneasy about these societies, as its reaction to the Bacchanalia crisis showed, because it did not know what they were up to. At times of political upheaval, they might conspire against good order. But potentially subversive "horizontal" social structures were counteracted by the "vertical" pyramid of the *clientela.* As we have seen, everyone, except those at the very pinnacle of society, was a *cliens* helpful to and dependent on one or more richer patrons. The relationship was hereditary and recognized, albeit not enforced, by law. If a man was lucky enough to be the client of a senator, he was expected to call on this person at home first thing in the morning and accompany him to the Forum; the more followers in a great man's train, the greater his prestige. In return, he could expect a *sportula*—some food or pocket money.

This system of mutual exchange of goods and services bound

society together and made revolt from below or the emergence of reform movements unlikely. Of course, patrons could sometimes be mean or fall on hard times for one reason or another. Plautus imagines an unemployed and half-starved client lamenting his fate:

> Why, just now in the Forum I worked on a couple of
> fellows I knew, young lawyers, and, "Going to lunch, then?"
> I in my innocence ask. And a terrible silence
> settles upon us. Does anyone say "You come too!"?
> Heads begin shaking. I tell them a nice little story,
> one of my best. God knows how often it's fed me.
> Laughter then? No. Smiles? No.

Rome was a great and growing community, it was the center of government, it was where the action was. In fact, its inhabitants often dispensed with its name and instead referred to it as *urbs*— not any ordinary city but *the* city. However, urban life was corrupting; money made the rich idle, and unemployment did the same for the moneyless. Responsible citizens believed that the countryside was a far, far better place. After all, it was to his small farm that the dictator Cincinnatus retired after saving the state, eschewing glory and wealth. It was from smallholders that the Republic's victorious legions were recruited. Cicero's friend the antiquarian and polymath Varro wrote in *De re rustica,* his compendium of country lore: "It was not without reason that those great men, our ancestors, put the Romans who lived in the country ahead of those who lived in the city."

An ordinary Roman farmer has left us his summary of the good life in his own words, found on an inscription at Forlì, in Italy. It expresses the tough, hardworking, sober values of the countrymen:

> Take all this as true advice, whoever wants to live really well and freely. First, show respect where it is due. Next, want what's best for your master. Honor your parents. Earn others' trust. Don't

speak or listen to slander. If you don't harm or betray anyone, you will lead a pleasant life, uprightly and happily, giving no offense.

A new generation of politicians emerged after the end of the wars with Carthage, the most able but most unlikable of whom was Marcus Porcius Cato (called the Elder, or the Censor, to distinguish him from his first-century namesake). He came from yeoman stock and spent the earlier years of his adult life, when not fighting in the army, tilling his own fields, just like a latter-day Cincinnatus. Plutarch said of him:

> Early in the morning, Cato went on foot to the [local] marketplace and pleaded the cases of all who wished his aid. Then he came back to his farm, where, wearing a working blouse if it was winter, and stripped to the waist if it was summer, he worked alongside his slaves, then sat down with them to eat the same bread and drink the same wine.

Talent-spotted by an aristocratic neighbor, he was introduced to Roman politics in the capital and soon rose to the top.

For Cato, there was something unforgivably Greek about the sophisticated self-indulgences of city life. Every true Roman's moral guide, the *mos maiorum,* was a treasury of rural virtues. In his book on farming, *De agri cultura,* Cato observed that trade was more profitable than farming, but too risky; the same went for banking, with the addition that it was more dishonorable. By contrast, he wrote, "it is from the farming class that the bravest men and the sturdiest soldiers come, their calling is most highly respected, their livelihood is most assured and is looked on with the least hostility." The citizen, in the field with his plow and on the battlefield with his sword and spear, stood for all that was best about Rome.

Cato did in fact farm his own acres himself, but only when he was young and poor. An austere hypocrite, he lived very simply but amassed a fortune, against his fine principles, as a moneylender and a property investor. Once he had made his way in the world, he ran his estates as an absentee landlord. He gives the game away in his book. In it, he offers copious practical advice to a landowner like himself, who pays his farm only the occasional visit. The overseer or bailiff, who runs the business on his behalf and manages the workers, some of them slaves and others freeborn, is to be kept on a tight rein:

> He must not be a gadabout; he must always be sober, and must not go out to dine. He must keep the farm laborers busy, and see that the master's orders are carried out. He must not assume that he knows more than the master. . . . He must not consult a fortune-teller, or prophet, or diviner, or astrologer {an echo here of official fears of Bacchic cults and the like}. . . . He must be the first out of bed, the last to go to bed.

Cato is unsentimental. He wants the laborers to be well enough looked after to function efficiently, but that's all. They should be either at work or asleep. Failure or illness, even old age, is not to be tolerated:

> Sell worn-out oxen, blemished cattle, blemished sheep, wool, hides, an old wagon, old tools, an old slave, a sickly slave, and whatever else is superfluous. The master should have the selling habit, not the buying habit.

We can blame Cato for his mean-spiritedness and intellectual dishonesty, but the fact is that the heyday of the independent small-holder, tilling his own soil and sending his sons to war, was over. Sixteen years of burning, looting, and destruction by Hannibal's army had emptied much of the Italian countryside and swelled the

population of Rome. It would take many years for the land to recover, and in some parts of the south it never did.

POVERTY WAS PARTLY alleviated by fun, albeit in the cause of
religion. Throughout the year, groups of days were dedicated to the
gods and set aside as holidays. In the city, public and commercial
business was suspended, the Senate did not meet, and the city's
routine was interrupted by festivals, or "games." The oldest were
the *ludi Romani* (Roman Games), founded in the days of the kings
and celebrated in September. They featured pantomime dances set
to flute music, which doubled as both ritual and entertainment,
and from 240 B.C. plays were added to the schedule. The other
games were founded during the nerve-racked time of the war with
Hannibal and its aftermath, and were attempts either to placate the
menacing supernatural order or to express heartfelt thanks for victory.

As already noted, the *ludi Plebeii,* or People's Games, were established in 221 by the plebeian leader Gaius Flaminius. The *ludi
Apollinares,* the games of Apollo, followed in 208; the *ludi Cereales,*
the games of Ceres, in 202; and in 194 the *ludi Megalenses,* held in
honor of the Magna Mater in front of her new temple on the Palatine.

Antiquarians like Varro were fascinated by the origins of live
performance. They posited archaic rituals in the countryside, with
dances and crude verses. Italians, wrote Virgil on the back of antiquarian speculation, were

> accustomed to hold a
> Beano, their poems unpolished and unrestrained their jokes:
> They wear the most hideous wooden
> Masks, and address the Wine-god in jovial ditties, and hang
> Wee images of the god to sway from windy pine-boughs.

Professional dance companies were imported from Etruria, but (we
are told) the Roman youths began to imitate them, adding obscene

verses of their own composition. This blend of words, music and gesture was cleaned up and professionalized, and led to the presentation of written comedies, which were performed at the *ludi.* (The young amateurs maintained their tradition of ribald songs regardless.)

The first proper plays to appear at the Games were written by Livius Andronicus, a half-Greek who was sold into slavery when Rome captured Tarentum after the defeat of King Pyrrhus. He tutored his master's son and wrote a translation into Latin of Homer's *Odyssey;* Cicero thought it poor stuff, but it became a set text that hapless schoolboys had to learn by rote. Little of his work survives except for a few titles—farces inspired by Greek models such as "The Gambler" and "The Dagger." His plots centered on rich young men's love affairs with prostitutes (who invariably turned out to be wellborn) and clever slaves who ran rings around their masters. His more famous successors, Plautus (Latin for "flatfoot," c. 254–184), a stage carpenter and sceneshifter from Umbria, and a young Carthaginian slave, Terence (195/185–159), used much the same kind of material.

Tragedies on Greek mythological themes (the adventures of Trojan heroes, for example) were also popular, as was an authentic Roman form, *fabulae praetextae,* poetic dramas about "documentary" or real-life subjects. These celebrated great moments in Republican history, such as the *devotio* of Decius Mus at Sentinum and Manlius's duel with a Gallic chieftain.

Plays were presented in the open air, and the audience sat on the grass or on temporary bleachers in front of a wooden stage. They fulfilled a useful social function, for they appealed to all classes, each of which was allocated special seating. A Roman could look around the audience and see all Rome represented, from a senior senator to a slave who had been given some time off.

Conservative politicians felt that the performing arts were a decadent, Hellenic innovation and blocked all attempts to build a permanent theater with more convenient and comfortable facilities.

At one point, a senatorial decree was passed banning the erection of seats for shows on the risible grounds that "mental relaxation should go together with the virility of a standing posture proper to the Roman nation."

The atmosphere at the *ludi* could be rowdy. Terence was furious that noise and commotion made a play of his, in which he was acting, fail:

> When I first began to perform it, there was talk of a boxing match, and there were hopes of a tightrope walker, too. Slaves were arriving; there was a din, women were shouting—these things made me leave the stage before I'd reached the end.

When he revived the play, the first part went well, but then the performance was disrupted by the rumor of a gladiatorial show, a spectacle that was much in demand.

Fights to the death as public display were akin to human sacrifice. Their origin is uncertain; perhaps Rome borrowed them from funeral rites in Etruria (along with wild-animal hunts) or came across them in Campania. The killing of prisoners of war to mark the passing of great men was not unknown. Homer, that universal maker of classical precedents, reports that the grief-stricken Achilles "hacked to pieces with his bronze [sword]" twelve young Trojans at the pyre of his dead friend or lover, Patroclus.

However, physical combat was unusual. The first report we have of it dates from 264, the year that the First Punic War began. At the funeral of a former consul, Decimus Junius Brutus Pera, his sons presented three pairs of slaves, selected from a group of prisoners of war, who fought one another in the Forum Boarium. By 216, the number of fights in a single program had risen to twenty-two, and in 174 seventy-four men fought over a period of three days.

As we saw with drama, entertainment and religion marched hand in hand, and it was not for nothing that a gladiatorial show was called in Latin a *munus*—a service or gift to a man's ancestors and to the gods. Until the first century, it always marked the death of a male relative, and was often staged in the Forum in a temporary arena. As violent death became an increasingly popular spectator sport, Romans offered a rational justification of its purpose. Gladiators were expected to act bravely and give up their lives with grace. They were an inspiring example of bravery, it was said, which citizens were to learn from and imitate. They were a metaphor for Rome's martial spirit—in a word, for *virtus.*

Munera were regularly programmed in December, especially during the festival of Saturnalia. This prototype of Christmas was the celebration to end all celebrations, and was introduced in 217. It had about it more than a whiff of misrule. Whereas the *ludi* affirmed social class, the Saturnalia temporarily subverted it. For up to a week, beginning on December 17, the ordinary rules of social interaction were turned upside down. Slaves were excused from work, and their owners would serve them a meal (often actually prepared by the slaves). They were allowed to gamble. Even Cato gave his slaves an extra ration of wine. Citizens were not obliged to dress in togas and everyone wore the *pileus,* the felt bonnet denoting a slave's manumission. Gifts were exchanged—wax candles and small pottery figurines, or *sigillaria.*

Rome's frequent festivities certainly mitigated the pain of life, but to the slave and the jobless citizen or part-timer the city was a cramped, crowded, smelly, unhealthy habitat. The rich and powerful enjoyed a high level of comfort and ease, but wisely kept a weather eye on the discontents that surrounded them in every street, alley, or crossroads.

IF THERE WAS one man Cato could not stand, who was the epitome of the decadent Greekness of which he so passionately disapproved, it was the hero of Zama, the all-conquering Scipio Africanus. Cato devoted much of his time attempting to discredit him.

There was an annoying grandeur about Scipio. He came from an extremely distinguished patrician family with many consulships to its credit. As we have seen, his father and uncle had been distinguished generals. Since being given command of an army himself at the early age of twenty-five, he had never lost a battle or seen a Roman force defeated. When abroad on foreign commissions, he tended to give himself the airs and graces of a Hellenistic monarch. He did not have the patience or the moral flexibility to thrive in the noisy rivalry of the marketplace; the first-rate general was a third-rate politician.

Worst of all, from Cato's point of view, Scipio was an unrepentant lover of Hellenic culture. He enjoyed wearing Greek fashions (and when he did put on a toga he draped it in an unusual and, unfriendly commentators said, effeminate manner). He wrote a memoir in Greek and spoke the language fluently. He gave his two sons a Greek education, and probably his two daughters, too, for one of them, Cornelia, the wife of that stickler for religious rules, Tiberius Sempronius Gracchus, had a reputation in adult life as a highly cultivated woman and an intellectual.

IN 204, THE two men's paths crossed for the first time. Scipio was in Sicily, assembling his consular army for the invasion of Africa. Cato was one of his quaestors, a junior elected official with financial duties. He argued that his commander was indulging in typically lavish personal expenditure and overpaying his troops. (Many of them were volunteers, so, if there was truth in the claim, the high command was very probably conceding to market forces.) They received much more money than was needed for the necessaries of life, it was said, and were spending the surplus on luxuries and the pleasures of the senses. In other words, Scipio was corrupting the "natural simplicity of his men"; the phrase is Plutarch's, but it rings true of Cato's self-serving self-righteousness.

Scipio replied tartly that he had no use for a cheese-paring quaestor, and Cato returned home to stir things up at Rome. He helped Fabius to attack the consul's waste of immense sums of money. They deplored Scipio's "boyish addiction to Greek gymnasia and theatrical performances. It was as if he had been appointed the director of an arts festival, not a commander on active service." A board of inquiry was sent to Sicily, but found nothing to substantiate the charges. The army was in excellent shape, as Scipio showed when he quickly went on to destroy the power of Carthage. He had won this round against his critics, but they would return. The squabbles and maneuvers of domestic politics bored and irritated him. His enemies were always lying in wait for any slip they could exploit.

And, reluctant though some might be to admit it, the suspicion in which Cato and his friends held Scipio was by no means irrational. So great now and so far-flung were the challenges and opportunities facing the triumphant Republic that a general could spend years away from Rome and the picky oversight of the Senate. (Scipio fought in Spain and Africa for almost all of a decade starting in 211.) He commanded soldiers who expected to spend many seasons far from home; in the past, they had been farmers who would leave their fields for only a few months, but now their link with the soil was becoming more and more tenuous. When Scipio demobilized his forces, he was obliged to ask the Senate to give them smallholdings from the *ager publicus* (state-owned land) so that they had somewhere to live and some means of making a living. If their general did not look after his landless legionaries, who would?

Scipio posed a potential danger to the state, given that he was the master of a great army whose first loyalty was to him. Had he so wished, he could have overshadowed the Senate and even established a formal or an informal despotism. In fact, he did not so wish. He remained at heart loyal to the constitution, that haphazard cocktail of oligarchy moderated by democracy and peopled by an annual procession of temporary monarchs. But it must have occurred to observant senators that a less scrupulous man could accumulate sufficient power with which to subvert the Republic.

It was also true that Rome's transformation from a middling Italian city-state into an invincible superpower had a coarsening impact on standards in public life. Vast quantities of wealth began to flow not only into the treasury but also into the pockets of the senatorial élite. Bribery during elections began to be widespread, and elected officials recouped the expenditure by extorting money from the provinces—to begin with, the two Spains (Near and Further), Sardinia, Corsica, and Sicily—which they went on to govern after their year of office as consul or praetor was over.

As censor in 184, Cato did his best to discourage high living and set punitive taxes on expensive clothing, carriages, women's ornaments, furniture and plate. Many young men paid fortunes for a rent boy or for highly fashionable pickled fish. In a public speech, Cato said, "Anybody can see that the Republic is going downhill when a pretty lad can cost more than a plot of land and jars of fish more than plowmen." In no way did Scipio and his family have anything to do with that kind of behavior, but to judge by Polybius's account of his wife's appearances in public at religious services there was little attempt to cut costs:

> [It was] her habit to appear in great state. . . . Apart from the magnificence of her personal attire and of the decorations of her carriage, all the baskets, cups and sacrificial vessels or utensils were made of gold or of silver, and were carried in her train on such ceremonial occasions, while the retinue of her maids and manservants who accompanied her was proportionally large.

Scipio's critics regarded the extravagant splendor of his lifestyle as part of the same general picture of moral decline.

Cato was disgusted by the abuses of power he came across as censor and ruthlessly weeded out the unworthy when he scrutinized the membership lists of the Senate and the class of *equites*. One particular case that Cato exposed concerned a former consul, Lucius Quinctius Flamininus, and horrified public opinion. Flamininus was conducting an affair with an expensive and notorious male prostitute named Philippus the Carthaginian. He persuaded Philippus to join him on campaign in Cisalpine Gaul (today's Po Valley). The boy used to tease his lover for having made him leave Rome just before the gladiatorial games, which, as a result, he had had to miss. One evening they were having a dinner party and were flushed with wine when a senior Celtic deserter arrived in the camp. He asked to see the consul, with a view to winning his personal protection.

The man was brought into the tent and began to address Flamininus through an interpreter. While he was speaking, the consul turned to his lover and said, "Since you missed the gladiatorial show, would you like to see this Celt dying?"

The boy nodded, not taking the offer seriously. Flamininus then drew his sword, which was hanging above his couch, struck the Celt's head while he was still speaking, and ran him through as he tried to escape. This breach of good faith toward someone seeking Rome's friendship was shocking enough, but what was really dreadful to the Roman mind was the casual ending of a life at a *convivium*, a boozy party.

Had the virtuous Republic of Cincinnatus come to this?

AS THE GLORIOUS victory over Hannibal receded into history, Cato and his friends sought every occasion to muddy the reputation of the Scipios. Africanus responded to these attacks with the clumsiness of a hurt lion trying to fend off a pack of hyenas. Matters came to a head when he and his brother Lucius returned to Rome in 190 after a successful campaign against Antiochus the Great of Syria. (I describe this in the next chapter.)

A few years later, during a meeting of the Senate, a hostile tribune, eager to stir up trouble, asked Lucius to account for the sum of five hundred talents, the first installment of a vast Syrian indemnity of fifteen thousand talents. There seems to have been no real suspicion of fraud; the money probably went to pay the soldiers' wages. In any event, while Lucius, as consul and commander-in-chief, was under a legal obligation to account for state funds, he was much less accountable for moneys won from the enemy.

Whoever was in the right, Africanus—then *princeps senatus,* or honorary leader of the Senate—lost his temper. Realizing that he was the indirect target of the intervention, he asked for the campaign books to be brought to him and tore them up in front of the Senate. The affair was allowed to drop, but the Scipios had been shown to be high-handed and possibly light-fingered. The opposition under Cato soon resumed their assault; another tribune was found who laid the question before the People. When Lucius still refused to account for the five hundred talents, he was fined, with a threat of imprisonment if he declined to pay. However, yet another tribune entered a veto. Cato was satisfied that enough had been done to discredit the brothers and no further action was taken.

When the Bacchanalia scandal broke in 186, Cato (of course) blamed Scipio and his circle for having opened the doors to Greek cults and influences, which now posed such great danger to the security of the Republic.

The final onslaught came in 184, and this time Scipio himself was accused (with a farrago of old charges). A huge crowd of clients and friends accompanied him to the Forum. According to Polybius, he spoke only briefly and with typically lofty sangfroid: "The Roman People are not entitled to listen to anyone who speaks against Publius Cornelius Scipio, for it is thanks to him that they have the power of speech at all."

The hearing was adjourned to a new date, which happened to be the anniversary of the Battle of Zama. This was too good an opportunity to be missed. Scipio arrived in court and announced that he was going to climb up to the Capitol to render thanks to the gods for the victory. Anyone who wished to accompany him would be very welcome. With one accord, the crowd left the Forum and followed in Scipio's footsteps. The master publicist did not stop at the Capitol but spent the rest of the day visiting other temples in the city. It was indeed as if Rome were celebrating a festival, with Scipio Africanus as its impresario. Cato's old insult had become reality.

But the lordly patrician had had enough. He retired to his villa at Liternum, a town on the sandy shore near Cumae, and refused to appear at the trial when it resumed. He pleaded sickness; this may have been a truthful rather than a diplomatic excuse, for within a year he was dead, at the comparatively early age of fifty-two.

He left instructions that he should be buried on the grounds of his villa, rather than in the Scipio mausoleum on the Via Appia. Rome's most talented commander wanted nothing more to do with his ungrateful city, even in death.

15

The Gorgeous East

THE WAR WITH HANNIBAL WAS OVER AND PEOPLE were worn out. The Italian countryside was devastated, the economy wrecked, the public finances deep in the red, and hundreds of thousands of citizens and allies had lost their lives in eighteen years of fighting. Victory was usually sweet, but this time it tasted bitter. There was no life-threatening enemy in sight, and for once Romans had had enough of the battlefield. Everybody was looking forward to a period of peace and recuperation. And yet, within a couple of years of the Battle of Zama, the Senate entered into a major new war. The People vetoed the enterprise when the question was broached, but, when invited to return to the subject, gave its reluctant consent.

How could this be?

THE REPUBLIC WAS unprepared for greatness. As the heir of Carthage, it now controlled the islands of the Western Mediterranean and most of Spain, but it had no other territorial ambitions. The old enemy was allowed to manage its own affairs in northern Africa but could not act independently at home or abroad without the Senate's express permission. Italy, although not yet the Celtic Po Valley, was well used to the yoke and after Pyrrhus and Hannibal the legions were invincible. Now in charge of half the known world, Rome had become a superpower, without being fully aware of what this might mean.

For many of its citizens, by contrast, the Eastern Mediterranean was terra incognita. Of course, traders traded and from time to time inquirers made the arduous trip to Delphi to learn about the future. In the third century, the Senate entered into friendly but remote relations with Egypt, but otherwise it had little direct experience of the world of Hellenic politics, and little interest in acquiring more. However, this was about to change.

Rome was now more open than ever to foreign, especially Greek, cultural influence. This seemed to some dangerously intoxicating, and to others an irresistible means of civilizing a provincial people. The contradiction in Roman attitudes was a proxy for a deeper uncertainty. Was the Republic to hoard its new power and live within an old, comfortable but limited mindset? And would the outside world allow it to do so? Multiple appeals for political and military assistance from across the known world began to pour into Rome. Cato and his puritans were fighting against human nature when they argued that these things had to be rejected. If a state has power and refuses to use it, it may create a vacuum that other unfriendly interests will seek to fill.

Was the Republic to welcome the prospect of empire and a *mission civilisatrice*? If so, somehow traditional ways would have to be adapted to new conditions. Men like Scipio Africanus envisioned a Hellenized Rome ready to embrace cultural diversity, to police the Mediterranean, and to operate a disinterested hegemony. Of course, this was a utopian vision. Imperialists may comfort themselves with their benevolence, but it is in their nature to intrude, to decide from a distance, to believe that the consent of provincials to foreign rule is freely given and not simply a rational response to the use of force.

Cato and Scipio represented two different responses to Rome's

military successes. The former inherited the native, negative caution of Fabius Maximus the Delayer, of whom he was an admirer:
he was a narrow nationalist and had no ambition for a wider empire. Although he knew a good deal more about Greek language
and literature than he let on, he wanted nothing to do with Hellenic culture and the East. It was enough to have expelled Hannibal
from Italy. By contrast, Scipio was a natural expansionist. The two
men embodied the dilemmas facing the Republic—between tradition and innovation, Hellenism and the *mos maiorum,* patriotism
and internationalism, superstition and mysticism, severity and tolerance, self-denial and extravagance. Which direction would Rome
take? Cato and his principles won many supporters, but, with his
acceptance of Rome's imperial destiny, Scipio saw a long way further into the future.

MORE THAN A century had passed since the death of Alexander
the Great, and his Oriental empire had broken down into three
large pieces—the kingdoms of Macedonia, Syria, and Egypt, which
jostled among themselves in an uneasy balance of power. To them
should be added some smaller fragments—including the mercantile island of Rhodes and the compact but wealthy kingdom of
Pergamum, in Asia Minor. The tiny city-states of Greece had long
since lost their international importance and dwelled reluctantly in
the chilling shadow of Macedon, which kept them under control by
garrisoning three strategic fortresses, nicknamed the "fetters of
Greece," at Corinth, Chalcis, and Demetrias. Some of them gathered together into federations—the most important being the Aetolian League, in the northern half of Greece, and the Achaean
League, in the Peloponnese. Athens lived off its past glories and
had dwindled into a center for the ancient equivalent of postgradu-
ate studies, especially in philosophy.

The intervention of Pyrrhus had been an unpleasant introduction to Hellenic belligerence, but, as already noted, Rome's first

military operation on Greek soil had been against the Illyrians, a half-Hellenized and piratical kingdom along the Dalmatian coast-line, which in the mid-third century expanded downward into to-day's Albania. No doubt they were alarmed by the establishment, in 244, of a Latin fortress-colony just across the strait at Brundis-ium, one of the finest harbors on the peninsula's east coast. During the Second Punic War, the murder of a Roman envoy at the hands of Illyrian privateers led the Senate to authorize a decisive interven-tion on their home territory.

This annoyed the king of Macedon, Philip V, a ruthless and im-pulsive ruler with a black sense of humor. He objected to intrusion into what he regarded as his sphere of influence. The Battle of Can-nae persuaded him to join what he wrongly guessed would be the winning side, and he concluded a treaty of mutual assistance with Hannibal. Nothing very much happened as a consequence except for some desultory fighting on the Greek mainland. By 205, with Scipio on the point of invading North Africa, the king realized that he had misjudged the situation and negotiated a peace. He was in a strong military position at the time. The Romans usually dis-cussed terms only when they were the victors, but on this occasion they were too busy to pursue Philip and agreed a treaty. However, they had not closed their account with Macedon.

Philip was always on the lookout for an unfair advantage. When a six-year-old boy acceded to the throne of the Ptolemies, he judged that the time was right to grab some of Egypt's overseas posses-sions. Not for nothing did the (possibly contemporary) author of Ecclesiastes write: "Woe to you, oh land, where your king is a child." In the winter of 203–202, the Macedonian monarch reached an understanding with his royal colleague and competitor, Antio-chus the Great of Syria, according to which they would share the spoils.

While Syria marched southward, Philip indiscriminately as-saulted unoffending cities on the Bosphorus, annexed the Cyclades,

and took the island of Samos. Pergamum and Rhodes were outraged, and it was not long before the king went on to attack them,
too. This uncalled-for aggression infuriated his victims, but what
could they do? Macedon and Syria were in cahoots, and Egypt was
impotent. Philip would not have had to answer for his crimes had
it not been for the arrival of Rome as a new actor on the geopolitical
stage.

Pergamum and Rhodes appealed to the Republic for assistance.
The Senate was minded to send out an expeditionary force at once,
but the Assembly's opposition made it hold its hand. The truth was
that Philip had acted perfectly properly toward Rome, and none of
the complainants were officially allies, requiring or permitting intervention. This was awkward if the law, the *ius fetiale,* was to be
obeyed. It stipulated that war could be declared only in the Republic's or its oathbound allies' self-defense.

So in 200 the Senate sent Philip an ultimatum so severe that he
would be compelled to reject it. The king duly obliged. In a sharp
exchange, a senior senatorial envoy blamed him for his aggression,
to which the king replied that if there had to be war his Macedonians would give a good account of themselves. The envoy broke
off the discussion and reported unfavorably to the Senate in Rome.
Philip had to be taught a lesson. When the subject was broached a
second time the People gave way and war was declared.

The sequence of events is clear, but no record survives of the Senate's debates which might explain its motives. So we have to specu-
late. Some have argued that this was a case of naked imperialism.
But there is little evidence that the ruling élite was set on a course
of territorial enlargement. It had annexed no Carthaginian land in
North Africa, and at present its hands were full dealing with recal-
citrant Spaniards and unsettled Celts in northern Italy. Senators
were as reluctant to go to war as the rest of the population.

Others have said that the Senate was packed with idealists who
wanted to free Greece from its Macedonian despot, that it was will-

ing, for no advantage, to be the known world's "policeman." Certainly aristocrats like Scipio Africanus were steeped in Greek culture, but they had no special fondness for modern Greeks and deployed their philhellenism strictly for Rome's benefit.

We must not exclude the possibility that miscalculation played a part in the slide towards conflict. Neither side knew enough about the other; Rome may have exaggerated the threat Macedon posed, and Philip simply would not take the Senate's interference in his own internal affairs seriously until it was too late.

In all likelihood, there was one main reason for the outbreak of hostilities, and two subordinate background motives. The Senate took the long view and was anxious to allow no hostile power to gather strength in the Eastern Mediterranean, as Carthage had done in the West. The military partnership between Macedon and Syria might well now be directed against Egypt, but it was easy to imagine Rome becoming a target in the future. It was wise to cut Philip down to size when the opportunity offered. After all, he had already fought a war against Rome, and (here was one of the secondary motives) he had not yet been punished for it.

Finally, there were the individual ambitions of those who governed the Republic. They were essentially a closed group of about two thousand men, a gentlemen's club, to which only a few "new men" (such as Cato) were admitted. Competition among them was more or less friendly, but at any given time most would be without a public commission. Following the defeat of Hannibal, Rome's new possessions in the Western Mediterranean (Near Spain and Further Spain, Sicily, Corsica, and Sardinia) all required governors and other officials, opening new opportunities for political action, military adventure, and self-enrichment. And now that the complicated, glamorous polity of the Orient had come within the Republic's purview there were jobs as ambassadors, advisers and, it could safely be predicted, army commanders. Roman travelers—officials and businessmen—stepped expectantly into this new world, and it is easy to imagine their mixed feelings of excitement and greed as they explored great cities such as Athens, Antioch, and Ephesus, toured the Seven Wonders of the World, and admired the amenities of Hellenic civilization.

AS USUAL, THE legions were slow off the mark, and Philip's energy and his willingness to deploy pillage and massacre as tools of policy gave him the initiative.

In the second year of the war, the tempo changed when an attractive and talented young man took over command of the Roman war effort. He was Titus Quinctius Flamininus (brother of the Flamininus who killed a Celt to amuse his lover and the same man who, later in his career, pursued Hannibal to his grave—see pages 279 and 280). Charismatic, charming, and a philhellene, he was a Scipio mark two. Against some opposition, he was elected consul at the unusually early age of twenty-nine.

Consul and king met for a conference at which Flamininus bluntly told Philip to unlock the fetters of Greece (in other words, withdraw his garrisons) and compensate the states whose lands and cities he had plundered. The king replied that he would never free cities that had previously been under Macedonian control, and that any claims for damages should be submitted to arbitration. The consul hit back: "There is no need for referees; it is obvious who is the aggressor." Philip lost his temper. He objected to being treated as if he had already been defeated, he said, and stormed out.

It was clear that Flamininus intended to eject the Macedonians from their three fortresses and then chase them from Greece altogether. Philip knew he did not command the manpower to survive a war of attrition and, betting on a quick victory, took the offensive. However, the Romans, supported by the Aetolian League, drove him back into Thessaly. The furious king adopted a scorched-earth policy as he withdrew, while the more astute Flamininus avoided looting and atrocities. Although one or two of his allies in the Peloponnese remained loyal, Philip could see that Greece was slipping from his grasp. He asked for another conference.

Someone at the meeting took notes, and a detailed account has survived that throws light on how international relations were conducted in those days, and on Philip's personality. The subtext is that, despite his readiness to talk, Flamininus never had any intention of agreeing a peace, whereas the king was eager for one, provided he could avoid complete capitulation.

THE ENCOUNTER TOOK place in the open air on a beach near Thermopylae. Captains and kings did not trust one another, and it was essential to choose a spot where the chances of an ambush were reduced to a minimum. A built-up area was risky, and in any event it would be hard to find a town or city that was reliably neutral. The coast had the advantage that one party could travel to the rendezvous by land and the other on water. This meant that neither could easily pursue and capture the other.

On this occasion, Flamininus and various delegates from Greece, Pergamum, and Rhodes gathered on the beach and waited for Philip to turn up. He arrived in a warship escorted by five galleys. He sailed close to the shore but refused to disembark.

The consul asked, tactlessly, "What are you afraid of?"

"I fear nothing but the gods, but I don't trust many of those present, especially the Aetolians," the King replied.

This was an inauspicious beginning, but Flamininus invited the king, who had requested the meeting, to raise whatever topics he wished.

"It is not for me to speak first, but rather for you. Kindly explain what I must do to have peace."

The consul set out his terms, of which the most important was that Philip should withdraw completely from Greece. Then the other representatives itemized detailed shopping lists. So, for example, the envoy from Pergamum wanted the king to restore the sanctuary of Aphrodite and the Temple of Athena the Bringer of Victory, near Pergamum, both of which he had destroyed during his foray into the kingdom.

A certain Phaeneas from the Aetolian League spoke at great length, making the point, with copious examples, that Philip had a habit of impartially devastating the territories of friends and allies as well as foes. This riled the king, who approached closer to the shore and criticized Phaeneas for speaking in "typically theatrical and Aetolian style." He went on to reject his charges, while conceding that commanders sometimes had to do things they would rather not do.

Phaeneas, who had very poor eyesight, interrupted and pointed out that words were not the issue: "The truth is that you must either fight and conquer, or else obey those who are stronger than you."

Philip, who had a reputation for being more satirical than was entirely suitable for a king, could not resist a sarcastic (and unamusing) joke at the speaker's expense: "Yes, even a blind man can see that!"

A disjointed conversation followed, in which the king continued to grumble about the Aetolians. He then put a clever question to those at the meeting: "In any case, what is this Greece you want me to evacuate? Most of the Aetolians themselves are not Greek." He cited other territories that were not regarded as genuinely Hellenic. "Am I allowed to stay in *these* places?" he asked.

He then turned his attention to the other speakers, dealing brusquely and mordantly with each issue they raised, point by point: "As for the damage done to the sanctuary of Athena and the shrine of Aphrodite, I can't help with the restoration, but I'll send some gardeners to look after the place and see to the growth of the trees that were cut down." Flamininus smiled.

Finally, Philip turned to the consul. "Is it the general's wish that I should withdraw from those towns and places I myself conquered, or that I should leave those which I inherited from my ancestors?" Flamininus remained silent, although some of his delegates were ready and primed to reply. However, the hour was getting late and Philip concluded by asking all the parties present to give him written statements of their positions. "I am alone and have no one to advise me," he explained. "I would like to reflect on your various demands."

The consul was amused by the mockery in Philip's tone of voice. He replied, "Of course you are alone by this time, Philip, for you have killed off all those friends who could give you good advice." The king grinned sardonically and said nothing. Everyone agreed to meet again the next day.

The Romans arrived punctually, but there was no sign of the king. They waited all day, and at last the Macedonians arrived just before dusk. Philip said in excuse that he had been delayed studying all the submissions. This was gamesmanship, for what he wanted was to finesse a tête-à-tête with Flamininus. The hour being late, the assembled dignitaries agreed that the two men, accompanied by only a few members of their staffs, should confer privately. The king disembarked and he and the consul talked together for a long time in the fading light.

Flamininus reported back to his delegation on the complicated but limited concessions the Macedonians were prepared to make. All present loudly declared their dissatisfaction with the proposals. Philip could see that an animated discussion was going on and proposed another adjournment to the following day.

The next morning, the king arrived on time. He gave a short speech, in which he said that he would be willing to send an embassy to the Senate for these matters to be determined if agreement was not possible now. Flamininus was happy to concede the point, for he wanted time to arrange for the Senate to approve the extension of his command. One may surmise that the idea of a reference to Rome had been mooted in quiet conversation on the darkened beach the night before.

THE SENATE DEBATED Philip's peace proposals, rejected them, and gave the consul the extension he was seeking. For all his cleverness, the king's diplomacy had failed and hostilities resumed. By the spring of 197, Flamininus had won over almost all of Greece, except for the fetters. More than twenty-three thousand Macedonians marched south into Thessaly, where they approached a Roman army of about the same size. The ground was unsuitable for a battle and Philip and Flamininus led their men along each side of a chain of hills called Cynoscephalae (Greek for "dogs' heads"). They collided more or less by chance. A battle ensued on uneven ground, which suited the flexible legion more than the unwieldy phalanx. A Roman detachment managed to outflank the enemy and fell on their rear. The day was won.

Since the reigns of Alexander the Great and his talented father, Philip, during the fourth century, the Macedonian phalanx had been insuperable. Now, to the amazement of the Hellenic world, it was destroyed as a fighting force. The initiative had shifted decisively to the still unfamiliar invaders from the west.

The ambitious and overbearing Aetolian League, whose soldiers had fought alongside the Romans, wanted to see Philip's power destroyed, but Flamininus knew better. It was enough that Macedon had been humbled and pushed back behind its borders. Its complete elimination would create a vacuum, upsetting the balance of power in the Eastern Mediterranean and encouraging Celts in the north to march down into Greece. A tamed Philip was left on his throne, stripped of his external dependencies, including the fetters, and bound into an alliance with Rome. Nothing if not a realist, he accepted his new, reduced status.

The senatorial decree that laid down the peace terms was more than a treaty with the king of Macedon; it was also a manifesto, which announced that Greeks everywhere (that is, in Asia Minor as well as the Balkans) were to be free. Rome was arrogating to itself the authority to determine the governance of Alexander's fractured empire. It not only decided the fate of Philip, its defeated enemy, but also warned Antiochus, whose path it had never crossed, to behave himself.

But what, exactly, was freedom to mean? As soon as Philip had withdrawn his garrisons from the fetters, the Senate substituted its own. Cynics wondered if one despot was to be replaced with another. Rome wanted to avoid military occupation and direct rule, which would bring much convenience and no obvious advantage, but was worried by a possible threat from Antiochus in the east; without the deterrent fortresses manned by Romans, he might be tempted to invade. Also, there were a number of awkward disputes that only Rome was in a position to settle. An ambitious king of Sparta needed to be restrained. The Aetolians were furious that the Senate had not rewarded them generously enough for their help in the war; they wanted additional territory, even though this was obviously inconsistent with giving the Greek city-states their independence. They put it about that the plan to free Greece was a fraud, claiming, "Flamininus has unshackled the foot of Greece only to put a collar round her neck."

There was something in these rumors. Ten senatorial commissioners advised Flamininus on the details of the settlement of Greece, and took the view that the fetters *should* remain in Roman hands. This would be a disaster, the commander felt, for when announced it would justify the suspicions of the Aetolians. With some difficulty, he persuaded the commission to change its mind.

Flamininus decided to dispel the fractious mood by staging a public-relations spectacular in Corinth, the wealthy entrepôt on the isthmus connecting the Peloponnese to northern Greece and the capital of the Achaean League. The Isthmian Games, an athletics and arts festival, were held there every two years (before and after the quadrennial Olympic Games) in the summer. A general truce was declared, to guarantee free passage to athletes, and people came from all over Greece to watch chariot races, boxing, wrestling, and the *pankration,* a blend of boxing and wrestling but with no rules except for a ban on eye-gouging and biting. There were also poetry and music contests, in which women were, apparently and unusually, allowed to compete.

At the Games of 196, the first peacetime festival for some years, a large crowd gathered in the stadium. Flamininus arranged for a trumpeter to signal a general silence. A public crier then stepped forward and announced:

> The Senate of Rome and Titus Quinctius Flamininus the procon-sul, having defeated King Philip and the Macedonians in battle, leave the following states and cities free, without garrisons, sub-ject to no tribute and in full enjoyment of their ancestral laws: the peoples of Corinth, Phocis, Locri, Euboea, Phthiotic Achaea, Magnesia, Thessaly and Perrhaebia.

The states and cities mentioned were all those which had recog-nized claims to independence and had been directly governed by Philip.

At the beginning of the proclamation, there was a deafening shout and some people did not hear what was said. Most did, though, and could not believe their ears. Polybius writes:

> What had happened was so unexpected that it was as if they were listening to the words in a kind of dream. They clamored and shouted, each of them moved perhaps by a different impulse, for the herald and the trumpeter to come forward into the middle of the stadium and repeat the proclamation. They wished, no doubt, not only to hear the speaker but to see him, so difficult did it seem to believe what he was saying.

As requested, the trumpeter blew his trumpet and the crier read out the text for a second time. A tremendous burst of cheering arose, so loud that it was heard at sea, and the entire audience got to its feet. Eyewitnesses many years later said it was difficult for those who could only read of the event in the present day to imagine how it sounded. Some ravens that happened to be flying over the stadium were so startled by the unexpected noise that they fell out of the sky.

When the shouting finally died away, it was replaced by a hubbub of excited chatter. Nobody paid the slightest attention to the athletic contests, but mobbed Flamininus. People pressed forward to touch his hand, garlands and headbands made from ribbon were thrown over him, and he was hailed as the savior of the Greeks. He only just escaped from the congratulations unharmed.

This was the reception that every liberator throughout history has dreamed of, but, as so many benevolent invaders have found to their cost, the moment of joy was shortlived.

The Greek cities, now to be freed, were as unquenchably quarrelsome as ever; Flamininus and his commission had to spend a year adjudicating and settling various disputes. Inevitably, this was unpopular work, not helped by the proconsul's de haut en bas manner, but once it was completed the Senate fervently hoped that it would not have to concern itself any more with Greek affairs. In the fall of 194, the Romans at last removed their garrisons from the fetters, and evacuated from Greece. Flamininus brought back cartloads of Greek art and much treasure, which decorated his triumph.

PHILIP OF MACEDON'S onetime partner in crime, Antiochus the Great, was tired of Rome's intrusion into what he regarded as his sphere of influence—namely, Asia Minor. For its part, the Senate feared that he planned to attack Rome—a fear much enhanced by Hannibal's arrival at his court. In fact, the Syrian monarch had no such intention. His vision was to restore the empire that his dynastic ancestor, Seleucus, had carved from the dead Alexander's

domains, and that was the extent of his ambitions. As far as the
Romans were concerned, he simply wanted them to leave him
alone. If only a pact could be agreed, along with a few platitudes
about perpetual friendship, the two states could pursue their separate courses unhindered.

On the face of it, Antiochus was a highly successful ruler. Born
in about 241, he was a young man when he inherited the throne
and a disorganized realm from his elder brother, who had been assassinated. He and the other Successors were of Macedonian or
sometimes Greek stock. They were absolute despots, devoted to the
perpetuation of their dynasties and to enriching themselves at
the expense of their subjects. Seleucus told his army bluntly toward
the end of his reign, "And I tell you that it is not the customs of the
Persians and other such nations that I shall impose on you rather
than this one law, common to them all, that whatever the king
decides is always right."

Philosophers developed a meritocratic theory that kingship was
a reward for noble deeds, and the next natural step upward (not unlike the *cursus honorum* for elected magistrates in Rome) was promotion to godhead. Heracles (the Greek version of Hercules) had
pointed the way, transcending his mortality. Homer had given his
imprimatur to the concept of a divided self, when his wanderer
Odysseus descends into hell and meets the hero's ghost:

> I observed the powerful Heracles—
> his image, that is, but he himself banquets at ease
> among the immortal gods.

Some monarchs reserved their divinity à la Heracles until after
their death, but alive they were at least *isotheoi,* or godlike. Others
put in a claim to deification before the tomb. A king of Macedon in
the previous century was greeted on his entry into Athens by a
choir singing a specially written hymn:

> The other gods are far away,
> or cannot hear.
> Or are non-existent, or care nothing for us;
> but *you* are here, and visible to us,
> not carved in wood or stone, but real.
> So to you we pray.

This attitude, which combined rational skepticism with divine worship, was widespread in the sophisticated East among rulers such as Antiochus and his subjects.

On his accession, the energetic and ambitious Antiochus set about rebuilding his empire. He failed to take back from the Ptolemies Syrian lands into which they had encroached, but he had more success in pressing his cause in Asia Minor. Then he decided to follow in Alexander's footsteps and marched east into Parthia and Bactria. He crossed into the Kabul Valley and descended into India, where he made friends with an Indian king, Subhashsena, from whom he procured elephants for his army. After a short expedition down the Persian Gulf, he returned home to general applause. He had restored his father's empire and on his return acquired the complimentary title of "the Great." He took to styling himself the Great King, after the long-gone Persian monarchs.

Antiochus's reputation was at its height, and from Rome's viewpoint he presented a serious threat. He was apparently an able general and now commanded a supply of manpower that outmatched that of the Republic. In fact, though, his seven-year *anabasis* ("journey up-country") had as much to do with public relations as with actual conquest. We do not know whether the Senate had any inkling of this, but the king had managed only to win friendly allies rather than to impose satrapies or annex provinces. He controlled nothing much beyond Persepolis. What he had done, admittedly with some skill, was to erect a sword-and-sandals film set, impressive from a distance but lath and plasterboard in close-up.

Having won the coastal cities of Asia Minor, the spoils of his mutual aggression pact with Philip, he decided to fit into place the last piece of the Seleucid imperial jigsaw—Thrace, Greece's unruly, semi-barbarous neighbor. To secure this, he crossed the Bosphorus onto European soil in 196. It was a truly momentous mistake, made from nostalgia rather than necessity.

Understandably, the Romans were displeased. In their view, Thrace was the essential no-man's-land between their sphere of influence and that of Antiochus. But the Syrian king located his neutral buffer zone somewhere west—the liberated Balkans. The sooner the Senate pulled back its troops from there, the better. This mismatch of understandings led inexorably to war.

The king opened negotiations with the Romans, but to little purpose. His embassies were rebuffed and he was infuriated by the Senate's patronizing assumption that it had the right to tell him how to govern in his own lands. Meanwhile, Pergamum, as alarmed by Syrian expansionism as it had been by that of Philip, dripped poison about his hostile intentions into the Senate's receptive ear. It was against its better judgment that it had endorsed the evacuation of Greece.

In 193 Flamininus, now back in Rome and speaking with the full authority of the Senate, at last offered Antiochus, through his envoys, a clear if cynical deal: "If he wishes us to take no interest in the concerns of the [Greek] cities of Asia, he on his part must keep his hands off any part of Europe." In other words, provided that Antiochus gave up Thrace, Rome would give him a free hand in Asia Minor (so much for the liberty of the Greeks!). But this was the one thing he would not do, so dear to him was his dream of reassembling Seleucus's vast domain.

It was at this awkward moment that the leaders of the Aetolian League moved to avenge themselves on an ungrateful Rome. They looked about for allies, and first of all they made overtures to King Philip. But bitter experience had taught him to stay in the Senate's good books, and he declined to join any insurrection. Finally, the Aetolians invited Antiochus to liberate Greece from the Romans. Most observers would have thought that it was not the Republic that posed any threat (after all, the legions had left), but, rather, the Aetolians themselves, ambitious to fill the space left by the Romans and a reduced Macedon.

While waiting for an answer, they set about making trouble. They assassinated the—admittedly annoying—Spartan king. The league then tried to capture Chalcis, one of the fetters, but was told sharply by its inhabitants that since Chalcis was already free it did not need freeing. The port of Demetrias, whose citizens were nervous that Rome might hand them back to Philip as a reward for his loyalty, was another of the fetters, and here the Aetolians were successful.

After a pause for thought, the Great King accepted the invitation. What persuaded him to take such a foolhardy step? Surely he could see that the Aetolians were unreliable, and that the Romans, who had already defeated the Hellenic phalanx, would return to Greece in force. In the autumn of 192, his fleet arrived at Demetrias and a small body of only ten thousand men and six of his famous elephants disembarked. This would hardly frighten off the Romans. It seems that all he wanted was respect.

Antiochus spent a lazy winter enjoying his recent marriage to a pretty local girl from Chalcis, and a more trying spring being unceremoniously chased out of Greece. A Roman army thrashed the invaders so overwhelmingly at that most symbolic of locations, Thermopylae, that the king lost no time in setting sail for home. If he hoped that the legions would now leave him be in his eastern empire, he was to be disappointed.

The Senate intended to teach him a lesson. Lucius Scipio, consul, with his much more famous brother Africanus as his deputy, or *legatus,* headed an army of about thirty thousand men. They were assisted by Philip, who, as a token of gratitude, had his war indemnity reduced and his son Demetrius, a hostage in Rome, sent back to Macedon. Pergamum and Rhodes were, of course, on Rome's side. Despite some setbacks, the legions crossed over into Asia for the first time and in December 190 met Antiochus's host, twice their number, at Magnesia, a city in Lydia not far from Smyrna.

The Great King, on his army's right wing, led a successful cavalry charge and galloped off in hot pursuit of the enemy. Meanwhile, the Romans routed and methodically butchered the phalanx. Antiochus only turned around when he met resistance at the Roman camp. He presumed that he was the victor and rode back in a haughty frame of mind. But when he saw the battlefield strewn with the dead bodies of his own men, horses, and elephants and his camp captured, he precipitately fled. Darkness fell, but still he rode on, reaching the Lydian capital, Sardis, and safety at midnight.

This was the end of Syria as a great power. Rome set an indemnity at fifteen thousand talents, the highest ever recorded. Antiochus was barred from Greece and most of Asia Minor, and was compelled to abandon his ancestral claim to Thrace. But, as with Philip, he was left on his throne. At this time, the Senate preferred to neutralize a fallen enemy, rather than to totally destroy him. In that way, it ensured the region's stability without being obliged to govern it itself.

That said, the message of Magnesia was unmistakable. The Successors to Alexander were no longer free agents. Rome insisted on obedience to its wishes, so they had to think twice before doing anything that might disturb the always uneasy equilibrium in the region.

By contrast, Pergamum, Rhodes, and the free Greek cities along the Aegean coastline had cause to be thankful to their protector. The Senate could depend on them to keep a watchful eye on behalf of Roman interests.

A small town off the beaten track on the coast of Phrygia was surprised to receive largesse from the victors, in the form of an exemption from taxes. This was Troy, now a mound of multidated ruins beside an unimpressive village that made a living from tourism. It had rendered no recent services to merit the award. But for Romans this was their once-upon-a-time *patria,* their land of lost content.

And what a pleasure it was to enjoy at leisure the humiliation of the once triumphant Greeks!

PHILIP'S SON BY a legal wife, Demetrius, now back home, was a charming and attractive young man. During his enforced stay in Rome, he had become popular in leading circles. How much more congenial it would be, senators mused, if they could deal with *him* on the Macedonian throne rather than with his prickly father or the heir apparent, his older brother Perseus, the offspring of a mistress. Perseus became convinced that Demetrius was plotting to oust him from the succession; he may well have been right in suspecting that attention and flattery had turned the inexperienced prince's head.

Unfortunately, there was no evidence, so Perseus manufactured some. He produced a forged letter from Flamininus spelling out Demetrius's treasonable plans. The king was taken in, and in 180 arranged his son's murder. At a dinner party, poison was added to Demetrius's drink. Draining the cup, the boy instantly realized what had happened and before long the pains began. He withdrew to his bedroom and raged against his father and brother, whom he correctly blamed for his death. The noise was embarrassing, and a man was sent in to smother him.

Too late, Philip became convinced that the letter was a fabrication. He blamed Perseus, who was fortunate that the king soon died. Apparently, his final illness was psychological rather than physical: he could not sleep for remorse.

Safely enthroned, Perseus did all he could to calm any fears the Senate might harbor about him. But he was an energetic ruler, determined to turn over a new leaf after his father's long reign. His aim was to reestablish Macedon's good name in Greece and the wider East. Openness and generosity marked a break with his father's caustic *machtpolitik*. Measures such as an amnesty for debtors signaled support for the democratic masses rather than the local aristocracies with whom the Senate preferred to do business. His marriage to Antiochus's daughter and his half sister's union with the king of Bithynia improved his international standing. While keeping carefully to the terms of the treaty with Rome, the king built up and trained his army.

All this activity disturbed the Senate. In recent years, it had become much more aggressive in Greece, irritated by the city-states' endless sniping at one another and, in particular, the ambition of the Achaean League to take over the entire Peloponnese. But Perseus's new popularity was a sign of something much more serious. Pergamum still had the Senate's ear, into which it continually whispered far-fetched accusations, and did all it could to turn opinion against the king.

Was a revived and renewed Macedon preparing a fresh challenge to the Republic? Yes and no. Perseus certainly wanted to improve his kingdom's political position, but Philip had recognized that Macedon could not compete with Rome, and so, surely, did his son. The Romans reacted evasively to requests for dialogue and agreed to a deceitful truce to allow time to recruit troops. It was as if they wanted war however weak the case for it. Eventually, in 171, the Senate sent an expeditionary force to Greece.

As in the conflict with Philip, the campaign got off to a desultory start, but in 168 Perseus, who was not a confident commander, lost a decisive battle at Pydna. This was the end of Macedon as a political entity. The kingdom was split up into four self-governing republics and its former ruler walked in his victor's triumphal procession. Perseus spent the rest of his days under house arrest in a small hill town not far from Rome. He was allowed to live in some comfort, supplied with palace furniture from Macedon and served by former court attendants. A disappointed man, he lasted for only a couple of years, starving himself to death in 166.

By an irony of fate, his throneless son was named Alexander, a sad echo of the most glorious of Macedonian monarchs. He was left to make his own way in the world. He learned Latin, and made a living as a skilled metalworker in gold and silver and as a public notary.

THE MAN WHO broke the phalanx at Pydna was a veteran Roman general, Lucius Aemilius Paullus. On his way back to Rome, he received an appalling instruction from the Senate. Epirus had not distinguished itself greatly since the days of its glamorous king Pyrrhus, and had unwisely favored Perseus in the war now ended. In order to supply the legions with booty, the Senate instructed Paullus to pillage every Epirote city, town, or settlement that had come out for Macedon. The general was a connoisseur of all things Hellenic and had just finished a sightseeing tour of Greece, but he set his hand to this new task with a will.

Leading men from each community were ordered to bring out the silver and gold in their houses and temples; legionary detachments spread out across the territory to collect this treasure. This they did, and then simultaneously and without warning overran and sacked each settlement. In a single day 150,000 men, women, and children were made slaves and Epirus became a wasteland, a condition from which it never fully recovered.

There had always been slaves in Rome—serfs, bankrupt citizen peasants who sold themselves as labor, and, as the legions marched through Italy, captured enemies. They were a common feature of life—noticeable but not dominant. It was only when the Republic fought and won its overseas campaigns that the number of slaves rose to the point that it transformed the city's way of life—that, in a word, Rome became a slave society.

It has been estimated that the first Carthaginian war produced some seventy-five thousand slaves. In the struggle with Hannibal the capture of a single city, Tarentum, saw the sale of thirty thousand prisoners. Now, with the collapse of Macedon and the defeat of Syria, slaves and money flooded into Italy. People could also be purchased through organized piracy and trafficking.

A slave had no rights: he or she was a *res mancipi*—the property of an owner who was entitled to do with it as he liked, including inflicting death. Varro said, with a Roman's carelessly brutal frankness, that, along with a propertyless farmworker, a slave was "a kind of speaking tool."

A wealthy man would dispose of many, perhaps hundreds, of slaves, but even a lowly artisan owned one or two. The worst fate was to lead a short life working in the mines. Diodorus Siculus observed that many of these slaves preferred death to survival:

> Day and night they wear out their bodies digging underground, dying in large numbers because of the terrible conditions they have to endure. They are allowed no restbreaks or holidays and under their overseers' whiplashes are forced to suffer the most dreadful hardships.

Almost as bad as the mines was hard labor on the great landed estates that were replacing peasant smallholdings across the peninsula.

To be a house servant was also bad, but better. Owner and slave could get close. Good-looking boys and girls fetched large sums at auction, and a master might well expect sexual favors. "I know of a slave who dreamed that his penis was stroked and aroused by his master's hand," wrote an expert on the interpretation of dreams, adding ominously that this meant he would be bound to a pillar and "receive many strokes." In this way, the dream elided many slaves' two recurring fears—of sexual and physical abuse.

Slaves often managed to have a family life, even if it was the master who allocated partners. But, having produced children, they had to live with the permanent anxiety that their offspring might be sold off or, conversely, that the children might have to watch their old or sick parents auctioned or abandoned.

Open resistance was dangerous, although unhappy slaves sometimes absconded. This was a dangerous thing to do, though, for the reach of the Roman state was long. Cicero, in the following century, was upset when his highly educated slave, Dionysius, ran off with some books from his library. The man was tracked down to the province of Illyricum, and his disgruntled owner asked two successive governors to help him retrieve the fugitive. History does not record the outcome, but the incident shows how hard it was for a man on the run to vanish without trace.

Uniforms were forbidden on the grounds that this would show slaves how many of them there were and encourage solidarity and conspiracy. And indeed a slave revolt would occasionally terrify the authorities, but they all failed and were savagely put down. The most famous was that of Spartacus, a Thracian slave who led a revolt that began in 73 at the gladiatorial school at Capua. He routed three Roman armies before being cornered and destroyed in 71. Interestingly, rebels did not criticize the "peculiar institution" as such; they merely wanted to escape its grip.

One of the most remarkable, and in part mitigating, features of the Roman slave system was the widespread practice of manumission. Slaves were often freed, although they were likely to remain in their former owner's employ and were bound by the *clientela* system of mutual obligations. Affection may often have been the motive (although freedom was sometimes bought with hard-won savings), but liberation as a promised ultimate goal was a means of ensuring obedience and hard work.

Former slaves automatically became Roman citizens and (in theory, at least) their male progeny could stand for public office, although in practice a man's servile origin was remembered negatively for generations. The Romans had no concept of racial purity and, just as they had welcomed conquered states into partnership with them since the days of Romulus, so they invited individuals whom they had oppressed and degraded to join them as collaborators in their imperial project. Over time, Rome became the most culturally diverse of cities and its population mirrored the ethnic composition of its growing empire.

AT SOME POINT in the 190s, when the memory of the war with Hannibal was still sharp, Plautus wrote a comedy called *The Little Carthaginian* (in Latin *Poenulus*). What is striking is that the juvenile leads are sympathetically drawn in spite of the fact that they are all Carthaginian. One of them is a young man who is sold into slavery and adopted by his wealthy purchaser, and the other two are kidnapped girls bought by a pimp for prostitution.

A businessman named Hanno, the girls' father, has long been looking for them and arrives from Carthage. He gives his opening speech in the Punic language before slipping into fluent Latin. He is a typical, shrewd, polyglot Carthaginian who astutely conceals his linguistic ability, but he is also an affectionate parent and a man of authority. The play leaves the impression that the Carthaginians were regarded as a clever race but had had bad luck. There is no residual enmity from the years of war, and we may suppose that this reflected the general opinion among Plautus's audiences.

It was not at all how the eighty-one-year-old Cato the Censor saw things. A member of a senatorial commission, he visited Carthage in 157, and was shocked by what he found. The city had recovered from its defeat and was enjoying an economic boom. It no longer had to bear the costs of running an empire and hiring mercenaries. In the old days, its wealth derived from trading in the Western Mediterranean, but Rome had annexed its possessions in Sicily, Spain, Corsica, and Sardinia and its prosperity now depended on the agriculture in its North African hinterland. It exported foodstuffs and developed a thriving trade with Italy. The envoys were disturbed by the evidence of revival. Appian writes:

> They carefully observed the country; they saw how diligently it was cultivated, and what great estates it possessed. They entered the city and saw how greatly it had increased in wealth and population since its overthrow by Scipio not long before.

On their return to Rome, Cato and his colleagues reported what they had seen and argued that Carthage would once again become a threat to the security of the Republic. The aged censor would not let the matter drop. On one occasion, he spoke on the subject from the speakers' platform in the Forum; he took a large and appetizing Punic fig from the folds of his toga. The country where it grew, he said, was only three days' sail from Rome. At the end of every speech he made in the Senate, he added the sentence *"Ceterum censeo Carthaginem esse delendam"* ("In addition, it is my opinion that Carthage must be destroyed").

This is very odd. Carthage had behaved toward Rome as a faithful and assiduous ally for half a century and had made no attempt to run an independent foreign policy. It supplied large amounts of grain as gifts during the Macedonian Wars and the war with Antiochus. It also helped stimulate the Republic's economy by importing vast quantities of ceramics and kitchenware from Campania and elsewhere in central Italy. Although the city restored its great military and commercial harbors at about this time, it had adhered to the terms of the peace treaty. Hardly a single Carthaginian citizen had done any serious military service since Zama. What's more, it was obvious that, without an army and with no fleet to speak of, Carthage no longer had the resources, let alone the will, to mount a serious challenge against Rome.

There was one difficulty, which took the form of the irrepressible Numidian ruler Masinissa, now an old man in his late eighties. He had lost little of his energy over the passage of time; in his personal life he was philoprogenitive, having sired fifty-four children by numerous women, of whom the youngest was an infant. The king had a policy of settling and uniting the nomadic tribes over which he ruled; he admired Punic cultural values and wanted his subjects to adopt them. But he coveted Carthaginian land. According to the peace treaty of 201, he was entitled to claim back any territory that lay outside Carthage's borders and had originally been a part of his domain. Unfortunately the terms were vaguely expressed and Masinissa constantly encroached on real estate that the Carthaginians knew was theirs. The Council of Elders regularly complained to the Senate, which sent out delegations to arbitrate, including the one on which Cato served. These invariably found for the king or suspended judgment, whatever the rights and wrongs of the particular case.

However, despite this open wound Carthage continued to thrive and to do all it could to placate the Senate. Why, then, was Cato so monomanic on the subject? He had fought in the war against Hannibal and his memories were bitter. He may have seriously believed that the old enemy was making a comeback. His political opponents did not disagree with his analysis of Carthage's growing strength, but they argued that without a strong potential enemy Rome would grow soft and decadent.

A growing number of Romans supported Cato, but for more cynical reasons. They were aware that war was a highly profitable business. Carthage was a ripe fruit ready to fall from the tree into their grasping hands. Plutarch tells the story of a rich young Roman who held an extravagant dinner party. The centerpiece was a honey cake designed to look like a city. He said to his guests, "This is Carthage, please plunder it." Rome was becoming both greedy and ruthless. As with Philip of Macedon the Senate secretly made up its mind for war and waited for an excuse to act.

Two events precipitated the crisis. In 151, Carthage paid its last installment of reparations, so a useful source of income for the Republic now dried up. And then, with the self-confidence and independence of spirit of a house owner who has paid off a mortgage, the Council of Elders lost patience with Masinissa, who had made an encroachment too far.

THE 150S WERE an uneasy time. The men who had defeated the Carthaginians were leaving the stage. They had had quick and easy successes in the Eastern Mediterranean and long, hard campaigns as they slowly Romanized Cisalpine Gaul in the north of the peninsula, but now their experience and skills gradually faded away. There was less fighting to be done, and in the absence of grand campaigns the Republic's legions were demobilized. When an army was needed, the business of training had to start again from scratch. Younger commanders placed less emphasis on discipline, development, and high-quality logistics.

Since acquiring Spain from the Carthaginians and establishing two provinces, the Romans had had trouble taming the Spaniards, who resented being plundered by venal governors. Cato campaigned successfully there in the year after his consulship and was awarded a triumph, but trouble continued. A great insurrection broke out in 154 and raged until 133. Roman generals combined incompetence with treachery. Even the Senate was shocked when a proconsul invaded Lusitania (roughly today's Portugal) and agreed to a peace treaty with the rebels. On his promise of resettling them on good farming land, he persuaded them to gather on three separate plains, where he would assign them their new territories. He asked the Lusitanians to lay down their weapons, an order they unwisely obeyed, for, one after another, each group was massacred. Back in Rome, the proconsul was brought to trial and Cato spoke against him, but he deployed his ill-gotten gains to procure an acquittal.

One of the few to escape the butchery was a shepherd and hunter, who carried on the struggle. A stickler for fair dealing and true to his word, Viriathus was a shining and shaming contrast to his Roman opponents. He was also a guerrilla fighter of genius, who deployed small bands that made sudden raids and then disappeared into the sierra. Eventually, in 140, a proconsul bribed three of Viriathus's senior followers to kill him while he slept. This they did, but when they asked for their money the general refused, saying, "It never pleases the Romans that a general should be killed by his own soldiers." The remark was a fine example of that fusion of high-mindedness and fraud that was becoming a routine feature of Roman public life.

The great hill fortress of Numantia (Cerro de la Muela, near Soria), which stood at the junction of two rivers running between steep banks through wooded valleys, repelled Roman attacks for ten years. Bungling legionary commanders behaved with their usual bad faith, but eventually, in 133, Numantia fell to the able Publius Cornelius Scipio Africanus Aemilianus: he was the birth son of Aemilius Paullus and had been adopted by Scipio Africanus's childless son (hence the "Aemilianus" at the end, to signal the original genetic connection). Noble families often helped out those facing extinction because of an absence of male heirs by allowing one of their boys to be adopted. Without consulting the Senate, Scipio razed the town to the ground, as a layer of burned material found on the site testifies to this day.

At last, Rome had a firm hold on Spain.

WITH APPALLINGLY BAD judgment, the Carthaginians laid a trap for themselves and then, eyes wide open, walked into it.

They had agreed never to make war without the Senate's permission. In 152, they raised an army to put an end to Masinissa's depredations and went on the offensive. They did not inform Rome. Scipio Aemilianus happened to be in the country and tried unsuccessfully to mediate a cease-fire. The Numidian king then cornered and besieged the Punic forces, which were gradually weakened by disease and shortage of food and forced to capitulate. Harsh terms were agreed, and the Carthaginians were allowed to march away with nothing but a tunic each. As they were leaving, Numidian cavalry fell on the defenseless men and massacred most of them. Of an estimated twenty-five thousand men, only a handful returned to Carthage.

When the Senate learned of these events, it began to raise troops without offering an explanation, except to say that it was "just in case of emergencies." The Council of Elders was not deceived and immediately sent envoys to Rome. They explained that the war with Masinissa had not been approved by the government and that those responsible for it had been put to death. The Senate, aware that it now had its casus belli, refused to be appeased. Why, a senator inquired, had Carthage not condemned its officers at the first opportunity instead of waiting until they were beaten? It was an unanswerable question. The envoys asked what they could do to win a pardon. "You must make things right with the Roman People" was the alarmingly obscure response. A second embassy pleaded for specific instructions. The Senate dismissed it with the words "You know perfectly well what is necessary."

The Carthaginian authorities were at their wits' end. Their only hope, they decided, lay in unconditional surrender. A third delegation made its way to Rome to announce this, only to find that war had already been declared. Neverthess, the Senate cynically accepted the surrender and demanded three hundred child hostages.

There was no difficulty in attracting recruits to the legions, for it was clear to everyone that Carthage could not conceivably achieve victory and soldiers could expect rich pickings, treasure, and slaves. In 149, an unusually large army of eighty thousand infantry and four thousand cavalry crossed the sea to Africa. The two consuls were in command and carried secret orders to destroy the city utterly when they captured it. Very helpfully, the important Phoenician port of Utica, a few miles from Carthage, which was "well adapted for landing an army," came over to the Romans.

The Punic leadership was appalled by news of the invasion and was willing to do almost anything to avoid fighting an unwinnable war. Yet more envoys were dispatched to plead for peace, this time to the Roman camp. When they arrived, the consuls, surrounded by their chief officers and military tribunes, were seated on a high dais. The entire army, with polished armor and weapons and erect standards, was drawn up to attention. A trumpet blew and, in dead silence, the Carthaginians were then obliged to walk the length of the camp before they reached the consuls. A rope cordon prevented them from drawing near.

They asked why an expeditionary force was necessary to defeat an enemy that had no intention of fighting. Carthage would submit willingly to any penalty. In response, the consuls demanded the city's complete disarmament. This was at once conceded, and soon a line of wagons brought to the camp armor and weapons for twenty thousand men and many artillery pieces.

Only then did the consuls show their hand. They complimented the Carthaginians for their obedience so far, and asked them to accept bravely the Senate's final commands: "Hand over Carthage to us, and resettle yourselves wherever you like inside your own borders at a distance of at least nine miles from the sea, for we have decided to raze your city to the ground."

This was unendurable. The people would wither away if banished from their traditional element, the sea. They rose up in rage and grief. They stoned to death the hapless envoys on their return and any pro-Roman politicians they could find. Roman traders who by ill chance happened to be in the city were set upon and killed. With magnificent, despairing defiance, Carthage made the decision to resist Rome.

If the Carthaginians knew they could not vanquish their opponents, they were no walkover. They were greatly assisted by the poor quality of the Roman commanders. The city's triple defenses, its high walls, and its fortified towers presented the besiegers with a very considerable challenge. Two years of hard but inconclusive fighting ensued. From the Roman perspective, the only bright spots were the valor and presence of mind of Scipio Aemilianus, who at this point in his career was a military tribune in his mid-thirties. Among other things, he arranged the defection of Carthage's Numidian cavalry.

The two very old men who were largely responsible for the war, Cato and Masinissa, died before its outcome was known. They shared a high opinion of young Scipio. Despite his dislike of the Scipio clan and his destruction of the grandfather Africanus's career, Cato recognized talent when he saw it. He campaigned successfully for Scipio's election as consul and army commander, despite the fact that he was officially too young to hold the post. Giving the lie to his pretended ignorance of all things Greek, Cato quoted the *Odyssey:*

Only *he* has wits. The rest are fluttering shadows.

The Numidian monarch, anxious to protect his hard-won kingdom, decided that it should be divided among three of his sons. Wiser than King Lear, he knew that he would need external guarantees. So in his will he charged Scipio with the disposal of his territories and powers.

Now that Scipio had consular *imperium,* he tightened the discipline of his troops and in lieu of training launched some exploratory assaults on the walls. He completely blockaded the city by building vast fortifications on the isthmus that connected it to the mainland and a mole across the harbor entrance. Once that was done, the fall of Carthage was only a matter of time. Food grew short and the Punic commander-in-chief, Hasdrubal, seized autocratic powers.

Before the final assault, Scipio conducted an *evocatio,* as Camillus had done before the sack of Veii, luring the Punic divinities to desert their temples and migrate to new homes in Rome. Carthage was now a godless community on which any kind of misery could be inflicted. Then the legions marched from the Roman mole along the twin harbors and up the narrow streets leading to the city's high place, the Byrsa. Scipio fired and demolished houses to make space for the advancing infantry. The grim, methodical fighting went on day and night for nearly a week. Some men were detailed as street cleaners, sweeping away rubbish, corpses, and even the wounded. Suppliants walked out of the Byrsa and asked Scipio for the lives of the survivors. The consul agreed, and fifty thousand exhausted and famished men, women, and children emerged, their ultimate destinies to be determined at slave auctions.

Only nine hundred or so Roman deserters remained, who could not expect forgiveness and had no choice but to make a last stand. They occupied the Temple of Aesculapius, the god of healing, which was built on a highly defensible rocky outcrop. They were joined by Hasdrubal and his family.

Hasdrubal could see that his position was hopeless and slipped across the Roman lines. Scipio accepted his surrender, despite the fact that he had committed atrocities and had tortured to death some prisoners of war, and showed him to the deserters. When they saw him, they asked for silence and hurled insults at him. They then set the temple on fire. Hasdrubal's wife was made of sterner stuff than her husband. After reproaching him, she killed her children, threw them onto the flames, and plunged in after them. The deserters, too, burned themselves to death.

Now that resistance was over and the war won, Scipio surveyed the scene and, like Marcellus at Syracuse, burst into tears. The long, proud history of Carthage was at an end. He stayed wrapt in thought for a long time, reflecting on the mutability of fortune. He thought of the rise and fall of great cities and empires—Troy, the Assyrians, the Babylonians, the Persians, and, most recently, the dominions of Alexander. Did a similar fate in some future age await Rome?

He turned to a friend who was with him, the historian Polybius, and, as educated Romans tended to do in moments of high emotion, quoted some lines from Homer. They appear in the *Iliad* and are spoken by Hector, Troy's leading soldier, on the eve of his death:

> For in my heart and soul I also know this well:
> the day will come when sacred Troy must die,
> Priam must die and all his people with him,
> Priam who hurls the strong ash spear.

This outburst of fine feeling did not deter the victorious general from razing the city to the ground and uttering a solemn curse that where Carthage once stood should forever be pasture for sheep.

THE ROMANS HAD behaved very badly toward Carthage. They had, in truth, no real justification for the Third Punic War, and even less for the city's annihilation. As we have seen, they liked speaking sarcastically of *Punica fides,* but their own reputation for fair and honest dealing took many knocks in the second century. They must have felt uneasy about what they had done. So it is no accident that they began to rewrite the legendary past, in an attempt to retrieve their good name.

The early histories of Rome were written in Greek. In the opening chapters of this book, I showed how the Romans linked themselves to the myths and legends of the Greeks. In this way, they acquired Hellenic credentials and proved that they were not barbarians beyond the pale of civilized life. Of course, in reality they had no connection that we know of with Trojans and (if it ever took place) the Trojan War.

Cato was the first to write a history of Rome in Latin: this was *Origines* (Origins), a substantial prose work of seven books that have, unfortunately, been lost. From what is known of it and the fragments that survive, it was a massive exercise in collective self-justification. The man who willfully advocated the destruction of Carthage highlighted the typical Roman virtues of valor, obedience to law, honesty, and respect for the family, the state, and the gods.

Two books were devoted to the beginnings of the peoples of Italy, perhaps to assert Rome's national integrity and right to leadership. The early centuries were described in only one book, while the two wars with Carthage were allocated one book each, and finally two books covered the first half of the second century down to the fateful year 149. This emphasis on the recent past no doubt reflected reader interest, but it also gave the author an opportunity to explain, excuse, and celebrate Rome's genocidal victory. He presented a dossier of seven alleged breaches by Carthage of its obligations to Rome. We may surmise that the Punic version of events received little notice.

Rome's first epic poets, Gnaeus Naevius and Quintus Ennius, from Calabria, also focused on the Punic Wars. Their poems have been lost, but we know that they interwove historical events with the legends of Greece and made much of Rome's genetic link to Troy. In Naevius's *Bellum Punicum* (*Punic War*), one or two fragments reveal Venus, Rome's traditional protectress, begging her father, Jupiter, to calm a storm that threatens to destroy Aeneas's fleet. We can just detect, offstage, the malign presence of Juno, for it appears that one hundred and fifty years later Virgil, in his masterpiece the *Aeneid,* which we have in full, lifted the entire episode from Naevius. Virgil blames the storm on the Queen of Heaven, and so, no doubt, did his predecessor. The earlier version probably also has Aeneas being blown off course onto Dido's shore. Their tragic relationship sets the stage for the struggles between their descendants.

Ennius, friend and admirer of Cato, saw himself as a second Homer. His masterpiece, *Annales,* or *The Annals,* took as its subject the whole of Roman history from the fall of Troy in 1184 (according to the calculations of Eratosthenes, a famous Greek mathematician and the inventor of the word and discipline of geography) to Cato's censorship in 184. It was a remarkable compliment to close his thousand-year saga at this apex of the aged statesman's career. Ennius's theme was the unending growth of Roman rule and the eventual defeat of the Greek powers that had once destroyed Troy. Three books, or chapters, are devoted to the Carthaginians; in one fragment, they are "boys in frocks," and in another "wicked haughty foes" who hamstring their opponents. The poet shows that during the Second Punic War Juno at last moderates her wrath and shows goodwill; and he has her all-powerful husband, Jupiter, swear the overthrow of Carthage.

The underlying purpose of the poets and early historians is to maintain an artificial equivalence between the two nations; this is why Dido and Aeneas were wrongly made out to be contemporaries. The argument is that the quarrel between Rome and Carthage had nothing to do with the motives of greed, fear, or self-interest among mortals but was a foreordained encounter governed by the loves and hatreds in the Olympian pantheon.

Fate follows a circular or repetitive course. Thus Hannibal is Dido's avenger and Flamininus and his successors have paid back the Greeks with interest for their capture of Troy. No wonder Scipio Aemilianus feared for the future, for he knew the wheel of fortune would continue turning.

BY A MACABRE coincidence, Rome destroyed another famous and outstandingly beautiful city in the same year that Carthage met its end. With the ruin of Corinth, the Greeks lost their freedom. By a savage irony, it was here that Flamininus had told the Greeks, exactly fifty years earlier, that Rome would guarantee it.

In 167, after the Battle of Pydna, the Romans decided to teach the disputatious and unreliable Greek states a lesson. Their conduct during the Third Macedonian War had fallen below expectations. Of the two leagues, the Aetolians fared worse, for more than five hundred of their leading men were liquidated. As for the Achaeans, one thousand named individuals, whose loyalty was suspected, were deported to Italy (history is grateful, for the list included Polybius, who spent many years in Rome studying its politics and, as already noted, became a close friend of Scipio Aemilianus).

A generation passed without incident. It was not until 150 that the surviving exiles, now well on in years, were allowed to return to their homes. The Senate discussed the topic at length, and Cato was moved to complain, "Just as if we had nothing else to do, we sit here all day debating whether some ghastly old Greeks should be buried in Rome or in Greece." In fact, the men's long absence had serious consequences, for it fanned the flames of anti-Roman feeling.

In the following year, a pretender to the throne of Macedon turned up out of the blue. He quickly took control of the four miniature republics; these had been designed to be unable to harm Rome, but by the same token they were unable to protect themselves. The revolt was soon put down, but the Senate realized that the only way to ensure stability was to annex Macedon and turn it into a province. A great road, the Via Egnatia, was built from the western coast of Greece to the Bosphorus, linking Roman colonies and enabling rapid access to trouble spots in the Balkans and the Hellenic kingdoms of the East.

In Greece, a quarrel with the embittered Achaeans led to an international incident. Some Roman ambassadors visited the capital, Corinth, and were beaten up. Rome's patience snapped. In 146, a consular army defeated the Achaeans in battle and entered the undefended city. To set an example, all the inhabitants who had not already fled were sold into slavery and its buildings and temples were leveled. Its treasures and centuries' old works of art were looted. A century later, the place was still deserted. Greece was added to the province of Macedon. It has been estimated that during the first half of the second century the region lost one quarter of its inhabitants.

The fates of Macedon, Carthage, and Corinth taught the world that the Romans were changing. Wealth beyond imagination and the absence of any enemy that could seriously imperil their military dominance lured them to act without restraint. They were no longer willing to tolerate dissent. Diodorus Siculus, perhaps drawing on Rome's affectionate but honest critic Polybius and writing from the vantage point of the first century B.C., remarked that the Republic used to be noted for "the kindest possible treatment of those whom it defeated." He continues:

> In fact they were so far from acting out of cruelty or revenge that they appeared to deal with them not as enemies, but as if they were benefactors and friends. . . . Some they enrolled as fellow citizens, to some they granted rights of intermarriage, to others they restored their independence, and in no case did they nurse a resentment that was unduly severe. Because of their exceptional humanity, kings, cities, and whole nations went over to the Roman standard. But once they controlled virtually the entire inhabited world, they confirmed their power by terrorism and by the destruction of the most illustrious cities.

This new brutality was accompanied by rising corruption in public life. Sooner or later, it would corrode the institutions of the Republic. The bacterium of self-destruction began to multiply beneath the glittering carapace of glory.

Cato was a humbug and a hypocrite, but when he denounced the moral devaluation of his times he spoke of what he knew.

16

Blood Brothers

CORNELIA WAS A VERY GRAND LADY INDEED. AS THE second daughter of Scipio Africanus, she belonged to one of Rome's wealthiest and most aristocratic families. Well educated, she cultivated intellectual pursuits and, Plutarch writes, "always had Greeks and literary men about her."

Her lifestyle was one of some splendor, although, like many millionairesses of taste, she dressed with elegant simplicity (as the poet Horace famously put it, *simplex munditiis,* or "casually chic"). Once, she was entertaining a woman friend from Campania, where bling or deluxe display was de rigueur. Her guest drew particular attention to the fine jewelry she was wearing. Cornelia waited until her two sons came home from school, and then said, "These are *my* jewels."

Noblemen's daughters seldom married for love, and the Scipiones were no exception. Cornelia's husband, Tiberius Sempronius Gracchus, had been a political opponent of her father but had objected to the attempts of Cato and his friends to bring her uncle Lucius to trial for corruption. Cornelia was his reward. When they married, sometime after Africanus's death in disappointed retirement, she was in her teens and Gracchus was in his forties.

Despite the disparity in their ages, the union was a happy one and Cornelia gave birth to twelve children, although only three reached adulthood—a daughter and the boys, Tiberius and Gaius. Gracchus loved his wife, as a curious anecdote bears witness. One day he discovered two snakes on his bed. Being a typically superstitious Roman, he saw this as an alarming prodigy and consulted the appropriate religious authority. The advice he received could not have been more awkward if that had been the intention. He was neither to kill the snakes nor to let them go; rather, he should kill one or the other of them. An unhelpful caveat was added: if the male snake was killed, *he* would soon die, and if the female snake was killed, then Cornelia would die. Because Gracchus was so much older than his wife, he decided that it was fairer to sacrifice himself, so he killed the male and let the female slither away.

Whatever the truth of the story, Gracchus did die sometime after his second consulship in 163, leaving his young widow to bring up the children alone. We have observed that Africanus conducted himself as the equal of an eastern monarch, and his daughter was the nearest thing the Republic had to an international royal celebrity. The pharaoh of Egypt, Ptolemy VIII, offered her his hand in marriage. Nicknamed Physcon (Greek for "sausage," "potbelly," or "bladder"), he was an unappealing prospect, and Cornelia politely declined. She decided not to marry again, but to manage her estates and devote herself to the education of her children. She lived the blameless life of a Roman matron. It was unusual for aristocratic widows to remain unmarried, but Cornelia was that rare thing in the ancient world—an independent woman.

HOW CORNELIA BROUGHT up her sons is uncertain, but at some point in the third century educational practice in Rome changed. Originally, it was based on an apprenticeship supervised by the father—in working families probably linked to agriculture or a trade, in more aristocratic homes to military training and an induction into public life in the Forum. Gradually, a Greek model came to be followed. Greek-speaking tutors were employed (for example, the poets Livius Andronicus and Ennius), who taught both Latin and Greek. This is no doubt what a wealthy Hellenistic family such as the Scipios would have done.

At about the same time, elementary and secondary schools opened, to which Cornelia could have sent Tiberius and Gaius. In that case, a *paedagogus,* usually a slave, would have taken them to and from their classes and generally supervised their behavior. A secondary school master, or *grammaticus,* taught language and poetry, and was sometimes a distinguished intellectual in his own right. For children in their mid to late teens, the principle of apprenticeship was maintained, with boys being attached for a time to a leading senator, rather like today's interns. Oratory was a highly developed art form and was essential to a political career. Teachers of rhetoric offered advanced training in the elaborate techniques of persuasion.

THE STATUS OF women in ancient Rome was mixed. Their main task was to bear legitimate children, and chastity outside the marriage bed was essential to achieving that aim. They had no political rights; they could not attend, address, or vote at citizen assemblies, and they could not hold public office.

As a rule, a girl married young, between twelve and fifteen years of age, but her husband was often a man in his twenties or older. Irrespective of whether she had passed puberty (generally thought to begin in the fourteenth year), it seems that she was expected to have, or perhaps to endure, sex immediately upon marriage. There were different kinds of contract. A wife might be passed into the *manus,* or hands, of her husband, but this was becoming increasingly unpopular. Otherwise, she remained under her father's nominal *patria potestas* or, if he was dead, she controlled her affairs *sui iuris,* by her own legal authority, albeit under the guidance of a guardian or *tutor.* This was Cornelia's situation.

Divorce was easy, and because of the age difference there was a large number of widows. While many remarried, Romans rather admired the *univira,* the woman who, like Cornelia, stayed true to the memory of one man.

(Boys, of course, enjoyed greater license than girls. They were expected to sow their wild oats, within reason. Once, when Cato saw a young nobleman emerge from a brothel, he told him, "Keep up the good work." When he came across the young man a short time later, in similar circumstances, he remarked, "When I complimented you on 'good work' I didn't mean you should make this place your home.")

In spite of legal constraints, women were able to play an important role in family and public life if they wished, provided they obeyed the conventions of modesty and respectability. Within her household, a wife was the *domina,* or mistress, and she was regarded on an equal level with her husband. She led a full social life, visiting friends, patronizing the Games, and attending her husband's dinner parties. She was able to exert political influence through her husband, whose career she promoted. Although marriages were often cool, professional affairs, we know of many happy couples.

Cornelia was not alone in seeing so many of her children die in their early years. The duty to produce progeny was hampered by primitive medical knowledge. The upper classes seem to have practised birth control and abortion, although it is unclear how effective their methods were. Techniques such as washing out the vagina, coating it with old olive oil, inserting sponges soaked in vinegar, or jumping up and down after intercourse are unlikely to have done much good. Doctors did their best to encourage fertility and were not meant to facilitate abortion, but in Hippocratic medicine a substance known as *misy* was claimed to prevent pregnancy for a year; unfortunately, we do not know what it is (some have suggested yellow copperas). Various plants were commonly used for birth control, and some have been found in modern times to have contraceptive properties—*Daucus carota,* or Queen Anne's lace, for example.

Women who broke the rules of propriety received no mercy. In the first century, a certain Sempronia met the full force of male condemnation. It has been speculated that she was Cornelia's granddaughter and, whether or not this was so, was similarly well-endowed with charm and intellect. She married well and received a good education in Greek and Latin literature. She wrote poetry, had a ready wit, and was an amusing conversationalist.

However, according to the historian Gaius Sallustius Crispus (whom we know as Sallust), there was another side to her personality:

> She had greater skill in lyre-playing and dancing than there is any need for a respectable woman to acquire, besides many other accomplishments such as minister to dissipation. There was nothing that she set a smaller value on than seemliness and chastity, and she was as careless of her reputation as she was of her money. Her passions were so ardent that she more often made advances to men than they did to her. Many times . . . she had broken a solemn promise, repudiated a debt by perjury, and been an accessory to murder.

It is a curiously unconvincing passage: venial sins such as being a lively partygoer are gradually amplified into an unsubstantiated accusation of involvement in murder, as if one thing naturally led to the other. Some of Sempronia's excesses echo those of Tanaquil and Tullia, perhaps because historians from the late Republic borrowed her traits in order to flesh out their portraits of those early fictionalized queens. As in their cases, Sempronia's real offense seems to have been that she openly supported a dissident politician, an impermissible intervention into an exclusively masculine sphere of activity. Charges of sexual promiscuity and criminality, invented or exaggerated, were her punishment, for they would destroy her social standing.

CORNELIA MARRIED HER daughter, another Sempronia of course, to her celebrated cousin, Scipio Aemilianus. Her two boy jewels were the center of her attention. They shared a family resemblance, but their personalities were very different. Tiberius, the elder by nine years, was "gentle and sedate," their biographer Plutarch writes, "while Gaius was highly strung and impetuous. When addressing the assembly one stood composedly on the spot, while the other was the first Roman to walk up and down the speakers' platform and pull his toga off his shoulder as he spoke." As regards food and lifestyle, Tiberius lived simply, while Gaius was ostentatious and picky.

As descendants of the most famous Roman of his day, the young men had distinguished political and military futures ahead of them. Cornelia used to tease them, complaining that she was still known as Scipio Aemilianus's mother-in-law, and not as the mother of the Gracchi. Tiberius's career nearly ended as soon as it began. He was appointed quaestor, or finance officer, to a consular general in Spain. The campaign against guerrilla insurgents went very badly. The Romans were comprehensively outmaneuvered and took refuge in their camp. Hearing that the enemy expected reinforcements, the consul had all fires put out and led his army of twenty thousand men out into the dead of night. He hoped to find safety at a remote former campsite. However, the Spaniards followed and soon had the Romans at their mercy. The consul, seeing that his situation was hopeless, agreed a surrender, to which he bound himself by oath. Thanks to his father, who had once commanded in Spain, Tiberius had excellent connections and played a leading part in negotiating the terms.

The Senate was outraged when it heard what had happened. Legions did not surrender. A tribunal with Scipio Aemilianus among its members ruled that the treaty should not stand. But sworn agreements could not be abrogated with impunity. In expiation for the religious offense of the breach, the consul was sent back naked and bound and handed over to the Spaniards. (They refused to accept him, in a faint echo of the Caudine Forks fiasco.)

Tiberius got off scot-free, despite the fact that he had been instrumental in making the treaty. Some put it down to the influence of Scipio, his adoptive uncle. His popularity with the troops may have counted for something, too. Cicero writes that the scandal was "a constant source of grief and fear to Tiberius Gracchus; and this estranged him, brave and famous as he was, from the wisdom of the Senators." He was not simply unnerved but mortified that his *fides,* his good faith, had been sabotaged.

Tiberius's politics changed. From being a political conservative, he began to promote the interests of the People. There was one issue in particular that drew his attention—land reform.

ON THE LONG overland journey to Spain to take up his quaestorship, Tiberius had passed through Tuscany on his way north. He was struck by how few people there were in the fields. Those he did see, tilling the soil or tending flocks, were foreign slaves rather than native Italians or Roman citizens. On his return in 137, he looked further into the matter.

What he found was a situation that needed to be addressed. As Rome vanquished its enemies in the peninsula, it confiscated a proportion of the land of defeated communities. Some of this was made over to smallholders and *coloniae,* but the rest remained *ager publicus,* or publicly owned land. After the end of the struggle with Carthage, the authorities had been preoccupied with new wars in Greece, Asia Minor, and Spain; and in southern Italy a great deal of *ager publicus* remained undistributed.

Wealthy landowners, especially profiteers from the lucrative wars of the second century, bought up the farms of soldiers who had been absent for years on distant campaigns and also silently expropriated public land. Hannibal had laid waste thousands on thousands of acres and substantial investment was needed to rebuild the farming industry. Large estates, or *latifundia,* were created rather than single farms. They were more often devoted to animal husbandry than to the labor-intensive production of crops and were staffed by teams of slaves.

The net result of these changes was the gradual disappearance of the sturdy peasant farmer, who earned enough to qualify for recruitment into the army. (As we have seen, the very poor—*capite censi,* or the "head count"—were not allowed to serve.) This applied not only to Romans but also to the citizens of allied communities, liable as they were to provide troops for the Republic's wars. One obvious solution to the problem was to open the legions to the head count, but it was a firm and traditional belief that only those with property, who had something to lose, would fight bravely for their country. So that exit was barred.

Tiberius was not alone in believing that the situation was untenable and urgently needed correction. Thoughtful Romans were less worried about economic change in the countryside (for they increasingly imported grain and other foodstuffs from northern Africa and Sicily) than they were about the decline of the social class that stocked the legions. They also feared the large and growing population of disaffected slaves who were replacing freemen throughout the peninsula. This was no nightmarish fantasy but a real threat, for in 133 a great slave revolt broke out in Sicily that took more than a year to put down. Senior politicians supported change, and a friend of Aemilianus had suggested reform when he was consul a few years previously, but he met with furious resistance and withdrew his plans; for this he was rewarded with the sarcastic nickname Sapiens, or the Wise. Many senators were illegally squatting on *ager publicus* and were vehemently opposed to any interference.

Tiberius decided that the time for action had arrived. He was too junior a figure to get his hands on the official levers of power as praetor or consul, but he was well liked by the People and was entitled to stand for tribune. As already explained, the tribuneship was not a governmental position conferring *imperium,* and appointments were made by the *concilium plebis.* Its purpose was to promote popular sovereignty and public accountability. Tribunes could propose laws and summon meetings of the Senate. However, they had become an accepted part of the political scene and were sometimes even used by the Senate to veto the plans of unruly elected officials. They were not as radical as they used to be, until the arrival of Tiberius Sempronius Gracchus.

He was elected one of the ten tribunes for 133 and put forward a land-reform bill, or *lex agraria.* He knew there would be fierce and self-interested opposition in the Senate and was careful to design a balanced package. He renewed an old law, which had fallen into disuse, banning the occupation of more than five hundred *iugera* of land—that is, about three hundred acres. But he sweetened the pill by allowing an additional two hundred and fifty *iugera* for each landowner's son (the concession was withdrawn after it failed to win over critics) and by offering all the land as freehold in perpetuity. Also, the fertile fields of Campania were excluded from the legislation. The territory so reclaimed was to be distributed to Roman citizens in up to thirty-*iugera* parcels. These could not be sold (although presumably they could be inherited), and a small rent would be payable.

So far, so reasonable. But Tiberius then made a fateful decision. A convention had grown up that all new legislation was first presented to the Senate for its consideration before being taken to the Assembly for enactment. The bold tribune decided to sidestep the obstructive Senate and proceed directly to the People. This was legal but highly unusual: such a thing had not happened for almost exactly a century.

Tiberius ran a vigorous campaign to promote his proposal, which was hugely popular. In an ancient equivalent of a poster campaign, graffiti were written on walls, monuments, and porticoes or colonnades, which were busy gathering places. "Wild beasts who roam over Italy all have caves and lairs to lurk in," he would say, "but the men who fight and die for Italy enjoy the common air and light, but nothing else." This high-flying oratory went down well with his audiences, but a young fellow tribune, Marcus Octavius, indicated that he intended to use his official powers to veto the legislation. Tiberius did his best to make him change his mind. He pointed out that Octavius was a large-scale occupier of *ager publicus*, but that he would pay him from his own resources the value of any of his land that was confiscated.

All to no avail. Tiberius convened an Assembly in the Forum and had the clerk read the bill. Octavius told the man to be silent. Tiberius postponed the meeting to another day, and again tried to have the bill read, with the same result. He took his cause to the Senate in the Senate House nearby, where he was treated contemptuously. He hurried back to the Assembly, where he took his next fateful step. He announced a further postponement, but warned that he would not only put his bill to the vote but also table a motion on whether Octavius should continue to hold office. He was as good as his word, and at the following meeting the vote on Octavius's deposition was taken, although there was a delay because the voting urns had been stolen. The ballot was conducted by tribes, and one after another they voted to remove Octavius. As each tribe reported, Tiberius turned to Octavius and asked him to reconsider his position. "Do not throw into chaos a project that is morally right and of the greatest utility to all Italy," he pleaded. Octavius refused, and when a majority against him had been reached he was dragged down from the speakers' platform. His friends rushed him away from the Forum or he might well have been lynched. The land-reform bill was then passed and a commission to implement it was established, of which the two Gracchus brothers were members.

At about this time the king of Pergamum died and, to avert a civil war, bequeathed his kingdom to Rome, which now became the province of Asia. The contents of the Pergamum treasury were paid into the Roman exchequer, and Tiberius had the bright idea of passing a law that distributed this money to the new smallholders, so that they could stock up on seed and equipment.

In his handling of the Octavius crisis, Tiberius had, once again, probably broken no law, but the deposition of a tribune was unprecedented. Even if land reform was a worthy cause—and many believed it was—it began to look as if its supporters were willing to subvert the constitution in order to achieve their ends. They had upset the delicate balance between the Assembly and the Senate, which had served the Republic well for centuries.

With all the postponed Assembly meetings, it was now summer and the victorious Tiberius feared that when he left office at the end of the year his law might be repealed before it had been put into full effect. All his good work would have gone for nothing. Also, he was worried about his security and, as an elected guardian of the People, his person was inviolable. He took his third and last fateful decision. Although once again it broke convention, he stood for a second year as tribune. For conservatives in the Senate, this was too much.

Voting began at the election, which was held on the Capitol, but order soon broke down. The presiding officer handed over to another tribune, who was a friend of Tiberius. Noisy objections were raised. Tiberius put off the voting until the next day. He and his followers got up early to occupy the assembly-place in front of the Temple of Jupiter Best and Greatest before the opposition arrived. When leaving his house, he accidentally stubbed his big toe on the threshold and blood was noticed leaking from his sandal—not a good omen.

A meeting of the Senate was also held that day in the tiny Temple of Fides, Good Faith, at the edge of the assembly-place. It was dominated by Tiberius's enemies, in particular a cousin of his who was another of Africanus's grandsons. This was Publius Cornelius Scipio Nasica ("big nose"). A senior politician who had held all the great offices of state and was now *pontifex maximus,* or high priest, he had a high opinion of himself: at a noisy public meeting, he once said, "Be quiet, please, citizens. I know more about the public interest than you do."

Nasica tried to persuade the consul to call a state of emergency, but the consul declined to use force or kill a citizen without trial. Meanwhile, a fight started outside between supporters of the different sides. Confusion reigned. The tribunes deserted their places, priests closed the Temple of Jupiter, and many people ran wildly about trying to escape. In the noise, Tiberius signaled that he was in personal danger by pointing to his head. This was reported to the Senate, which decided that the gesture meant that he wanted a diadem (a white cloth headband signifying royal power) and was aspiring to be king.

Throughout the history of the Republic, this ambition was the ultimate crime. Would-be tyrants deserved no mercy. Nasica seized his moment. "Since the Consul betrays the state, anyone who wants to save the constitution, follow me," he declared. The *pontifex maximus* then pulled a fold of his toga over his head, as if he were about to conduct a sacrifice, and ran out of the temple followed by senators and their attendants.

The Gracchans were startled by the sight of so distinguished a company rushing at them and lost their nerve. Nasica and his people snatched the makeshift weapons with which their opponents had armed themselves—sticks, rods, and the like—and broke up the benches that had been laid out for the meeting. They then chased the Gracchans over the precipitous edges of the Capitoline Square. Somebody grabbed at Tiberius's clothes. He let his toga fall and ran off. With bitter symbolism, he was caught, this (allegedly) potential despot, beside a cluster of statues of Rome's kings. An assailant hit him on the head with a bench leg; others piled in, and the sacrosanct tribune was beaten to death. He was not quite thirty years old. When the riot was over, all the corpses were thrown into the Tiber under the cover of darkness.

The death of Tiberius was an earthquake that shook the pillars of the state. Reactions were contradictory. Tiberius's cousin and the leading man of his day, the cultured Scipio Aemilianus, gave the deed his cautious approval. The Senate instructed the consuls for 132 to investigate and execute those who had conspired with Tiberius. However, Nasica was the object of popular fury and was challenged even in the Senate to justify his actions. His continued presence in Rome was an embarrassment. He was sent off on a foreign assignment and soon conveniently died in Pergamum.

Tellingly, no one challenged the land-reform legislation, and the implementation commission got on with its work unhindered. It was Tiberius's methods, not so much his policies, that had incensed Rome's élite. Furthermore, repeal could well lead to dangerous public disturbances. Best to leave well enough alone.

ONE DAY A Roman consul paid a visit to Teanum Sidicinum (modern Teano), an Oscan-speaking settlement on the borders of Samnium. His wife accompanied him, and said that she wanted to bathe in the men's baths. (These seem to have been something of an attraction, and the remains of extensive baths can be seen by today's visitors.) A certain Marcus Marius, the town treasurer, was instructed to send the bathers away so that she could have the place to herself. Later, she complained to her husband that the baths were not cleared quickly, and that they were not clean enough.

The consul had a stake planted in the main square and Marius, Teanum's leading citizen, was led to it. Then his clothes were stripped off and he was whipped with rods. When news of this reached a nearby municipality, its Assembly passed a law forbidding anyone to use the public baths when a Roman elected official was in town.

Gaius Sempronius Gracchus told this story in a speech complaining of the outrageous behavior of senior Romans when traveling in Italy. It was not only officeholders who acted with criminal insolence. "I will give you a single example of the lawlessness of our young men, and their complete lack of self-control," Gracchus said on another occasion. "Not many years ago a young man who had not yet held public office was sent as an envoy to the province of Asia. He was carried in a curtained litter. A herdsman from Venusia in southern Italy [presumably, the Roman was on his way to the port of Brundisium] met him and, not knowing who the passenger was, asked as a joke if the litter-bearers were carrying a dead body. The young man heard this. He ordered that the litter be set down and that the peasant be beaten to death with the leather thongs by which it was fastened."

Rome's allied communities were seething with resentment. They not only complained of arrogance by roaming dignitaries; they felt that the historic concordat between them and their conqueror all those centuries ago was breaking down.

The system of some one hundred and fifty bilateral treaties between Rome and each of them had worked well. As we have seen, they were obliged to supply troops on request to help fight Rome's many wars. In return, allies were guaranteed security and a share of the very considerable spoils of victory. They also had the right to benefit from land assignations and to join or found *coloniae*.

With the acquisition of a large overseas empire, the terms of advantage changed. The regular taxes paid by new provinces were monopolized by the Roman exchequer. Colonization dried up and, although Tiberius Gracchus recognized that Italians were as much in need of succor as Roman citizens, his reforms had meant a loss of *ager publicus* in their territories.

Just as observant Romans recognized the case for land reform, they also saw that something would have to be done to quiet the allied communities and compensate them for their economic losses. One of these was Scipio Aemilianus, to whom allied landowners made representations. They objected to having a *Roman* commission interfere with their local property rights, and Scipio arranged for their cases to be considered by the consul; that official, however, knew what a thankless task he had been given and immediately went abroad to his province.

Scipio had already caused offense by his opposition to Tiberius Gracchus, and his sympathy for the allies only compounded his unpopularity with the urban mob, which saw no reason to make concessions to "foreigners." His political enemies claimed that he was set on undoing Tiberius's agrarian law and was plotting an armed massacre. With the city in this ill-tempered mood, few were surprised when, in 129, Scipio was found dead, his body unmarked. Intending to write a speech that night which he was due to deliver at a meeting of the Assembly, he had a notebook beside him.

The rumor mill got to work. Perhaps Cornelia, the mother of the Gracchi (as she now certainly was known), had killed Scipio to prevent a repeal of her son's legislation. Very probably, word went, her daughter Sempronia had aided and abetted her; she was Scipio's wife, but unloved because of her ugliness and her childlessness. Others claimed that Scipio had committed suicide in the realization that he could not accomplish what he had undertaken to do. Apparently, Scipio's slaves were put to the torture (this was the rule when a paterfamilias was murdered). They confessed, it was said, that strangers had been brought into the back of the house and had strangled their master.

Scipio may have been murdered, but if the reports of how he was found and the appearance of his body are correct, it is more likely that he succumbed to a heart attack or a stroke. In any case, he was dead, and despite the distinction of his career public opinion would not allow him the honor of a state funeral.

FOR SOME YEARS after his brother's killing, Gaius had stayed away from the Forum and the alarms of public life. But he disliked having nothing to do and was uninterested in the sexual promiscuity, drinking, and moneymaking practiced by many of his peers. He enjoyed army life but lost his temper when his commission as quaestor in Sardinia was unfairly extended. He sailed away to Rome in a rage. Charged with dereliction of duty, he easily cleared himself with a powerful speech in his defense. He had already served longer than the law required, he pointed out, and added, "I am the only man in the army who entered the campaign with a full purse, and left it with an empty one. My colleagues brought amphorae of wine with them which they drank on service, and then took back home with them, stuffed with silver and gold."

Supporters of reform kept prompting him to stand for tribune, and conservative senators let it be seen how much they feared that he would. Tiberius was said to have appeared to Gaius in a dream and said, "However much you try to defer your destiny, you must die the same death that I suffered." His mother was no ghost, and expressed her disapproval. A letter of hers has survived in which she tells her son, "Apart from those who killed Tiberius Gracchus, no enemy has caused me so many troubles and so many labors as you. As my only surviving son, you should have taken trouble and care that I should have the fewest anxieties in my old age."

Gaius refused Cornelia's pleas and bowed to the inevitable. He was elected tribune in 123.

In a sign that times were slowly changing, he had no trouble getting reelected for a second year and he introduced a far-reaching catalog of reforms. First of all, he appeased his brother's spirit by introducing two new laws. The first banned anyone who had been deposed from public office from serving again in any capacity. This was obviously aimed at Octavius, but, according to Plutarch, Cornelia made representations and persuaded her son to withdraw it. This magnanimous gesture delighted public opinion.

Second, a bill was passed forbidding any capital trials without the Assembly's approval. Anyone found to have deprived a citizen of his civic rights through execution or exile, as if he were an enemy of the state, was to be arraigned before the People. The prohibitions were retrospective, and the former consul who chaired the commission that persecuted Tiberius's followers in 132 was driven into exile. It was not simply that revenge was sweet; reactionary senators needed to be reminded of the dangers they faced if they ignored the will of the People.

Gaius reaffirmed Tiberius's land act but exempted some *ager publicus* from redistribution, perhaps so that it could be leased to non-Romans. He also announced the foundation of three *coloniae* in Italy and one in northern Africa, on the desolate site of Carthage. This last was to be named Junonia, or Juno's Place (a tactful nod in the direction of the goddess?). It was a controversial project to countermand the recently dead Aemilianus's curse and, in the event, the sheep pastures of Carthage were left undisturbed. Plans were commissioned for the building of new roads across Italy. All these measures would have the effect of alleviating unemployment.

The burgeoning city of Rome required reliable and copious supplies of grain, imported from Africa and Sicily. When harvests failed, famine followed. Food riots imperiled government. Gaius arranged permanent stockpiles of grain as an insurance policy against shortages and set a bargain price for its sale to citizens.

The tribune turned his attention to corruption in public life. He passed laws against fraud and theft by governors of provinces, and a special extortion court, *quaestio de repetundis,* heard cases in front of a jury of senators. The conviction rate was low, because the jurors were often friends of the defendants. Gaius decided to put this right by asking *equites,* originally Rome's cavalry but now men possessing the next property qualification beneath that of senators, to share jury service. Then, on second thought, senators were barred altogether from serving on juries, which now consisted entirely of *equites.*

This was not all that Gaius did to the advantage of *equites*. The class had grown in economic importance in recent years. Some were country landowners uninterested in entering national politics, but a growing number were prosperous businessmen. The Republic had little in the way of a civil service, and indirect revenue collection (customs dues and the like) was contracted out to companies, or *societates* of *equites;* they also won commissions for public works, the construction of public buildings and roads, and the provision of military supplies. Of course, senators were not allowed to engage directly in trade, but provincial governors, proconsuls, and propraetors were responsible for the collection of direct taxes, a profitable opportunity for the practise of extortion. However, to ensure an adequate inflow to pay for his reforms, the tribune put the collection of direct taxes in the wealthy new province of Asia up for auction. This was a plum concession for commercial interests, as well as a vote of no confidence in senatorial probity.

These measures all served immediate, sometimes urgent purposes, but in the longer run Gaius probably intended to encourage the growth of a wealthy nonpolitical class as a counterweight to the aristocracy in the Senate, and if that was not his intention it was certainly the result.

Other constitutional and administrative changes were made. As ever, honesty and efficiency were the watchwords. Gaius had a larger and more all-embracing vision than his brother. His reforms were a comprehensive political program. In fact, when he was out and about in the Forum it was as if he were a government; Plutarch reports him as being "closely attended by a throng of contractors, technicians, ambassadors, officials, soldiers and literary men." Although nowhere did he say this, it is clear that he was aiming to rebalance the constitution in the direction of popular sovereignty.

However, there is no evidence that he wanted to emasculate or even abolish the Senate; rather, his idea was to purify the Senate and make it more responsive to the interests of the People. He shared something of Cato's disgust with the activities of the ruling élite and of Scipio Aemilianus's commitment to fair treatment for the provinces. He was a radical, not a revolutionary.

DURING HIS SECOND term, Gaius grasped the nettle of allied resentment. He could see from Aemilianus's fate that it would be hard to win public opinion to the Italian cause. A colleague of his on the tribunician bench had tabled a proposal, while serving as consul a few years earlier, to grant citizenship to any allied community that wanted it and, for those who didn't, the right of appeal against Roman officials. The Senate was nervous and dispatched the consul to Gaul in response to a conveniently timed call from the port of Massilia for military assistance. The matter had had to be dropped.

The tribune would have been wise to let leave well alone, but the danger of serious disaffection across Italy was too great to ignore. He proposed that communities with Latin status (that is, a second-class citizenship—see pages 153–154) should be awarded the full franchise, and that plain and simple allies should receive Latin status. The Roman mob was displeased, and there was heated opposition in the Senate.

One of the consuls led the assault, deploying the fear-inducing slogans of the anti-immigrant campaigner through the ages. He declaimed:

I suppose you imagine that, if you give Latins the citizenship, there will still be room for you in the Assembly where you are standing now, and seats at the games and festivals. Don't you realize that they will swamp everything?

A fellow tribune, working for the Senate, trumped Gaius with a populist package designed to satisfy both the People's Assembly and Italian opinion. This was approved but (as intended, no doubt) never implemented, and Gaius's bill failed. The only practical result of the initiative was his rising unpopularity among the city's masses.

He failed to win a third term as tribune, and his opponents at once began to unpick his legislation. He had recently returned from a visit to Carthage to make arrangements for the building of Junonia, and at a crowded Assembly on the Capitol one of the new tribunes for 121 attacked the law authorizing it. Now that the crisis had arrived, Cornelia set aside her opposition to her son and helped him recruit bodyguards. These hired men lurked on the outskirts of the meeting, with Gaius walking up and down a portico in a nervous frame of mind. He may have intended only to observe the debate, but it is possible that he planned to disrupt the meeting.

Fate then played a wild card. A servant of Lucius Opimius, one of the consuls, bared his arm and made an insulting gesture. An overexcited Gracchan stabbed him fatally with a writing stylus. This was just the pretext the consul was hoping for. He immediately went to the Senate and persuaded it to vote a state of emergency. This was the first time that what came to be called the Final Decree, or *senatus consultum ultimum,* was passed. The Senate resolved: "Let the consuls see to it the Republic comes to no harm," (*"Videant consules ne quid detrimenti res publica caperet"*).

This vague formula was understood to give senior officeholders the power to use lethal force against malefactors who were endangering the state. But did the Senate actually have the power to suspend a Roman citizen's constitutional rights? The answer depended on a man's political point of view, on the emotion of the moment. If we look at the issue dispassionately, the Senate was, in the final resort, an advisory body and its resolutions had no legal force. A consul had *imperium,* but the law insisted that he could not execute citizens without trial (reinforced by Gaius Gracchus's own recent legislation); this was because they had the right of appeal, of *provocatio,* to the People. In practice, few would disobey a serving consul's command, but he was wise to remember that, once out of office, he was subject to the courts and the anger of the Assembly.

Such fine considerations were of little interest in the heat of the present moment. Opimius called on senators to arm themselves, and for all *equites* to turn up the following morning with two armed servants. Rome passed an uneasy night. In the morning, the Gracchans seized the Aventine Hill, the traditional refuge of plebeian agitators through the ages. Gaius refused to arm himself (except for a dagger) and left home wearing a toga as if it were a normal day and he were just going down to the Forum on routine business.

After unsuccessful negotiations, Opimius had some archers loose their arrows into the crowds on the Aventine, throwing them into confusion. Gaius, furious at what was happening, took no part in the fighting. He walked up the broad steps of the Temple of Diana, standing high on its plateau on the hilltop, and entered the precinct. Ironically, the shrine was devoted to community, sanctuary, and arbitration, attributes not on offer that day. Gaius was so depressed that he considered taking his own life, but his companions confiscated his dagger and urged him to escape.

With enemies close behind, Gaius, a slave, and two friends ran across the narrow wooden footbridge spanning the Tiber, the Pons Sublicius. The friends halted and turned round at the head of the bridge, where, like Horatius and his companions, they fought their pursuers in order to give Gaius time to make a getaway. But they were soon overwhelmed.

Bystanders watched Gaius run to the other side of the river. They told him to hurry up, but offered no help. When he called for a horse, nobody gave him one. On being caught, the slave with him threw his arms around his master and had to be killed as well. (Another version of Gaius's end has him finally succeed in committing suicide.) Gaius's head was cut off and taken to Opimius, who had promised to reward the bearer with its weight in gold. Some say Gaius's killer gouged out his brains and replaced them with lead to make the head heavier.

FOR ALL THE brothers' good intentions the Gracchan episode was a disaster. Their policies were rational, and ultimately much of their legislation passed into the body of Roman law. The economic consequences of their land reforms were beneficial. The Senate reacted to the brothers rather like a general faced with a mutiny, who concedes most of the grievances but executes the ringleaders.

However, the constitutional results of their efforts were overwhelmingly negative. The Italians were more embittered than ever, through the Assembly the People had stretched their muscles, and for the first time the *equites* had become aware of their own strength vis-à-vis the Senate. Before the Gracchi, nobody had realized that the Republic could be governed from the tribunes' bench. Both the Senate and the People had been shown to act with breathtaking selfishness, always consulting their own rather than the public interest.

The Roman constitution was a complicated contraption of levers and balances, with obsolete pieces of machinery left in place alongside modern additions. Its management called for sensitivity, imagination, and, above all, an ability to accommodate, to concede, to compromise. For centuries, these qualities among Rome's politicians had drawn the admiration, reluctant or full-hearted, of friend and foe.

Now, though, the tragic trajectory of the Gracchi exposed the Republic for what it had become, an unstable and uncreative monster. It is no accident that, in his *Civil Wars,* Appian chose this moment at which to begin his story. He observed:

No sword was ever brought into the assembly, and no Roman was ever killed by a Roman, until Tiberius Gracchus . . . became the first man to die in civil unrest, and along with him a great number of people who had crowded together on the Capitol and were killed around the temple. The disorders did not end even with this foul act; on each occasion when they occurred the Ro-

mans openly took sides against each other, and often carried dag-
gers; from time to time some elected official would be murdered
in a temple, or in the assembly, or in the Forum—a Tribune or
Praetor or Consul, or a candidate for these offices, or somebody
otherwise distinguished. Undisciplined arrogance soon became
the rule, along with a shameful contempt for law and justice.

The mother of the Gracchi left Rome after Gaius's death. She settled in Misenum, a narrow isthmus culminating in a rocky outcrop
at the northern end of the Bay of Naples. It had beautiful views and
was off the beaten track. However, Cornelia did not hide herself
away and made no alteration to the gregarious brilliancy of her
lifestyle. Plutarch reports: "She had many friends and because of
her love of visitors kept a good table. She always had Greeks and
intellectuals as guests, and all the reigning monarchs exchanged
gifts with her."

It made her happy to reminisce about her father's life and character. Remarkably, she spoke of her sons without any tears or dis-
plays of emotion and discussed their careers and sad ends as if she
were referring to immemorial statesmen from Rome's first centuries.

Cornelia survived her lost jewels for more than ten years, dying
at the turn of the century. She was lucky not to witness the fulfillment of their legacies.

17

Triumph and Disaster

THE TWO MEN WERE, TO PUT IT MILDLY, UNPROMIS-
ing and even distasteful specimens of humanity.

The older one was Gaius Marius. He was born in 157 in a small
village near Arpinum, a hill town in Latium of Volscian and Samnite origins, some sixty miles southeast of Rome. He was lucky to
be a voting citizen of Rome, for the full franchise had been awarded
the town only thirty years earlier.

According to his biographer Plutarch, the boy's parents lived in
very humble circumstances and he is said to have worked for wages
as a simple peasant. He may have been a blacksmith for a time. He
grew up rough and uncouth and lived frugally. He seems to have
been proud of his modest background. When campaigning later in
life for public office, Marius certainly made the most of it, and
liked to compare himself, a little in the manner of Cato, with effete
aristocrats:

These proud men make a very big mistake. Their ancestors left
them all they could—riches, portrait busts, and their own glorious memory. . . . They call me vulgar and unpolished, because I
don't know how to put on an elegant dinner and don't have actors at my table or keep a cook who has cost me more than my

farm bailiff. All this, fellow citizens, I am proud to admit. For I was taught by my father and other men of blameless life that, while elegant graces befit woman, a man's duty is to labor.

The teenage Marius chose the only escape route from provincial isolation that was open to him, the army. His exceptional ability soon allowed him to shine. It is possible, too, that despite his poverty his social status was higher than he cared to admit and that he came from an equestrian family that had fallen on hard times; if so, that would have helped speed promotion.

He had a fierce temper. Plutarch once saw a statue of him at Ravenna and wrote: "It very well expresses the harshness and bitterness of character that are attributed to him." Military life suited him. He refused to study Greek literature and never spoke Greek; he could not see the point of having anything to do with the culture of a subject people. Some critics regarded him as a hypocrite who would say anything to get his way and was not above employing blackmail; to their annoyance, Iago-like, he actually won a reputation for honest dealing.

What nobody could deny was Marius's combination of fortitude and realism. Later in life, he suffered from varicose veins in both legs. Disliking their ugly appearance, he decided to undergo surgery to remove them. Anesthetic had not been discovered, but he refused to be tied down, as was the practice, to keep himself still. He endured the excruciating pain from the knife in silence and without moving. But when the surgeon proceeded to the other leg, Marius stopped him, saying, "I can see that the cure is not worth the pain."

LUCIUS CORNELIUS SULLA could not have been more different in background and personality from a bright country lad with rough edges. Nearly twenty years Marius's junior, he was born into a patrician family of little distinction and less money. His only ancestor of whom anything was known had been expelled from the Senate. He inherited so little from his father that he lived in a cheap ground-floor apartment in an unfashionable part of town.

Sulla loved literature and the arts, and before he had any money he spent most of his time with actors and actresses. He liked a good time and enjoyed drinking and joking with the most indiscreet theater people; once seated at a dinner table, he categorically refused to discuss any serious topic, although when on business he was severe and unyielding.

The young nobleman seems to have got on well with older women; his stepmother loved him as if he were her own son and left him her estate. He fell in love with a wealthy courtesan, a certain Nicopolis, and his charm and youthful grace eventually led her to return his feelings; on her death, he inherited again. In this way, he became moderately well-off. However, Sulla was bisexual and the true love of his life was Metrobius, a celebrated tragic actor who specialized in women's roles, of whom he remained passionately fond until his dying day.

Sulla's most remarkable feature was his appearance. He had gray eyes and a sharp and powerful gaze. His face was covered with an ugly birthmark—coarse blotches of red interspersed with white. An Athenian wit wrote a famous verse about him:

Sulla is a mulberry sprinkled with barley meal.

Marius and Sulla came to represent two emerging groups in Roman public life. On the one hand, the *populares* spoke for the People; in the footsteps of the Gracchi, they supported the sovereignty of the Assembly against the authority of the Senate. They were inheritors of the centuries-old campaigners for the rights of the plebs. Then there were the *optimates,* the soi-disant "best people," who distrusted democracy and spoke for the predominance of the great families that monopolized the offices of state.

These groups were not disciplined political parties with agreed programs, as in today's parliamentary democracies. Rather, they were fluctuating factions. Their methods varied; a *popularis* leader tended to be an individualist who sought power for himself, whereas the *optimates* defended a collective interest. Although the occasional *novus homo*, "new man," such as Marius, was admitted via elections into the ruling class, the membership of both groups was drawn from the aristocracy. Ordinary citizens were allowed to vote, but otherwise their participation in politics did not extend much beyond watching and waiting, receiving bribes from candidates for public office, and, when they lost patience, rioting.

THE PATHS OF Marius, the unpolished commoner, and Sulla, the hard-up sensualist, crossed for the first time in northern Africa. They were fighting Jugurtha, a very able but unscrupulous grandson of the old Numidian king Masinissa, who had helped the Romans defeat Hannibal at the Battle of Zama nearly a century earlier. As a young man, he had served in Spain under Scipio Aemilianus, and won golden praises. He was ambitious and very free with his money. Scipio gave him some avuncular advice. In a private meeting, he told Jugurtha to cultivate Rome's friendship, not that of individual Romans, and to suppress his habit of offering bribes. The prince paid absolutely no attention to these wise words.

When the current king of Numidia died, he bequeathed his realm to his two sons and to Jugurtha, his nephew. A similar tripartite division had worked well enough on Masinissa's death, probably because it had been guaranteed by the Romans. But Jugurtha did not want to share power. He had one brother assassinated and the other, Adherbal, fled to Rome. The Senate misguidedly decided that Numidia should be bisected between the two surviving rivals. Jugurtha refused to accept the settlement and besieged Adherbal in his capital. A resident community of Italian merchants persuaded the beleaguered king to give himself up on condition that his life be spared.

Jugurtha accepted the terms, but as soon as he had his cousin in his possession he put him to death—and many of the Italian merchants were massacred, too, for good measure. This was an irreparable mistake. Rome never forgave the murder of its citizens. War was declared and the Senate dispatched an army to Africa. However, Jugurtha soon agreed to surrender to a Roman general on condition that he keep his throne.

This was a completely unexpected outcome, and it was widely supposed that Jugurtha had bribed every Roman official with whom he had come into contact. The Senate set up a board of inquiry and Jugurtha was invited to Rome under a safe-conduct to reveal the identity of all those he had suborned. Incorrigible as ever, he bribed a tribune to prevent him from announcing any names. He was also responsible for the assassination of a cousin, who was living in Rome and had been invited by one of the consuls to claim the Numidian throne for himself. By now it was obvious that Jugurtha was a man with whom it was impossible to do business. He was sent back to Africa, and the fighting resumed.

An incompetent Roman army was soundly beaten by the Numidians and forced to march under a yoke of spears, as in the bad old days of the Samnite Wars. It was obliged to evacuate Numidia. At long last in 109, the Senate was persuaded to treat Jugurtha seriously and a competent and incorruptible general was sent out to rescue the war.

He was Quintus Caecilius Metellus, a member of a leading senatorial family. Marius was among Metellus's clients and served as his *legatus,* or deputy. Now in his late forties, he had made reasonable progress up the political ladder for a *novus homo,* having been elected praetor in 114 and appointed governor of Lusitania. He was ambitious for the top job, even if it meant offending his longtime patron.

Metellus was winning the campaign, but slowly. Jugurtha had not been captured. Marius began to agitate that the war was being spun out unnecessarily. He was popular with the army rank and file and with Roman traders, not to mention voters at home. He asked Metellus for permission to return to Rome so that he could run for the consulship and take over the command. Being the aristocrat that he was, an irritated Metellus could not resist cracking a joke at his deputy's expense. "So you are going to abandon us, are you, my dear fellow?" he asked. "Wouldn't it be a better idea to delay your campaign until you can stand at the same time as this boy of mine?" Metellus's son was only twenty.

Eventually, Marius was allowed to take his leave. In Rome, he raised enough popular and equestrian support to win the consulship. The Assembly disregarded the Senate's decision to prolong Metellus's command and appointed Marius in his place. This usurpation of the Senate's traditional role in deciding provincial commands set a dangerous precedent. It paved the way for extraordinary commands for ambitious politicians who were willing to bypass the usual constitutional limitations.

Marius was determined to finish off Jugurtha at the earliest opportunity, so he levied more troops. However, he found the going as difficult and time-consuming as his predecessor had. He reduced stronghold after stronghold, but the legions were hard put to worst a highly mobile enemy on land well suited to the deployment of cavalry. Jugurtha strengthened his position by an alliance with his neighbor, Bocchus, the king of Mauretania. At long last a pitched battle was fought, which Marius won decisively—thanks in large part to Sulla, who commanded the cavalry, turning up at just the right moment.

However, the slippery Numidian king was still at large. He was not so slippery, though, as his new friend Bocchus, who decided to surrender him to the Romans. Simultaneously and falsely, the king promised Jugurtha to hand Sulla over to *him;* with such a distinguished captive, the Numidian calculated, he would easily be able to negotiate a peace with Rome. Bocchus invited the two men to a conference. Sulla, taking his life in his hands, rode to the rendezvous with only a few followers. At the last minute, the Mauretanian king had second thoughts and wondered anxiously whether, after all, he should favor Jugurtha. He eventually decided that the Roman was the better bet, and Jugurtha was arrested.

Jugurtha was taken to Rome and paraded in Marius's triumph. Defeat made him lose his mind. When he was inserted, naked, into Rome's main prison, the Tullianum, a tiny drumlike cellar with a shaft leading into the Cloaca Maxima, he said, "God, this Roman bath is cold." He lasted six days in the dark and without food before dying.

Much to Marius's fury, Sulla made the most of his coup and was widely credited with winning the war. He had a seal ring made that depicted Bocchus delivering, and Sulla receiving, Jugurtha.

We may imagine a smile lighting up Metellus's face.

MARIUS WAS CREDITED with being a great military innovator, although it may be that the ancient sources have used him as a clotheshorse on which to hang a number of important reforms agreed at different times.

As the Gracchi had discovered, the days of the reasonably well-off yeoman were closing and, when he raised his additional troops for Africa, Marius recruited directly from the head count, Rome's lowest economic and social stratum, who owned little or nothing and by law could not be drafted. This was not as revolutionary a step as might at first appear, for the prescribed property qualifications for legionaries had been falling for some time, and Marius was careful to ask for volunteers rather than conscripts.

One way or another, many recruits could no longer afford to pay for their own gear, as they had been expected to do in the past, and had no farms to return to. What had once been a militia was mutating into a near-professional army. This had one very dangerous consequence: soldiers became increasingly dependent on their commanders, both to ensure that they were well equipped and, already a problem in the age of Scipio, that they had somewhere to go when they were demobilized after their six to sixteen years' term of service.

The system of maniples, the three lines of infantry and the forward screen of light-armed skirmishers, gave way during the second and first centuries to the cohort, a grouping of four hundred and eighty foot soldiers equivalent to three maniples. Not as complex and decentralized as the old arrangement, a legion of ten cohorts was more readily responsive to its commander during battle.

Marius standardized uniforms and weapons and, to foster esprit de corps, introduced the *aquila,* a silver eagle carried on a pole. It symbolized the legion, and its capture by the enemy conferred lasting shame on all its soldiers.

An ingenious technical device helped make survival on the field of battle a better bet. The heavy javelin, or *pilum,* was an essential part of the legionary's armory. But when he threw it at his opponents, they often picked it up and hurled it back. Its iron head was attached to a wooden pole by two metal rivets. One of these was now replaced by a wooden dowel, so that the head was bent or snapped off entirely when the pilum reached its target or fell to the ground. This meant that it could not be reused.

Marius reduced the number of camp followers, making individual legionaries more self-reliant. In addition to their weapons, they had to carry on their backs emergency food rations and essential equipment for cooking and entrenching. With their bent, ungainly gait, infantrymen looked like beasts of burden. They were nicknamed Marius's mules.

A TERRIBLE THREAT to Rome's very existence suddenly materialized. Every Roman remembered the horror story of the Battle of the Allia and the capture and looting of their city by the Celts in the fourth century. Barbarian hordes pressing down from the dark forests of central Europe into the sunlit lands of the Mediterranean remained figures of nightmare, lurking just beyond the direct field of vision.

Every now and again, the Celts reappeared. In 279 they invaded Greece, reaching as far as Delphi before being repulsed. Immigrant Celts settled in Galatia (in what is today's central Anatolia). Rome did what it could to reduce the risk of further incursions into Italy by creating buffer territories. In 120, southern France became the province of Gallia Transalpina, later Narbonensis. Over the years, many consular armies marched north to reduce the Celtic communities in the Po Valley; eventually, in the first century, the region became the province of Cisalpine Gaul.

Alarming reports reached Rome in 113 that two Germanic tribes, the Cimbri and the Teutones, were emigrating en masse with their women and children southward from their homelands in or near Jutland. The record of incompetence and corruption in Rome's political class continued; somewhere in the eastern Alps, a consul crashed to defeat at the hands of the tribal wanderers. Most fortunately for the Republic, they turned westward toward Gaul, which they reached in 110.

A succession of consuls suffered further routs, culminating in 105 at Arausio (modern Orange, not far from Avignon), in Rome's greatest military disaster since Cannae, with a reported loss of eighty thousand men. Italy lay at the invader's mercy. Men under the age of thirty-five were forbidden to leave the country. Rome prepared for the worst.

Marius was still in Africa when the news of the catastrophe reached Rome. On a wave of popular enthusiasm, he was reelected consul in absentia for the following year. This was against all the conventions, but the Assembly had had enough of hopeless aristocrats and wanted a commander who had a chance of repulsing the Celts.

The Celts were in no hurry to do anything in particular and rambled around the Gallic countryside. This gave Marius breath-

ing space, during which he introduced his military reforms (or re-
fined earlier ones) and honed his troops into an efficient fighting
force. He went on being elected consul for six years in a row. This
was unprecedented, but it was evidently more sensible to keep the
Republic's most able general in place than to insist on an annual
change of command just for the constitutional principle of the
thing.

The Celts split their forces into two. The Teutones (alongside a
fellow tribe, the Ambrones) intended to enter Italy via the seacoast,
while the Cimbri would descend on the peninsula through the
Brenner Pass. Marius was waiting for the former, but did not immediately give battle. The Celts were a terrifying sight, and their
vast numbers covered the plain. The Romans stayed in their camp
and watched them pass by; if we are to believe Plutarch, this took
six days.

Marius shadowed the enemy until he found a suitable site for a
battle. A skirmish led to a successful engagement, and on the following day the Roman army deployed for battle. A force of three
thousand men hid in ambush behind the Celts. In the face of an
onslaught by the Teutones, the legions more than held their ground;
astounded by an attack on their rear, the enemy panicked and fled.

The bodies of the Celtic dead were left where they were. They
fertilized the ground, and the people of Massilia used their bones to
fence fields. For some years, it was said that the grape harvests were
unusually rich.

Marius quickly joined the consular army confronting the Cimbri
in the Po Valley, and in 101 the combined forces met the enemy
outside Vercellae (today's Vercelli, in Piedmont) on a hot midsum-
mer's day. The armies raised such a cloud of dust that at the beginning they missed each other. The Celts were unused to the
sweltering temperature and were soon cut to pieces. Their disgusted womenfolk killed any fugitives who came their way, and
many of them strangled their children and cut their own throats.

Rome had outfaced an external challenge, but it was to have no peace. Now it was to risk destruction from enemies within.

MARIUS WAS NOT much of a politician. A man without grace, he was happier giving orders to troops than compromising with civilians. While serving his successive consulships and campaigning against the Celts, he needed political support in the Forum. He found it, unwisely, in an embittered and daring tribune, Lucius Appuleius Saturninus, a nobleman who turned against his class and became a *popularis* after being sacked from his job as quaestor in charge of managing Rome's grain supply at the port of Ostia.

A fine public speaker and a clever fixer, Saturninus was elected tribune in 103. His policy was uncomplicated: it was to be as disobliging as possible to the Senate. He entered into a partnership with Marius and on his behalf passed a law settling the general's veterans from the war with Jugurtha on land in the province of Africa. He had no qualms about using violence. When a fellow tribune tried to interpose a veto, Saturninus got his followers to drive him off with a hail of stones. He also helped Marius win his fourth consulship in 102.

After his victories over the Celts, Marius returned to Rome and entered into a new compact with Saturninus. The tribune and the consul shared a hatred for Metellus, who had not only patronized Marius in Africa but also tried to remove Saturninus from the Senate on the grounds of immorality. They laid a trap for him.

A proposal was put to the Senate that all soldiers, Latins as well as Roman citizens, demobilized after the defeat of the Cimbri and the Teutones, should be given allotments in Transalpine Gaul and colonies in various places across the Mediterranean. A controversial clause was added that each senator should swear to observe the new law. Everyone knew that for Metellus this was an unconstitutional infringement of senatorial independence.

Marius assured all and sundry that he would never bind himself in this way. Then, a few days later, just before the legal deadline for taking the oath, he unexpectedly convened the Senate and said that because of popular pressure he had changed his mind. But he had worked out an ingenious formula that would address Metellus's objection. He would swear to obey the law "insofar as it *was* a law." A nervous Senate followed his lead, except for Metellus. He was outmaneuvered and isolated, but, having taken a stand, he refused to backtrack. His punishment was exile.

Marius, although cussed, was no revolutionary and could see that the *populares* were running out of control. Saturninus won a third term as tribune, and a colleague of his ran for consul. When a leading rival for the consulship was beaten to death in public, it was clear that a line had been crossed. Popular support for Saturninus evaporated.

For the second time, the Senate passed the Final Decree. The tribune and his friends occupied the Capitol. Abandoning them to their fate, Marius put together an armed force and cut off their water supply. This was a turning point in the history of Rome, for soldiers in uniforms and carrying weapons were strictly forbidden within the city boundary; also, the ease and speed with which the consul found and deployed these men strongly suggests a personal loyalty to him rather than to the state.

The parched revolutionaries soon surrendered. Promised their lives would be spared, they were locked up, as a temporary expedient, in the Senate House at the foot of the Capitol. But a furious lynch mob climbed onto the roof, stripped off the roof tiles, and threw them down onto the rebels until most of them were dead.

That was the end of the affair. Marius completed his term as consul, but his lack of political skill and principle were embarrassingly obvious, and thereafter he was frozen out of public life. As Plutarch put it: "He lacked the abilities others had of making themselves agreeable socially and useful politically. So he was left on the side like military equipment in peace-time." He traveled to the East, apparently on private business, and disappeared from view.

Ancient historians have not been kind to Saturninus, and we cannot now judge his value as a statesman. He may have been no more than an upper-class monster with a chip on his shoulder, or a worthy successor of the Gracchi, or a bit of both. But one truth stands out: where the old Republic used to solve problems through discussion, now the *optimates* and the *populares* had acquired an addiction to violence that they were unable to shake off.

IF THE ENTENTE in the Forum was dissolving, so, too, were relations between Rome and its allies throughout Italy. For years there had been talk of offering them full Roman citizenship, but proposals had always lapsed. The urban masses who voted at assemblies in Rome would not allow any measure that benefited others than themselves.

In 91, a bright young optimate, Marcus Livius Drusus, was elected tribune. He was hardworking but self-important. From his boyhood, he refused to take holidays. When he was building a house on the fashionable Palatine Hill, his architect thought of a way of designing it that would prevent it from being overlooked. "No," replied Drusus. "Build it so that my fellow citizens are able to see everything I do."

The tribune had a solution to every political conundrum, and a talent for putting backs up—in the Senate and among the People and the *equites*. He correctly judged that the Italian allies should be given what they wished, and proposed that they should be enfranchised. But the opposition was too strong. Drusus was suspected of conspiring with allied leaders, some of whom he was known to have entertained in his house—no doubt because of its openness to observers. It was there, too, that he paid for his plans with his life. One evening, after conducting business in a portico, he dismissed the crowd. Then, suddenly, he shouted that he had been stabbed, and fell to the ground with the words on his lips. He had been fatally wounded in the groin. A leather worker's knife was found, but not the assassin.

The allies laid secret plans for an uprising but awaited the outcome of Drusus's attempts at reform. With his death, they abandoned negotiation for armed force. Their war aim was, to put it mildly, unusual: most of them sought not to overthrow the Republic but to join it. They intended to force the Romans to be their friends and equals, and to give them the vote. There was one exception, a community that had harbored hatred for their conquerors through long, bitter centuries of servitude. These were the Samnites. They had never accepted the verdict of defeat after defeat after defeat two centuries earlier. Whenever the opportunity arose, they enthusiastically took up arms against their ancient enemy once again.

By mischance the allies' plans were detected too soon, and they were obliged to launch their attack rather late in the campaigning season. However, they held the initiative and swept all before them. After all, they regularly supplied more than half of Rome's ever-victorious armies and knew all there was to know about their methods. The legions were fighting against old comrades.

Rome had the winter to gather its forces, and by spring of 90 put fourteen legions into the field. Every Roman of good family was called up. (Even the unmilitary young Cicero served as an officer.) There were two theaters of war—north-central Italy and Samnium. In both of them, the Italians scored a catalog of victories culminating in the defeat and death of a consul. Marius was recalled and held off the onslaught in the north (he soon retired, ostensibly on grounds of ill health, but perhaps because, as a man of Arpinum, he was not altogether trusted). Although much of the peninsula was in flames, the Latin and Roman fortress *coloniae* remained true.

As one disastrous month followed another, the revolt spread southward, and toward the end of the year the Etruscans and Umbrians in the north demanded the franchise. The Senate made a historic decision. The only way Rome could win the war was by conceding the main point at issue. A law was passed granting full

Roman citizenship to any Latin or Italian communities that either had not revolted or had laid down their arms.

The war carried on for another two years, but this timely concession, later extended to everybody, threw a blanket over the flames. Sulla was successfully active in the south. The legions began to win victories, and even the Samnites lost heart. Gradually, the fighting petered out.

It had been a terrible convulsion. Many thousands of lives had been lost, and it was said that the devastation of the countryside exceeded that wreaked by Pyrrhus and Hannibal. In the long run, there were both positive and negative consequences. Every man south of the Po became a Roman citizen, and there was a growing sense of Italy as a single nation. Local identities continued to flourish, but within a larger commonwealth that the *civitas Romana* brought into being and guaranteed.

However, Italian enfranchisement weakened a constitution that had been designed for a city-state where most citizens were within a day or two's traveling distance of Rome, and so were able to cast their democratic vote. In future, the interests of those attending Assembly meetings in Rome were not necessarily the same as those of the new larger, far-flung citizenship.

A FLAMBOYANT NEW actor now strode onto the stage— Mithridates, the king of Pontus, a remote realm on the southern littoral of the Black Sea. For the ordinary Roman, this was near the edge of the known world, but it had formed part of Alexander's empire and had been duly Hellenized. The official language was Greek, and city-states in the Greek manner lined the coast. In the interior, mountains stood guard over a large, high plateau where Persian aristocrats presided over a native peasantry.

The royal house claimed descent from Darius, the luckless King of Kings whom the Macedonian conqueror overthrew in the fourth century. The character of Mithridates' home life can be gauged by a glance at his family tree. His father was murdered, and his mother died in prison. Five siblings (from a total brood of seven) met untimely ends, all of them at the hands of their brother Mithridates, who was also responsible for the deaths of two of his own sons. None of this was particularly unusual in Hellenistic monarchies, where a ruler's greatest enemies were usually his closest relatives.

Mithridates was born in about 120, the elder of two boys. When he was eleven, his father was poisoned at a banquet. The beneficiary, and perhaps the assassin, was his wife, a daughter of Antiochus the Great, who took over the reins of power during her sons' minority. She seems to have preferred her youngest child, Chrestus, to Mithridates, or (just as likely) had no intention of letting either of them reach adulthood and claim the crown back from her.

By the age of fourteen, Mithridates began to fear for his life. He rode off on a hunting trip, and did not return for seven years. He seems to have spent the time in the valleys and forests of Pontus's massif central, and became a romantic folk hero in the popular mind. When he eventually came back to Sinope, the capital of Pontus, he had the support of the masses and his mother gave herself up without making trouble. He agreed to rule with Chrestus, but the boy became a focus of palace intrigue. Mithridates was too strong-willed to bother with the constraints of a dual monarchy. He gave Chrestus a show trial and a public execution.

Traditionally, Pontus pursued a pro-Roman policy, but the young king intended to challenge the new imperialists from the west. Calculating that the Republic would hardly notice, he began by creating an empire up the eastern coast of the Black Sea as far as Colchis, the legendary birthplace of Medea and once the home of the Golden Fleece.

In 104, he and the neighboring king of Bithynia invaded and annexed Galatia and Paphlagonia. They then marched into Cappadocia but quarreled over who should control it. Mithridates sent an embassy to Rome to bribe senators to tolerate his interventions and to take his side on the issue of Cappadocia. In 99 or 98, Marius, who was in the region on his eastern travels as a *privatus,* warned Mithridates to take care. "Either be greater than the Romans," he advised, "or else obey them."

The Senate found the whole business tediously complicated and ordered both kings to withdraw, which they did. Sulla, who was the propraetor of Cilicia at the time, installed a new king of Cappadocia, chosen by the local nobility.

In 90, with Rome preoccupied by its war with the Italian allies, Mithridates went on the offensive again. This time he occupied Bithynia and (for a second time) Paphlagonia. The Senate sent out a commission to deal with this turbulent despot, led by a certain Manius Aquillius. Backed by a small military force, the commissioners ordered Mithridates to return to Pontus forthwith. Again, he obeyed. The Romans were not offering a free service and asked their protégés for payment. To raise the necessary cash, they recommended an invasion of Pontus. Bithynia reluctantly complied.

This was too much for Mithridates. He had always taken care to avoid a direct military confrontation with Rome, but now he felt that he had no choice but to resist. In short order, he defeated three armies sent against him. Aquillius was captured and put to death; as punishment for his greed, gold was melted and poured down his throat.

The king had reached a point of no return, and felt obliged to go to a further extreme. He marched on the Roman province of Asia, promising freedom for the Greek city-states and canceling debts. He accepted an invitation from Athens to liberate Greece. But what was he to do with the many thousands of Roman and Italian businessmen in the cities of Asia? If they were left alone, they would be a potential fifth column, but it was impractical to gather them together and expel them.

Mithridates made the most dangerous decision of his long career. He sent a round-robin letter to Asia's local authorities, in which he instructed them, in exactly thirty days from the date of writing, to kill all people of Italian birth—men, women, and children—and, in the ancient world the ultimate insult, to leave them unburied. Almost everyone obeyed with enthusiasm, although at least one municipality used hired killers. There were terrible scenes. Once the slaughter began, many victims ran to temples for sanctuary. In Ephesus, fugitives in the world-famous Temple of Artemis (the Greek equivalent of Diana) were torn from statues of the goddess, and in Pergamum those who had fled to the temple of the god of healing, Asklepios, were shot with arrows. In total, about eighty thousand people lost their lives.

The king knew that Rome would never forgive him, or anyone complicit in the extermination. The citizens of Asia were now bound to follow the fortunes of Pontus. From the Senate's point of view, there was a painful lesson to be learned: the zeal with which the population took to mass murder exposed the widespread hatred of Roman corruption and cruelty.

THE SENATE PLAYED a dirty trick when it offered the full Roman franchise, in effect, to all the allied communities south of the river Po. The many thousands of new citizens were enrolled in only a few of the thirty-five tribes, instead of being distributed among them all; this meant that, despite their large numbers, they would never be able to win a majority for their views. (It should be remembered that each tribe cast only a single collective vote.)

In 88, the conservative-minded Sulla was consul, a reward for his distinguished record in the Italian war. He was allocated the province of Asia—in other words, the potentially very lucrative command against Mithridates. So far, so straightforward.

A tribune of the same year, Publius Sulpicius Rufus, was one of the finest public speakers of the day. Cicero in his youth witnessed him perform. "Sulpicius of all the orators I have ever heard was the most theatrical," he claimed. "His voice was strong but pleasing and noble." Now in his mid-thirties, Sulpicius had been a brilliant and influential *optimate,* but as soon as he was elected tribune he switched loyalties and joined the *populares.* This probably had something to do with his close friendship with the assassinated Drusus. He was a warm supporter of the Italian allies and set himself the difficult task of passing a law that distributed Rome's new citizens fairly across all the thirty-five tribes.

Sulpicius could count on opposition in the Senate and among the People, so he struck a deal with Marius, who was still bitter that he had been excluded from public life and, at seventy, eager for one final military adventure. Marius was a popular figure among ordinary voters and could also muster backing for Sulpicius from the *equites.* In return, the tribune would repeal the law giving Sulla the eastern command and transfer it to Marius.

An outraged Sulla called a halt to public business (a *iustitium*). In reply, Sulpicius brought his mob onto the streets. Fighting broke out in the Forum, and an attempt was made on the consuls' lives. Sulla was able to make his escape but was forced, humiliatingly, to take refuge in Marius's house near the Forum. His pursuers ran past the building and Marius let him out by a back door. Sulla stayed in the city long enough to call off the *iustitium* and then slipped away to join the six legions he was to lead against the king of Pontus.

Sulpicius passed his legislation, and some of Sulla's supporters were killed. As soon as the consul learned that he had lost the command he convened a meeting of the army. The soldiers were looking forward to a profitable war and feared that Marius might recruit other men in their place. Sulla reported the violence to which he, a consul of Rome, had been subjected. He asked the men to obey orders, without specifying exactly what these were likely to be. They could read between the lines, though, and when Sulla commanded them to march on Rome they did as they were told. Their officers, however, could not stomach leading an army against their own country and fled the camp.

Another of Rome's great turning points had been reached. Politicians had now graduated from roughing up their opponents, and from time to time killing them, to out-and-out civil war. Appian writes bluntly: "The murders and civil disturbances had so far been internal and sporadic; but after this the faction leaders struggled against each other with great armies in military fashion for the prize of their native land."

THERE BEING NO garrison and so no official resistance, Sulla entered Rome at the head of two legions. This was sacrilege. A strict and ancient taboo forbade soldiers to enter the city (except for a triumph). Never before had it been so comprehensively broken. As the men filed down the narrow street to the center, shocked citizens flung stones and roof tiles on their heads, until Sulla threatened to set fire to their houses.

Once master of Rome, the consul had no trouble annulling Sulpicius's legislation. He also pushed through a few measures to strengthen the Senate and limit the power of tribunes. The consular elections took place, but he had no time to manage the results and one of the two new consuls, Lucius Cornelius Cinna, was a *popularis* and not to be trusted. Too bad, for Sulla was in a hurry to reach the East and deal with Mithridates.

Sulpicius was found hiding in a villa and put to death; the slave who betrayed him was given his freedom and then flung from the Tarpeian Rock. Marius, however, made good his escape, but not without some unpleasant ordeals as he tried to elude his pursuers. He set sail for Africa but became seasick and made landfall near the seaside resort of Circeii, sixty miles south of Rome. Fainting from hunger, he and his companions wandered about aimlessly in a forest. At the seashore again, they were alarmed to see a troop of horsemen in the distance and swam out to some merchant ships that, luckily, happened to be sailing by. These reluctantly took their celebrated but unwanted guest aboard, and soon dropped him off again with some provisions.

The old man stripped off his clothes and hid in a muddy marsh. He was discovered and dragged out naked and covered in slime. He was taken to a nearby town and handed over to the local council, which decided that he should be put to death. A Celt (perhaps a member of the Cimbrian tribe that Marius had destroyed in battle more than ten years earlier) was ordered to do the deed. He entered the darkened room where Marius was lying. A loud voice roared from the shadows: "Man, do you dare kill Gaius Marius?"

The Celt threw down his sword, ran out of doors, and said, "I can't kill Gaius Marius!" Consternation was followed by a change of heart. Marius was taken back to the coast, a ship was found for him, and he made his way to the province of Africa, where he had settled many of his veterans. At last, he was among friends.

WITH SULLA SAFELY in the East, the new consul, Cinna, tried to reintroduce Sulpicius's legislation for the new citizens but was declared a public enemy by the Senate and driven out of the city. Marius, tormented by his trials, returned to Italy and raised troops. He was soon joined by Cinna. For the second time in its history, the legions marched on Rome.

The two men launched a massacre of *optimates*. Soldiers were allowed to loot and kill at will. Among the many statesmen who lost their lives was Quintus Lutatius Catulus, who had been Marius's fellow consul in 102, when they had jointly fought off the Celtic hordes. He averted murder by suicide, suffocating himself by burning charcoal in a newly plastered room. No one was allowed to bury the dead, so birds and dogs tore apart the corpses. After five days, Cinna called a halt.

Marius won an unprecedented seventh consulship for 86, but within seven days of taking office he was dead. Old, sick, and mad, he fell into a delirium. According to Plutarch:

He imagined that he was the commander-in-chief of the war against Mithridates and then behaved just as he used to do when really in action, throwing himself into all sorts of attitudes, going through various movements, shouting words of command and constantly yelling out his battle cry.

Three years passed, with Cinna retaining the consulship and Italy remaining at peace. There appears to have been good government; useful laws were passed to alleviate indebtedness and restore the quality of a debased coinage. But, at last, Sulla, victorious over the Pontic king, returned to Italy. He had vengeance in mind. Cinna was killed by his own troops, who then switched sides. A short civil war put paid to the *popularis* administration.

For the very last time the Samnites, still bleeding from the war of the allies, rose again. They joined a consular army, which Sulla defeated. Many prisoners were taken and the victor, to settle the matter once and for all, had any Samnites put to death. After this atrocity, the Samnite nation could foresee its ultimate fate and made one final bold throw of the dice. Its forces made a dash for Rome. But Sulla rushed back and intercepted them just in time outside the city's Colline Gate. The fighting went on all day and lasted well into the night. Although at one point the Samnites gained the upper hand, they went down in defeat. It was their last battle. An invasion of their homeland followed, and much of the population was put to the sword. Samnium became a desolation.

Once in Rome, Sulla launched a domestic pogrom, the Proscription (as we have seen, names of the doomed were listed on a public notice board). He decided to liquidate all the political opponents he could find, and the butchery went on for months. Victims' heads were displayed on the speakers' platform in the Forum. Their estates were confiscated and used to finance the settlement of demobilized veterans. According to Appian, ninety senators died, and about sixteen hundred *equites,* but we may guess that the final total was much higher. Many Italians also suffered. The Senate, usually about three hundred strong at this time, was reduced to a hundred and fifty members. Marius's remains were disinterred and scattered.

Sulla freed himself of any legal checks by reviving the all-powerful post of dictator, which had been in abeyance for more than a century. He was elected *dictator legibus scribundis et rei publicae constituendae* ("dictator for the writing of laws and organization of the Republic"). His term of office was not the traditional six months but for an indefinite period.

This gave the new master of Rome as much time as he needed to reform the constitution. In his view, the Senate was broken and needed to be mended. The tribunes were overmighty and needed to be tamed. In a word, the world was to be made safe for *optimates.* Above all, Sulla sought to prevent the emergence of another Sulla.

The Senate was increased to six hundred members. A ladder of political progression—the *cursus honorum,* or "honors race"—was clearly laid down, with minimum ages for magistrates. A man qualified for election as quaestor, a junior treasury official, from the age of thirty; as aedile, from thirty-six (this post was optional); as praetor, from thirty-nine; and, finally, as consul, from forty-two. The number of quaestors was raised from eight to twenty; they automatically joined the Senate once their term of office was over. So the membership would be regularly refreshed. New law courts were established that covered a range of crimes. Jurors were no longer to be *equites* but exclusively senators again.

In an attempt to control unruly generals, such as Sulla himself had been, governors were forbidden to leave their provinces or make war outside them without explicit permission from Rome. The charge for disobedience was to be treason, *maiestas minuta populi Romani* (literally, "the diminution of the majesty of the Roman people").

The veto of tribunes was restricted, and they were no longer allowed to promote bills without the Senate's prior authorization.

To universal astonishment, the dictator resigned his office on completing his legislative program, and in 80 retired into private life. He seems to have had a wonderful time. According to Plutarch, his wife died and he remarried a younger woman, who had picked him up at a gladiatorial show. In spite of that, Plutarch writes:

> He still kept company with women who were ballet-dancers or harpists and with people from the theater. They used to lie drinking together on couches all day long. The men who were now most influential with him were Roscius the comedian, Sorex the leading ballet dancer, and Metrobius the female impersonator. Metrobius was now past his prime, but throughout everything Sulla continued to insist he was in love with him.

Curiously, when he walked about the city with his friends nobody arrested or physically attacked him. The worst that happened to him were the insults of a teenage boy who once trailed him all the way to his house. The former dictator put up with this patiently, only remarking (presciently), "This lad will stop anyone else from laying aside such power."

Throughout his life, Sulla believed in his luck and added the cognomen Felix, or Lucky, to his name. In this he resembled the legendary king of Rome Servius Tullius, who also made much of his good fortune. As with the king, Sulla's luck abandoned him at the end. His retirement was brief. In 78, after a very unpleasant illness, entailing an ulcerated bowel, malodorous discharges, and worms guzzling on necrotic flesh, he died. He was about sixty years old. The early symptoms of a terminal disease may help to explain his unexpected abdication.

IN THE FOURTH century A.D., when the Roman Empire in the west was within a century of its fall, a collection of eighty-six short biographies of famous Romans was published: *De viris illustribus urbis Romae* (*Famous Men of the City of Rome*). All the most celebrated names of Roman history were there, from Romulus and Remus to Mark Antony. The list also included five foreigners, those who had been the Republic's most dangerous enemies: they were Pyrrhus, Hannibal, Viriathus (the Spanish guerrilla fighter), Cleopatra— and Mithridates.

The king of Pontus spent a long lifetime opposing Rome, and came close to destroying its power in the Eastern Mediterranean. When Sulla left Italy to campaign against him, Mithridates was in command of the Balkans and Asia Minor, and disposed of vast financial and manpower resources. But after two great battles the legions drove him out of Greece and captured Athens, which had invited the king to free it from Roman rule. Much of the city center was destroyed and many Athenians were put to the sword.

In 85, Sulla crossed into Asia Minor, but instead of continuing the fight he negotiated a quick settlement at a place called Dardanus, near the ruins of Troy. Mithridates agreed to surrender a fleet, evacuate all the territory he had conquered in Asia Minor, and pay an indemnity of two thousand talents. In return, he not only kept his throne but was granted "most favored nation" status as a Friend and Ally of the Roman People. Under the circumstances, not a bad result. But the ghosts of eighty thousand businessmen remained unappeased.

In 75 or 74, the king of Bithynia, at various times the friend and the enemy of Pontus, died. He bequeathed his realm to Rome. The Senate accepted the legacy, careless of the impact this would have on the balance of power in the east. To have Rome right on his doorstep was more than Mithridates could bear, and he invaded the new province.

Two proconsuls were appointed to Bithynia and Asia. Mithridates defeated the former but was worsted by the latter—Lucius Licinius Lucullus, a talented but haughty general. Two years of fighting saw the destruction of a large Pontic army. Mithridates escaped to the safety of his own kingdom.

Lucullus was in no hurry and refused to countenance a compromise peace, as Sulla had done; he moved against Pontus itself. The campaign was hard-fought, but by 70 he had the kingdom at his mercy. Mithridates fled to Armenia, where his son-in-law Tigranes was the ruler and gave him refuge. The Roman commander sent an envoy to the Armenian court to demand the Pontic king's surrender. While waiting for an answer, Lucullus reorganized the finances of his province, which was laboring under a high level of indebtedness. His reforms infuriated extortionate Roman tax collectors, who were used to excessive profits. They instigated a whispering campaign against Lucullus, alleging that he was prolonging the war for his own glory.

Tigranes refused to hand over his father-in-law, who returned to Pontus. Lucullus invaded Armenia, but after winning some important victories his troops refused to carry on the war. An effective commander, he was a poor manager of men. Much to his annoyance, he was replaced by a onetime favorite of Sulla, Gnaeus Pompeius, known to us as Pompey the Great. He had little trouble finishing off what Lucullus had almost concluded.

Betrayed by two of his sons, Mithridates was holed up in a castle in the Crimea. He no longer had any hope and took poison, but even though he walked around quickly to hasten the effect of the drug, it failed to work. Apparently, as an unsurprising precaution for an eastern monarch, he had regularly consumed small doses of various poisons for many years and had inured himself to their effect. So the king of Pontus had a servant dispatch him. He was about seventy years old and had been troubling the Romans for the better part of five decades.

POMPEY WAS NOT only a competent soldier but an administrator of genius. Before returning to Italy, he reconstructed the East in a settlement that lasted for many years. He established a line of directly governed provinces that ran from Pontus on the Black Sea, down the Eastern Mediterranean to the frontier of the still independent kingdom of Egypt. Alongside, a band of free states, governed by client kings, acted as a buffer between Rome's sphere of influence and the great Parthian Empire, which stretched from the Euphrates to India.

On 29 September 61, his forty-fifth birthday, Pompey celebrated the most splendid of triumphs, mainly for his victories in Asia Minor but also for a successful earlier campaign against pirates in the Mediterranean. A long line of horse-drawn carriages and litters carried a fabulous quantity of precious metals. It included more than 75,000,000 denarii's worth of silver coins (probably equivalent to Rome's entire tax income for a year); Mithridates' throne and scepter as well as a statue of the king, more than twelve feet high and made of solid gold; and chariots of gold and silver.

Among other exotic exhibits were a moon of solid gold, an outsize chessboard in precious stones and, writes the encyclopedist Pliny the Elder, a "square mountain of gold, with stags and lions on it and all sorts of fruit, framed by a golden vine." This mysterious object was perhaps a table decoration for a banquet. All in all, the Roman public was offered a display of Oriental luxury at its most extravagant.

Large paintings illustrated high points in the campaigns. Tigranes and Mithridates were depicted fighting, defeated, and in flight. The Pontic king's death was shown, too. Tigranes had been taken alive and he, with his wife and daughter and other captives, walked in the procession. Once the triumph was over, he was put to death in the Tullianum, according to custom.

A proud notice board boasted:

Ships with brazen beaks captured, 800;
cities founded in Cappadocia, 8;
                     in Cilicia and Coele Syria, 20;
                     in Palestine the one which is now Seleucis.
Kings conquered: Tigranes the Armenian,
                     Artoces the Iberian,

Oroezes the Albanian,

Darius the Mede,

Aretas the Nabataean,

Antiochus of Commagene.

The general himself rode a chariot studded with gems and wore a cloak that had once belonged to Alexander the Great—"If anyone can believe that!" remarked a skeptical Appian. Apparently, it was found among Mithridates' possessions. Pompey was a great admirer of the Macedonian king, and somewhere in the procession there was a portait bust of him, ingeniously made from pearls and showing him, in imitation of Alexander, with his hair thrown back from his forehead.

WITH POMPEY'S RETURN from the East, the rise of Rome was complete. The Republic had destroyed the last of its external foes, and its position as proprietor of the largest empire the classical world had seen was secure. Except for desolate stretches of northern Africa, the Republic controlled the full extent of the Mediterranean coastline.

The next one hundred and fifty years would see further acquisitions. In the main, these were a form of extremely aggressive consolidation. They guarded against the Celtic threat from the north, Rome's recurrent nightmare since the capture of the city in the fourth century. In the 50s, Gaius Julius Caesar conquered and annexed Gaul (roughly equivalent to France), and that was followed a century later by the invasion of Britannia under the emperor Claudius. During the same period, the conquest of all Spain was finally concluded and Rome's northern frontier was extended to the banks of the Rhine and the Danube, a strong defensive position. With the death of Cleopatra, Egypt changed from being a client kingdom to a Roman province. The empire had found its natural frontiers.

SULLA'S HOPES WERE posthumously dashed; by reducing the power of the People, reinforcing that of the Senate, and curbing that of overmighty proconsuls at the head of armies, he had intended to restore constitutional stability. But the bad example he set by marching on Rome was more attractive to his successors than were his good intentions. The Proscription (and Marius's earlier massacres) revealed a fateful truth: the ruling class had forgotten the imaginative tolerance it showed during the Conflict of the Orders.

The reforms Sulla introduced came too late to do any good. The governing system had broken down beyond repair. For this, there were interlocking reasons. First, as noted, the enfranchisement of all Italy meant that a People's Assembly, suitable for a small city-state, lost its democratic legitimacy, because most citizens were unable to attend its meetings. From being guardians of the popular interest, tribunes became managers of the city mob and so were able to hijack the powers of government from the Senate. This upset the balance between the "mixed" constitution's three component parts (as Polybius and Cicero saw it)—namely, the principles of monarchy, oligarchy, and democracy as represented by the consuls, the Senate, and the People.

The arrival of empire greatly complicated the business of government. An arrangement whereby all executive posts were subject to annual election made strategic planning difficult, if not impossible. There was not enough talent in the aristocracy to ensure competent administration. It proved impractical to supervise provincial governors and prevent them from making fortunes through extortion and fraud. In theory, the Senate was a forum where long-term issues could be thrashed out, but the attacks on it by populist tribunes weakened its authority.

Major crises in distant corners of the Mediterranean meant that the rules had to be bent. A handful of able and ambitious men, supported by the People, were able to insist on special commands that would inevitably last for a number of years (for instance, both Sulla's and Pompey's eastern commissions to suppress Mithridates).

The decline of the class of rural smallholders, which used to supply the legions with recruits, and the transformation of a citizens' militia into a professional army with long terms of service meant that soldiers were no longer primarily loyal to the state. Rather, they relied on their generals to look after their interests. The selfish reluctance of senators to reward demobilizing soldiers with grants of farming land only made the situation worse.

IT DID NOT take long for Sulla's legislation to be unpicked. Pompey entered into a political alliance with a daring financial speculator, Marcus Licinius Crassus. The Senate was too weak to prevent them from becoming consuls in 70 (although they were conspicuously unqualified to stand) and from restoring the powers of the tribunes of the plebs.

However, it was not too weak to snub them. The latest in a series of special commands was the conduct of the war against Mithridates. After Pompey's spectacular triumph, he was due to disband his army, but the Senate refused to help. The most brilliant politician of the age was a blue-blooded *popularis,* Gaius Julius Caesar. He persuaded Pompey and Crassus, who had fallen out, to join him in a secret alliance, which came to be known as the First Triumvirate.

Pooling their resources—clients as well as cash—the three men took control of the state. Caesar was elected consul for 59. Ignoring his consular colleague's attempts at obstruction, he passed a law settling Pompey's soldiers and obtained special commands for Crassus and himself. Crassus led an expedition against the Parthian Empire but found that his reach failed to exceed his grasp. In short order, he was defeated and killed.

Caesar did much better. He spent ten years conquering the Celtic tribes of Gaul, showing himself to be as brilliant in the field as he was in the Forum. He only returned to domestic politics in 50. He intended to stand for the consulship again, but the Senate blocked him on an electoral technicality. So Caesar led his legions across a little stream called the Rubicon, which marked the frontier between the province of Cisalpine Gaul and Italy itself. "The dice have been thrown," he remarked dryly. The Senate won Pompey to its side and fought back, but Caesar defeated his old partner in a great battle at Pharsalus, in central Greece. Pompey fled to Egypt, where the nervous authorities had him killed.

By 45, the war was over and Caesar was master of the Roman world. He did not intend to repeat Sulla's mistake and retire early. He appointed himself dictator for life. This was tantamount to being king, the unforgivable crime. On the Ides of March in 44 B.C., during a meeting of the Senate, he was stabbed to death by angry aristocrats. He collapsed at the feet of a statue of Pompey the Great.

Another fourteen years were to pass before peace returned to the empire. Caesar's adoptive son, Octavian, an inexperienced but clever eighteen-year-old, and Mark Antony, an able but idle military commander who had been one of Caesar's henchmen, launched a Proscription as savage as that of Sulla. After defeating Caesar's assassins at Philippi, they divided the empire between them. Octavian took the West and Antony the East. As far as they were concerned, the Republic was dead. They, too, then fell out, however. Another civil war ensued, which Octavian won at the sea battle of Actium.

In 27, with breathtaking dexterity, he brought back the Republic—but in name only. Renamed Augustus, the Revered One, he restored elections, and political life seemed to return to normal. However, he made sure to maintain control over the legions, and he was given a tribune's powers regularly renewed—the veto, authority to table laws, personal inviolability—but without the tiresome obligation of actually having to hold the office. The ruling class, decimated in the wars, accepted the pretense.

A little more than one hundred years had passed since the tribuneship of Tiberius Gracchus and almost exactly fifty years since the reign of Sulla, the *Sullanum regnum*. Like the inexorable plot of a Greek tragedy, the consequences of the constitutional breakdown they brought about had finally worked themselves out.

18

Afterword

I T HAS OFTEN BEEN SAID THAT HISTORY IS WRITTEN by the victors, but in the case of Rome it was the losers who commandeered the narrative. Even those who published under the severe gaze of the emperors looked back on the Roman Republic with respect and nostalgia. For this, Cicero and Varro can take much of the credit. They committed scholarly errors and misjudgments, but, like a sacred flame, they preserved the spirit of the Republic that was dying.

They were political failures. Enemies of Julius Caesar, they witnessed the destruction of all their hopes. Varro made his peace with the great dictator, won over by a commission to establish Rome's first public library; he died in his bed at the ripe age of eighty-nine. Cicero was made of sterner stuff. After the Ides of March, he bravely returned to politics. He tried to save the Republic, but fell victim to Octavian and Mark Antony's Proscription.

As authors, though, the two friends excelled. Their rural retirement was not wasted. They wrote much on the rise of Rome, excavating and analyzing the past as best they could. Cicero said of Varro:

We were wandering and straying about like strangers in our own city, and your books led us, so to speak, right home, and enabled us at last to realize who and where we were. You have revealed the age of our native city, the chronology of its history, the laws of its religion, its civil and military institutions, the topography of its districts and sites . . . and you have likewise shed a flood of light upon our poets and generally on Latin literature and the Latin language.

Cicero was less of a scholar than Varro and more of a controversialist. He noted: "Like the learned men of old, we must serve the state in our libraries, if we cannot do so in the Senate or the Forum, and pursue our researches into custom and law." His main contributions were *Republic* and *Laws,* two substantial tomes in which he examined the history of the Roman constitution and, while allowing for reforms, commended its virtues. A moderate conservative, he believed that "excessive liberty leads both nations and individuals into excessive slavery."

Cicero had sharp eyes, and it seems strange that his books do not offer a more accurate perception of what was really happening. The explanation is that, like most of his contemporaries, he saw politics fundamentally in personal rather than ideological or structural terms. There had been a decline in moral standards in public life. All would be well if only there was a return to traditional values, to the *mos maiorum.* Caesar disagreed. With the insight of genius, he saw that incremental reforms would not save the day, nor would a return to the ideals of Cincinnatus. An altogether new system of government was required.

Grief-stricken by his daughter's death in 45, Cicero went on to write a series of books that presented Greek philosophy to Latin readers. They form the basis of his reputation with posterity and, in the past two millennia, empowered the thinking of generations of European readers.

Cicero regarded Julius Caesar as a second Hannibal, but though the dictator manipulated and bullied him as a politician, he held

Cicero in the highest esteem as an author. He once wrote of him that he was "winner of a greater laurel wreath than any gained by a triumph, insomuch as it is greater to have advanced the frontiers of Roman genius than those of the Roman empire."

Praise from one's worst enemy is the most annoying, but also the most credible, of compliments.

SO THE LONG, slow collapse of the Roman Republic had one positive consequence. The uncertainties of the age impelled men like Cicero and Varro to inquire into their collective past—to find an explanation for the crisis and, as a kind of antidote, to reveal the basis of their country's vanishing greatness. They evoked an idea of Rome that still lives and breathes two thousand years later.

But what was gone was gone, and they knew that. Cicero wrote the epitaph:

> The Republic, when it was handed down to us, was like a beautiful painting, whose colors were already fading with age. Our own time has not only neglected to freshen it by renewing its original colors, but has not even gone to the trouble of preserving its design and portrayal of figures.

TIME LINE

Dates in italics are traditional and legendary. Some traditional dates are judged likely to be historical. Some people and places are listed here whose names, to avoid an excess of detail, do not appear in the main text.

1084	Fall of Troy.
753	Romulus founds Rome.
c. 625	Earliest evidence of contact with the Etruscans.
753–715	Romulus.
715–673	Numa Pompilius.
673–642	Tullus Hostilius.
642–616	Ancus Marcius.
617–579	Tarquinius Priscus.
579–534	Servius Tullius.
534–510	Tarquinius Superbus.
509	Fall of the monarchy. First treaty with Carthage.
494	First secession.
493	Treaty of Spurius Cassius with the Latins.

491	Coriolanus marches on Rome.
From 486	Wars with the Aequi and Volsci from time to time over the next fifty years.
479	Battle of the Cremera; sacrifice of the Fabii.
474	Etruscans defeated off Cumae by Hiero I of Syracuse.
471	*Concilium plebis* and tribunes recognized.
451–450	Rule of the decemvirs. Twelve Tables published.
449	Secession. Valerio-Horatian laws. Rights of tribunes legally defined.
447	Quaestors elected by the People. *Comitia tributa* probably established.
445	Military tribunes with consular powers replace the consulship.
443	Censors appointed for the first time.
431	Dictatorship of Cincinnatus. Battle of Mons Algidus. Aequi decisively defeated.
396	Pay for soldiers introduced. Fall of Veii.
390 (or 387)	Battle of the Allia. Sack of Rome.
378	Construction of Rome's Servian walls starts.
367	Licinio-Sextian Rogations passed. Consulship restored. Curule aediles elected for the first time.
366	First plebeian consul elected. First praetors elected.
358	Treaty with the Latins renewed.
356	First plebeian dictator.
354	Alliance with the Samnites.
348	Treaty with Carthage renewed.
343–341	First Samnite War.
340–338	Latins revolt. Latin League dissolved.

337	First plebeian praetor elected.
326–304	Second Samnite War.
323	Alexander's death.
321	Roman defeat at the Caudine Forks.
312	Censorship of Appius Claudius.
298–290	Third Samnite War.
295	Battle of Sentinum.
287	Lex Hortensia makes resolutions of the *concilium plebis* binding on all citizens.
282	Tarentum attacks Roman naval squadron.
281	Rome attacks Tarentum, which seeks help from Pyrrhus of Epirus.
280–275	War with Pyrrhus.
279	Battle of Asculum.
278	Roman treaty with Carthage. Pyrrhus goes to Sicily.
276	Pyrrhus returns to Italy.
275	Pyrrhus defeated at Malventum, returns to Greece.
272	Surrender of Tarentum. Livius Andronicus brought to Rome.
264	First Punic War starts. Mamertines of Messana appeal to Rome for assistance against Carthage. Rome sends an expeditionary force. First gladiatorial show at Rome.
263	Hiero II changes sides, and allies Syracuse to Rome.
263/62	Sicilian city-states come under Roman control.
262/61	Siege and fall of Acragas.
261	The Carthaginian navy raids the Italian coast from Sardinia. Rome builds a fleet.
260	Naval victory off Mylae.

259	Hamilcar Barca campaigns in Sicily; also, fighting in Corsica and Sardinia.
258	Rome attacks Panormus. Carthaginians defeated off Sulci, in Sardinia.
257	Rome raids Malta and wins minor victory at Tyndaris.
256	Regulus defeats Carthaginian fleet at Ecnomus and sails to North Africa, where he defeats a Punic army and takes Tunis.
256/55	Peace negotiations fail.
255	Spartan Xanthippus leads Carthaginian army to victory near Tunis over Regulus, who is taken prisoner. Roman fleet victorious off Cape Bon. Survivors of Regulus's army are rescued. Storm inflicts great losses on a Roman fleet.
255/54	Roman fleet rebuilt.
254	Rome captures Panormus; Carthage holds Drepana and sacks Acragas.
253	Rome fails to take Lilybaeum. Major Roman naval losses in a storm.
252	Rome captures Thermae Himerae and the Lipara Islands.
251/50	Hasdrubal defeated near Panormus.
250–241	Roman siege of Lilybaeum.
249	Carthage wins a great sea victory off Drepana over Claudius Pulcher. Heavy Roman losses in a storm near Camarina. Rome seizes Eryx.
248	Mutiny by Carthaginian mercenaries is put down.
248–244	Punic raids on the Italian coast.
247	Hamilcar Barca arrives in Sicily and sets up camp on Mount Heirkte.
244	Hamilcar captures Eryx.
242	New Roman fleet blockades Drepana and Lilybaeum.
242/41	Decisive Roman victory off the Aegates Islands.

241	Peace gives Rome control of Sicily. First Punic War ends.
241–237	Mercenary War at Carthage.
238–225	Invasion and annexation of Corsica and Sardinia.
236	Hamilcar Barca and his son Hannibal go to Spain. Barca launches a war of conquest.
231	Roman embassy to Hamilcar Barca in Spain.
229–228	First Illyrian War.
228	Hamilcar Barca killed in battle. His son-in-law, Hasdrubal, succeeds to his command.
226	Roman embassy to Hasdrubal in Spain. Ebro treaty.
225	Celtic invasion halted at Battle of Telamon.
221	Hasdrubal assassinated. Hannibal succeeds to the command. Saguntum appeals to Rome.
219	Second Illyrian War. Hannibal storms Saguntum.
218–201	Second Punic War.
218	Hannibal climbs the Alps and enters Italy. Battles of the Ticinus and the Trebia.
217	Battle of Lake Trasimene.
216	Fabius Maximus, dictator. Battle of Cannae. Large-scale defections in southern Italy; revolt of Capua.
215	Partial Roman recovery. Hiero of Syracuse dies.
214	Roman successes in Spain. Syracuse defects to the Carthaginians.
214–205	First Macedonian War.
213	Marcellus besieges Syracuse.

212	Hannibal takes Tarentum. Marcellus takes Syracuse. Scipios take Saguntum.
211	Hannibal marches on Rome. Capua recaptured. Scipios defeated and killed.
210	Young Scipio (later Africanus) arrives in Spain.
209	Scipio takes New Carthage.
208	Marcellus ambushed and killed. Scipio wins Battle of Baecula. Hasdrubal disengages and marches to Italy.
207	Hasdrubal defeated and killed at the Battle of the Metaurus.
206	Scipio wins Battle of Ilipa, leaves for Italy.
205	Scipio elected consul, wins African command. Scipio in Sicily.
204	Scipio lands in northern Africa. Ennius brought to Rome. Cult of Great Mother introduced in Rome.
203	Carthaginian and Numidian camps destroyed. Battle of the Great Plains. Peace negotiations. Hannibal recalled to Carthage.
202	Last dictator appointed before Sulla. Battle of Zama. Carthage capitulates. Fabius Pictor writes first prose history of Rome.
201	Rome negotiates peace treaty. Carthage becomes a client state.
200–196	Second Macedonian War.
197	Philip V of Macedon loses Battle of Cynoscephalae. Peace agreed with Philip.
196	Flamininus announces liberation of Greece at Corinth. Hannibal elected *sufet* at Carthage.

195	Hannibal exiled from Carthage.
	Masinissa begins encroachments on Punic territory.
194	Rome evacuates Greece.
192–189	War with Antiochus.
	Antiochus in Greece.
191	Battle of Thermopylae. Antiochus driven from Greece.
189	Antiochus loses battle of Magnesia to the Scipios.
188	Settlement of Asia.
187	Criticism of the Scipios.
186	Bacchanalian conspiracy.
184	Scipio withdraws from Rome.
	Cato elected censor.
181–179	First Celtiberian War in Spain.
179	Philip V of Macedon dies, succeeded by Perseus.
173	Embassy sent to arbitrate between Masinissa and Carthage.
172	Two plebeian consuls, for the first time.
172–167	Third Macedonian War.
168	Perseus defeated at Battle of Pydna.
167	Macedon divided into four republics.
	One thousand Achaeans deported to Italy (including Polybius).
166–159	Production of Terence's comedies.
153–151	Second Celtiberian War.
151	Carthage declares war on Masinissa.
149–146	Third Punic War.
149	Publication of Cato's *Origines*.
147	Macedon becomes a province.

146	Sack of Carthage. Africa becomes a province. War between Rome and the Achaean League. Sack of Corinth.
143–133	Third Celtiberian War.
133	Tiberius Gracchus elected tribune. Land-reform law passed and land commission created. Pergamum bequeathed to Rome by King Attalus III. Gracchus murdered by rioting senators. Scipio Aemilianus takes Numantia. Spain settled. Slave war in Sicily continues.
132	Special court set up to punish Gracchus's supporters. Secret ballot for legislation votes in the People's Assembly. Slave war in Sicily ended.
129	Scipio Aemilianus dies mysteriously.
125	Proposal to enfranchise the Latins fails.
123	Gaius Gracchus elected tribune for the first time. Proposes many laws this year and in 122. Tiberius's land reform confirmed. Special courts barred from imposing death penalty unless approved by the People. Judicial reforms: extortion court juries to comprise *equites* only. Large overseas *coloniae* planned, including Junonia, on the site of Carthage. Grain supply and distribution improved. Many construction and road-building projects commissioned. Proposal to extend citizenship to all Italian allies rejected.
122	Gaius Gracchus elected tribune for the second time. Gracchus opposed by Tribune Marcus Livius Drusus. Fails to win reelection for 121. Senate passes the Final Decree (state of emergency) for the first time. Gracchus and followers defeated by force of senators and *equites*. Gracchus killed or commits suicide.

116	Problem of Jugurtha begins. Senatorial commission of inquiry partitions Numidian kingdom between Jugurtha and Adherbal.
112	Jugurtha besieges Adherbal, who surrenders and is put to death. Italian merchants in Numidia massacred. Rome declares war on Jugurtha.
111	Jugurtha surrenders but keeps his crown. Visits Rome, where he has a Numidian opponent murdered.
110	War with Jugurtha resumes.
109	Metellus campaigns against Jugurtha.
107	Marius, elected consul, replaces Metellus.
106	Marius advances into western Numidia. Bocchus, king of Mauretania, surrenders Jugurtha to Sulla.
105	Cimbri and Teutones defeat two Roman armies at Arausio, near the river Rhône.
104	Marius, Consul II, reorganizes Roman army equipment and tactics. Jugurtha starved to death after appearing in Marius's triumph. Second Sicilian slave war.
103	Marius, Consul III, trains army in Gaul. Saturninus elected tribune, works in partnership with Marius. Land allotments in Africa assigned to Marius's veterans.
102	Marius, Consul IV, defeats Teutones at Aquae Sextiae (Aix-en-Provence).
101	Marius, Consul V, and Catulus defeat Cimbri near Vercellae (Vercelli).
100	Saturninus, Tribune II. Marius, Consul VI, breaks with Saturninus. Rioting in Rome. Senate passes the Final Decree. Marius restores order. Saturninus and his followers lynched. Second Sicilian slave war ended.
98	Marius leaves politics and travels to Asia as a *privatus*.

97–92	Sulla, as proconsul of Asia, orders Mithridates, king of Pontus, out of Paphlagonia and Cappadocia. Mithridates obeys.
91	Marcus Livius Drusus, Jr., elected tribune. His plans to enfranchise the Italian allies fail. Drusus assassinated. War of the Allies (Social War) breaks out. Mithridates takes Bithynia. Aquillius incites invasion of Pontus.
90	Roman reverses in the Social War. Legislation grants Roman citizenship to Italian allies.
89	Roman victories in Social War.
88	Social War restricted to the Samnites, who yield. Sulla Consul I. Sulpicius Rufus, tribune, proposes to transfer command of war against Mithridates from Sulla to Marius. Sulla marches on Rome, captures the city, repeals Sulpicius's legislation. Marius flees to Africa. Mithridates overruns Asia Minor, orders massacre of Romans and Italians. Mithridates invited to "liberate" Greece.
87	Cinna and Marius seize Rome, massacre opponents. Sulla lands in Greece, besieges Athens.
86	Fall of Athens. Pontic army evacuates Greece after two defeats. Marius, Consul VII, dies. Cinna sends army to Asia (taken over by Sulla in 84).
85	Sulla negotiates peace treaty with Mithridates at Dardanus, near Troy.
84	New Italian citizens distributed among all the tribes. Cinna murdered by mutineers.
83	Sulla lands in Italy. Second Mithridatic War (to 82).
82	Civil war in Italy. Sulla wins battle of the Colline Gate. Proscriptions start.

81	Sulla appointed dictator, reforms the constitution and the criminal law.
80	Sulla Consul II.
79	Sulla resigns as dictator.
78	Sulla dies.
75 (or 74)	King Nicomedes bequeaths Bithynia to Rome.
74	Mithridates invades Bithynia. Lucullus given command against him.
73–71	Slave revolt in Italy, led by Spartacus.
68	After successful campaigning against Mithridates, Lucullus's troops become restless.
67	Pompey given command against pirates, whom he clears from the Mediterranean.
66	Pompey given command against Mithridates.
63	Mithridates commits suicide. Cicero elected consul.
62	Pompey's eastern settlement; he returns to Italy.
61	Senate refuses to confirm Pompey's settlement and land allocations for his soldiers.
60	Julius Caesar, Pompey, and Crassus agree alliance, known as the First Triumvirate.
59	Caesar elected consul.
58–50	Caesar's conquest of Gaul.
49–45	Civil war.
48	Battle of Pharsalus.
44	Caesar assassinated.
43–33	Octavian, Mark Antony, and Marcus Aemilius Lepidus establish Second Triumvirate. Proscription. Cicero put to death.
32–31	Civil war.

31	Antony and Cleopatra defeated at the Battle of Actium.
30	Antony and Cleopatra commit suicide.
27	Octavian/Augustus establishes new constitutional settlement.
43	Invasion of Britannia.

ACKNOWLEDGMENTS

My faithful twin props in England have been my agent, Christopher Sinclair-Stevenson, and the London Library. My exemplary editor on the far side of the Atlantic, Will Murphy, ably supported by assistant editor Katie Donelan, has tolerated broken deadlines and been a fountain of wise advice. As with my previous books, Professor Robert Cape of Austin College, Texas, has kindly read a draft and offered valuable comments and suggestions.

I am indebted to the dentist Shahin Nozohoor for advice on the state of Pyrrhus's teeth.

I am grateful to Penguin Books for permission to quote extensively from its translations of Livy and Polybius.

SOURCES

The main evidence for our knowledge of the history of the Roman Republic is books, mostly written from the first century B.C. to the period of the high empire in the third century A.D. Monkish summarizers and authors of miscellanies of various kinds stretch into the Byzantine era. Most offer narrative accounts, but those which address Rome's beginnings do not succeed in distinguishing fact from legend and, where there are gaps in the records, tend to fill them in with what was thought to be appropriate rather than with what actually happened. Events from the Republic's declining years are allowed to reshape early stories. Sometimes an incident that took place in one era is copied and inserted into a previous one.

Livy (59 B.C.–A.D. 17), a northern Italian and an almost exact contemporary of the emperor Augustus, wrote a vast history from Rome's foundation to his own day. When complete, it comprised 142 "books" (that is, long chapters). However, much ancient literature failed to survive the fall of empire and the judgments of Christian monks. Today, we have only thirty-five of Livy's books. He was a literary artist of a high order, and some of his set pieces are gripping to read, but he added moral color and drama to his canvas; this needs to be cleaned off before the bare essentials of a partial truth can be discerned.

By contrast, the Greek Polybius (about 200–118), who spent much of his life as an exile in Rome, where he mixed in leading circles, wrote of the (for him) recent past. He investigated the period between 264 and 146, when Rome emerged as a leading Mediterranean power. No great stylist, he was a stickler for accuracy. He spoke to survivors of the events he described, examined documents (for example, treaties), paid attention to geography (often visiting sites in person) and was present at some occasions himself. "The mere statement of a fact may interest us," he remarked. "But it is when the reason is added that the study of history becomes fruitful." His general attitude resembles that of Thucydides, the historian of the Peloponnesian War in the fifth century. Of the original forty volumes of his History, only the first five are extant in their entirety; much of the work has come down to us in collections of excerpts that were kept in libraries in Byzantium.

Another talented Greek was Plutarch, whose life straddled the turn of the first century A.D. He had the off-the-wall idea of writing "parallel" lives of famous Greeks and Romans—for example, Alexander the Great and Julius Caesar. These comparisons threw little new light on Plutarch's subjects, but each biography is a fascinating stand-alone text. The author profitably plundered every source he could lay his hands on, although he did not always sufficiently assess their reliability. He made no claim to be a historian and was, rather, a moralist who explored the impact of character on men's destinies. He had a sharp eye for the telling anecdote. Plutarch was also a copious essayist, and his works bring together a wide range of useful information on the Greek and Roman world.

Toward the end of the first century, a Greek, Diodorus Siculus, published a "universal" history, although in fact it concentrates on Greece and his homeland of Sicily, and later Rome. Fifteen of a total of forty books survive, and others in fragments. He is a rather careless writer and is only as trustworthy as his often unnamed sources, which he tends to follow closely.

Cassius Dio (about 164 to after 229) was a Greek who became a Roman senator and consul. He wrote an eighty-book history of Rome from its foundation to A.D. 229. Ten books on the Punic Wars are lost. The part dealing with the period from 69 B.C. to A.D. 46 survives, although with gaps after A.D. 6. The rest has come down in fragments and summaries. He is stolid, usually sound but unexciting.

In the shadows, behind the writers we have are those numerous historians on whom they depended, but whose work has disappeared. One of these was the first Roman to compose a history of the city, a Roman senator named Quintus Fabius Pictor, who lived in the second half of the third century. He wrote in Greek, partly because he wanted to apply Greek principles of historiography to Rome and partly to acquaint the Hellenic world with this newly emergent state.

Quintus Ennius (230–169) wrote an epic, *Annales* (*Annals*), which tells the story of the Roman People from the fall of Troy and the wanderings of Aeneas down to his own times; only tantalizing fragments remain. His friend Marcus Porcius Cato, the Censor, did much the same with his *Origines,* also lost; his originality was to write in Latin prose.

A number of important, but lost, Greek historians took notice of Rome, among them Hieronymus of Cardia and Timaeus of Tauromenium (a Sicilian whose alleged distortions aroused the ire of Polybius).

But where did the first Roman historians find the information they needed to fill their narratives? Family tradition was a useful source: the great aristocratic houses preserved details of their ancestors, of the offices they held and of the triumphs they celebrated. However, caution was needed, for the spirit of emulation often led to exaggerated claims.

Then there must have been oral traditions, which may have expressed themselves as dramas performed during the *ludi:* for instance, the story of the overthrow of the first Tarquin reads like a theatrical farce. (We know that in the *late* Republic, plays that dealt with Roman themes were regularly presented—for example, about Romulus, the overthrow of the kings, and the Battle of Sentinum during the Samnite Wars.)

Officials of the Republic kept archives. The *pontifex maximus* was responsible for the *annales maximi,* annual accounts of important events and the names of officeholders. Other institutions may also have kept records, and the plebs had their own files in the Temple of Ceres on the Aventine Hill. These documents probably went back to the beginning of the Republic and in the early centuries were thin and basic. Treaties, laws, and dedications were also written down, sometimes as inscriptions on stone or in bronze.

From the second century B.C., educated Romans became interested in antiquarian studies. It has been wittily said that an antiquarian can be defined as "the type of man who is interested in historical facts without being interested in history." Cicero's friend Varro was the greatest antiquarian of his age and an indefatigable author. Ancient texts such as the Twelve Tables, the buildings and monuments of Rome, the state archives, the Latin language, the calendar, religious cults, family histories, social customs, place names, and ritual formulas fell under his scrutiny. Unfortunately, some interpretations were wildly off the mark, especially in the field of etymology, but much curious and interesting information was gathered. Another copious antiquarian was Dionysius of Halicarnassus, who flourished at about the same time as Augustus; his aim was to reconcile the Greeks to the rule of Rome. He is a prosy bore, but his lengthy *Roman Antiquities* is a treasure-house of curious detail about Rome's legendary beginnings.

Cicero makes useful comments in his *Republic* on the city's early history, which are not only interesting in themselves but reveal what was the received narrative in the first century. In *Laws,* he studies the nature of law and proposes detailed reforms of Rome's constitution.

Roman and Greek historians had little to say about social matters, the arts and design, the role and status of women, and economic development. They focused their attention on political and military affairs and on the deeds of great men. Fortunately, much of Cicero's private correspondence has survived, and illuminates what it was like to live through the destruction of the Republic. So have a variety of medical texts—for example, the writings of Celsus. Some poets in the late Republic and the empire evoke the upper classes at leisure. However, for a broader picture of how the Greco-Roman world functioned, we must depend on the increasingly sophisticated and instructive findings of the archaeologist and on a multitude of carved inscriptions, which throw a fascinating light on the doings of local authorities across the Mediterranean region and on the day-to-day lives of ordinary people. This material is fragmentary and can be hard to interpret but is nonetheless valuable for that.

BIBLIOGRAPHY

Ancient Texts

Sources not cited here are published both in the original language and in translation by Loeb Classical Library, Harvard University Press, Cambridge, Massachusetts, and are listed under Abbreviations in the Notes section. Other translations I have made use of or consulted appear below.

Artemidorus, *Oneirocritica,* trans. R. J. White, *The Interpretation of Dreams* (Park Ridge, 1975).

Asconius: Commentaries on Five Speeches of Cicero, trans. and ed. Simon Squires (Wauconda, IL: Bolchazy-Carducci Publishers, 1990).

Aurelius Victor (attributed), *De viris illustribus,* Andreas Schottus (8 vols., Antwerp, 1579).

Aurelius Victor (attributed), *De Caesaribus,* www.roman-emperors.org/epitome.htm.

Bible (*Good News Bible,* 1966; New York: American Bible Society).

Catullus, *Carmina (Odes),* trans. James Michie (London: Rupert Hart-Davis Ltd., 1969) (Also in Loeb).

Corpus Inscriptionum Semiticarum {CIS}. Pars Prima Inscriptiones Phoenicias Continens (Paris, 1881).

Eutropius, Flavius, *Breviarium (Abridgement of Roman History),* trans. H. W. Bird (Liverpool: Liverpool University Press, 1993).

Festus, *Breviarium rerum gestarum populi Romani (Summary of Roman History),* ed. W. Förster (1874), C. Wagener (1886).

Horace (Quintus Horatius Flaccus), *Carmina (Odes),* trans. James Michie (Harmondsworth, UK: Penguin Books, 1967) (Also in Loeb).

Horace, *The Complete Odes and Epodes,* trans. W. G. Shepherd (London: Penguin Books, 1983).

Horace, *Satires and Epistles*, Persius, *Satires*, trans. Niall Rudd (London: Penguin Books, 1973).

Inscriptiones Latinae Selectae, H. Dessau (Berlin, 1891–1916).

Livy, *The Early History of Rome*, trans. Aubrey de Selincourt (London: Penguin Books, 1960).

Livy, *Rome and Italy*, trans. Betty Radice (Harmondsworth, UK: Penguin Books, 1982).

Livy, *The War with Hannibal*, trans. Aubrey de Selincourt (Harmondsworth, UK: Penguin Books, 1965).

Livy, *Rome and the Mediterranean*, trans. Henry Bettenson (Harmondsworth, UK: Penguin Books, 1976).

Orosius, Paulus, *Historiarum Adversum Paganos Libri VII ("Seven Books of History Against the Pagans")*. See the Latin Library, www.the latinlibrary.com/.

Plautus, *The Comedies*, trans. various hands, 4 vols. (Baltimore and London: Johns Hopkins University Press, 1995).

Pliny the Elder, *Natural History: A Selection*, trans. John F. Healy (London: Penguin Books, 1991).

Plutarch, *Makers of Rome*, trans. Ian Scott-Kilvert (Harmondsworth, UK: Penguin Books, 1965).

Plutarch, *Fall of the Roman Republic*, trans. Rex Warner (Harmondsworth, UK: Penguin Books, 1958).

Polybius. *The Rise of the Roman Empire*, trans. Ian Scott-Kilvert (Harmondsworth, UK: Penguin Books, 1979).

Propertius, *The Poems*, trans. W. G. Shepherd (London: Penguin Books, 1985).

Sallust, *The Jugurthine War, The Conspiracy of Catiline*, trans. S. A. Handford (Harmondsworth, UK: Penguin Books, 1963).

Terence, *The Comedies*, trans. Peter Brown (Oxford: Oxford University Press, 2006).

Virgil, *The Aeneid*, trans. C. Day-Lewis (Oxford: Oxford University Press, 1986).

Virgil, *The Aeneid*, trans. W. F. Jackson Knight (London: Penguin Books, 1956).

Virgil, *The Georgics*, trans. C. Day-Lewis (London: Jonathan Cape, 1940).

Selected Modern Studies

Citations are usually the author's surname.

Balsdon, J. P. V. D., *Roman Women: Their History and Habits* (London: The Bodley Head, 1962).

———, *Life and Leisure in Ancient Rome* (London: The Bodley Head, 1969).

Briquel, Dominique, *Les Étrusques* (Paris: Presses Universitaires de France, 2005).

Briscoe, John, *A Commentary on Livy Books XXXI–XXXIII* (Oxford: Oxford University Press, 1973).

———, *A Commentary on Livy Books XXXIV–XXXVII* (Oxford: Oxford University Press, 1981).

———, *A Commentary on Livy Books XXXVIII–XL* (Oxford: Oxford University Press, 2008).

The Cambridge Ancient History, vols. 7.2, 8, and 9 (Cambridge: Cambridge University Press, 1989, 1989, and 1992).

Champion, Jeff, *Pyrrhus of Epirus* (Barnsley, UK: Pen and Sword Books, 2009).

Collins, Randall, *Violence: A Micro-sociological Theory* (Princeton, NJ: Princeton University Press, 2008).

Cornell, T. J., *The Beginnings of Rome: Italy and Rome from the Bronze Age to the Punic Wars (c.1000–264 BC)* (London: Routledge, 1995).

Duggan, Alfred, *He Died Old: Mithradates Eupator, King of Pontus* (London: Faber, 1958).

Dyson, Stephen L., *Rome: A Living Portrait of an Ancient City* (Baltimore: Johns Hopkins University Press, 2010).

Flaubert, Gustave, *Salammbo,* trans. Robert Goodyear and P. J. R. Wright (London: New English Library, 1962).

Frost, H., "The Prefabricated Punic Warship," in H. Devijver and E. Lipiński, eds. *Punic Wars* (Louvain: Peeters Press, 1989).

Goldsworthy, Adrian, *The Roman Army at War: 100 BC–AD 200* (Oxford: Oxford University Press, 1996).

———, *In the Name of Rome: The Men Who Won the Roman Empire* (London: Weidenfeld and Nicholson, 2003).

Grant, Michael, *Gladiators* (London: Penguin Books, 1991).

———, *The History of Rome* (London: Weidenfeld and Nicolson, 1978).

Green, Peter, *Alexander of Macedon,* (Harmondsworth, UK: Penguin Books, 1974).

———, *From Alexander to Actium: The Hellenistic Age* (London: Thames and Hudson, 1990).

Holleaux, Maurice, "L'entretien de Scipion l'Africain et d'Hannibal," *Hermes* 48, no. 1 (1913): 75–98.

Hopkins, K., and M. Beard, *The Colosseum* (London: Profile Books, 2006).

Jaeger, M., *Livy, Hannibal's Monument, and the Temple of Juno at Croton,* Transactions of the American Philological Association, vol. 136, no. 2 (Autumn 2006): 389–414, University of Pennsylvania, Philadelphia.

Keppie, Lawrence, *The Making of the Roman Army* (London: B. T. Batsford, 1984).

Lancel, Serge, *Carthage: A History* (Hoboken, NJ: Wiley-Blackwell, 1995).

Leigh, Matthew, *Comedy and the Rise of Rome* (Oxford: Oxford University Press, 2004).

Macaulay, Thomas Babington, *Lays of Ancient Rome,* 1842.

Miles, Richard, *Carthage Must Be Destroyed: The Rise and Fall of an Ancient Mediterranean Civilization* (London: Penguin Books, 2010).

Momigliano, Arnaldo, *Alien Wisdom: The Limits of Hellenization* (Cambridge: Cambridge University Press, 1975).

Mommsen, Theodor, trans. W. P. Dickson, *The History of Rome* (Gloucester, UK: Dodo Press, originally published 1894).

Oakley, S. P., *A Commentary on Livy, Books 6–10* (Oxford: Oxford University Press, 2008).

Ogilvie, R. M., *A Commentary on Livy, Books 1–5* (Oxford, 1965; repr. with addenda, 1970).

Potter, T. W., *Roman Italy* (London: Guild Publishing, 1987).

Richardson, L. Jr., *A New Topographical Dictionary of Ancient Rome* (Baltimore: Johns Hopkins University Press, 1992).

Salmon, E. T., *Samnium and the Samnites* (Cambridge: Cambridge University Press, 1967).

Scullard, H. H., *Scipio Africanus: Soldier and Politician* (London: Thames and Hudson, 1970).

———, *A History of the Roman World 753 to 146 BC* (London: Routledge, 1935; 4th ed. 1980).

———, *From the Gracchi to Nero: A History of Rome 133 BC to AD 68* (London: Routledge, 1988).

Stambaugh, John E., *The Ancient Roman City* (Baltimore: Johns Hopkins University Press, 1988).

Toner, Jerry, *Popular Culture in Ancient Rome* (Cambridge: Polity Press, 2009).

Walbank, Frank W., *A Historical Commentary on Polybius,* vol. 1 (1957), vol. 2 (1967), and vol. 3 (1979), Oxford University Press.

Warmington, B. H., *Carthage* (Harmondsworth, UK: Penguin Books, 1960).

NOTES

CAH	*Cambridge Ancient History*
Cat	Catullus, *Carmina* (*Odes*)
Cat Agr	Cato, Marcus Porcius, *De agri cultura* *(*On Farming*)
Cic Acad	Cicero, Marcus Tullius, *Academica*
Cic Att	Cicero, Marcus Tullius, *Epistulae ad Atticum* (*Letters to Atticus*) [I use the order and numbering of the D. R. Shackleton Bailey Loeb edition.]
Cic Balb	Cicero, Marcus Tullius, *Pro Balbo* (*In defense of Balbus*)
Cic Brut	Cicero, Marcus Tullius, *Brutus*
Cic Div	Cicero, Marcus Tullius, *De divinatione* (*On Divination*)
Cic Fam	Cicero, Marcus Tullius, *Epistulae ad familiares* (*Letters to His Friends*) [I use the order and numbering of the D. R. Shackleton Bailey Loeb edition.]
Cic Fin	Cicero, Marcus Tullius, *De finibus bonorum et malorum* (*On Ends of Good and Evil*)
Cic Har	Cicero, Marcus Tullius, *De haruspicum responsis* (*On the Responses of the Omen-Diviners*)
Cic Invent	Cicero, Marcus Tullius, *De inventione* (*On Rhetorical Invention*)
Cic Off	Cicero, Marcus Tullius, *De officiis* (*On Duties*)
Cic Phil	Cicero, Marcus Tullius, *Philippicae* (*The Philippics*)
Cic Rep	Cicero, Marcus Tullius, *De re publica* (*The Republic*)
Cic Rosc Am	Cicero, Marcus Tullius, *Pro Roscio Amerino* (*In Defense of Roscius Amerinus*)
Cic Sen	Cicero, Marcus Tullius, *De senectute* (*On Old Age*)
CIL	*Corpus Inscriptionum Latinarum*
CIS	*Corpus Inscriptionum Semiticarum*
Col Re Rust	Columella, Lucius Junius Moderatus, *De re rustica* (*On Agriculture*)
Corn Nep Ham	Cornelius Nepos, *Lives of Great Foreign Leaders, Life of Hamilcar*
Dio	Cassius Dio, *Roman History*
Dio Chrys	Dio Chrysostom, *Orations*
Dio of H	Dionysius of Halicarnassus, *Roman Antiquities*
Dio Sic	Diodorus Siculus, *Historical Library*
Eccl	Ecclesiastes, Book of, Bible
Enn	Ennius, Quintus, *Annales* (Annals)

Eutrop	Eutropius, Flavius, *Breviarium* (*Abridgement of Roman History*)
Ezek	Ezekiel, Book of, Bible
Fest	Festus, *Breviarium rerum gestarum populi Romani* *(*Summary of Roman History*)
Flor	Florus, Publius Annaeus, *Epitome de T. Livio Bellorum omnium annorum DCC Libri II* *(*Epitome of Livy's Histories*)
Her	Herodotus, *The Histories*
Hom Il	Homer, *Iliad*
Hom Od	Homer, *Odyssey*
Hor Car	Horace (Quintus Horatius Flaccus), *Carmina* (*Odes*)
Hor Ep	Horace (Quintus Horatius Flaccus), *Epodon Liber* (*Epodes*)
Hor Epist	Horace (Quintus Horatius Flaccus), *Epistulae* (*Epistles*)
Hor Sat	Horace (Quintus Horatius Flaccus), *Sermones* (*Satires*)
ILS	*Inscriptiones Latinae Selectae*
Jer	Jeremiah, Book of, Bible
Livy	Livy (Titus Livius), *Ab urbe condita* (From the Foundation of the City)
Macr	Macrobius, Ambrosius Theodosius, *Saturnalia*
Oros	Orosius, Paulus, *Historiarum Adversum Paganos Libri VII* (*Seven Books of History Against the Pagans*)
Paus	Pausanias, *Description of Greece*
Pet	Petronius, Gaius, *Satyricon*
Pind	Pindar, *Nemean Odes*
Plaut Capt	Plautus, Titus Maccius, *Captivi* (*The Captives*)
Plaut Curc	Plautus, Titus Maccius, *Curculio* (*The Weevil*)
Plaut Poen	Plautus, Titus Maccius, *Poenulus* (*The Little Carthaginian*)
Plin Nat Hist	Pliny the Elder, *Naturalis Historia* (*Natural History*)
Plut Alex	Plutarch, *Life of Alexander*
Plut Cat Maj	Plutarch, *Life of Cato the Elder*
Plut Cor	Plutarch, *Life of Coriolanus*
Plut Fab	Plutarch, *Life of Fabius Maximus*
Plut Flam	Plutarch, *Life of Flamininus*
Plut G Grac	Plutarch, *Life of Gaius Gracchus*
Plut Mar	Plutarch, *Life of Marius*
Plut Marc	Plutarch, *Life of Marcellus*

Plut Mor Plutarch *Moralia*
Plut Pom Plutarch, *Life of Pompey*
Plut Popl Plutarch, *Life of Poplicola*
Plut Pyr Plutarch, *Life of Pyrrhus*
Plut Rom Plutarch, *Life of Romulus*
Plut Sul Plutarch, *Life of Sulla*
Plut Tib Grac Plutarch, *Life of Tiberius Gracchus*
Polyb Polybius, *The Histories*
Prop Propertius, Sextus Aurelius, *Carmina*
Sall Sallust (Gaius Sallustius Crispus), *Bellum Iugurthinum* (*War Against Jugurtha*)
Sall Hist Sallust (Gaius Sallustius Crispus), *Histories*
Strabo Strabo, *Geographica* (*The Geography*)
Suet Caes Suetonius (Gaius Suetonius Tranqillus), *Life of Julius Caesar*
Suet Tib Suetonius (Gaius Suetonius Tranqillus), *Life of Tiberius* (*de vita Caesarum, The Twelve Caesars*—lit., "On the Life of the Caesars")
Tac Hist Tacitus, Publius (or Gaius) Cornelius, *Historiae* (*Histories*)
Ter Ad Terence (Publius Terentius Afer), *Adelphi* (*The Brothers*)
Ter Hec Terence (Publius Terentius Afer), *Hecyra* (*The Mother-in-Law*)
Theo Theophrastus, *De Causis Plantarum* (*On the Origins of Plants*)
Val Max Valerius Maximus, *Factorum et dictorum memorabilium* (*Memorable Acts and Sayings*)
Var Ling Lat Varro, Marcus Terentius, *De lingua Latina*
Var Rust Varro, Marcus Terentius, *De re rustica*
Virg Aen Virgil (Publius Vergilius Maro), *Aeneid*
Virg Geo Virgil (Publius Vergilius Maro), *Georgica* (*Georgics*)
Zon Zonaras, John, *Extracts of History* (Cassius Dio epitomes)

Dedication, p. vii: Translation of "La Trebbia"

The dawn of an ill-omened day has whitened the heights. The camp awakes. Below, the river swirls and roars where a squadron of Numidian light cavalry waters its horses. Everywhere sounds the clear call of Roman buglers, for in spite of Scipio's disapproval, the lying auguries, the Trebbia in flood, the wind and the rain, Consul Sempronius, new to office and vainglorious, has ordered the symbols of his authority, the bundled axe and rods or *fasces,* to be raised and his state attendants to advance.

On the horizon, Gallic villages were on fire, reddening the dark sky with baleful bursts of flame. In the distance the trumpeting of elephants could be heard, and there, under a bridge, leaning with his back against an arch, Hannibal was listening, thoughtful and exultant, to the muffled tread of legions on the march.

Introduction

Cicero's wonderful letters allow us insight into the quality of life in the late Roman Republic.

xxvii *"I am coming to hope . . ."*   Cic Fam 175 (9 1).
xxviii *Eventually, a young man*   Plut Sull 31 1–2.
 xxix *"What a disaster!"*   Plut Sull 31 6.
 xxix *"And look at the man himself"*   Cic Rosc Am 46 135.
  xxx *"Only let us be firm on one point"*   Cic Fam 177 (9 2).
  xxx *a handbook on agriculture*   Var Rust De re rustica.
 xxxi *"If I have leisure to visit Tusculum"*   Cic Fam 179 (9 5).
 xxxi *"If you don't come to me"*   Op. cit., 180 (9 4).
 xxxi *"These days you are now spending"*   Op. cit., 181 (9 6).
 xxxi *"To every man"*   Macaulay, Horatius stanza 27.

1. A New Troy

Variants of the Aeneas story were current. I have mostly depended on Virgil's canonical account, his epic poem the *Aeneid,* but have also made use of a somewhat different version of events in Dionysius of Halicarnassus.

 7 *(some said) the celebrated Palladium*   According to other traditions, the Palladium had been stolen by Ulysses and the Greek hero Diomedes, and ended up variously at Athens, Sparta, or Rome.
 7 *According to another narrative*   Dio of H 1 46.
 8 *Aeneas looked wonderingly*   Virg Aen 1 421–25.
 9 *"Now this second Paris"*   Ibid., 4 215–17.
 9 *Aeneas the True*   Virg Aen passim.
 9 *"So stop upsetting yourself"*   Op. cit., 4 360–61.
10 *Neither love nor compact*   Ibid., 4 624–29.
11 *a memorial was still standing*   Dio of H 1 64 4–5.
11 *Seven years had passed*   Ibid., 1 65 1.

2. Kings and Tyrants

The story of the birth and early days of Romulus and Remus is drawn from Dionysius of Halicarnassus, Plutarch, and Livy. The basic story is unchallenged, but the details vary and were hotly debated.

13   *"Hercules, who was the greatest commander"*   Dio of H 1 41 1.

15   *They were on friendly terms*   Plut Rom 6 3.

15   *an ancient festival*   The appearance of the Lupercalia in the story is attributed to Cicero's friend the historian Aelius Tubero. Dio of H 1 80 1.

17   *"nothing bordering on legend"*   Dio of H 1 84 1.

18   *A river enables the city*   Cic Rep 2 5 10.

19   *Faustulus's grave*   Dio of H 1 87 2.

19   *Eteocles and Polynices*   See, for example, *Seven Against Thebes* by Aeschylus.

19   *Cain murdered Abel*   Genesis 4:9–16.

20   *was conceived in his mother's womb*   Plut Rom 12 2–6.

20   *little more than three thousand Latins*   Dio of H 1 87 2.

21   *Consus, the god of good advice*   Originally a god of the granary.

24   *"I have chosen you"*   Dio 1 5 11.

24   *He presented himself*   Ioann. Laur. Lyd., De magistr. rei publ. Rom. 1 7.

24–25   *"the shrewd device"* and *"my Rome"*   Livy 1 16 5–7.

25   *one of Rome's earliest historians*   Fabius Pictor.

25   *"great inclination to the invention"*   Cic Rep 2 10.

25   *a new comet*   Suet Caes 88.

26   *He wanted the proper performance*   Cic op. cit., 2 14.

26   *a sacrifice was conducted thirty times*   Plut Cor 25 3.

27   *"So perish all women"*   For the story of Horatius, see Livy 1 26

27   *The timber is still to be seen*   Livy ibid.

28   *"Every building, public and private"*   Op. cit., 1 29 6.

28   *Pons Sublicius*   See Richardson under heading.

29   *"Hear me, Jupiter"*   Livy 1 32 6.

3. Expulsion

Livy and Dionysius of Halicarnassus are the main literary sources, with useful commentary from Cicero's *Republic*.

32   *on a par with the name of Hecuba's mother*   This was Theodor Mommsen's view. See Mommsen 1 9, p. 121, referring to Suet Tib 70 3. Hecuba was the wife of King Priam of Troy.

32   *"deeply learned as they were"*   Livy 5 1 6.

32 *"rules concerning the founding"*   Festus 358 L.

32 *Inside every ordinary object*   This paragraph is indebted to Heurgon, 224–25.

33 *gold ornaments*   Heurgon, p. 152 (citing Raniero Mengarelli).

34 *Theopompus, has left a frank*   Cited in Ath 12 14 517d. It is hard to know what weight to place on this testimony. It receives some confirmation from Posidonius via Diodorus Siculus 5 40. Posidonius puts this decadent behavior down to Etruscan weakness in the centuries following the Roman conquest. But sexual promiscuity is not in itself inconsistent with military prowess.

35 *between about 620 and 610*   The traditional date is 657 B.C., but recent scholarship has pushed the date of Cypselus's accession further forward. See Cornell, p. 124.

35 *the geographer Strabo*   Strabo 8 c. 378.

36 *"It was indeed no little rivulet"*   Cic Rep 2 19 (34).

37 *Genial, well-informed*   Ibid., 2 19 34.

39 *"This statue remained"*   Dio of H 3 71.

39 *"not a Roman, but some newcomer"*   Ibid., 3 72 5.

40 *This was Servius Tullius*   The emperor Claudius (first century A.D.) was an Etruscan expert and tells a completely different and probably more historical story about Servius's rise to power. According to him, Servius was an Etruscan adventurer who came to Rome at the head of an army. See a speech by Claudius preserved in an inscription. Table of Lyons ILS 212 1 8–27.

40 *son of a slave woman*   Some ancient historians felt that for a Roman king to have been a slave's offspring was *infra dignitatem,* and suggested that she had originally been a noblewoman before being captured in a war. See Livy 1 39.

40 *Though he was brought up as a slave*   Cic Rep 2 21 (37).

41 *"The king has been stunned"*   Livy 1 41 5.

42 *believed devoutly in his luck*   For example, Sulla and Julius Caesar in the first century B.C.

42 *special relationship with Fortuna*   See Cornell, p. 146.

44 *"{The king} put into effect the principle"*   Cic Rep 2 22 39–40.

45 *about 80,000 citizens*   Livy 1 44 2. The number given by Dio of H 4 22 2 is 84,700.

45 *a population of about 35,000*   On Rome's population, see Cornell, pp. 204–08.

46 *base-born himself*   Livy 1 47 11.

47 *At the top of Cyprus Street*   Ibid., 1 47 6–7.

48 *the Sibyl used to sit in a bottle.*   Pet 48.

48 *discovered by a modern archaeologist*   Amedeo Mauri in 1932.

48 *understand "the regular curving path"*   Cic Rep 2 25 45.

48 *Tarquin was no delegator*   For this paragraph, see Dio 2 11 6.

49 *"In the sweetness of private gain"*   Livy 1 54 10.

51 *"through country which Roman feet"*   Ibid., 1 56 6.

51 *"difficult even for an active man"*   Paus 10 5 5.

52 *Bronze Charioteer*   Now in the Delphi Archaeological Museum.

52 *The Pythia was a local woman*   In fact, there were three of them, two who alternated and the third being a reserve. The Delphic oracle was a cottage industry.

53 *a sex scandal*   I follow Livy's more composed, even theatrical version of events (1 57–59), rather than that of Dionysius, who moves the key personalities to and fro between Ardea and Rome, to no great purpose, except for a veneer of verisimilitude.

4. So What Really Happened?

Livy, Dionysius of Halicarnassus, and Cicero are the main literary sources.

57 *"old tales"*   Livy 1 Preface 6–7.

57 *"a nation as truly Greek"*   Dio of H 1 61 1.

58 Romulus *means "founder of Rome"*   Ogilvie 1 p. 32.

60 *"the spirit of tranquillity"*   Cic Rep 2 14 27.

61 *"religious ceremonial {and} laws"*   Ibid., 2 14 26.

5. The Land and Its People

The poets Virgil, Horace, and Propertius evoke Rome's prehistory. For a more detailed account see Scullard, *A History of the Roman World 753 to 146 B.C.,* Chapter 1.

67 *a shower of stones*   Livy 1 31 1.

67 *Laurel, myrtle, beech, and oak*   Theo 5 8 3.

68 *"All Latium is blessed"*   Strabo 5 3 5.

69 *"In general, Etruria"*   Dio Sic 5 40 5 (citing Posidonius).

70 *{He} avoids the haughty portals*   Hor Ep 2 7–16.

70 *This is what I prayed for*   Hor Sat 2 6 1–4.

70 *The Curia, now standing high*   Prop 4 1 11–14.

75 *Homer probably wrote his great epics*   Homer, of course, may have been one or more authors—even a woman. Samuel Butler argues that the writer of the *Odyssey* was a young Sicilian woman (see *The Authoress of the Odyssey,* 1897).

76 *"We Romans got our culture"*   Cic Rep 2 15 29.

76 *had no settled / Way of life*   Virg Aen 8 315–18.
76 *"intractable folk"*   Ibid., 321.
76 *The Capitol, "golden today"*   Ibid., 348.
76 *"Cattle were everywhere"*   Ibid., 360–61.
76 *an assemblage of wattle and daub*   Modern archaeologists have found postholes and cuttings for several huts, and more than one may have survived. A duplicate was maintained on the Capitol.
77 *the foundations of a village*   See Stambaugh, pp. 11–12.

6. Free at Last

Livy, Dionysius of Halicarnassus, and Cicero are the main sources, together with Cassius Dio. Plutarch's life of Publicola describes the execution of Brutus's sons.

79 *quite possibly because of a sex scandal*   Ogilvie, pp. 94–96, 218–20. He argues that it is possible that Lucretia committed suicide, anticipating an unfavorable verdict by a court of family members headed by her plenipotentiary husband. (This was how adultery was then dealt with.)
80 *two officials called consuls*   Their powers probably took some time to develop; I describe them at their complete extent. They were perhaps originally named as praetors. Some moderns have argued that there was an interim period after its birth when the Republic was governed by one official. But there is little evidence for this and the tradition of two consuls/praetors is strong.
80 *took office in 509*   This was the traditional date, and is probably (give or take a year or two) accurate. To what degree Brutus, one of the first pair of consuls, is a fully historical figure is moot.
80 *invented the post of dictator*   Consuls convened elections for their successors, but in their absence a dictator could be appointed to fulfill this task.
80 *ad hoc collection of patricians*   For the structure of the early Senate see Cornell, pp. 248–49.
81 auctoritas *"was more than advice"*   Mommsen, *Römisches Staatsrecht,* vol. 3, chap. 2 (1887).
82 *lower their rods*   Cic Rep 2 31 54.
82 *final court of appeal*   A right of appeal existed under the kings and probably did not have to be conceded.
82 *"though the People were free"*   Cic Rep 2 31 (57).
83 *The conspirators decided they should swear*   The story of the unmasking of the traitors bears an uncanny resemblance to Cicero's exposure of the Catilinarian conspiracy in the first century B.C.

84 *"Come, Titus, come Tiberius"*   Plut Popl 6 1.

84 *"cruel and incredible"*   Dio of Hal 5 8 1.

84 *"performed an act"*   Plut Popl 6 3–4.

86 *swam back to the Roman shore*   Polybius 6 55 ends the story differently. Horatius drowns.

86 *A statue of Horatius was erected*   Aul Gell 4 5.

86 *its presence is attested*   Pliny Nat Hist 16 236.

86 *Porsenna settled down*   For the siege, see Livy 2 12 1.

88 *an Athenian king*   Codrus, last of the semi-mythical kings of Athens, who was succeeded by the new post of archon.

88 *"Porsenna, when the city gave itself up"*   The great historian is Tacitus in Tac Hist 3 72.

88 *"In a treaty granted by Porsenna"*   Pliny Nat Hist 34 139.

89 *named after them,* vicus Tuscus   Dio of H 5 36 2–4. Of course, it could well be that the story was invented to explain the street name.

89 *an old custom at public sales*   Livy 2 14 1–4.

7. *General Strike*

Livy and Dionysius of Halicarnassus are the main sources, and Plutarch's *Life of Coriolanus.* The Coriolanus episode is almost certainly fictional; Cicero in *Brutus* 41–43 observes: "Coriolanus is obviously a second Themistocles." Themistocles was the savior of Athens during the Persian invasion; he was exiled and then plotted against his native country.

90 *climbed a sparsely populated hill*   Some ancient sources, e.g. Plut Cor 6 1, identify the hill as the Sacred Mount three miles from the city beside the river Anio. But the Aventine, a place closely associated with popular politics, seems a more likely candidate.

90 *This was a mass protest*   The consensus of contemporary opinion is that this secession was a historical event, caused indeed by a debt crisis.

91 *"Once upon a time"*   Livy 2 32 9 12.

92 *a Temple of Mercury*   See Ogilvie, pp. 22–33.

92 *"The People, freed from the domination"*   Cic Rep 2 33.

93 *the story of a victim*   Livy 2 23 (and for the quotation that follows). This incident may or may not have occurred. It resembles the kind of rhetorical exercise that would-be orators used for training. But it was certainly typical.

94 *Appius Claudius*   Appius was a first name, or praenomen, that was exclusive to the Claudians.

94 *members of a gathering called the* plebs   I follow Cornell, pp. 256–58.

95 *a state within a state*   A phrase from Mommsen 3 145, who himself followed Livy 2 44 9.

95 *first tribunes to take office*   Dionysius gives these perhaps fictitious details about the first two tribunes—Dio of H 6 70. Brutus may have really been Lucius Albinius, according to Asc, p. 117.

96 *"lynch law disguised as divine justice"*   Cornell, p. 260.

96 *it was not for another two decades*   In 471 B.C.

96 *the right to "intercede"*   Valerio–Horatian Laws in 449.

97 *No reports of their proceedings*   Livy 3 55 13.

97 *"so that nothing that was transacted"*   Zon 7 15.

99 *"Unless you stop disturbing the Republic"*   Dio of H 7 25 4.

99 *"Any such measure on our part"*   Plut Cor 16 4.

100 *The stalemate was broken*   Volumnia's meeting with Coriolanus can be found in Plut Cor 33–36.

101 *"You were elected as Tribunes of the plebs"*   Livy 3 9 11.

101 *A leading statesman, three times a consul*   This was Spurius Cassius, consul in 502, 493, and 486. Some modern scholars do not believe the story of his ambition and fall.

101 *its text could still be seen*   Cic Balb 53.

102 *once his father had given evidence*   Our sources may be confused. Spurius Cassius could have been condemned by a family court of his own relatives, with his father, the all-powerful paterfamilias, presiding.

102 *a spirited resistance*   It is said that in 454 a delegation of three was sent to Athens to study the laws of Solon (638–558). This is most unlikely to have taken place; Pericles was in power and would hardly have shown the visitors such old-fashioned and outmoded legislation. However, it *is* credible that consideration was given to the laws and constitutions of Greek cities in Italy. An alternative tradition has a Greek philosopher in exile advise the decemvirs.

103 *ingenious speculations*   For example, Ogilvie p. 452 says firmly that "the second college is fictitious from start to finish."

103 *"The Decemvirate, after a flourishing start"*   Livy 3 33 2.

104 *"ten Tarquins"*   Ibid., 3 39 3.

104 *As with the fall of the kings*   Modern scholars look on the approximate "rhyme" with the rape of Lucretia with suspicion. Perhaps rightly so, but Cornell p. 275 argues that the story of Appius Claudius and Verginia may be very old and that its main elements could have a basis in fact.

105 *"I have incontrovertible evidence"*   Livy 3 48 1–3. This speech is drawn from Livy's imaginative reconstruction.

106 *encamped on the Aventine*   Livy 3 52 2 says that they moved on to the Sacred Mount, probably an unnecessary elaboration of the story.

106 *"I know well enough what is coming to us"*   Ibid., 3 54 3–4.

106 *"wisely favored popular measures"*   Cic Rep 2 31 54.

106 *haughty manner of a Claudian*   It is odd that, for centuries, the Claudian *gens* produced generation after generation of impossible men. Some assert that this was all made up by hostile Roman historians. Maybe, but (for example) we have reliable evidence of bad behavior by Claudians in the late Republic (witness Cicero's relations with Clodius Pulcher and Appius Claudius, as set out in his correspondence). Genetics are less likely to be responsible than the not entirely unwelcome obligation to live up to other people's expectations.

106 *killed himself*   Dio of H 9 54 3–6. Another imaginative reconstruction, no doubt.

107 *The consuls had three important laws passed*   The ancient sources give differing accounts of the Valerio-Horatian legislation. The difficulty is that real constitutional changes did take place, but it is not at all clear exactly when. I follow mainstream modern opinion. Those wishing to delve more deeply into this dry earth may do so at CAH, pp. 227–35.

108 *"still today the fountainhead"*   Livy 3 34 6.

108 *"A man might gather up fruit"*   Table 7 10 (according to the traditional tabulation).

108 *"Let them keep the road in order"*   Table 7 1.

108 *"Where a party is delivered up"*   Table 3 10.

8. The Fall of Rome

Livy and Dionysius of Halicarnassus are the main sources, with contributions by Cicero and Polybius.

111 *fifteenth of July in the year 496*   This is the date given by Livy 2 42 5.

111 *the spring that rose just by the Temple of Vesta*   The Pool of Juturna.

112 *Castor and Pollux*   Castor and Polydeuces, in their Greek incarnation.

112 *"It made a fine sight"*   Dio of H 6 13 5.

112 *Livy's "great astonishment"*   Livy 6 12 2.

113 *The Carthaginians shall do no injury*   Polyb 3 22 11–13. This treaty is historical. The reliable Polybius reports what he surely saw for himself, that the treaty was preserved in bronze in the treasury of the aediles beside the Temple of Jupiter Best and Greatest. He confesses to having some trouble translating the archaic Latin, but the text as he gives it is plausible and rational.

113 *boundaries of Latium at this epoch*   Latium Vetus, Old Latium.

114 *still there in Cicero's time*   Cic Balb 53.

114 *Let there be peace between the Romans*   Dio of H 6 95 2.

115 *Etruscan ruling class of Capua*   Livy 4 37 1–2.

116 *Lucius Quinctius Cincinnatus*   Livy 3 26–29.

118 *"most opulent of all Etruria's cities"*   Ibid., 5 22.

118 *its forces reached Rome*   The First Veientine War, 483–74.

118 *As you know, gentlemen*   Livy 2 48 8. A Livian reconstruction.

119 *replaced their kings with elected officials*   Briquel, p. 44.

120 *Aulus Cornelius Cossus*   Livy 4 19. A vivid account.

120 *a linen corselet*   The inscription and corselet had probably been restored in 222, when the third winner of *spolia opima* made his dedication at the temple. See Ogilvie *Livy* 1–5, pp. 558–65.

121 *expanded from four thousand to six thousand men*   Keppie, p. 18.

122 *priestess straightforwardly suggested*   According to Livy 5 16 9–11.

122 *designed to prevent seepage*   See Ogilvie 1, pp. 658–59.

122 *This work was now begun*   Livy 5 19 10–11.

123 *archaic wooden statue*   Dio of H 13.3. A *xoanon,* or carved wooden image. A contemporary sculpture would have been made of terra-cotta.

123 *"leave this town where you now dwell"*   Livy 5 21 3.

123 *"too much like a romantic stage play"*   Ibid., 5 21 8–9.

124 *the only civic status available, Roman citizenship*   For this plausible speculation, see CAH 7 2, pp. 312–13.

124 *We are told, too, that words were uttered*   Ibid., 5 22 6.

124 *"How sad, ancient Veii!"*   The poet was Sextus Propertius. See Carmina 4 10 27 30.

125 *"Calamity of unprecedented magnitude"*   Livy 5 37 1.

125 *{They} had no knowledge of the refinements*   Polyb 2 17 8–12.

126 *were usually tall*   This paragraph draws on Dio Sic 5 28 and 32.

127 *A foolish story is told*   If there is any truth in this, it could be that the Celts were invited to intervene in some internal quarrel in Clusium.

127 *about ten thousand Romans faced thirty thousand Celts*   Scullard, p. 103.

128 *a rout with high casualties*   Livy exaggerates the disaster for dramatic effect. From what followed, it seems clear that much of the army must have managed to escape.

128 *Livy describes what happened next*   Livy 5 39–49. He overdoes the damage caused by the Celts.

129 *a strange ritual called* devotio   For this interpretation see Ogilvie, p. 725. Also Livy 5 41.

129 *Many public and private records*   Livy 6 1.

130 *It was the geese that saved them*   Ibid., 5 47.

130 *Juno's sacred geese*   Juno had no special interest in geese. The birds were probably those kept in the *auguraculum,* or space for augury, on the Capitol, where the mood of the gods was divined from the way the birds ate their food. See Ogilvie, p. 734; the story is "the authentic stuff of history."

131 *Insult was added*   Livy 5 48 9.

132 *barbarians may have gone, but not forever*   See Oakley 1, pp. 360–65 for a discussion of "Gallic attacks on Rome between the Allia and Sentinum."

132 *king of the Visigoths, the fearsome Alaric*   Alaric captured Rome in A.D. 410.

132 *"at that moment an invasion"*   Polyb 2 18 3.

133 *All work was hurried*   Livy 5 55. The story may be an ancient urban myth, invented to explain the haphazard layout of Rome's drains.

133 *work began in 378*   Ibid., 6 32.

134 *"giving the beholder the impression"*   Dio of H 4 13 4.

9. *Under the Yoke*

Livy is the main source, with contributions by Cassius Dio, Cicero, and Dionysius of Halicarnassus.

135 *the Caudine Forks*   The opening section of this chapter discusses the *clades Caudiana,* the Caudine catastrophe, which is recounted in Livy 9 1.

137 *The Consuls, pretty much half-naked*   Ibid., 9 6 1–2.

138 *"You are never without a reason"*   Ibid., 9 11 6–7.

138 *far from being grateful to the Samnites*   Dio 8 36 21.

139 *speaks of a* foedus   Cic Invent 2 91–94.

140 *in 319, a Roman general is recorded*   CAH 7, pt. 2, p. 371.

140 *"It is not inevitable"*   Dio 8 36 21.

140 *Some fifty-three patrician clans*   Grant, p. 61.

141 *"Very well," shouted Sextius*   Livy 6 35 8.

141 *tribunes aborted the elections*   Roman historians, including Livy, reported a five-year vacation of magistrates. This is most unlikely, and was probably proposed to correlate the disjunction between traditional dates in the early Republic and the accurate dates from the middle Republic onward.

142 *reserved for patricians*   The praetorship was opened to plebeians in 337.

142 *"Camillus, conqueror of the Veian people"*   Ovid 1 641–44.

143 *"the liberty of the Roman People"*   Livy 8 28 1. Livy claims that *nexum* was abolished, but he was probably overstating the case.

143 *"Every man is the maker"*   Sall *Epist ad Caesarem senem,* I.1.2. Napoleon famously made the same point when he was considering a candidate for the post of maréchal of France: *"A-t-il de la chance?"*

143 *his famous censorship of 312*   See Livy 9 29 and Dio Sic 20 36.

147 *In my opinion, the three most magnificent works*   Dio of H 3 67 5.

148 *resolutions of the Plebeian Council*   Livy 8 12 15–17 writes that Quintus Publilius Philo passed such a law about the *concilium plebis,* but it seems more likely that Publilius recognized the validity of *concilium* resolutions, provided they received *patrum auctoritas*—that is, senatorial approval—and that the full measure was taken in 287. See Oakley 2, pp. 524–27.

150 *"Our own commonwealth was based"*   Cic Rep 2 1 2.

150 *"not by abstract reasoning"*   Polyb 6 10 13.

150 *Titus Manlius*   Livy 8 7 tells the story.

152 *Janus, Jupiter, father Mars, Quirinus*   Livy 8 9 6–8. It is uncertain whether this is an accurate citation of the ritual text, or invented by Livy. However, it would certainly have looked convincing to his readers, familiar as they were with the many ceremonies that framed their lives.

153 *Did these episodes take place?*   See CAH 7 2, p. 362.

154 *the borders of Latium*   "Old" Latium, smaller than today's Lazio.

155 *the extent of territory*   CAH 7 2, p. 367.

155 *According to a modern calculation,*   CAH 7 2 353. Apparent precision masks clever guesswork.

155 *If ever a landscape made its people*   See Salmon pp. 14–27 for a fuller description of Samnium.

156 *about 450,000 persons*   Ibid.

157 *They had their pubic hair shaved*   Ath 12 518b.

157 *The Samnites have a splendid law*   Strabo 5 4 12.

157 *the first-century poet Horace*   Hor Car 3 6 39–41.

158 *invented by Oscans*   For the origins of gladiatorial contests, see Grant, *Gladiators,* pp. 19 and 55.

158 *A short first war*   Some modern authorities have argued that this war never took place, but see Oakley vol. 2 pp. 307–11.

161 *"Let us pitch camp facing each other"*   Livy 8 23 8–9.

162 *greater number of troops contributed by the allies and the Latins*   Ibid., 10 26 14.

162 *A female deer*   Livy 10 27 8–9.

162 *"nearest run thing"*   Thomas Creevey, Creevey Papers, p. 236 (London: John Murray, 1903).

162 *followed his father's example*   Some modern opinion challenges the historicity of this *devotio;* however, there is abundant testimony for both of the Decius Mus *devotiones,* and it is beyond doubt that the younger Decius Mus fell at Sentinum. See Oakley 4, pp. 290–91.

163 *They could carry on no longer*   Livy 10 31 15.

163 *For an individual Roman soldier* The paragraphs about the experience of battle are indebted to Randall Collins's *Violence*, which summarizes much research about modern warfare. With caution, I have assumed that some basic findings can plausibly be applied to the emotions of a Roman legionary.

164 *von Clausewitz's fog of war* Carl von Clausewitz, *On War*, Book 2, chap. 2, paragraph 24.

166 *Battles often have a rhythm* Collins, p. 40.

166 *only a quarter of them actually attack* Ibid., pp. 44ff., regarding fighting in the Second World War.

166 *A paralysis of terror* Ibid., p. 47.

166 *about one-third of combatant soldiers* Ibid., p. 69. The percentages are based on a review of photographic evidence of Second World War fighting.

166 *"in ancient and mediaeval warfare"* Ibid., p. 79.

167 *The Romans look not so much* Polyb 6 24 8–9.

167 *its territory had grown* See Oakley 4, p. 3.

167 *twenty-five percent of all adult male citizens* CAH 7 pt. 2, pp. 383ff.

10. The Adventurer

Arrian, Plutarch, and Quintus Curtius wrote lives of Alexander. Embedded inside the fanciful Greek Alexander Romance are quotations from the court day book covering the king's last days. Plutarch is the main literary source for Pyrrhus.

173 *What, exactly, was the matter is unknown* Some time after his death, it was alleged that Alexander had been poisoned. This is unlikely, because he survived for nearly a fortnight after being taken ill, and the ancient world almost certainly did not have access to very slow poisons. Unexpected deaths from disease were often wrongly put down to foul play.

174 *"There will be funeral 'games'"* Arr 7 26 3.

174 *He would never have remained idle* Arr 7 1 4.

175 *"to strive, to seek, to find"* The final line of Alfred Lord Tennyson's poem *Ulysses*.

175 *"The same wickedness"* Cic Rep 3 14 24.

176 *killed its aged king, Priam* Readers will recall the Player's speech in Hamlet act 2, scene 2, which describes the deed.

178 *Alexander called to him in a dream* Plut Pyr 11 2.

178 *his appearance "conveyed terror"* Ibid., 3 4–5.

178 *sufferers from depression* Ibid., 3 4–5.

178 *the king wore a bone or ivory denture* An alternative suggestion (see

Champion, p. 19) is that Pyrrhus had fused teeth, but these usually come only in pairs and not as a complete row of teeth.

178 *naturally brilliant*   Dio 9 40 3–4.

179 *ate his heart away*   Hom Il 1 491f.

179 *The city was "leafy"*   Hor Epist 1 16 11.

179 *"mild winters"*   Hor Car 2 6 17–18.

179 *To me the bonniest square miles*   Ibid., 13–16. Hymettus is a mountain range in Attica famous for its bees. Venafrum is a plain in central Italy crossed by the river Volturnus, where olive trees flourished.

180 *army of more than thirty thousand men*   Strabo 6 3 4.

180 *Later, because of their prosperity*   Ibid.

180 *offered their services as neutral mediators*   Livy 9 14 1.

182 *Postumius was invited*   The episode that follows was recorded in Dio 9 39 3–10 and Dio of H 19 5 and 6.

183 *"This time they did not laugh"*   App Samn 7 3.

184 *a famous anecdote of Plutarch's*   Plut Pyr 14 2–7.

185 *Archaeologists have discovered some of the tablets*   This paragraph is indebted to E. S. Roberts, "The Oracle Inscriptions Discovered at Dodona," *Journal of Hellenic Studies,* vol. 1, 1880.

185 *"Lord Zeus, Dodonean, Pelasgian Zeus"*   Hom Il 16 233ff.

185 *During the great war*   Paus 8 11 12. According to Peter Levi, "Sicily" is probably one of the small hills above Syngrou Street, on the way to the Piraeus.

186 *"construe the advice according to his wishes"*   Dio 9 40 6.

187 *Those issued under Pyrrhus's aegis*   See CAH 7 pt. 2, pp. 4636.

188 *By this time the elephants were boxed up*   Arr 5 17.

189 *Pyrrhus jumped up*   Plut Pyr 15 3–4.

189 *"the mass of people were incapable"*   Ibid., 16 2.

189 *"they fought out their country's battles"*   Ibid., 16 2.

190 *King Pyrrhus to Laevinus, Greeting*   Dio of H 19 9–10. Whether Dio is quoting from the original correspondence or making it up, the sense of the exchange is historical.

191 *"The discipline of these barbarians"*   Plut Pyr 16 5.

191 *Granicus*   The accounts are contradictory. The best hypothesis has Alexander send his army to cross the river Granicus uncontested downstream at night, surprising the Persians in the morning. See Green, *Alexander of Macedon,* Appendix.

193 *"Another victory like this"*   Plut Pyr 219.

193 *"King Pyrrhus and the Epirotes"*   CAH 7 pt. 2, pp. 468–69.

193 *"He is like a player with dice"*   Plut Pyr 26 2. The speaker was Antigonus Gonatas, the king of Macedonia.

194 *"After being cut to pieces"*   Zon (Dio) 8 4.

194 *"I commend you, Pyrrhus"*   Ibid.

195 *"His words have won me"*   Plut Pyr 14 2.

195 *Cineas brought with him*   Ibid.

195 *fashionable women's dress*   Zon (Dio) 8 4.

195 *The terms he proposed*   App Samn 10 1.

196 *"Up to this time, I have regarded"*   Plut Pyr 19 1.

196 *"council of many kings"*   Ibid., 19 5.

196 *"ready speaker"*   Cic Brut 14 55.

196 *archaeologists unearthed a stone box*   For this paragraph, see CAH 7 pt. 2
     pp. 471–72.

199 *He had lost a great part of the forces*   Plut Pyr 21 10.

201 *Whichever party may need help*   Polyb 3 25 3–5.

201 *Punic*   Carthaginian. Latinization of *phoinix,* the Greek word for Car-
     thaginian.

203 *Wheeling round he pushed through*   Plut Pyr 24 3.

205 *"Many roads to death"*   Ibid., 31 2.

206 *with their purple costumes*   Plut Pyr 8 1. For "the poise of his neck," see
     Plut Alex 4 1.

207 *"My friends, what a wrestling ring"*   Plut Pyr 23 6.

11. All at Sea

Livy is still absent. Polybius, most accurate of ancient writers of Roman history, arrives in force. Cassius Dio, Diodorus, and Appian assist. An inscription describes Hanno's travels. The Bible throws light on Punic religion.

208 *the fleet sailed out*   The account of Hanno's journey is given in full in
     Warmington, pp. 7 4–6. (Müller, K. [1965]: *Geographi graeci minores.*
     1 1–14). The inscription, on which Hanno's dispatch was recorded and
     which has now disappeared, was translated from Punic into Greek.
     Scholars have disagreed about its authenticity, but the story it tells is
     internally consistent and fits the geography. Since the dispatch was
     made public, it is reasonable to assume that some details were altered
     or omitted to deceive any potential rivals, especially in the earlier
     parts.

208 *western limits of the known world*   Pind 4 69.

209 *They unload their goods*   Her 4 196.

209 *lack of water and blazingly hot weather*   Arr Ind 43 11–13.

210 *Thirty-five days had elapsed*   Ibid.

211 *an Egyptian Pharaoh with a penchant*   Her 4 42

211 *quoted by a fourth-century* A.D. *Latin author*   Avienus in his geographi-
     cal poem, *Ora Maritima* ("Sea Coasts"), pp. 114–29, 380–89, 404–15.

211 *"I will stop the music of your songs"*   Ezek 26:13–14.

212   *"transformed from Tyrians into Africans"*   Dio Chrys 25 7.

212   *"If you have bought land"*   Col Re Rust 1 1 10.

212   *often cited by Greek and Latin authors*   Especially Col Re Rust.

213   *"getting bees from the carcass"*   Ibid. 9.14.6.

213   *By comparison, Rome's walls*   See Dyson, p. 18.

213   *Beyond {the wall}, the city rose in tiers*   Flaubert, p. 44.

214   *On the island was built*   App Pun 96.

215   *{They} are a hard and gloomy people*   Plut Mor 7990.

215   *"so that no one could sacrifice his son"*   2 Kings 23:10 (*Good News Bible*).

215   *"They have built altars for Baal"*   Jer 19:5.

216   *In their anxiety to make amends*   Dio Sic 20 14 4–6.

216   *parents saved their own infants*   Plut Mor 171 C-D.

216   *"It was to the lady Tanit"*   CIS i 5507.

217   *"an excellent form of government"*   Arist Pol 2 8.

219   *"Carthage would not have maintained an empire"*   Cic Rep 1 frag 3.

219   *They followed up this action*   Polyb 1 7 3–4.

221   *"pity for those at risk"*   Dio Sic 23 1 4.

221   *"they would prove the most vexatious"*   Polyb 1 10 6.

221   *"for want of judgment and courage"*   Ibid., 1 11 5.

222   *"The truth is otherwise"*   Dio fragment 11 43.

224   *Two men rowed with each of the top two oars*   Possible alternative arrangements were five men rowing with one oar or three men to an upper and two to a lower oar.

224   *It was not a question*   Dio fragment 1 20 12.

225   *A Punic quinquereme*   Some have questioned this story, arguing that Rome could have borrowed the naval skills of the Tarentines. But it would seem that they did not have quinqueremes (if they had, surely they would have lent them to Rome with their other ships). Carthaginian ships were recognized as being the best afloat.

225   *{The trainers} placed the men*   Dio fragment 1 21 2.

227   *perhaps by stoning*   Oros 4 4 8.

229   *They locked him in a dark and deep dungeon*   Aul Gell 7 4 3. The historian was Quintus Aelius Tubero, either father or son. Polybius does not mention the story of the return to Rome, which surely he would have done if it had taken place, and so it has been discredited. As for Regulus's torture, this may have been confected to justify his widow's alleged torture of two Carthaginian POWs. See CAH 7, pt. 2, p. 556.

230   *"Let them drink"*   Suet Tib 2 2 2.

231   *"If only my brother were alive"*   Suet Tib 2 4.

231   *"It is perfectly proper to assist"*   App Sic (Constantine Porphyrogenitus, *The Embassies:* 1).

232   *In the end the contest was left drawn*   Polyb 1 58 5–6.

234 *"Even though my country submits"*   Corn Nep Ham 1 5.
234 *"the longest, the most continuous"*   Polyb 1 63 4.

12. "Hannibal at the Gates!"

Polybius is the main and most reliable source, with Livy telling much the same story, but his is more highly colored. Cautious use is made of Dio, Diodorus Siculus, and Appian.

236 *"I was nine years old"*   Polyb 3 11 5–7. In the original, this passage appears in indirect speech.
237 "Hannibal ad portas"   Cic Fin 4 9 22.
237 *became besotted with an attractive young aristocrat*   Corn Nep Ham 3 2.
238 *charges of maladministration*   App Han 2 2.
238 *"inflicted on him all kinds of torture"*   Polyb 1 88 6.
238 *A child tore his ear*   Flaubert, pp. 245–46.
239 *"It is impossible to discover"*   Polyb 3 2 8 1.
240 *Later on after the conclusion*   Dio Sic 25 8.
241 *labor force of forty thousand slaves*   See Miles, pp. 219–20.
241 *an embassy to Hamilcar*   Dio 12 48.
242 *"fast asleep"*   Polyb 2 13 7.
243 *Reckless in courting danger*   Livy 21 4 5–8.
243 *notorious among his fellow citizens*   Polyb 9 26 11.
245 *"We will not overlook this breach"*   Ibid., 3 15 7.
245 *driven by starvation to cannibalism*   Aug Civ 3 20.
245 *When the women watched the slaughter*   App Span 12.
246 *The senior member of the delegation*   Polyb 3 33 2–4.
247 *Twenty years had passed*   It is an oddity of history that the Second Punic War began after the same interval as that between the First and Second World Wars of the twentieth century and that, like the Germans, the Carthaginians felt that they had not been truly defeated, had been forced to pay excessive reparations, and had unfairly forfeited sovereign territory.
248 *ninety thousand infantry and twelve thousand cavalry*   All the numbers in this paragraph come from the usually numerically conservative Polybius (Polybius 3 35).
248 *A legendary personality*   This section is indebted to Miles, pp. 241–55.
249 *He saw a vast monstrous wild beast*   Cic Div 1 24 49.
250 *He issued silver shekels*   CAH 8, p. 39.
251 *It was necessary to cut through rock*   Livy 21 37.
251 *"a kindlier region"*   Ibid.
252 *Scipio had put his son in command*   Polyb 10 3 4–5.

254 *A spring sacred to Hercules*   Livy 21 62 9 and 22 1 10.

255 *This was a correct judgment*   Flaminius's contemporaries were unkind to him, and classical historians perhaps exaggerated his failings. There is no good reason, though, for rejecting the charge of impatience. It explains his actions.

256 *The Consul's death was the beginning*   Livy 21 6.

256 "Magna pugna victi sumus"   Ibid., 22 7.

257 *because of his gentle and solemn personality*   Plut Fab 1 3.

257 *he had read a lot "for a Roman"*   Cic Sen 12.

259 *"because he had not despaired of the Republic"*   Livy 22 61 14.

13. *The Bird Without a Tail*

Livy and Polybius follow the Second Punic War to its close. The latter is especially useful on Rome's military organization.

262 Unus homo nobis cunctando   Cic Off 1, 24, 84.

262 *He threw a spear over the wall*   Plin Nat Hist 34 32.

263 *he looked down on the city*   Plut Mar 19 1.

263 *he looted so many paintings*   Ibid., 21 5.

263 *"The Tarentines can keep their gods"*   Livy 27 16 8.

263 *the Senate was unable to make up its mind*   Ibid., 26 18 3.

264 *"If the People want to make me aedile"*   Ibid., 25 2 6.

265 *Polybius was a friend of the Scipios*   Polyb 10 2 5.

266 *"I am happy to be spoken of as kingly"*   Ibid., 10 40 6.

268 *Hasdrubal's army was already drawn up*   Livy 27 47.

269 *When fortune had deprived him*   Polyb 11 2 9–10.

269 *"Now, at last, I see plainly the fate"*   Livy 27 51 12.

269 *"it had an enclosure surrounded by dense woodland"*   Ibid., 24 3. The discussion of the Temple of Juno was informed by Jaeger.

269 *If we can believe Cicero*   Cic Div 1 24 48.

270 *pro-Carthaginian original source*   From Hannibal's personal historian, Silenus, via Coelius Antipater.

272 *some Italian soldiers in the Punic army refused*   Livy 30 20 6.

274 *You must pardon me*   Polyb 15 19 5–7.

275 *the Republic's military dispositions*   Ibid., 6 19–42.

276 *"When we consider this people's almost obsessive concern"*   Ibid., 6 39 11.

277 *a huge number of olive trees*   Aur Vic Caes 37 3. A late source, but consistent with the nature of Carthage's economic renaissance.

277 *He ordered a treasury official to appear*   Livy 33 46 1–7.

278 *"We should be satisfied with having defeated him"*   Ibid., 33 47 5.

279 *Scipio laughed and asked*   App Syr 10.

279 *Scipio seems to have been in Carthage*   See Lancel, p. 195; Holleaux, pp. 75–98.

280 *His only remaining option was suicide*   Plut Flam 20 4–6 (including Hannibal's last words).

280 *he took poison*   Aconite was the deadliest known toxin in the ancient world, and usually takes an hour to begin to take effect, although a large dose can be fatal almost immediately. The symptoms are unpleasant. It might not have been easy to obtain a large dose, and to be certain of its effect. Suicide by slave was the surer choice.

280 *"like a bird who is too old to fly"*   Plut Flam 21 1.

14. Change and Decay

The sections of Polybius that cover this period have been lost, and Livy is the main source. Plautus and Terence evoke daily life in Rome.

282 *a workshop of corruptions*   Livy 39 10 6–7.

283 *There were more obscenities*   Ibid., 39 13 10–12.

283 *An inscription has survived*   CIL i2 2, 581.

284 *"no slur or disgrace"*   Livy 39 19 5.

285 *"would jeer at their habits and customs"*   Ibid., 40 5 7.

285 *"method of infecting people's minds"* and *"Greek of humble origin"*   Ibid., 39 8 3–6.

286 *moved by madness*   Cat 63 6–10. Catullus wrote in the first century, but he echoes what was believed and practised in the third.

286 *Whenever a magistrate*   Plut Marc 5 1–2.

287 *The image consists of a mask*   Polyb 6 53–54.

289 *Rome was more than a space*   For a fuller account of urban living see Stambaugh, passim.

289 *a tour of the Forum*   Plaut Curc 461ff.

289 *"From virtue down to trash"*   This description of the Roman Forum is drawn from Plautus's *Curculio,* pp. 462–86. In theory, both Plautus and Terence (see below) set their plays in Greek towns, but their urban descriptions are evidently Roman.

289 *there was room, at a squeeze,*   Dyson, p. 49.

290 *Most thoroughfares in the city were unpaved*   The paving of streets began in 174.

291 *the title of street, or via*   Var Ling Lat 7 15.

291 *"Do you know that arcade by the market?"*   Ter Ad 573–84.

295 *"Why, just now in the Forum"*   Plaut Capt lines 4 78–84.

295 *"It was not without reason"*   Var Rust 2 Preface 1.

295 *"Take all this as true"*   CIL 11 600.

296 *Early in the morning, Cato went on foot*   Plut Cat Maj 3 1–2.

296 *"it is from the farming class"*   Cat Agr intro 4.

297 *He must not be a gadabout*   Ibid., 5 2, 4, and 5.

297 *"Sell worn-out oxen"*   Cat Agr 2 7.

298 *the origins of live performance*   Livy 7 2 3–13. Livy probably drew on Varro's (lost) writings on theater. The explanation is plausible.

298 *accustomed to hold a/Beano*   Virg Geo 2 384–88.

300 *"mental relaxation should go together"*   Val Max 2 4 2.

300 *When I first began to perform it*   Ter Hec Prologue 33ff.

300 *"hacked to pieces with his bronze"*   Hom Il 23 175.

301 *an extra ration of wine*   Cat Agr 57.

302 *"natural simplicity of his men"* and *"boyish addiction"*   Plut Cat Maj 3 6–7.

304 *"Anybody can see that the Republic"*   Polyb 31 25 .

304 *"{It was} her habit to appear"*   Ibid., 31 26 3–4.

305 *One particular case that Cato exposed*   Plut Cat Maj 17. There are variations on this story, one being that the boy was a girl, another that the man killed was a condemned criminal rather than a distinguished Celt, a third that the prostitute requested the execution and, finally, that the deed was done by a lictor, not by the consul himself. However, in his account of the affair, Livy (39 42) claims to have read the speech Cato made about the affair, and there is no reason to doubt him. Cato's version is likely to be the nearest to the truth.

305 *Matters came to a head*   The surviving accounts of the Scipionic trials are confused. I follow what I hope is a plausible narrative.

306 *"The Roman People are not entitled"*   Polyb 23 14 3 (Suid).

307 *He left instructions*   As always, there are different stories. But Livy visited a tomb with a statue of Scipio at Liternum. Although another statue was erected on the family mausoleum at Rome, this was probably a memorial. It seems most likely that Liternum was Scipio's last resting place. Whom else could the tomb there have belonged to?

15. The Gorgeous East

Livy and Polybius begin to fade. Plutarch's lives of Cato and Aemilius Paulus are useful. We rely heavily on Appian for the fall of Carthage.

308 *The Gorgeous East*   William Wordsworth, *On the Extinction of the Venetian Republic.*

310 *"fetters of Greece"*   Polyb 18 11 5.

311 *"Woe to you, oh land"*   Eccl 10:16. This Old Testament book may have been composed in about 200 B.C.

314 *Consul and king met* Livy 22 10, for the entire paragraph, including the consul's retort.

315 *The encounter took place in the open air* Polyb 18 1–12. Also Livy 32 32–36. Other examples of similar conferences between enemies include the triumvirs' negotiations in 43 B.C. on a river island near Bologna and Sextus Pompey's encounter with Octavian and Mark Antony at Cape Misenum in 39 B.C.

319 *"Flamininus has unshackled the foot"* Plut Flam 10 2.

320 *The Senate of Rome* Polyb 18 46 5.

320 *What had happened was so unexpected* Ibid., 7.

321 *Some ravens that happened to be flying* Plut Flam 10 6.

322 *"And I tell you that it is not the customs"* App Syr 61.

322 *I observed the powerful Heracles* Hom Od 11 601–3.

323 *The other gods are far away* Ath 6 253 b-f. See Green, *From Alexander to Actium,* p. 55.

324 *"If he wishes us to take no interest"* Livy 34 58 2.

326 *A small town off the beaten track* Ibid., 38 39 10.

327 *He produced a forged letter* Ibid., 40 23 4–9. Livy was certain that it was a forgery, and there are no good grounds for thinking otherwise.

327 *his final illness was psychological* Ibid., 40 56 8–9.

330 *"a kind of speaking tool"* Var Rust 1 17 1.

330 *Day and night they wear out their bodies* Dio Sic 5 38 1.

330 *"I know of a slave who dreamed"* Art 1 78. Cited in Toner, p. 71. Artemidorus lived in the second century, but he used material from earlier writers and his examples do not appear to be time-sensitive.

332 The Little Carthaginian Plaut Poen. The play is officially set in Aetolia, in northwestern Greece; as ever with Plautus, one cannot avoid the feeling that the characters resemble everyday Romans.

332 *opening speech in the Punic language* It is not quite certain whether Hanno speaks in proper Carthaginian Punic, a lost language, or in a comedy pastiche.

333 *They carefully observed the country* App Pun Wars 69.

333 *a large and appetizing Punic fig* Plut Cat Maj 27 1.

333 *"Ceterum censeo"* This famous sentence appears in various forms in Plut Cat Ma 27 (δοκεῖ δέ μοι καὶ Καρχηδόνα μὴ εἶναι), Pliny NH 15 74, Florus 1 31 4, Aur Vic Vir ill 47.8.

334 *"This is Carthage"* Plut Mar 200 11.

336 *"It never pleases the Romans"* Eutrop 4 16.

337 *"just in case of emergencies"* App Pun 74.

337 *"You must make things right"* and *"You know perfectly well"* Ibid., 75.

338 *"well adapted for landing an army"* Ibid.

339 *Only he has wits* Hom Od 10 495.

340 *Scipio surveyed the scene* App Pun 132. Appian says this comes from Polybius, who heard Scipio say it.

341 *For in my heart and soul* Homer, Il 6 448–49.

341 *the day will come* The day did indeed come. It was 24 August A.D. 410, when Alaric the Visigoth sacked Rome.

341 *where Carthage once stood* App Civ 1 24.

341 *The Romans had behaved very badly* This section is indebted to Miles, pp. 348–51.

342 *lifted the entire episode from Naevius* Macr 6 2 31.

343 *"boys in frocks"* Enn 8 270. Loeb reference numbers, for this and the following two citations. Skutsch, *The Annals of Ennius,* OUP; 1985.

343 *"wicked haughty foes"* Ibid., 282.

343 *at last moderates her wrath* Ibid., 293.

344 *"Just as if we had nothing"* Plut Cat Maj 9 2.

345 *Greece was added to the province of Macedon* Greece had to wait until the nineteenth century A.D. before it regained its full freedom.

345 *"the kindest possible treatment"* Dio Sic 32 4 4–5.

16. Blood Brothers

Appian, here admirably well informed, and Plutarch's lives of Tiberius and Gaius Gracchus are the chief sources.

346 *"always had Greeks and literary men"* Plut G Grac 19 2.

346 simplex munditiis Hor Car 1 5 5. "Casually chic" comes from James Michie's translation.

346 *Once, she was entertaining* Val Max 4 4 praef.

346 *Cornelia was his reward.* The story of Cornelia's marriage to Gracchus has echoes of her son's and may be unreliable.

347 *a curious anecdote* Plut Tib Grac 1 2–3.

349 *"Keep up the good work"* Cit. Balsdon, *Life and Leisure,* p. 119 (Porphyrio and Ps) Acron on Hor Sat 1 2 31f.

350 *Cornelia's granddaughter* See Balsdon, *Roman Women,* p. 48.

350 *She had greater skill in lyre-playing* Sall Cat 25 1–5.

351 *"gentle and sedate"* Plut Tib Grac 2 2.

351 *still known as Scipio Aemilianus's mother-in-law* Ibid., 8 5.

352 *a faint echo of the Caudine Forks* It may be that the Caudine Forks story was rewritten in the light of this latest debacle.

352 *"a constant source of grief"* Cic Har 43.

355 *"Wild beasts"* Plut Tib Grac 9 4.

355 *pay him from his own resources* Ibid., 10 5.

355 *"Do not throw into chaos"*   App Civ 1 12.

356 *the assembly-place*   I assume that this was in front of the Temple of
     Jupiter. See Richardson fig. 19, p. 69.

357 *"Be quiet, please, citizens"*   CAH 9, p. 60.

357 *"Since the Consul betrays the state"*   Plut Tib Grac 19 3.

359 *"I will give you a single example"*   Aul Gell 10 3 5.

361 *"I am the only man in the army"*   Plut G Grac 2 5.

361 *"However much you try to defer your destiny"*   Cic Div 1 26 56.

361 *"Apart from those who killed Tiberius"*   Corn Nep Fragment. Scholarly
     opinion inclines toward the genuineness of the fragmentary letters.

361 *Cornelia made representations*   Plut G Grac 4 1–2.

363 *"closely attended by a throng"*   Ibid., 6 4.

364 *I suppose you imagine*   CAH 9, p. 83.

365 *a visit to Carthage*   This is a little odd, for tribunes were not meant to
     cross the city boundary. Perhaps Gaius received some kind of special
     dispensation.

365 *helped him recruit bodyguards*   Plut G Grac 13 2.

366 *Gaius's head was cut off*   Ibid., 17 4.

367 *The Senate reacted to the brothers rather like a general*   I am indebted for
     this admirable simile to Andrew Lintott, CAH 9, p. 85.

367 *No sword was ever brought into the assembly*   App Civ 1 2.

368 *"She had many friends"*   Plut G Grac 19 2.

17. Triumph and Disaster

Plutarch's lives of Marius and Sulla are important sources (also, to a lesser
extent, those of Caesar, Cicero, and Pompey). Sallust is essential for the Jur-
gurthan War. Appian, assisted by Cassius Dio, carries along much of the
main narrative. Keppie is valuable on military matters.

369 *He may have been a blacksmith*   Aur Vic Caes 33. A late source, so we
     cannot be certain of the claim.

369 *These proud men make a very big mistake*   Sall Hist 85 29–40. Gaius Sal-
     lustius Crispus, whom we know as Sallust, will have written up this
     speech; but if these are not Marius's words, they well represent his
     embittered feelings.

370 *"It very well expresses the harshness"*   Plut Mar 2 1.

370 *"I can see that the cure"*   Ibid., 6 3.

371 *Sulla loved literature and the arts*   This account of Sulla's personal life,
     including the verse, is taken from Plut Sul 2.

371 *Then there were the* optimates   This Latin word is found only in the
     plural; when using the singular, I adopt an Anglicized version of the
     word: optimate.

372   *served in Spain under Scipio*   Sall 7–8.
374   *"So you are going to abandon us"*   Plut Mar 8 3.
375   *"God, this Roman bath"*   Ibid., 12 3.
376   *Marius's mules*   Plut Mar 13 1.
378   *this took six days*   Ibid., 25 1.
380   *"insofar as it* was *a law"*   Ibid., 29 4.
380   *"He lacked the abilities others had"*   Plut Mar 32 1.
381   *"No," replied Drusus. "Build it"*   Plut Mor 800f.
382   *The allies laid secret plans for an uprising*   The ensuing war is known as the Social War (from *socius,* the Latin for "ally").
383   *the devastation of the countryside*   Florus 2 6 11.
384   *He rode off on a hunting trip*   This Robin Hood–like tale may be a legend.
385   *"Either be greater than the Romans"*   Plut Mar 31.
386   *"Sulpicius of all the orators"*   Cic Brut 203.
388   *"The murders and civil disturbances"*   App Civ 1 55.
389   *He imagined that he was the commander-in-chief*   Plut Mar 45 6.
390   *According to Appian, ninety senators died*   Ibid., 1 103. Elsewhere, Appian gives the number as forty (App Civ 1 95).
392   *He still kept company with women*   Plut Sul 36 1.
392   *"This lad will stop anyone else"*   App Civ 1 104.
395   *the most splendid of triumphs*   The details are largely drawn from App Mith 1 116–17, Plut Pom 45 and Plin Nat Hist 33 151 and 37 13–14.
395   *Ships with brazen beaks captured*   App Mith 1 117.

18. Afterword

Cicero's letters and his *Republic* and the *Academics* are the main sources.

401   *We were wandering*   Cic Acad 1 3 9.
402   *"Like the learned men of old"*   Cic Fam 177 (9 2).
402   *"excessive liberty leads"*   Cic Rep 1 68.
403   *"winner of a greater laurel wreath"*   Plin Nat Hist 7 117.
403   *The Republic, when it was handed down to us*   Cic Rep 5 2.

Sources

419–420   *"The mere statement of a fact"*   Polyb 12 25b.
421   *"the type of man"*   Cited in Cornell, p 2.

INDEX

ABOUT THE AUTHOR

ANTHONY EVERITT, a sometime visiting professor in the visual and performing arts at Nottingham Trent University, has written extensively on European culture and is the author of *Cicero, Augustus,* and *Hadrian and the Triumph of Rome.* He has served as secretary general of the Arts Council of Great Britain. Everitt lives near Colchester, England's first recorded town, founded by the Romans.